CLEVER HEARTS
Desmond and Molly MacCarthy – a biography

CLEVER HEARTS

Desmond and Molly MacCarthy
a biography

Hugh and Mirabel Cecil

LONDON
VICTOR GOLLANCZ LTD
1990

First published in 1990
by Victor Gollancz Ltd, 14 Henrietta St, London WC2E 8QJ

© 1990 by Hugh and Mirabel Cecil

The right of Hugh and Mirabel Cecil to be identified
as authors of this work has been asserted by them
in accordance with the Copyright Designs and
Patents Act 1988

A CIP catalogue record for this book
is available from the British Library

ISBN–0–575–03622–2

Typeset at The Spartan Press Ltd, Lymington, Hants
Printed in Great Britain by St Edmundsbury Press Ltd
Bury St Edmunds, Suffolk

FOR SELINA HASTINGS

Contents

List of Illustrations

Acknowledgements

This book was written with the help and encouragement of the MacCarthy family, in particular the late Dr Dermod MacCarthy (Desmond and Molly's younger son) and his wife, Marie-France; the late Lord and Lady David Cecil (Desmond and Molly's son-in-law and daughter); and Mrs Michael MacCarthy and her son, Desmond, who have been unfailingly hospitable and helpful to us.

In addition, thirty years ago, at the request of the family, Mrs Frances Partridge collected and copied letters from Desmond to his chief correspondents; these copies, now part of the Desmond MacCarthy papers, are an important part of this book. Mrs Partridge also lent us the correspondence between Desmond and Molly and herself and her husband, Ralph, as well as talking to us at length about the MacCarthys and their circle, which she knew so well.

Professor Quentin and Mrs Anne Olivier Bell have given invaluable advice and encouragement to us at all stages of writing this book.

Other members of the Warre-Cornish and MacCarthy families have been informative and helpful, in particular Molly's nieces, Mrs Horatia Buxton and the late Mrs Clare Sheppard, and the grandchildren of Desmond and Molly MacCarthy, Jonathan Cecil and Laura Hornak.

We are grateful to the following for their help in supplying information, manuscript and photographic material, and in some cases, copyright permission:

Mrs C. Beauman; Lord Bonham-Carter; Michael and Eleanor Brock; Nathalie Brooke; Dr Helen Chambers; Paul Chipchase; the Hon. Mrs Chippindale; Ewan Cooper-Willis; Viscount Esher; Richard Garnett; Johnny Gathorne Hardy; Lady Harrod; Jonathan Hunt; Louis Jebb; Professor Charlotte Jolles; John Kynaston; the late Jack Lambert; Paul Levy; Francis Noel-Baker; Belinda Norman-Butler; the late Lady Phipps; Sheila Pitt; Lord Ponsonby of Shulbrede; Dilys Powell; Sheila, Lady Powerscourt; James Reeve; Lady Ritchie; Kenneth Rose; Catherine and Ian Russell; George Rylands; Anne Sebba; Barbara Strachey; the Hon. Guy Strutt; the late Julian Vinogradoff; Eleanor Winthrop Young.

We wish to thank the staff of the following libraries: King's College,

Cambridge (Dr Michael Halls); Eton College (Dr Paul Quarrie); Trinity College, Cambridge (Alan Kucia); Girton College, Cambridge (Mrs Kate Perry); Sussex University (Elizabeth Inglis); the Harry Ransom Humanities Research Center, University of Texas, Austin (Cathy Henderson); the BBC Written Archives Centre, Caversham (John Jordan); Rhodes House Library (Dr Alan Bell); the London Library.

Further acknowledgements for publication rights, copyright permission and information are due to: Messrs Collins Ltd (Fontana Books) for quotes from Harold Nicolson's *Diaries*; Penguin Viking for Virginia Woolf's *Diaries* and for Harold Hobson, Leonard Russell and Phillip Knightley's *Pearl of Days* (Hamish Hamilton); Faber & Faber Ltd for Ottoline Morrell's *Memoirs*; Constable Ltd for Mary MacCarthy's *A Nineteenth Century Childhood* and David Cecil's *Max*; OUP for David Garnett (ed.), *Carrington, Letters and Extracts from her Diary* and Leonard Woolf's *Autobiography*; Heinemann Ltd for Enid Bagnold's *Autobiography*; Random Century for Cynthia Asquith's *Diaries* (Hutchinson) and *The Letters of Virginia Woolf* (Chatto & Windus); the Society of Authors for the Shaw Estate for Bernard Shaw; the Estate of Mrs Dugdale for the Hardy papers; Colby College, Maine, for the Vernon Lee papers; Timothy Jones for the Enid Bagnold papers; McMaster University for the Bertrand Russell papers; John Russell for Logan Pearsall-Smith; Trekkie Parsons for Leonard Woolf; Nigel Nicolson; James MacGibbon; Lady Mary Clive; Tony Witherby; and Michael Asquith.

We are also grateful to the Leeds Philosophical and Literary Society for funds towards arranging the MacCarthy archive, and the British Academy, towards studying material at Austin, Texas.

Finally, we are deeply indebted to the following for their advice: the archivist of Hatfield House, Robin Harcourt-Williams; the late Stanley Olson; the Lady Selina Hastings; colleagues at Leeds University; Elfreda Powell, our editor, and to Miss Sue Estermann for unravelling this manuscript on to a word processor.

Hugh and Mirabel Cecil
London, January 1990

Desmond and Molly

Desmond MacCarthy was one of the most perceptive literary and dramatic critics of the twentieth century, though he is now less well-known than he deserves. He had a strong, humorous, idiosyncratic personality, but he was neither flamboyant nor in the vanguard of any modern movement. Besides, the art of the literary journalist is of its nature ephemeral.

Desmond was deeply learned in British and Continental literature over the past 250 years and understood its impact on the thought of the modern world. His judgements combined commonsense with imagination; to read his work is an education in the values that sustained the civilised western world before the First World War.

Sadly, however, he himself never thought much of his journalistic achievement. He set out to write a great novel, to match Tolstoy, Henry James or Proust in its scope, and he talked frequently of this ambition to his friends. To them – as to himself – he seemed indeed to possess real creative powers. His conversation was famous; it was inventive, beautifully expressed and subtle. The enthralling stories he told were full of pathos and picturesque detail; and he possessed an extraordinary *élan vital*, even in old age, despite being often oppressed by doubt and ill-health. His love of life lay at the root of his exceptional popularity, earning him, he claimed, one new great friend every year from seventeen to fifty. He had the gift of making his friends feel better about themselves: "You always manage", Bertrand Russell told him, "to cheer me up when I see you."[1]*

Yet he also gave an impression of muddling through life. His sage appraisal of plays and books contrasted with the chaos of his daily existence, his forgotten appointments, his too hectic social life, his postponed debts. Besides, when he lamented his inability to write the great works he had planned, his friends took his belittling estimate of himself at face value, instead of reassuring him that what he actually did was worth doing. So he has gone down in the diaries and memoirs of

*Sources are given on pp. 303–311.

intimates like Leonard and Virginia Woolf as a brilliant failure whose early promise was never fulfilled.[2]

On the other hand, those two austere critics – and many others – have also left a picture of someone who inspired the greatest affection: "and a delightful man you are," Sean O'Casey told him when they corresponded in 1942. "I love lovable men."[3] Desmond had none of the wintry or exclusive character of many members of the literary intelligentsia whom he knew so well. His capacity for friendship was wide and embraced even as prickly a character as Somerset Maugham. It was the same with his cultural tastes: he found things to enjoy in most theatre, for example, even when he knew it was flawed.

He died in 1952. There are few left now who can recall the charm of his company or who remember his engaging appearance – the long bald cranium, the thick eyebrows; the good, though shabby, suit and the bow-tie – suggesting someone always ready for a party; the voice melodious, a cigarette held between strong fingers. Even in his old age he could dominate a conversation, in his unassertive way, with the skill of one who has excelled in the art over a lifetime.

His wife Molly who seemed diffident, to some, on first acquaintance, was also original and unconventional. She had an astringent sense of the ridiculous and she wrote with a clever, fluent pen, producing two books of lasting quality and many fascinating letters. She had a sensitive, attached nature, which could make her anxious and, at times, violently jealous; but it also forged a deep, permanent bond between her and her easily diverted, though affectionate, husband.

When they married, in 1906, rather than be pinned down by a regular job, Desmond was anxious to take his chance as a writer, like the poet Coleridge whom he described as living "like a true man on the decks of the world, not shut in a warm, tidy little cabin, satisfied with a porthole glimpse of the flying sea."[4] Molly had agreed to take the chance with him; the waters they embarked on together were indeed uncharted and for long stretches of the voyage she had both to navigate and take the helm.

Their lives, though not outwardly eventful, were full of vivid person-alities and passionate friendships; they reflected the pleasures and preoccupations of a cultivated society which came to flower in the late nineteenth century and has now vanished.

Both Desmond and Molly possessed an instinctive power of sympa-thetic understanding – a quality they prized above all else in others. It was central to all they valued in friendship and family ties, and it sustained their marriage, through many vicissitudes, for nearly fifty years: to describe it, they coined the phrase "a clever heart".

1 A Nineteenth-Century Childhood

Unlike Desmond, an only child, Molly came from a large family, and her happy childhood was to dominate her whole life – an idyll which could never be regained nor recreated. She was the seventh of the eight children of Francis and Blanche Warre-Cornish. She was born on a wet August afternoon in 1882 in the little village of Lynton, on the North Devon coast.

She "is the sweetest little creature . . ." her mother wrote. "She is so fair and healthy that I think we shall all play at dolls with her perpetually, and she will be quite a Devonshire girl."[1] Her mother was right; all her life Molly loved her birthplace and frequently returned to "sweet heavenly Lynton" as Blanche called it. It is a romantic and spectacular spot: 800 feet above the sea, Lynton stands on high cliffs between the broad sweep of the Bristol Channel and the lonely heights of Exmoor. Inland, it is a secret part of the world, where deep, overgrown, twisting lanes lead to hidden farmsteads; where the tall hedges are spangled with violets, primroses and cowslips in spring, and luxuriant with honeysuckle and brilliant fuchsia in summer; where in the autumn, the red apples from which the famous Devon cider is made grew in diminutive orchards.

The Warre-Cornish's house, the Chough's Nest, took its name from the species of red-legged crow which frequented such rocky heights, along with gulls, kittiwakes, and curlews. It was built a few years before Molly was born by the architect Basil Champneys who was noted for his "Queen Anne" style of domestic architecture: but in this case he designed a simple family house of local stone roofed with slate. With sweeping views of the sea and the cliffs, this unadorned building seemed to the Warre-Cornish children to extend a magical welcome when they arrived there: "Twice a year the whole household, numbering about 15 souls, with about 20 trunks, was transported" to the west country.[2] Her early memories of Lynton planted an ideal of family life in Molly's mind which remained there always. She and her brothers and sisters hunted for fossils and birds' eggs and explored the rock-pools. If they felt brave, they swam in the breakers which rolled into the bays. The boys fished for the brown trout which leapt in the clear streams on the moors; they all rode on donkeys and shaggy Exmoor ponies whose sturdy, sure-footed legs negotiated the cliff paths down to the sea. In the evenings they read by lamp-light, played the piano, or sang, for they were a very musical family. And always in the background was the sound of the sea, hundreds of feet below; of the sea-birds wheeling round the cliffs; of the streams rushing down from the moor: "as I lie down in my bed, with the murmur of the sea in my ears, I am as happy as a little caterpillar on a fresh green leaf," wrote Molly.

She enshrined the Devonshire countryside in her novel, *A Pier and a Band*; and in her memoir, *A 19th Century Childhood*, she recounted that her father came from a long line of west country families, "very quiet, mild people. The bones of these small squires, ensigns in line regiments, lieutenants of marines, and scholarly country clergymen, lie buried in their own corners of that sleepy county."

Molly's father was similarly cultivated and God-fearing: he was the son of a clergyman and his mother, Louisa Warre, was the daughter of one. Fearing that it would otherwise die out, Francis Cornish added his mother's maiden name to the family surname. Frank, as he was commonly known, had toyed with the idea of taking Holy Orders, but contented himself with writing the definitive history of the Anglican Church in the nineteenth century. Born in 1839 he was educated at Eton and King's College, Cambridge. He returned to Eton to teach classics, becoming a Housemaster, and eventually, until his death in 1916, Vice-Provost and Librarian, living, appropriately, in the Cloisters. It was a sheltered life, yet not a narrow one: of Frank and his wife Blanche, another Eton master, the writer Arthur Benson, said: "They belonged to a larger sort of world, and were in touch with wider influences, both artistic and intellectual."[3]

A large part of the appeal, and singularity, of the household in which Molly grew up was due to Mrs Cornish. Marrying her was the most imaginative choice Frank Cornish ever made. As a young Eton master of twenty-seven, he met the romantic Miss Blanche Ritchie when she was only just eighteen. Her father had been Advocate-General of Bengal, and had died young, at 45, "eminent, and leaving a good fortune." "We belonged", said Molly, "to one of those now old-fashioned families with uncles and cousins meting out justice in India, who spent their lives in carefully weighing in the scales Queen Victoria against millions of natives . . . A mass of traditional prejudice, I still believe firmly that the English rule in India has been a most marvellous feat . . . and I am utterly insulted at hearing that fine volume of history closed with an ungrateful bang."

Blanche's widowed mother settled with her brood of nine children in a large house in the west of England. Blanche painted a characteristically romantic vision of her girlhood for her own children: "I could see her & her sisters flitting up & down the wide staircase in white muslins, with camellias in their hair & Beethoven scores under their arms," Molly wrote. Frank and Blanche had married in 1866. They were very much in love, and "Please God we shall love each other better every year," Frank wrote to his young bride just before the wedding. Their first daughter, Margaret, was born nine months after their marriage, followed by another girl, Dorothy; then came the three boys, and Charlotte and Molly; she was supposed to be their last child, but a final baby, Cecilia, arrived in 1886.

Coming as her mother did from a large family, Molly had many cousins: her grandfather, William Ritchie, was a favourite relation of the novelist Thackeray, and Blanche and her sister Augusta saw a good deal of his daughters Anny and Minny. It was through the Thackerays that they met Tennyson, then living on the Isle of Wight, and his neighbour on the island, Mrs Julia Margaret Cameron, the pioneer portrait photographer who several years later photographed Molly and her brothers and sisters looking like long-suffering angels.

Anny Thackeray was to marry Blanche's brother, Richmond Ritchie, seventeen years her junior, so that she became Blanche's sister-in-law; she was a great character in Molly's life until her death, aged eighty-two in 1919; and it was through Aunt Anny, too, that Molly was connected with the Stephen sisters, Virginia (Woolf) and Vanessa (Bell), who became lifelong friends. The ramified family backgrounds of Molly and of Virginia were similar. Virginia later described herself as "descended from a great many people, some famous, others obscure; born not of very rich parents, but of well-to-do parents, born into a very communicative, literate, letter-writing, visiting, articulate, late 19th century world."[4]

Few were more "communicative, literate, letter-writing, visiting, articulate" than Molly's mother, Blanche. She was an original, talented and complex woman, whose eccentricities of outlook and utterance made her a legendary figure at Eton. As a wife she was not always easy to live with, nor as a mother easy to live up to. She was commonly held to dominate her self-effacing, gentle husband, who was described by Arthur Benson as "leisurely, low-voiced, humorous, subtle rather than emphatic. But he assumed no direction – he aided & abetted rather than initiated; and Mrs. Cornish . . . was the moving spirit of the whole."[5]

Life at Holland House, Eton, where Frank was Housemaster must needs be arranged according to Blanche's highly developed aesthetic sense – as Molly described it: "It is a warm May late afternoon," she wrote of the year 1889 when she was seven. "The garden, with the lawn and the shrubbery, the quince, and the mulberry tree, is bathed in western sun – the lilacs are out. . . . In the drawing-room, with its French window open, sits my mother . . . under a great piece of romantic tapestry representing a woodland scene, making tea for Mr. Oscar Browning,[*] who is calling. . . . Her sister[†] has ceased her Brahms sonata, closed the piano, and joined them. . . . Absorbed in metaphysical speculations, [my mother] is like a swift fish rising out of a river of doubt to catch small flies of certainty. . . .

"In the quiet, comfortable study, with his white hair and a look of being half a medieval saint and half a country squire, my father sits correcting Latin verses at a great writing-table, while little boys knock at his door and come in, bringing him their books. He has a detached, imaginative grasp of all their characters . . . and says something always kind, but often too clever for them; some of them see what he means when they have left the room and thought it over; others give it up.

"Upstairs in her room Margaret is studying Greek . . . In the school-room tea is over, and Charlotte and Gerald are playing Diabelli duets together; two deathly pale children with any amount of vitality in their eyes. . . . They end in a wild noisy strumming, and then rush out into the garden to look for the strayed tortoise, to the relief of an elder brother, Hubert, who is quietly reading *Redgauntlet* in a rocking-chair.

"Upstairs in the nursery Cecilia and I are on the floor, playing on the Kidderminster carpet. She is four; I am seven. She is making a garden with dandelions and cow parsley. She is fond of bringing in bunches of wayside weeds from our walks. I am simply lying there, chaunting idly and looking at things upside down. Eva, our nurse, doesn't approve; lifts me up off the floor and tells me to tidy the dolls' house. . . ."

It was Eva who governed their nursery routine. After tea, the three youngest girls were sent downstairs decked in their sashes and coral necklaces for an hour with their mother before bedtime: she would read Grimm's tales aloud perhaps, and they would sing to her accompaniment on the piano: if, by an unfortunate chance, they sang hymns, Molly recalled she would be overcome with terror as soon as she got into bed: when her mother came upstairs to say goodnight "a little out of breath in her comfortable velvet dress," she would wail reproachfully at her "Oh, why did we have 'We are but little children weak'?" which always reduced her to misery; her mother soothed and comforted her, and "stroked her chin with a deliciously soft hand" until the three little girls dropped off to sleep peacefully.

Their father, though seeming remote and scholarly, was affectionate too: when, in their night-clothes, the little children "came softly to the

---

[*] Oscar Browning (1837–1923), scholar and teacher. See Ch. 3.

[†] Emily Ritchie, unmarried. Close friend of Edith Sichel, author, woman of letters, part of the Cornish intellectual circle.

study door" he would obligingly draw a picture – the same one every night if they wanted.

Blanche and Frank appeared to be preoccupied with affairs of the mind, but both believed that a household should be well-run, without pretension but with attention to detail. The rooms, even if simply furnished, should be well-arranged, comfortable and warm; the flowers fresh and abundant; the chair covers scrupulously clean, and colourful rugs on the polished floor boards. Blanche had a horror, which she passed on to her children, of "Bohemianism": happy-go-lucky artistic disorder had no charms for her, though she was artistic and imaginative to a degree. What she achieved, as Arthur Benson noted, was highly individual and appealing: "a fine taste expressing itself simply."[6] She liked the birds and plants of William Morris's patterns, predominantly blue and green; Medici prints of Old Masters, and Mrs Cameron's photographs, with a William de Morgan plate or a della Robbia plaque hung over the door here and there. When Frank Cornish was appointed Vice-Provost and Librarian to the school in 1893 the family moved to a house in the medieval Cloisters.

At the back of the Cloisters was the Fellows' Garden, running down to the Thames, with the castle at Windsor outlined against the horizon. Another of the attractions of the house was that in fine weather the French windows of the drawing-room on the first floor could be opened on to the "leads", a flat roof where the family could sit outside. Here Blanche would sit for hours writing her letters with a squeaky quill pen, her feet on a footstool and a board on her knees. The squeak was erratic with long interruptions while she gazed abstractedly at her surroundings or shut her eyes in reverie.[7]

Her flavour, or "atmosphere" to use a favourite word of hers, is conveyed by a privately printed collection of her utterances "Cornishiana": one of the most well-known of which was "In all disagreeable circumstances remember the three things which I always say to myself: 'I am an Englishwoman; I was born in wedlock; I am on dry land.'" Mrs Cornish was nothing if not outspoken. "When there was a scandal of the usual sort at Eton, and her young daughter expressed shocked feelings, 'Don't be a prig!' Mrs. Cornish answered. 'It's the traditional, ancient aristocratic vice of Eton. What do they know of it in those modern, sanitary linoleum schools?'"[8]

It is difficult now to realise in what spirit, or even tone, her remarks were made. All too often they stopped conversation; but that was far from her intention. They were usually the result of her enthusiasm for a topic: "she said exactly what came into her head. . . . Her mind worked very rapidly, and as it moved picked up many threads of allusion and suggestion, and omitting the obvious links and prosaic connections, came to the surface in a remark which often condensed a whole train of thought and summed up an unspoken reverie."[9]

To be commonplace was virtually a moral failing in Blanche's eyes; she hated and eschewed the ordinary. "She does not know how to come down to a below sea-level atmosphere. She insists on keeping on her fine imaginative plateau & expects people to come up & join her there," wrote Molly in her memoir.

This frequently made her difficult to live with: certain subjects such as servants, ailments or money were taboo except in a bedroom "tête à tête". Like her daughter Molly, neither her health nor her nerves were strong; and she had spent almost twenty years, from the age of eighteen, when she married, to nearly forty, when her last child was born, in being pregnant and bringing up her large family.

Blanche was an appreciative reader and some of her published writing on literature was capable and entertaining. She wrote novels too; her first, *Alcestis*, published in 1873, was a highly-coloured story of love and art told with the extravagance of Ouida, with settings like those of du Maurier's *Trilby*, decadent salons which the young wife of a schoolmaster can have visited only in her imagination. Her next novel was tamer, but none the better for that.

Molly's father too wrote novels of church life, short on plot, and dealing with religious debates of the time, but his books do not convey the breadth of his mind which Molly remembered: "I never asked him anything he didn't know; he knew all about birds and fish and beasts as well as ancient & obscure kings & popes & everything else, and his playing of Mozart operas, & Bach was perfectly charming."[10]

Although he had none of his wife's spectacular or dominating qualities, the Eton boys held Frank Warre-Cornish in great affection: "The existence of Cornish justifies Eton . . ." wrote the captain of his house, Arthur Ponsonby,* later with his wife, Dolly, a close friend of Desmond and Molly. "Very different types of boys seemed to find in him the sympathy they wanted. He by no means subscribed to the orthodox, almost universal public school habit of suppressing originality."[11]

Arthur Ponsonby's father, Sir Henry Ponsonby, was for many years Queen Victoria's private secretary, and the family lived in the Norman Tower, Windsor Castle. Arthur's mother, M'Aimée, a humorous, well-read woman, became a devoted companion of Blanche, and the Cornishes were often invited to the Castle – excursions which Molly and her brothers and sisters relished. M'Aimée was an aunt of Maurice Baring, a

---

*Arthur Ponsonby (1871–1946) later to be a leader of the peace movement in the First War; created Baron Ponsonby of Shulbrede.

future friend of Desmond's. In the '90s she introduced Baring, while still an Eton schoolboy, into the inner circle of the Cornish family.

The Baring and Ponsonby families had a phraseology of their own which became part of the Cornishes' language, too, and then of the MacCarthys, who invented their own variations and additions: from Eton days came, for instance, "Heygate" (variations "unheygate," "Heygatism" and "Arch-heygate") which they often noted on their letters to one another; named after an Eton Housemaster of great conventionality, it meant sticking to the commonplace rules of life: "baeger" and "Archbaeger" were also often noted on letters telling a long boring story with no point. This was a corruption of "Baker", one of the Barings' gardeners. "Hell's delights" were the plethora of domestic chores which had to be done, such as packing, tidying up or answering routine letters. Blanche once wrote to Maurice Baring describing the book she was reading as "like a lovely melody which makes one believe in another world in the midst of the mysterious hell's delights of life so much worse than its sorrows."

A large part of Blanche's life was spent in rising above "the mysterious hell's delights of life" to another, richer plane of sunsets, spring flowers and sweet music;[12] but from time to time, her husband was brought down to earth by a sense of his family's poverty and imminent ruin, feelings which intensified after he became Vice-Provost of Eton: for this post, though elevated, was like that of a lay canon at a cathedral. It had no educational function and almost no salary. He received a stipend of £25 with a pension of £400. (The Provost's stipend was £2,200.)

When in the grip of financial agitation, he would call a family conference, flinging piles of bills upon the dining-room table and bringing out an enormous account book. "This was known as 'Le Grand Livre'. It was kept on a cryptic system devised by my father and mother in collaboration, and rigidly adhered to in spite of the fact that no one, not even they themselves, could work the system of analysis devised. The family account-book may seem a trivial matter to mention, but 'Le Grand Livre' played so large a part in my life before marriage that it must be brought into the picture." These attempts at being businesslike were liable to end only in the conclusion that they should cut down on seed for the parrot. "'Now the parrot really *is* an expense,' I remember [my mother] saying." After one of these "Grand Livre" conferences efforts at economy would be made – for a while.

Molly and her sisters Cecilia and Charlotte – to whom she was closest all her life – had rooms at the top of one of the Tudor towers. They overlooked the meadow where a stream flowed beneath the willow trees on its way to join the Thames. Beyond were the turrets and battlements of

Windsor Castle: "on close summer nights, when sleep was slow in coming and we heard the college clock strike every quarter above our heads, one or other of us would be constantly out of bed, padding from window to window, to look out at the river in the moonlight; at the poplar tree that was scarcely stirring, at the grey Castle with its few twinkling lights, and at the brook gleaming behind the willows. The husky cough of one of the shabby old sheep in the meadow down below would suddenly break the romantic spell for me; after one last draught of all the loveliness I would get back into bed" remembered Molly.

By day, the life of the great school went on around them; the girls were more or less immune to it, "though it pressed upon us on all sides with its running, kicking, batting, rowing, loafing boys. . . . Charlotte & Cecilia agreed with me that our Elizabethan house with the library, the cloisters, the gallery and the river, made a paradise of a home, but that a boys' public school was a hampering place for a girl to live in."

Molly's brothers were educated at boarding schools: Francis went on from Winchester to Sandhurst; Hubert and Gerald from Eton to Cambridge, where they made great friends with Desmond MacCarthy – thenceforward a regular visitor to the Warre-Cornishes. The girls were educated mostly at home. To begin with her elder sister Margaret taught the younger girls, until eventually Molly was sent to an Anglican convent school on the outskirts of Windsor, St Stephen's, run by the Community of St John Baptist at Clewer; it had been founded in the mid-nineteenth century for the education of "the daughters of professional men and of others whose means are moderate". Blanche, of course, took a romantic view of the nuns, who "with their long black robes, fresh white caps under their flowing veils & their silver crosses, seemed to her angelic. The long, white dormitories, the bees-waxed floors, the incense-laden chapel, gave her a sense of that disciplined order & calm she herself longed for, and would love to have implanted to a daughter. But oh, mother! you did not inquire about the fellow-pupils, about the food, the hours of work, the walks 2 & 2 in a 'crocodile'. There & then she sealed my fate. I was to be incarcerated in this High Church stronghold as speedily as possible."

Here Molly endured the miseries of homesickness and the discomforts of school wintertime, with its attendant chilblains and ailments. Although it was only a short distance from Eton, the convent seemed to be in a different world, but gradually she responded to its religious ritual, and the spirituality of the nuns, her teachers, made an indelible impression upon the spiritual side of her own nature. Molly however only stayed for a brief year, 1895, at the convent; her education was completed by Miss Sophie Weisse, a passionate, determined German, who had long been a friend of the family – she was, in fact, Molly's godmother. When she started a girls' boarding-school, Northlands, in her large house at Englefield Green, across Windsor Great Park from Eton, Molly attended it.[13]

The daughter of a concert pianist, Miss Weisse was intensely musical; she often arranged concerts at Holland House and she brought the famous violinist Joachim to Eton. An integral part of Molly's childhood was the music-making of Miss Weisse, and of her protégé, Donald Tovey.* Miss Weisse undertook the musical education of the child prodigy Tovey when he was only five years old. He was brought up virtually as her son and he received lessons from the most illustrious musicians of the day – under her close supervision. Miss Weisse's was the only house the young Donald knew "where the chairs really creaked in time, or the drawing-room chintzes were not only in harmony, but what was, to him, an even more intimate necessity, in counterpoint with the dining-room wallpaper" as a friend, Eddie Marsh, once wrote in a literary game at the Cornishes, parodying Henry James.[14]

As Donald – always to Miss Weisse "my Donald" – grew up, his teacher's passion for him, in particular her consuming jealousy when he married, clouded her whole life. Listening to Miss Weisse on Tovey's marriage, said Desmond, one of the innumerable people to whom she vented her aggrieved feelings, was "like reading a dope-story by thunder and lightning. Sometimes the possession of a just mind seems but a tame property, but when it is altogether absent in anyone – how one misses it!"

But at Northlands during the last years of the nineteenth century, "Miss Weisse was in her heyday," said Molly, whose education there was, as might be expected, thoroughly musical. "We started the day with porridge and Gregorian chants," recalled another old pupil. Northlands did not prepare girls for the university, or a profession, but then not many of them wanted to go on to either. Their schooling was, however, on a broad cultural basis: all aspects of music – singing, playing and theory, predominated; Miss Weisse taught German, as well as employing teachers of other nationalities, French and Italian; like Blanche Warre-Cornish, she was enthusiastic about performing and the girls often acted plays – in French and in English. But above everything else, "It was Miss Weisse's remarkable, unexpected and terrific personality that kept us all alive when I was there; and Donald Tovey's music . . ." wrote Molly many years later.

Molly's formal education ended when she left the school in 1899, aged seventeen. There was no question of the university for her. Neither had there been for her eldest sisters, Dorothy and Margaret; the lives of these two were unfulfilled: Margaret, though good-looking and talented in so

*Donald Francis Tovey (1875–1940) was the son of a classics master at Eton; from 1914 he held the Chair of Music at Edinburgh. Knighted 1935.

many ways – in painting, teaching, and music, particularly – never found
anything to occupy her wholeheartedly and was disappointed in love. She
and Dorothy dwindled into delicate and sad old maids.

Molly did not "come out" in the accepted sense of being presented at
Court, but there was plenty of social life for her and her sisters Charlotte
and Cecilia to enjoy: at the end of the London season her parents used
regularly to exchange their house at Eton for one in Stratford Place, off
Oxford Street. Molly and her sisters window-shopped in Bond Street to
start with and then drove on in a hansom to Knightsbridge: "In the end
we spend a great deal, and everything is put down to Mrs. Cornish's
account. It is 'feast' not 'fast' just now. 'Le Grand Livre' will lie in its
drawer for many a day after the exchange of houses . . . for no-one will
have the courage to bring it out."

Apart from her sisters, Molly had numerous cousins and aunts to go on
excursions with: she was devoted to her Aunt Gussie, her mother's sister,
Augusta, who was married to Douglas Freshfield, a rich traveller and
mountain climber, and she often visited the Freshfields in Kensington,
besides going on holiday with them to the Swiss mountains at Pontresina
in the Engadine, where Desmond MacCarthy was also invited. Then there
were Uncle Richmond Ritchie, now the permanent Under-Secretary for
India and Aunt Anny, Thackeray's daughter.

Charades and "theatricals" were constantly arranged and played with
the family and friends, such as Maurice Baring and Donald Tovey, as well
as Desmond MacCarthy and other companions of the Warre-Cornish
boys from the university; there were also literary games of great
complexity in verse, or in a foreign language, or in parody – preferably all
three.

Concerts and pageants were organised by Mrs Cornish, some impromptu, but most rehearsed. One pageant in the pre-Raphaelite vein
was dreamt up by her mother in the mid-1890s: "The room was filled
with beautiful young women metamorphosing themselves into months of
the year; there were young slips for the early months, voluptuous girls for
the hotter summer months, intense and spiritual creatures for those of the
dying year. August was making a poppy wreath, June was engaged with
roses; all were at work on properties – strawberries, blue and yellow
irises, holly and ivy and corn." Molly was February "in a pale-green
floating frock with long white petals. . . ."

The intense romanticism of this entertainment was typical of Blanche,
whose household with its theatricals, word games, literary conversations
and musical evenings was unique at Eton. There were times when the
Cornish children resented their mother's dictatorial ways, but their
devotion to their parents far exceeded any feelings of rebellion, and they

never departed from the aesthetic and transcendental vision of life that they had been taught with such conviction. The atmosphere entranced visitors.

During the early months of the new century, there were changes in Molly's family circle as her brothers and sisters grew up and left home. The Chough's Nest was sold, after almost twenty happy years, but Molly was often to revisit Lynton.

Charlotte was the first of Molly's sisters to marry, to Reggie Balfour, the clever undergraduate who shared her brother Gerald's rooms at Cambridge. His health was uncertain – he had a suspected tumour on the brain, a diagnosis which was to prove tragically correct, but Molly welcomed Charlotte's love-match, and was devoted to the four babies born to her over the next seven years.

Her sister's wedding marked a milestone for Molly between girlhood and growing up. The end of an era was symbolised by the death of the old Queen Victoria six months later. Not that Molly and Cecilia saw it in that light. They had been used to dropping curtsies to the old Queen when she passed them in her great Landau on their walks in Windsor Great Park; now, "'it is too lovely having mourning without any grief,' exclaims Cecilia, looking at herself in the drawing-room mirror in an inexpensive, but captivating, black coat & skirt. She felt what every woman in England felt. All had been delightfully occupied in getting themselves into histrionic and becoming black for three whole days . . ." wrote Molly in her memoir.

"'You look perfectly radiant, darling children, in your black,' says my mother."

Invited to the Norman Tower at the Castle by Lady Ponsonby, the girls viewed the royal funeral procession as it wound its way to the chapel, standing in the intense cold until the coffin drawn on a gun-carriage and all the mourners following it were lost from view . . .

In 1901 came the first great tragedy to affect the close-knit family circle at the Cloisters – the death of the oldest son, Francis, in India at the age of thirty. This dashing, high-spirited cavalry officer, who loved the army and horses, had been afflicted since childhood with recurring bouts of malaria. One morning in a fit of delirium, he shot himself. The shock to his family when the news was telegraphed by his colonel was terrible: they could scarcely comprehend his death by his own hand. As for Molly, though she was so much younger than him, Francis was her favourite brother. The day of his death, "our saddest anniversary", was long remembered by the family. The loss of her eldest son, his grave too distant to be visited by the family who mourned him, added a terrible poignancy to Mrs Cornish's evening ritual which Molly described: "as we sat late in the evening in the Cloisters drawing-room with the windows open to the still night, there would be wafted across the river, clear and faint, the enchanting lilt of the 'Last Post', sounded on the bugle from the Castle garrison. . . . Sitting alone sometimes, with my mother, at that moment, I noticed, she would shut her eyes, with a little intake of the breath, as though the distant music had lifted her suddenly out of the reverberating worries & dull exasperations of the past day, into romance; and the 'Last Post' would be an overture to a mood of reverie for both of us, as we sat there in silence, hearing now only the faint rush of the weir and the stir of the poplar tree."

2 "A Remarkable Child"

Eton College, where Molly spent her idyllic girlhood, had a central place in her future husband's early life as w_ll. Desmond MacCarthy spent nearly six years there as a schoolboy, from 1888, when he was eleven years old. Most of what he learnt, at that confidently philistine academy, was from the others boys, not from the masters: "I was almost entirely boy-educated. When I talk to a dog, I am sometimes reminded of myself and my masters. No animal could be apparently more responsive than the dog, but at the sound of a distant bark its whole being quivers with a very different sort of attention, and in an instant it forgets me. I, too, could only attend to barks. I could be made for a few seconds to sit up with pendant paws for a biscuit, and if scratched behind the ears I capered and ran in circles with delight; when my masters talked to me I heard them, but I only really listened to barks."[1]

The most useful lesson came on his first evening there, when he was teased about his new, monogrammed hairbrushes. Instinctively he hurled a well-aimed punch at his chief tormentor: "'You little devil,' he exclaimed, with his hand to his face. But my contrition was so obviously genuine that instead of retaliating (in spite of cries urging him to do so) he allowed me to open the wash-stand and bathe his swelling eye. . . . it turned out a blessed mishap: I was never ragged again. Looking back, I see now that the boys who suffered most at a public school were either the proudly independent boys, or the half-cracked ones, or the hot-tempered who were good sport to tease, or the very gentle boys who would stand anything and became bullies' prey. A flash-in-the-pan temper, usually followed by remorse, was about the happiest endowment for getting through school on the pleasantest terms."[2]

In fact, Desmond was always popular, both at Eton and at Stonehouse, the little preparatory school in Kent where he had been sent at seven years old to get away from the unhealthy smoke of Leeds, his northern city home. High-spirited, imaginative, responsive, he was an exceptionally attractive child, who easily drew friends to him, and whose social talents and athletic ability gave him a leading position in any company he kept.[3]

At Eton, even his developing love of language owed little to teachers.

He became a practised public speaker through debating societies run by
the boys themselves[4] – the foundation of his later success as a lecturer and
broadcaster; and independently of any official instruction he awoke, at
the age of fifteen, to the beauty of Latin. He was trying to read Horace's
odes on a holiday in the Alps:

"I came to four words: 'Uda mobilibus pomaria rivis.' I knew
'pomaria' meant an orchard. Only four words and behold I was *again*
standing in a steep mountain orchard. What a quick wriggling word it
was – 'mobilibus'! Only four words! I could *see* the irrigation runnels
twisting down through the lush grass beneath apple trees! Yes, it *was* 'a
good expression'! . . . henceforth in *Horace* who came round twice a
week, I was on the lookout for other examples."[5] He had already found
that "good expressions" in English literature gave him a similar pleasure
– whether in Milton, in Dickens, in Keats, in Kipling, or in Stevenson.

By the age of seventeen he had discovered that there was yet more to
literature than exciting plots or thrilling phrases; Henry James' novel *The
American*, taught him how to analyse what he saw around him.[6] Always
amused by the antics of his fellow human beings, he now became a
perceptive observer of life; his later memoirs of Eton were detached and
humorous – quite unlike the usual sentimental reminiscences of late
Victorian schooldays, such as those by his contemporary, Percy Lubb-
ock.[7] He drew striking vignettes of boys he had known – the ineffably
foolish "Ticky" Cavendish and the pathetic, insane Jakes, who smeared
marmalade on his door handle to keep away evil spirits.[8]

The influence of his parents, however, was far greater than that of Eton.
Not that C. D. MacCarthy (1833–1895) ever succeeded in transmitting
to his son the disciplined habits he had learned in his own profession as a
banker. Devoted though Desmond was to his father, he caused him
anxiety at school by his laziness,[9] which Mr MacCarthy correctly realised
might become a real problem in later life: "You have had the disadvantage of being an only child," he told him, "and it may be that you have the
germ of a slight mental weakness, as I have noticed that you still have the
nursery habit of dropping things anywhere without thinking of the
trouble you are giving."[10] Desmond was far from being overawed. He
used to tease his father for his own inconsistencies about the rules of
"form" which he urged Desmond to obey;[11] on one occasion he appeared
for the Fourth of June – Eton's chief annual festival – wearing a cap,
instead of the top hat which was correct: "there he was, his white hair
escaping from a deer-stalker, strolling about and joking among all the
fashionable parents on the river bank, long before darkness could cover
his and my shame."[12]

Mr MacCarthy's carelessness about dress was the more odd because he was a pillar of Britain's financial establishment. Like his own father before him he worked for the Bank of England, Britain's most important lending house, serving as sub-agent at Plymouth and Leeds, and returning in 1891 to Plymouth, with the superior status of Agent (manager). In those flourishing cities, at the height of Britain's commercial eminence, such posts carried great social prestige. Through his salary and a modest capital – part of the legacy of his maternal grandfather, an East India Company director – Mr MacCarthy could afford to entertain the local aristocracy – though the MacCarthys were not wealthy by the standards of his powerful, well-born associates.

Desmond was born in Plymouth on 20th May 1877. When he was only two, the family made the move up to Leeds. Over the next twelve years, they lived above the bank – a fine mid-Victorian building, opposite the town hall. Mr MacCarthy, for security's sake, slept with a magnificent ornamental truncheon by his bed. Among his friends he numbered members of leading Yorkshire families, such as the Becketts and the Marshalls; but he was a far from conventional banker. He and his wife sometimes visited Isabella Ford, the wealthy pioneer socialist; at her house Desmond and his parents met – with liking – Edward Carpenter, the pioneer of homosexual freedom, who preached the virtues of advanced democracy and home-made sandals.

Aside from a sentiment for Ireland – their forebears had been landowners in County Clare – neither Mr MacCarthy nor his tougher, evangelical father differed in style of life from the normal run of the Victorian English gentry. Both were devout Anglicans, with many Church of England clergy among their relations; they sent their sons to public schools and to the ancient universities. Yet Desmond – in whose veins their Irish blood was even more diluted – was often to be described as a "typical Irishman", on account of his easy charm, and readiness to wile away time in enthralling conversation. It would be unfair on the Irish nation, however, to blame it for his impractical, unpunctual nature. Both his father and grandfather, though they could behave illogically, were hard-working, capable men of business. Desmond's background on his father's side was in any case half-English, and on his mother's side, to all intents and purposes, wholly German. Judging by her family, it seems to have been rather from Germany, the nation commonly associated with orderliness and duty, that Desmond's more unworldly traits originated.

His mother, Louise de la Chevallerie (1854–1938), usually known as "Isa" or "Chen" ("little one"), was tiny and frail-looking, but built of some relentlessly enduring substance. "Chen" was elegant in dress and physique, with deep-set eyes, light brown hair and a pale complexion. Though not without perception, her fantastical and childish sides were dominant. Her own background was anything but straightforward. She was the daughter of an eccentric Prussian aristocrat, Otto de la Chevallerie, the legendary "Parent Bird", who was, as she once put it, "shock full of blue blood" and had, reputedly, sixteen quarterings. His family, after emigrating from France in the seventeenth century, had served for generations in the Prussian army and state service. From a misplaced sense of chivalry, Chevallerie had married, at the age of twenty-three, the daughter of the King of Hanover's coachman, a working-class girl who had been compromised by Chevallerie's elder brother. It was a Cinderella story gone wrong; for it meant immediate social disgrace for Otto de la Chevallerie, his resignation from his army commission, and, out of pride, withdrawal from Berlin, where he could no longer afford to live the smart society life of the exclusive *adeligefamilien* with whom he had associated earlier. The real tragedy of his life, however, so it was said, was his failure to achieve his high ambitions as a writer and philosopher.

He put the blame for this on his marriage and terrorised his unfortunate wife Wilhelmine and their four children with his rages against their "plebeian blood". By the time that Desmond was leaving Eton, Chevallerie's first and second wives had gone to their graves, worn out, Chen claimed, by his hysteria. He outlived a third wife. Chen revered him, but her feelings were ambivalent. There was much to admire – he was cultivated and refined; he was a courageous liberal, appalled by the militarism which dominated newly unified Germany after 1870; but he was deeply unbalanced and this, not his first feckless marriage, was the cause of his failure. Because he was terrified of flies, but insisted on fresh air, he could only work in a room with windows open and the venetian blinds down save for one slat, to admit light. In this half-darkness he would write until a fly found its way through the narrow aperture, after which all work was halted until he had slain it. Small wonder he spoke of being "kaputt" by 1871.[13]

"The Parent Bird" was too selfish to be a good father, though fond of Chen in his odd way. Poverty, and the desire to escape their neurotic parent drove Chen and her coarser-grained sister, Zelma, to seek good marriages in England – with success: Zelma married a well-off clergyman, Alfred Fuller, and became the mother of an eminent general, Fritz – later "John" Fuller, famous for his far-sighted views on tank warfare. Chen, at the age of twenty-one, met her husband, Charles Desmond MacCarthy, almost twice her age, warm-hearted and a haven of security. She was living, *en famille*, at Hardwick, the fine eighteenth-century Shropshire home of Mr Mac-Carthy's cousin, the Reverend Walter Kynaston.

With her romantic wedding from Hardwick in 1876, at which she was bedecked with emeralds and diamonds and surrounded by the neighbouring aristocracy, Chen felt that she had recovered caste; she had returned to the *vornehm* kind of people she had been brought up to admire – superior in rank, civilisation and virtue.[14]

She adored her husband without inhibition. Though not exactly humorous in outlook, she was as easy to amuse as a child, even in old age, if she could be coaxed out of her self-absorption; but like her father, she had moments of frenzied temper, which became known as "doing a Parent Bird". Because of the difference in age between herself and her patient husband, she fell rapidly into the role of a child-wife – an unfortunate preparation for the long widowhood she was to have, for it encouraged her dependent and self-centred tendencies; but she had a real talent for making a comfortable and attractive home for her husband and Desmond. She herself was always scrupulously clean and becomingly dressed.

The MacCarthys would have liked several children, but an attack of appendicitis after Desmond's birth seems to have affected Chen's ability to conceive. Prolonged cures in German spas fostered her hypochondria – the dominant note in her letters to her husband – and to everyone else: "my colon is my bitter enemy," she wrote to him from Bohemia; but, she added over-optimistically, "my womb is quite flexible enough for any purposes". She took Desmond to Switzerland with her when he was ten. He chased butterflies in the clinic gardens, while she immersed herself in the prescribed baths, in torrid German romances or in the cultivation of well-born fellow invalids.[15] Her infertility affected Desmond's life as much as her own. A new baby would have diverted a part of her uncontrolled maternal devotion, to which Desmond was to be exposed for over fifty years. During her lifetime, her "beloved Ifchen" (as she called him) must have received at least five hundred of her letters, of which about four hundred survive today. She never wrote one sentence or one letter where three could tell the same message.

Like so many late Victorians, she was obsessed with bowel movements – her own, and her family's. She herself took three globules nightly of the powerful purgative, Cascara, and Desmond was duly dosed for constipation. Even at Cambridge she pursued him with instruction: "I am sending an Enima [sic] and Vaseline . . . Never drink the water of yr bedroom bottle . . . Keep yourself in order with the Cascara. . . ."[16] Both his parents' hopes were vested in their only son. The spectacle of his German grandfather's wasted genius acted both as a warning and a promise of greatness. Their conviction that they had a remarkable child lay at the root of his own belief that he would one day be a great man – a politician, a sage, a doctor of genius – which later developed into the belief that he could write a great novel.[17]

Because he was so responsive, his parents fostered his literary interests.

In particular Chen encouraged him to read continental authors, and he became particularly fond of French and Russian writing. She also stimulated his poetical and romantic feelings, though he was not a romantic in his preferences. What came to fascinate him was how authors used words and how they interpreted the human condition. It was his father who instilled a love of language in him. Together they went to Shakespeare plays. A visit to *Macbeth* at the Lyceum Theatre in 1889 was intensely exciting to the eleven-year-old Desmond: "The witches were magnificent," wrote the future drama critic to his mother: "You cannot hear very well what Irving sayes [sic] he speaks so tragically. Ellen Terry was splendid; it was awful when he crept round the stairs and Lady Macbeth listen and you heard the door open and hear a cry. And the scenery, I never saw anything like the castle it made one long to explore it and then the storm was done so wonderfully and was so gaushtly." [18]

When he was older Mr MacCarthy often took him to the House of Commons. Desmond was profoundly impressed by the adroit wit of Sir William Harcourt and by Mr Gladstone speaking on Ireland, his voice "husky and like the dashing of a cascade at the end of a cavern". [19] His father was always drawn to eloquence and he also cultivated men of letters – including Oscar Wilde – who had this gift, imbuing Desmond with a lifelong curiosity about their characters and conversational style.

Of the greatest importance was Desmond's encounter, at the age of ten, with Samuel Butler, the author of *Erewhon* and *The Way of All Flesh*. That humorous, solitary, independent spirit, with his deep hatred of mid-Victorian Christianity, was to become one of the great influences of Desmond's life. He first met him at an hotel in the Valley of the Saas in Switzerland, where the MacCarthys were staying. "Opposite us at *table d'hote* sat an elderly man with very bushy black eyebrows, and with him, from time to time, there interchanged a few cheerful polite remarks."

A day or two later, Desmond was enjoying himself clambering about the valley rocks. He ignored the luncheon bell and was not surprised when Chen came impatiently out to fetch him: "What did surprise me was that she was presently followed by the old gentleman with the thick eyebrows. As we all three entered the hotel together he whispered: 'I thought I'd better come, with a stranger Mama couldn't be quite so angry.' It was only long afterwards that I realized how it was kind of an elderly gentleman to jump up from his midday meal and hurry out into the blazing sun to protect a small boy from a scolding: but when I did, I realized also that it was thoroughly characteristic of him to suppose that *every* child was likely to be bullied by its parents."

left
Desmond as a boy of 13

above
Desmond's father, D.C. MacCarthy

below
Molly MacCarthy in 1907, aged 25
(painted by Neville Lytton)

opposite top left Molly's father, Frank
Warre-Cornish, on 'the Leads' at the
Cloisters, Eton College

opposite top right Gerald Warre-Cornish,
Molly's brother who was to die in the
Battle of the Somme

opposite bottom Molly's mother, Blanche
Warre-Cornish, pictured with one of her
William Morris wall-hangings

above Samuel Butler (1835-1902), whom
Desmond first met when a small boy on
holiday in Switzerland

George Meredith (1828-1909) – the last portrait

With his father Desmond visited Butler's rooms at Cliffords Inn in London. "I ate nuts and apples and listened. Mr Butler would sometimes give me one of his books, always with strict instructions not to attempt to read it."[20] Only half-understanding what was said, Desmond was able to study his distinguished friend's memorable manner and appearance: "In stature he was a small man, but you hardly noticed that. His lightly built frame was disguised in clothes of enviable bagginess and of a clumsy conventional cut, and he wore prodigious roomy boots like the heads of miniature hippopotamuses. But it was the hirsute, masculine vigour of his head which prevented you from thinking him a small man ... his company manner was that of a kind old gentleman, prepared to be a little shocked by any disregard of the proprieties. . . . He spoke softly and slowly, often with his head a little down, looking gravely over his spectacles and pouting his lips, with a deliberate demureness so disarming that he was able to utter the most subversive sentiments without exciting more than a moment's astonishment."[21]

During Desmond's later teens, Butler undoubtedly affected his out-look. The novelist's unhappy childhood experience of religious bigotry made him dislike any view of the universe except a rational commonsense one. Desmond refused to dismiss the transcendental completely, but his attachment to Christianity declined in his last year at school; and he found Butler's impudent down-to-earth approach attractive, particularly as it did not exclude imagination or response to beauty. Though often unrealistic in his expectations of life, Desmond always came across in conversation as extremely sensible, with a distinct ring of Sam Butler – the same teasing mockery of pretension or illogicality, and the same emphasis on being true to one's nature.

Butler's views on riches and poverty met with his particular approval: for that writer believed the best moral qualities to be inseparable from wealth – "No gold", he declared, "no Holy Ghost".[22] The contempt for worldly success and smart society Desmond sometimes encountered among his Cambridge acquaintances would have infuriated Butler. It was not shared by the MacCarthy family and least of all by Chen. Ever since her marriage, her most passionate interest, after her husband and son, was in various members of the well-born circles into which she had been introduced: on these she lavished all the soulful energy and tenacity of her nature. On a particular pinnacle she placed the Earl Brownlow, a Victorian grandee whose immense landed wealth was matched by his godliness and public spirit. Chen's worship of Adelbert Brownlow and his wife Adelaide was almost indecent: "he has the most tremendous high thoughts about this life & the other," she wrote of the Earl; as for his wife, "the blessed A.B.," she told Desmond: "I think she is not of this world at all. . . . All her faults are to my mind more beautiful than other people's virtues for not one of these touch her soul or spirit."[23]

From early on Desmond was a frequent visitor with his parents to Brownlow family homes at Belton, Ellesmere, Ashridge and Carlton House Terrace. In those days such aristocratic establishments would readily have absorbed old family friends such as the MacCarthys on its periphery. Kindness and hospitality were an obligation. Besides, not even the mighty could have resisted flattery so lavish and heartfelt as Chen's.

Her feelings about the Brownlows' heir, the brilliant and ill-starred Harry Cust, were equally enthusiastic. As a fair-haired resplendent Etonian youth, Cust dandled the baby Desmond on his knee at Hardwick and corresponded soulfully with Chen in the summer of 1879.[24] She never forgot that romantic friendship; she followed the blossoming of Harry's career as an M.P. and as the lively editor of the *Westminster Gazette*, and afterwards his decline when he became increasingly an invalid. She mourned his death in 1917 at the age of 58, before he had come into his inheritance.

Chen's litany of her upper-class heroes and heroines: "the Brownlow Towers, the Tatton Bowers, the Cockburns and the Custs" – as Desmond's children later used to chant satirically – inevitably made its impact on her son. Though all his life strikingly catholic in his tastes, at home alike with Cambridge intellectuals, down-at-heel German musical students, South African millionaires, Irish poets and obscure psychological misfits, he had a taste for high society and was often rebuked for this by both his highbrow "Bloomsbury" friends, such as Virginia Woolf, and by his wife who regarded it as a waste of his time. Despite his impecuniousness as a journalist, his upbringing encouraged him to strike up friendships in wealthy houses where his conversational talents were particularly appreciated. His oldest friend, Arthur Paley, once described him as "a man who travelled first class through life on a third class ticket".

3 "A Really Strong Swimmer"

Desmond went up to Cambridge in October 1894.[1] University life suited him from the first: everything about it – the pursuit of friendship and of self-discovery; the social life, with its endless talk at a high intellectual level, light as well as serious; the public debates, the papers read to undergraduate clubs, and the leisurely reading parties – was congenial. The very lack of structure in an undergraduate's life agreed with him. Cambridge intensified his great strength – his talent for friendship – and his besetting weakness – his tendency to fritter away time. His surroundings were conducive to this, combining as they did privacy with the means of entertaining his fellow undergraduates. He was delighted with his suite of rooms at Trinity College, in the late Victorian Whewell's Court.

In general, the way of life there in Desmond's time bore no close relation to the Cambridge of today. The lovely old college buildings, medieval, Renaissance and classical, endure, but much of the peace and seclusion of those days has gone. Although women's colleges were founded before the end of the century, their social impact in Desmond's day was negligible. Social, intellectual and sporting life took place in entirely male company, except for the occasional tea with cucumber sandwiches or game of tennis at which the daughters of a tutor might be present. There were times when sisters and cousins joined the young men punting down the river Cam or danced with them at the May Week Balls. But these were special occasions, the more significant for their infrequency.

Among the more academically inclined undergraduates, this segregated existence favoured strenuous intellectual activity – poetry readings, discussions, debates, essays – which took place in each other's rooms, as early as breakfast time and late into the night over cocoa, after dining communally in the college halls. By modern – and earlier – standards, such a student way of life was extraordinarily sober – though there were dining clubs where alcohol was consumed. Desmond's father kept him supplied with wine during his first year, and he willingly accepted it from the more bibulous dons like Oscar Browning who were generous with their Chablis.

Segregation encouraged a network of male friendships, which often, notably in Desmond's case, lasted a lifetime. In his world practising homosexual attachments seem to have been uncommon; doubtless some undergraduates seethed under the weight of Victorian repression, but there seems to have been less preoccupation and torment about sex during the 1890s until the advent of Lytton Strachey in the last year of the decade raised the emotional temperature. On the whole, for these young men from refined and sheltered backgrounds, the scarcity of feminine company simply retarded sexual awareness. Most of Desmond's own circle, including himself, were sexually inexperienced and firmly under their parents' wings.

Apart from a smattering of poor scholars, most of the undergraduates and dons in Desmond's time came from the upper class or the upper sections of the middle classes and had been educated at public schools. Desmond's friends tended to be Liberals. Desmond's life at Cambridge can be summed up as chaste, relatively sober, intellectually, but not academically strenuous – and enjoyable.

Cambridge men were often charged, particularly by Oxford contemporaries, with being too priggish, too serious minded, too caught up in philosophy and mathematics. Desmond always defended "seriousness" in conversation – defined as a proper zeal for thorough discussion which he had imbibed at Cambridge.

The University's intellectual heart at the time was a select secret discussion society, "the Apostles". Over a year went by until Desmond was admitted fully to this select circle and until he came to know well the closest of all his friends, G. E. Moore; but before undergraduates could be chosen as Apostles they had to be identified as friends worthy of trust, and Desmond, unknown to himself, was being inspected from the time he arrived until he first learnt of his election in the spring of 1896.

As they had to many others his originality and intelligence had quickly brought him to the Apostles' notice. So, too, had his attractive personality, in which humour, joie de vivre, an athlete's vigour and a quickness of sympathy combined. These showed in his appearance – his robust physique and his open, handsome face, strong-featured but without harshness or angularity. As a talker he had already acquired a reputation. "One cannot accuse him of not being interesting", wrote one Cambridge contemporary, Molly's brother, Gerald Warre-Cornish, "& in fact the only fault I have to find with him is that we cannot talk together for more than five minutes without his plunging out of his depth, & dragging me with him; but he is a really strong swimmer even though the water is very deep."[2]

Mr MacCarthy had insisted on Desmond's studying History. Unlike many of his contemporaries, he quickly passed the "little go" examinations qualifying him to take the Tripos Honours Degree examinations at the end of three years' work, but he found "political economy", which he took in his first year, intolerably dull. He and his friends were more interested in talking about what made life worth living than what political structures were needed to make these ends attainable. Such limited enjoyment of history as he gained came from the private tutor he hired, as was the custom, at £9 a term. Wyatt Davies, a young Roman Catholic historian was humorous and companionable and Desmond ignored his father's stern warning that "the long struggle of our ancestors against priestly domination cannot be adequately viewed by a papist."[3]

Though he cast his intellectual net widely and energetically, Desmond neglected his degree work. He made a notable maiden speech at the Cambridge Union and was soon elected to the Union Committee. His senior tutor, *in loco parentis*, was the distinguished classicist, A. R. Verrall, a thrilling lecturer on the Greek language and literature. He watched Desmond's progress tactfully, praising his many interests, but warning his parents that he must eventually cultivate deeply rather than widely in order to do well in the Tripos.[4] Verrall was himself an Apostle and his influence was important in Desmond's election to the society; he introduced him to other notable figures in the circle; there was Oscar Browning, the most talked of, albeit not the most eminent Cambridge historian of his day.

He had arrived at Cambridge from Eton some twenty years back with a brilliant, tainted reputation as an inspired teacher with an inordinate fondness for clever, titled boys. Though Desmond could hardly ignore his snobbishness and the "dense rich egotism which exhaled from him," Browning's lifelong generosity, his political radicalism and his pioneering of teacher training – especially for poorer, non-university students – all proved, in Desmond's view, that he was genuinely disinterested and spontaneous in his deeper feelings. As a kind, older friend he gave Desmond the first jog that shook the prejudices of a public school boy out of him; showing him that "good" and "good form" were not necessarily the same thing. He encouraged him not to be overawed by other men's learning and to realise that his very youth could be an asset in enabling him to make new intellectual discoveries.

Above all, the excitement of Browning's Sunday soirées enlivened Desmond's years at Cambridge though the first that he attended, soon after coming up, gave him something of a shock. "Entering, I caught straight in the face a blast of native air from off the heights of Intellectual Bohemia, a country of which I was to become a denizen. I sniffed; I did not like it. It made me cough, a cough of bewildered decorum." The two large rooms, lined nearly to the ceiling with ten thousand dusky undusted books were thronged with guests. "Such an aquarium of strange people I had never yet seen. In one corner a man, whom I recognized as a famous metaphysician, was being badgered by a couple of undergraduates. 'What did he, what could *anyone* mean by the Unity of Apperception?' More unexpected was the spectacle of a soldier in a scarlet uniform shaking into the fire the spittle from the clarinet he had just ceased playing; while seated on the floor, pairs of friends conversed earnestly in low tones." The most astounding sight was the host himself: "a very short, globular old man with an enormous yellow bald head and a broken coronal of black, unpleasant curls, came rolling towards me as though the cup of his happiness was at last full. I was led with many pats and smiles up to a youth shrinking with shyness, who turned out to be a shorthand writer, a non-Collegiate student, one of 'O.B.'s' numerous beneficiaries. With an affectionate hand on the shoulder of each of us, and bringing us almost nose to nose, he seemed to be performing a sort of marriage ceremony; then with the confident assertion that two such charming people must like each other, he rolled off into the next room, throwing as he went a rapid Spanish sentence at a professor from Madrid, who remained for the rest of the evening sadly stinted of conversation."[5]

To his tutor, Verrall, Desmond also owed his introduction to the classicist and philosopher, Goldsworthy Lowes Dickinson, whom he saw often in later life with their great mutual friend, Roger Fry. Dickinson held a weekly symposium of cultivated youths to whom he preached a brand of Grecian rationalistic hedonism too mild to thrive anywhere save in that gentle adolescent atmosphere. Desmond admired "Goldie's" unpretentious goodness far more than his mind. The sensitive Dickinson knew nothing of the world though throughout his life he tried passionately to set it to rights. Faced with unsympathetic critics, "He would shake with laughter at them," Desmond recalled, "and his black eyebrows would rise to the extremity of surprise. But presently he would sigh, and rubbing a wrinkled forehead, he seemed to be peering out of a melancholy that nearly touched despair at the tangle of the world."[6]

However, the greatest influence on Desmond's intellectual development was the philosopher G. E. Moore, the leading spirit of the younger generation of Apostles, who became his greatest friend.

Moore presented an extraordinary contrast to Desmond: he was neither witty nor self-assured in company; his face was striking, and in his twenties had a gentle, cerebral beauty. Later, he became tubby and ungainly, puffing at a heavy pipe and dressed in stained, shapeless clothes; but when Desmond first met him, Moore, three years older than he, was an arresting figure, with his intense inward-looking gaze, his lofty forehead over which the fine hair hung untidily, his delicate features and charming smile. The initial impression he made was one of extreme shyness, and many were disconcerted by his prolonged contemplative silences.

Moore's passionate and persistent efforts to reach the truth through rational argument well matched the mood of the time, when intellectuals expected that the improvement of mankind would continue indefinitely once the first principles of things had been painstakingly established. The great task was to sweep away misconceptions and the obsolete religious and ethical cobwebs which still stood in the way of clear understanding and rational conduct. In this sense, though in little else, the writers George Bernard Shaw and H. G. Wells, both pre-eminent in that period, had much in common with the philosopher Moore.

Moore insisted that terms must be clearly defined and he chased propositions relentlessly if he suspected them to be false. "*Do* you *really* think *that?*" he would ask incredulously, his mouth agape and shaking his head in such vehement disagreement that his mop of brown hair flew up and down. His capacity to separate the irrelevant from the relevant and to detect an inconsistency was dazzling to his friends, all of whom, to some extent, began to adopt his ways of thought. His combination of simplicity with genius, and sweetness of nature with uncompromising intellectual standards, was irresistible to them. He provided them with an aesthetic and moral ideal, later expressed in his greatest work, *Principia Ethica* published in 1903, by which they could hope to live; in fact, it was so pure and rarefied that it bore little relation to real life, but it taught its disciples to recognise and reject triviality or coarseness of feeling.[7]

As a teacher, Moore was unsurpassed. It was delightful and exhilarating to explore philosophical questions with him. It was also alarming: "He enjoined on his disciples never to say anything at all unless they felt quite sure that it was both true and important," one of Desmond's friends recalled. "The consequence was that young men who had been quite happy chatting on were reduced to silence." This formidable side showed in his personal relationships. He could not conceal his dislike for his great contemporary and fellow Apostle, Bertrand Russell, because he sensed in him a ruthlessness which repelled him and which morally he condemned. There was jealousy, too, between the two men. Desmond, who was friendly with both eminent philosophers, found himself often having to act as an intermediary.[8]

Moore's influence on Desmond was to last a lifetime. The intellectual standard he set pervaded Desmond's literary and dramatic criticism. At difficult moments in his life, it led Desmond to try and solve his problems

through airing them with absolute honesty and openness. For years he
believed whole-heartedly that Moore's moral conclusions represented the
very best he knew. During his early twenties, Desmond could have been
described as an idealist, a "pure" and serious-minded, though light-
hearted, young man. In this sense he was as unworldly as Moore and as
many of his contemporaries at Cambridge.

In another sense, however, he was much more a man of the world than
they were. Love of Society at its wealthiest and most sparkling came
naturally to him. He was pleasure-loving in a way that G. E. Moore could
never be, though he revered the lofty ideals presented by his friend. His
exuberance and enthusiasm, his lack of shyness and his affectionate
nature, drew Moore out of the enclosed existence that he had hitherto
known. Desmond knew, more than anyone, how to amuse his brilliant
friend: "A frequent scene which I like to look back upon," wrote Leonard
Woolf, "is Desmond standing in front of a fireplace telling a long fantastic
story in his gentle voice and Moore lying back on a sofa or deep in an
armchair, his pipe as usual out, shaking from head to foot in a long
paroxysm of laughter."[9]

What Moore stood for quintessentially represented the Apostles'
purpose at that time: to pursue truth in an atmosphere of close,
unreserved friendship. Desmond's first paper to the society was on the
theme: "should realisation of death determine our projects in life?" It was
lively but discursive. Full of literary references, it was chiefly an attack on
"the practical man's view of life." A later talk he gave, on "humour",
began – like much of his later work – with an early reminiscence: he
described his fastidious disgust when he saw for sale a book with a picture
of "an odious laughing round faced man" on the cover, entitled "Laugh
and Be Fat". The brief, evocative vignette of childhood was the best thing
in a hastily composed and rambling paper.[10]

Membership of the Society was supposed to be a closely guarded secret,
which has contributed to its spurious mystique for later "spycatching"
commentators. When Desmond told his mother of his election, he
suggested that she should burn his letter. Normally those elected were
obliged to attend the meetings regularly for several years after they had
gone down from the university. Desmond, who left Cambridge in 1898,
kept on coming to them until May 1901. At that point he formally
resigned, as was the custom, and became "an angel". After "taking
wings" angels could still attend meetings, and the annual dinner held in
the summer was a gathering of many men of great distinction.

Over the years, the Society was the source of many additions to
Desmond's circle of friends. Through it he encountered the brothers
Theodore and Crompton Llewellyn Davies: Theodore was tragically

drowned in 1905; Crompton remained a great friend until his death in 1935. At Desmond's college, Trinity, he first met two young Apostles, George and Robert Trevelyan (pronounced "Trevillion"), the sons of Sir George Otto Trevelyan and the great-nephews of Lord Macaulay. He stayed often at their beautiful house, Wallington, near the Scottish border, where there was a good atmosphere for hard work and high thinking.

George Trevelyan was to become, during Desmond's lifetime, almost as famous an historian as his forebear; but it was his literary and aesthetic side which drew Desmond to him. They were at one in hating the jejune pseudo-science of Professor Seeley who had lectured them on political economy;[11] and they were both dedicated to the writings of George Meredith, one of the most important literary luminaries in Desmond's life. The Trevelyans, a Northumberland land-owning family, were pillars of the Liberal Party, and, though they eschewed religion, were as morally serious as the most pious mid-Victorian Christians. They, like the Apostles, set themselves the highest standards in telling the truth. Desmond once wrote to confess to George that he had told him a lie in an earlier conversation. Most people, George reassured him, occasionally told lies to avoid losing face. He had done so himself three years before and then took the same step as Desmond had done – "that is I went and told the man. He didn't seem more shocked than I am now, probably because he remembered about the stoning of the woman taken in adultery. I remember it was one of the most difficult things I ever did and one of the most salutary . . ."[12]

The two streams in George's nature, the one earnest and political, the other eloquent and poetical, converged in the wide-ranging historical works which he turned out all through his life and which earned him the Order of Merit and the Mastership of his beloved Trinity.

Desmond was even more attached to George's elder brother Robert, "Bob Trevy". The two brothers shared a love of the countryside and of discourse, and both were tall and big-boned. There, however, the resemblance ended. Where George was well organized and single-minded in his objectives, Bob was rambling and unrealistic. George had an air of distinction, Bob was engagingly undignified.

Bob Trevy was naïve, confident, unselfconscious: from his large, humorous mouth there flowed, noisily, "the disorderly riches of his mind which was a junk shop of wisdom and learning". In an undergraduate atmosphere, his incoherent, idealistic meanderings, his bursts of passion and his overstated intellectual arrogance had their place; and it was really the early impression he made that fixed itself in his friends' affections. "Bob in those days made one think of a charming woolly bear, all the more charming for not having been too thoroughly licked," wrote Eddie Marsh.[13] Throughout Bob's life, Desmond helped with his poetry and listened patiently to his diatribes against "ignorant and illiterate publishers".[14] Fondness made him overestimate his friend's talents: Trevelyan's verses, published at his own expense, were but a pale echo of Robert Bridges. Technically competent and pleasant in atmosphere, they were repetitive and seldom original. After the university, he had no distractions outside his marriage and his children. His small private income enabled him to take a house in Italy as well as the one near Dorking, "The Shiffolds", where Desmond was a frequent guest. Such a life was possible in those days for people of relatively slender means, and after old Sir George Trevelyan died, his income increased. All his life Bob Trevy remained essentially the irresponsible undergraduate, enthusiastic and innocent. His best writing was, significantly, on the happy boyhood he had never left behind.

Bob and George Trevelyan, Lytton Strachey and Leonard Woolf were among those invited on the select annual reading parties organised by G. E. Moore during the Easter vacations, which Desmond attended almost every year up until the First World War. Moore chose out-of-the-way, windswept spots for the beauty of their setting rather than for comfort – a cottage at Birdlip in the Cotswolds, overlooking a vista of ancient Roman villa sites and the spires of Gloucester; Wyngate Farm in North Devon, with snow storms blowing inland from the sea, and smoking fires in the sitting room; or a house by the Needles on the Isle of Wight. Desmond worked diligently for short periods on these occasions but much of his time was taken up in wild, rain-drenched football matches, in scrambling over the rocks, in playing sodden games of croquet and wiling away the evenings by firelight, with excited arguments, jokes, poetry reading and word games, while Moore played the piano and sang. Above all it was the chance to talk about whatever he had been reading – it might be *Tess of the d'Urbervilles*, or *Marius the Epicurean* or *The Ordeal of Richard Feverel*.[15]

For this was the time when Desmond, in literary terms, was coming of age. As an undergraduate, his most important "discoveries" were Henry James and George Meredith, closely followed by Thomas Hardy. The influence of James and Meredith on his Cambridge circle at the time cannot be exaggerated. They discussed Henry James's novels endlessly in their efforts to establish what constituted the highest forms of experience. "His philosophy", Desmond wrote, "amounted to this: to appreciate exquisitely was to live intensely. . . . Whether or not we always agreed with his estimate of values, he was pre-eminently interested in what interested us; that is to say, in disentangling emotions, in describing their appropriate objects and in showing in what subtle ways friendships might be exquisite, base, exciting, dull or droll."[16] At the time it did not worry Moore or Desmond or the Trevelyans that the characters in James's novels lived in a world consisting entirely of personal relationships and aesthetic emotions, untroubled by practicalities; what Desmond and his friends responded to were the lofty ideals which James presented to them – spiritual decency, the beauty of gentleness, aesthetic purity. He planted the notion of "moral vulgarity" deep in Desmond's mind.

Desmond shared both James' lack of interest in how wealth was accumulated and his strong admiration for "ancient riches" as an essential foundation of civilised sensibility. Though he came later to think that James excluded too much that was important in life, Desmond persisted in defending his view that it mattered more to achieve the right state of mind and feeling than any particular practical goal.

As for Meredith, that ardent genius seemed to Desmond, Moore and George Trevelyan to hold the secret of living. His optimistic stoicism was more attractive to them than orthodox religion and more positive. He was the first Victorian poet, Desmond observed, to absorb wholeheartedly the message of Darwin. His reputation was then at its zenith and his message was directed at the young: "Face the world with courage," his books told them, "pursue the finest, be true to yourself and to the 'comic spirit', the humorous commonsense that exposes false feelings as absurd; and just because the best things fade, that is no reason to lose faith in them or in life itself." Desmond's expectations were raised by Meredith's views about love – that it should be "a noble strength on fire", and nothing less. Meredith's radiant, sharp-witted heroines became his ideal. He was drawn to the novelist's unpuritanical moral system and the subtly conveyed aura of sex in his books, which as Meredith later told Desmond, "cannot be too spiritual or too sensual for me". He also liked the way Meredith enjoyed the eccentricities and arrogant self-confidence of the aristocracy, and the "patrician oxygen" they imparted to the spirits.

Though he recognised that it could be obscure and inconsistent, he admired Meredith's writing as much as his vision. His mannered, idiosyncratic style entranced, if it occasionally irritated him.[17] He admired, above all, the skill with which Meredith created a romantic harmony between the passions and personalities he described and surrounding nature; of the heroine in Meredith's masterpiece, *The Egoist*, Desmond wrote: "We remember Clara Middleton, because, besides being an extremely sensible, quick-witted young lady, she has reminded us of so many beautiful things, of summer beechwoods with brown leaves underfoot, of mountain echoes and torrents with their ravishing gleams of emerald at the fall."[18]

For much of his life Meredith's view of things was close to his heart – well into the time of the novelist's eclipse after the First World War. "He is sure to rise again," Desmond told an audience in 1928.[19] Later, however, after a second world war, he found that writers with a more sombre vision, like Hardy, or a more divided one, like Tolstoy, had, in the end, come to mean more to him.[20]

In one other important respect, membership of the Apostles was responsible for Desmond's intellectual development, for it was the beginning, through Leonard Woolf, Lytton Strachey and Thoby Stephen, of his close association with the brilliant circle that came to be known as "Bloomsbury". After he went down from Cambridge, he met Thoby's sisters, Vanessa (later Bell) and Virginia (later Woolf), at the London house of their father, Sir Leslie Stephen, and subsequently he became a friend of Clive Bell, the future art critic, another of the "Bloomsbury" nucleus. Clive was never an Apostle – a source of lasting chagrin, because he enjoyed close friendships with so many of them. Desmond first encountered Clive in 1901 on the train to Cambridge, while Clive was still an undergraduate.

"There was on this occasion one other occupant of the carriage that I entered that afternoon. He was a youth with a noticeable head of wavy auburn hair, and that milk-white skin which often goes with it . . . he was dressed with careless opulence, and . . . wore, flung open, a dark fur coat with a deep astrakhan collar. I thought his appearance distinctly enviable. . . ."

Even more than his appearance, Desmond was struck by Clive's eager and enjoying temperament. "I delighted in him because I could see in imagination the enormous rich hunk he was about to cut from the cake of life." The two young men – Clive was twenty, Desmond twenty-four – became friends at once after this first chance meeting. He accepted Clive's invitation to lunch the next day. On arriving in his rooms, he noticed his ease both among the rich sporting set and the intellectuals at the university: "I found my host in a white hunting-stock and a dressing gown. His aspect was reminiscent of a sporting young man in a Leach picture at that delicious moment when he has pulled off his top-boots and is about to take his hot shower-bath. That it was a Sunday and he could not have thrown a leg over a horse that morning, added to his character a touch of fantasy," that element of fantasy which always attracted Desmond in his friends.[21]

Until 1901, Desmond remained a constant visitor to Cambridge for these Apostles' meetings, delivering papers and attending Moore's philosophical lectures at Trinity where his friend had at last gained a prize fellowship. Early in 1900, Moore had expressed fears that his differences with Russell might split the society, and wondered whether he should resign. With George Trevelyan's support, Desmond, himself beginning to tire of the form of discussion, wrote a critical paper lamenting the Apostles' increasingly inward-looking attitude and their preoccupation with their personal relationships. This essay interested and disturbed Moore who arranged for it to be read aloud to "brothers" on several occasions.[22] Desmond's disenchantment grew as the years passed. After 1902, Lytton Strachey's influence accentuated the tendency away from philosophy and public affairs. Desmond's close Apostolic friendships survived, but his recollections of their proceedings – to Moore's regret – were tinged with embarrassment. Later, in 1907, E. M. Forster's gently satirical description in his novel, *The Longest Journey*, was to meet with Desmond's grudging approval. He thought the book soft-centred and full of unreal situations; but he recognised that Forster had "hit off those miserable muffs the Cambridge Apostles pretty well".[23]

Intellectual Cambridge of the 'Nineties was an eventful but thoroughly sheltered world. There were not even the crises of religious faith which had so much disturbed young men in the mid-Victorian period. Desmond and his friends slipped into a serene agnosticism. The unceasing discussions sharpened his perceptions and stimulated his mental agility to a high level. In his circle, however, scant consideration was devoted to the future that awaited them in the world outside. Most achieved a successful transition from Cambridge to a career, but it proved very hard for Desmond himself. It is possible too that the rarefied atmosphere of the Apostles conflicted with his inner nature. He was a more full-blooded figure than his Apostolic contemporaries. Their influence may have acted as a curb on his spirit, and ultimately weakened his creative powers.

4 Aspirations

Desmond decided to be a writer early on in his Cambridge career. His father, however, who had himself, as a young man, been ambitious to enter politics, steered him towards the more practical choice of reading for the Bar after university;[1] but Mr MacCarthy's death, in September 1895, following a heart attack and long illness, removed his guiding hand and Desmond soon abandoned the uncongenial idea of becoming a barrister. His father's sudden death in his mid-sixties shocked and saddened Desmond, but the longer-term effect was that he now became the central object of his mother's frenzied possessiveness.

His death meant, too, that they had to vacate the house at Plymouth which went with Mr MacCarthy's job. For some time they stayed with friends and relatives until they eventually (in 1898) settled in London. Their income was of course reduced, not least because Mr MacCarthy had sustained a large financial loss before he died;[2] but they had enough – about £800 a year – to live upon, as long as Desmond was unmarried. His father left him £5,000, yielding £150 per annum. Neither mother nor son understood the buying of stocks and shares.[3] Chen, who controlled the bulk of their capital, asked everyone in sight before making even the most cautious move. She also canvassed her friends at length about Desmond's choice of career; it was her patrician protector, Lady Brownlow, who suggested he should apply for a Clerkship in the House of Lords – just the thing for an intelligent young man who wanted to combine a literary life with a public position.[4] Lady Brownlow's cousin, the Clerk of Parliaments, interviewed Desmond late in 1896 and judged him a suitable candidate. All that was required of Desmond was to pass a testing examination, to be taken when the next clerkship vacancy arose in two or three years' time, in such subjects as Latin, Maths, German, French and History. To Desmond, this formidable hurdle seemed a long way off, and there were two ever-present distractions from serious work: his life with his friends and his mother's grief-stricken state.

Chen needed endless reassurance. Unfortunately, Desmond frequently forgot to answer her letters and at times ignored her advice. Consequently, even though he was more devoted than many sons, and wrote to her sympathetically during her repeated bouts of psychosomatic illness, she complained of neglect. She longed for Desmond to be older and more responsible in order to look after her and yet she did not want him to change from being the child she had known, because to her any change was another death. "Keep your body very pure and clean outwardly & inwardly & as to your sweet soul," she urged him, fearing loss of innocence, "of course you will. Father is quite near still with you."[5] Her long-lasting notion of her husband as a benign presence hovering over them stemmed from her reluctance to face the fact of his non-existence. She continued for years to treat Desmond as if he were almost a child. He never became a "mother's boy" but his mother's eagerness to supply his every practical need, and her continual greed for his confidence, at once perpetuated his irresponsible side and led him to cultivate an emotional detachment. These two characteristics, already within him, were intensified as a result of his father's death, and characterised all his future relationships, in particular with his wife.

At the start of 1897, he was with Chen on a bleak winter holiday at Seaford, on the Sussex coast. He had a lot of catching up to do on work for his history degree, the Tripos examination being only a few months away; but he was worn down by his mother's demands and her obsessive talk about the Clerkship, the prospect of which did not excite him. On top of that he was debilitated by an attack of shingles.[6]

As the warmer spring weather approached his spirits revived, while Chen, not content with nagging him, also extended her interference to his friends, hoping to use their influence to make him work harder. She visited an exhibition of French pictures with G. E. Moore and went on the river at Eton with Hubert and Gerald Warre-Cornish and their mother, who alarmed her: "I could never become at all a friend of hers," she complained.[7] Desmond's future brothers-in-law were learned and civilised young men. Neither were Apostles, but Hubert shared Desmond's literary and aesthetic interests while Gerald was quite as keen as any Apostle to get at the truth in his arguments with Desmond. His approach was religious and intuitive rather than analytical, but Desmond appreciated his unusual mental powers. Gerald's extraordinary short story, *Beneath the Surface*, written some years after he left Cambridge, shows him to have been a mystic with a powerful inner vision.[8]

For a while, Desmond seemed once more in bounding health, playing tennis with vigour and cat-climbing over the roofs of his college; but in the weeks immediately before the Tripos his shingles recurred; when the examinations started he was in a state of collapse. After a few days, his tutor Verrall and his colleague decided to call a halt to the proceedings.

Desmond was given an "aegrotat" degree – awarded to candidates too ill to complete their papers.[9]

Desmond spent three months with Chen recuperating and learning German near Dresden for the Clerkship examination. He persuaded his mother that he should return to Cambridge in the autumn of 1897 to read for a further degree in philosophy for which he would be examined the following summer. Moore, impressed by his powers of argument and his wide philosophical reading, undertook to be his tutor.

Desmond proclaimed an ambitious programme of work for his second degree: lectures three times a week with Professor Henry Sidgwick at 9 a.m. and with J. Ellis MacTaggart at 12 noon daily – philosophers of great eminence whom Desmond knew well as Apostles.[10] He was to be coached in German twice a week and to write to Chen or his grandfather, the "Parent Bird" weekly in that language. In between the usual instructions about applying Vinolia cream to his chin and getting his broken teeth crowned, Chen expressed reasonable doubts about his ability to rise early enough to carry out his studies. His prolonged visits to friends in the country, like the Trevelyans, continued to prevent a regular pattern of work.

The relations of mother and son were now entering a new phase. Her interest in his friends was turning into an obsession: "I find myself not only often thinking about them but actually sometimes dreaming of them," she said. Friendship with them was the way to bind Desmond to her more securely. Her outward expression of what she felt subconsciously was to knit all of them silk ties. Being able to talk about Desmond in his absence with Moore, or Hubert Cornish was the next best thing to having Desmond's own company. Desmond, though glad that his friends could divert her, was frequently embarrassed by her unbalanced behaviour towards them.

For example, there was her attempt to make Desmond feel guilty about her by enlisting the aid of a fellow-Apostle, Eddie Marsh (1872–1963). Marsh, the son of a distinguished surgeon, was already an energetic patron, spending a part of his modest income on works of art; after Cambridge, he joined the Colonial Office and went on to be Winston Churchill's secretary and literary amanuensis. Industrious and sure-footed, Marsh led a self-contained bachelor life which made few demands on his pocket or his emotions. He was nattily dressed, his fresh-faced good looks, with peaked eyebrows and retroussé nose, recalling the Westminster choirboy he had been a few years before. His erudition was impressive, his delivery witty – though his thin squeaky voice detracted from the otherwise impeccable impression he made. Chen was somewhat daunted by Marsh's precocious self-possession, when he came to see her.

However, as so often happened with those who possessed social glamour for her, admiration for him grew: "how wonderfully he *lights* up at night. He is not nearly as handsome by day as by night, but he is very good looking." She responded to his marked femininity. Eddie, Chen accurately observed, "is so tremendously sensitive on things which women care for so much more than men. He is *dainty* & so fond of beautiful dress & loves his surroundings to be luxurious. . . ."[11]

Predictably she poured out to him about Desmond's "neglect" of her. The punctilious Marsh, who was infuriated by Desmond's vagueness over time whenever they arranged to meet, seized the opportunity to tick off his friend in a letter ". . . . when I see such a relationship in danger of being the least bit injured by anything that can be avoided I can't bear not to rush in and give warning . . ."[12] Desmond was intensely annoyed by his mother's conduct in dragging Eddie into an intimacy which did not exist between him and the MacCarthys. Although they remained always on affectionate terms, in later years Desmond and Molly, in common with "Bloomsbury", tended to disparage Marsh and his scrupulously organised existence. For all his cultivation, they thought him unoriginal; but their objections were not based only on their exacting standards. Though honourable and good-hearted, he was governessy and tactless, besides being a great gossip; and he was prickly: Molly once offended him deeply by laughing when he solemnly confided to her that his mother had died of a heart attack at a party while struggling with the tongue twister "a noisy noise annoys an oyster" (a detail not recorded in his memoirs).[13]

In November 1897 Chen was living at 7 Old Paradise Street, Lambeth, where her husband's old Leeds friend, Bishop Talbot, had found her work with the Cambridge Mission. For Desmond, Chen's new way of life came as a great relief; the work satisfied her insatiable curiosity about her fellow human beings and her taste for the gloomy end of life's spectrum. She visited consumptives and the bereaved, and read to invalids on their deathbeds. Encouraged by the Bishop she began to turn more actively to religion. Desmond was sceptical about the value of her new-found faith, save as a placebo. Nonetheless she stuck to it.

This was more than could be said for Desmond over his philosophical studies. While Chen was in London, choosing a silver inkstand for his twenty-first birthday and joining the crowds filing past Mr Gladstone's coffin as he lay in state in Westminster Hall,[14] Desmond decided in May to leave Cambridge, abandon his degree and immerse himself in the German language at Leipzig University as part of his preparation for the Clerkship examination.

Early in June he was writing to his mother from under the cool of the trees in the Rosenthal, Leipzig.[15] He had just been to stay with Otto de la

Chevallerie at Naunhof. This was the last time Desmond came into close contact with his strange grandparent, whose unhinged character seems so much at odds with his own, but who appears to have left some relic of fantasy within Desmond's make-up. In old age the "Parent Bird" seemed as "cracky" as ever. He had long been convinced that he had explained the riddle of the universe but, unfortunately, as Desmond recalled, he had found it to be "of such a nature that anyone who had discovered it must perforce forget the steps by which he had arrived at it."

One typical Sunday at Naunhof Desmond came down to breakfast to find that the "Parent Bird" "had been up all night crashing and hacking through a jungle of syllogisms and intuitions and had only lain down on the sofa for an hour before breakfast. His pointed beard was tortuously twisted & there were large ink patches in his soft grey hair, but otherwise he showed no signs of fatigue unless his eyes seemed set even a little deeper than usual in their bony sockets." After gulping down his morning coffee Chevallerie would discourse about literature and politics "with that overwhelming vehemence which", Desmond recorded, "at once extenuated & stimulated me, though after Mittagessen, on hot German summer afternoons, there was no doubt that extenuation prevailed. . . ." Desmond would then take to the green velvet sofa leaving his seventy-five-year-old grandparent "to tear up & down the room with his hands behind his coat-tails making them stick out – & looking like a cock pheasant's tail, shouting poetry, accumulating invectives, and occasionally stopping to bend over me and with an odd affectionate gurgle stroke my cheek with the back of his long hand & call me 'an angel'."

It was impossible to follow the old man's line of argument as he used his own private philosophical terminology; but Desmond could not but admire his eloquent tirades, which were "full of nuggets, unusual phrases, which even when I did not understand had, I felt convinced, a concentrated imaginative quality".[16]

Desmond's failure over his degree had plainly demoralised him, and life in a staid German provincial town offered nothing to distract him from introspection. He took German lessons desultorily and loafed in cafés with a local cocotte, allowing the social pariahs of the university to sponge off him. The "Parent Bird" sent Chen frenzied reports of his grandson's idleness and his disrespect for his teachers.

Desmond's only moments of intellectual stimulation came when watching the playwright Franz Wedekind performing in his dramatic work the *Erd-Geist*. Wedekind appeared before the curtain went up, "a bewigged, heavy-eyebrowed man in a crimson satin jacket and limp thigh boots, with a revolver in one hand and a whip in the other," and launched into a tirade to rival the "Parent Bird". Desmond was the only one in the small, hostile audience who appreciated the performance. He went three times and sent Wedekind a note which led to them drinking a silent glass of beer together. Unfortunately his real interest in the theatre had not yet developed or, as he later ruefully reflected, he might have been the man who brought Expressionism to Britain.[17] From Germany he went to Paris to improve his French. He was usually happy in France, which he found sympathetic, but now he found the weather oppressively sultry and he could not work. Even so, Paris always has compensations. He went several times to watch the famous actress, Réjane, performing. He also made friends with the artist, Neville Lytton (1879–1951), the younger brother of Lord Lytton – an athletic, Byronically handsome youth. Eddie Marsh – who had introduced him – was sentimentally in love with him; for Desmond this was no recommendation, but he admitted to Moore that "For once, Eddie is quite right."[18]

While Desmond was abroad Chen kept up an incessant barrage of complaints by post. Desmond found a packet of her reproachful letters awaiting him when he first arrived in Paris; "You treat everything however great sacred and solemn the thing is just as you do yr toothbrush. If you had the smallest respect for your toothbrush or cleanliness or order you cld not trample on the feeling of a splendid old man of seventy-six like yr grandfather."[19]

She raised the topic of Desmond's ambitions to write a great novel, and here, in contrast with her uncontrolled rantings, she came out with an alarmingly acute analysis of his personality. "I do not think you have genuis. I think you have *grt* feeling & understanding of the powers, & greatness & genius in others, which is clever and delicious & will make yr life always interesting & delightful even in *yr* most despondent moments, but I do not think you have any creative power nor have you endurance enough to be a *grt* man. All those things show very early in people. Talent is always *there* – it does not grow suddenly – it grows rapidly but from the instant the child is born. You are in matter of thinking and appreciation rather above the average & that tempts you and others, those who love you, to be led to think at *first* you are much more clever than you are."[20]

Desmond's self-defence was characteristically Apostolic in its objective self-examination and lack of false modesty. It was a tone he adopted frequently throughout his life when asserting his point of view – particularly in personal relationships with women. "I think what you say of my literary power is quite true. I have neither the facility or the energy to make a good easy living by writing. I should be further handicapped by fastidiousness – not one of the necessary qualities of a successful journalist. I know I sometimes write well, but with regard to real talent, I am, I expect, even more doubtful than you.

"If you mean by 'cleverness' power of understanding – I've met very few people who are at all my equal. You don't expect I shall write a big book – you see how uncertain it is; but I think you can be sure that whether I wear a shabby coat or a smart one I shall make a good many people feel more clearly the true values of things – and occasionally I hope to bring uneasiness to one or two self-satisfied worthies. You often tell me you wonder I am not more grateful – you have given up a home for me – I cost four hundred a year. I sometimes wonder you are not more grateful to me. You have often said that a new world has come to you through me, but I don't think you understand that with all my feebleness that it is I just as much as father's death and your religion that have made you understand your life. Perhaps this seems to you blasphemous absurd conceit. If there is any such idea in your head as you read this, it is no use adding 'I am certain of it' – but I am."[21]

Undeterred by Chen's estimate of his literary chances, Desmond began to work out ideas for a novel as soon as he returned to England in the autumn of 1898, closely studying such authors as Ruskin, Coleridge and Matthew Arnold. By the end of 1899, he and his mother had moved into what was to be their permanent home for years: No. 8 Cheyne Gardens, a tall, commodious late-Victorian terrace house of red brick near the Chelsea Embankment. Chen was enraptured at having him more exclusively to herself. Less welcome was his abandonment of the Clerkship. In December 1900 he announced, amid a storm of protest from his mother and her friends, that what mattered to him was literature and writing and that to undertake any job would only frustrate his determination to be a novelist.

The MacCarthys' financial position was insecure. Their dividends had diminished. The rent of the house was high. Desmond's expenses – clothes, shooting, cigars, fares – were increasing. His mother asked him to give up travelling by cab. She went third class on the railway – which she hated – and resigned from her ladies' club, the Sesame, to economise. Chen prided herself on her ingenious household management. Her principal wish was to create an environment where her son could write and where they could both entertain his friends. She was still young and it meant much to her to have the company of attentive, clever, young men.

Desmond himself sought out a wider literary acquaintance, among his heroes like Henry James, from whom he hoped to learn more of the secret of artistic inspiration. He often visited Samuel Butler; and he met the poet, Wilfred Scawen Blunt, Herbert Paul, Matthew Arnold's biographer, and Sir Leslie Stephen, the eminent man of letters.

His first encounter with Henry James, at an evening party in 1901, made him realise how careful one had to be in ordinary small talk with him: "I asked him if he thought London 'beautiful' – an idiotic question;

worse than that, a question to which I did not really want an answer, though there were hundreds of others (some no doubt also idiotic) which I was longing to ask. But it worked. To my dismay it worked only too well. 'London? Beautiful?' he began, with that considering slant of his massive head I was to come to know so well, his lips a little ironically compressed, as though he wished to keep from smiling too obviously. 'No: hardly beautiful. It is too chaotic, too –'"

James thereupon launched into a massive discourse on London's appeal to the historic sense. Having set the author's mind working at such a pitch of concentration on a subject to which he himself was indifferent, Desmond quite failed to follow its rolling phrases; he was also longing to make his mark on James by thanking him for the inspiration he had given him: "At the end of a sentence, the drift of which had escaped me, but which closed, I think, with the words 'finds oneself craving for a whiff of London's carboniferous damp,' I did . . . interrupt him. Enthusiasm and questions (the latter regarding *The Awkward Age*, just out) poured from my lips. A look of bewilderment, almost of shock, floated for a moment over his fine, large, watchful, shaven face, on which the lines were so lightly etched. For a second he opened his rather prominent hazel eyes a shade wider, an expansion of the eyelids that to my imagination seemed like the adjustment at me of the lens of a microscope; then the great engine was slowly reversed, and, a trifle grimly, yet ever so kindly, and with many reassuring pats upon the arm, he said: 'I understand, my dear boy, what you mean – and I thank you'. (Ouf! What a relief!)"[22]

Subsequently, Desmond wrote to tell James that he was keen to renew their acquaintance: "It is such a satisfaction to meet or even to know, that there exists someone who takes things & above all personal relations more complicatedly, or as complicatedly . . . as one does one's-self. And one likes to share a bit of experience with him, even if it is only walking down the street."[23]

Even so, he hesitated to pester him and over the fifteen years that he knew him, he preferred to leave their meetings to chance. However on three occasions at least he visited "the Master" at his "quiet, dignified and gemütlich" home, Lamb House, at the top of Mermaid Street in the picturesque, erstwhile port of Rye, Sussex. They walked together down the steep cobbled streets and across the marshes, where the sea had formerly stretched, between Rye, with its bright irregular roofs and gaily decorated church tower, and the gaunter, greyer Winchelsea. James, lamenting the long departed greatness of these towns, observed: "Rye dares to be cheerful: Winchelsea has the courage of its desolation." During those dark winter afternoon walks, James ranged over many topics – the British Parliament, the Empire, women suffragists, the vulgarity of modern French literature, the personality of the novelist Gissing, the intellectual dilettantism of Lord Acton, George Meredith's inaccuracies and his poetical power.[24]

Like many of James' disciples, Desmond was terrified of boring him — which could happen all too easily. Worse still, James suffered from remorse over any lack of rapport: "if your talk with him had been something of a failure, his farewell expressed that what you had wanted, yet failed to get, he had also wanted[;] and that nothing must blind you to his recognition of any affection or admiration you might be so generous as to feel for 'your old Henry James'."[25]

5 Mother and Son

The path Desmond had chosen is notoriously hard. Writing a novel needs tranquillity and self-discipline. He had neither. He had long been convinced that he had something new and important to say in a novel, and that he was more responsive than anyone else he knew to certain aspects of *life*. He was exceptionally appreciative of many atmospheres and points of view. He was a collector of human "types". His interests ranged through philosophy, religion, aesthetics, criminology, blood sports, political ideas and medicine. All this, and his analytical powers, were qualities any novelist might envy; but he found it very hard – all too like the "Parent Bird" – to grasp and articulate the thrilling truths about life that seemed so tantalisingly close. After eight months' work at Cheyne Gardens he was still fumbling "at the lock of the precious chest where they lie hidden".[1] Why were his ideas not falling into place? he wondered. Why did his every change of mood interrupt the flow of his creative imagination? He put his difficulties down to having lost his way in life – and concluded that unless he achieved understanding through working out a philosophy for himself, he would never be able to focus his thoughts effectively.

He was confident, however, that whatever the outcome, he was right in dedicating himself for a few years to the ambitious task of sorting out his ideas and teaching himself to write: "I have no profession to shelter behind," he had declared at the outset, "and if I find I can't write, at least that is a very distracting delusion laid. However as long as I find I can go on with ardour and occasional gleams of happy enthusiasm, in spite of excruciating dissatisfactions and flat results, I shall continue to think it worthwhile."[2]

He was optimistic that it would all come right in the end; Tolstoy and Meredith had taken years before they had developed into great writers: "with this want and longing in my heart surely it is worthwhile trying," he told Chen. "All I can do is to try and open myself bravely and sincerely to every perception & experience wh: chance may blow upon my heart. . . ."[3] These were heroic words – but most of his experience at this time came from his reading. Yet lack of first hand knowledge of the world was not the chief problem. His central difficulty remained that his uncertainties about life inhibited him. Even when he took the plunge, and tried to write, the perfectionism of G. E. Moore and Henry James – whose minds he so much admired – was his enemy. His words never came out as he would have wished, so he destroyed them; nothing save a few fragments of prose, and an enormous literary knowledge, emerged from the four years from 1899 to 1903 when he tried to launch himself as a major novelist.

He often poured out his uncertainties to his friends. George Trevelyan who set himself more defined, though no less ambitious goals, was working on his famous *History of England Under the Stuarts*, when Desmond confided in him. Replying, Trevelyan advised him: "One of the reasons why I believe in methodical work at some carefully chosen object, is because it is also the chief condition of . . . a state of mind and soul.[4] . . . [in which] one can live and work and love . . . unafraid."

Rather than taking this sensible advice, Desmond tried to get over his difficulties by rearranging his day: "I find [I] get more work done if I telescope the morning into the afternoon. I begin at about twelve & work on to abt. 5 with a glass of milk & a few biscuits on a tray instead of lunch – & then go out when the street lamps burst into blossom – an arrangement of the day wh: lets me take a long night's reading whenever I feel inclined."[5]

The significance of this apparently undemanding programme lies in the last sentence. By contrast with Desmond's frustrated effort at creative writing, his reading was rigorous and concentrated. He read to gain inspiration, but it was what he eagerly absorbed, not what he tried to put out, which was the lasting monument to these years.

A diary he kept during the early part of 1900 gives a glimpse of how he habitually spent his time: on New Year's Day he first read *Jasper Tristram*, A. W. Clarke's disturbing novel of schoolboy love that Desmond always recommended to friends, and mulled over Meredith's *Diana of the Crossways* which he already knew well. On 5th January, he started Froude's *Carlyle* and Crabbe's poetry; he bought a volume of Bridges' poems and a copy of de Gramont's memoirs. On the 6th he began and finished Masson's life of de Quincy and read Bridges' poems. On the 9th he returned to Froude's *Carlyle* in earnest. On the 12th he began and finished the life of Lewis Carroll and read poems by Sturge Moore. For a week he went shooting, then on the 18th he recorded a morning spent on Browning's verse. On the 19th he launched into *Madame Bovary*, finishing it at one in the morning. The next day he re-read *Jasper Tristram*. On the 24th he began Swinburne's study of Ben Jonson. On the 26th he read Baudelaire's *Epaves*, on the 27th an English novel, and on the 29th most of a life of Tolstoy. On 2nd February he was deep in Dante. On the 3rd he read an article by Bradley on psychology; then after a gap of a week he began *Jude the Obscure*; on the 13th he devoted himself to Byron – *Childe Harold* and Arnold's essay on the poet; on the 14th it was the poetry of Verlaine; on the 15th he began Henry James' *The Awkward Age* for a second time. On the 16th he turned to a short story by Tolstoy. We may therefore guess that on average from 1899 until his marriage, he read every year between 100 and 150 important works of literature, biography or philosophy of varying lengths and languages – that is, between 600 and 800 works altogether; this leaves out the previous years at Cambridge which would raise the figure to about 1,200. Such wide reading gave him an exceptionally strong basis for his eventual career of a critic.

His was not altogether a sedentary life. He was a keen field sportsman, riding, hunting and shooting (inaccurately) with the Trevelyans at their Northumbrian home at Wallington, at Hardwick, at Crabbet Park with Wilfred Blunt,[6] at Ampton in Suffolk with his childhood friend Arthur Paley and wherever else the opportunity presented itself. He found the sport itself exciting and above all he loved the countryside: riding and roaming through it induced powerful aesthetic reactions.

Desmond often shared his excursions into the country with one of his most devoted Cambridge friends, Reymond Abbott. He had come to live at Cheyne Gardens largely because Chen took pity on his loneliness and this curious combination of Chen, Desmond and Reymond made for a turbulent ménage. He rapidly made his presence felt with his mania for fresh air, his late rising, his unaccountable moods, which during 1900 and 1901 often brought him close to madness.

Reymond de Montomorency Abbott (1870–1963) was a slender and delicate-featured young man, quivering with aesthetic rapture and appalled by any failure of sensibility; he could not bear to be shaved by a Cambridge barber and travelled instead up to London twice a week for the purpose.[7] Nor could he stand the gregariousness of the university clubs and societies. He dressed with great care and in due course settled on what was to be his style of clothes for life, regardless of changing fashion: a pepper and salt tweed suit and "wide awake" hat, both of excellent quality – the only thing, in his opinion, that a quiet gentleman should wear. He drank moderately but expensively and patronised an exclusive wine merchant. One of his favourite writers was the conservative intellectual novelist, W. H. Mallock, the fastidious astringencies of whose prose pleased him; he shared Mallock's view that "the world was indeed very bad and that society was on the point of dissolution".[8]

Though Abbott had a good, well-balanced intellectual judgement and was learned and scholarly, he was excessively critical of his own work. His Latin verse paper in the Tripos examination consisted of a few unfinished lines with some suggestions for possible endings and other scraps of information, finishing with the words: "these verses are not meant to scan".

Desmond delighted in his friend's Ruskinian sensitivity to literature, architecture and music, in his fantastical sense of humour, in his high, breathy laugh, and also in his courtesy and his air of distinction. Abbott's habit of sitting wide-eyed and rapt in thought earned him the nickname "The Owl"; but he was not a wise owl when it came to coping with life. His father, General Sir James Abbott, died while he was up at Cambridge, leaving him an orphan with a small private income on which he lived, without working, to the end of his days. "The Owl" had been devoted to his father, who was no ordinary soldier, but a poet and a hero of the North West Frontier in the romantic, adventuring mould. In the Peshawar province of Pakistan, a town, Abbottabad, commemorates his name and throughout "The Owl's" peripatetic life he carried with him like a campaigner's impedimenta the relics of his father's Indian life – a wonderful treasure hoard of jewelled weapons, rugs and carvings, along with the hero's sword, his documents and his diary.

Given his solitary, introspective existence it is not hard to see why "The Owl" was so fond of Desmond, but the amount of time that Desmond devoted to such peculiar and often blighted individuals as Abbott, requires explanation. A liking for oddities was something Desmond had acquired from his father.[9] Though Desmond got on with most people, as a rule, his greatest friendships were with people who appealed to his imagination. Even where he made particular friends associated with his professional work, it was because of their originality and personal idiosyncrasies, as in the case of Max Beerbohm, Hilaire Belloc and Vernon Lee, none of whom could fairly be described as "normal". Unaffected by worldly considerations, it was his genius to draw out what was most unusual and amusing in his companions' natures, and to act as their sympathetic guide and confidant. His detachment was an asset in a life so crowded with close companions; but he was far from cold-blooded, and as long as eccentrics like "Owl" – or anyone – needed him, he could not turn his back on them.

Chen came to believe that Reymond's oddity and inability to work were the consequences of having so old a father, of being the product of "exhausted loins", as she put it. Whatever the explanation for "The Owl's" peculiarities, this is clearly not it: for he was tough and wiry, under a fragile demeanour which fooled everyone. He never suffered from serious ill health, despite under-nourishment for most of his life, and periods of poverty and neglect as his tiny income dwindled away. He possessed, in fact, a good natural endowment of nervous vitality which showed in his bright eyes and lively expression. His chin, however, had a retreating, irresolute appearance, indicative of inner fears.[10]

The fact was that all his life "The Owl" was in the grip of an obsessional neurosis, which drained his energy and weakened his personality. He was tortured by fears of dirt and contamination and by suspicion of plots against him or attempts to steal his talismanic possessions. At the time when he first came to know Desmond, he had the hand-washing mania. He would put on a glove to turn a door handle for fear of contact with germs; all his life he would also cover himself with eau de cologne as a disinfectant and deodorant.

Because of his humour and ultra-civilised standards, Abbott was on the whole kindly. He was particularly sweet to small children; but he was not really a gentle character. So high were his expectations of human nature that his contempt was easily aroused and paranoia made him unpredictable. He ruined many evenings at Cheyne Gardens with sudden venomous attacks.

During 1899 Chen's feeling for "The Owl" passed from protectiveness and delight to an obsessive clinging. In this she convinced herself she was helping Desmond too, for "The Owl's" miseries worried him deeply. Abbott became almost a second child. As Desmond's intimate friend she could pour out to him her incessant worries about her son, at times playing the one off against the other. Besides, his affinities with her neurotic father had a compelling fascination for her. She was desperate for his good opinion and to be the woman in whom he confided. Being childish herself, she had none of the detachment that would be normal to an older person over a young friend. The confused Abbott sometimes encouraged her, but at other times was terrified that she would penetrate his defensive armour.

She did not recognise that his behaviour was psychotic. Her own language, mirroring his own, became frenzied and hysterical: "I have never felt any love such a reality as the love I feel I have for you . . . no-one has made up life for me *more* than you, not even Ifchen the blessed one. . . . I can't do without you . . . yr smile is the most beautiful I've ever seen in a human face."[11] Later, when they were estranged, she worried greatly about "The Owl's" possession of such letters: "They are not love letters, though very loving but everyone would think them love letters. . . . I love him more than anyone except you since father's death but I could never have married him. . . ."[12]

Whatever the true nature of her sentiments, under the onslaught of her money worries and hysteria about "the beloved Abbott", Desmond's normally robust spirits flagged: "Wednesday 14th February 1900: long gloomy talk with mother. Bad night."; "Abbott came. Doleful evening," were typical diary entries for this period. It was a relief to visit other friends, such as Hubert and Gerald Cornish, "for a few days' delicious change" at Wyngate Farm in Devon, or G. E. Moore, who greatly regretted Desmond's absence from Cambridge. Desmond was delighted whenever he saw his old friend again, finding his rational outlook a healthy antidote to Chen's nerve storms.

Finally, in the spring of 1901 while Chen took a cure in Switzerland, Abbott was persuaded to leave Cheyne Gardens. The following year, he settled in Dorchester, drawn by the presence of Thomas Hardy. Desmond shared Abbott's passion for Hardy's novels, and together they paid a literary pilgrimage to the writer's house, Max Gate.

When he saw Hardy, in his "little chintzified, cultured sitting room", Desmond was struck, as portrait painters who captured it were too, by "something . . . winning and somehow twisted both in his features and expression; something agelessly elfin in him . . . and a glint in his eye which one might have associated with slyness in a mindless and insensitive man. He was very small, very quiet, self-possessed and extraordinarily unassuming. I seem to remember that his laughter made no sound. As is usual with subtle people, his voice was never loud, and a gentle eagerness which was very pleasing, showed in his manner when he wanted sympathy about some point. He would instantly recoil on being disappointed. I observed in him once or twice a look, a movement, too slight to be called a wince, but not unlike the almost imperceptible change one sees in a cat when a gesture has perturbed it."

Desmond enjoyed nearly an hour's talk with Hardy "about – Shelley – & being clever – & telling stories in verse & animals – all easy & natural: hard to remember, but never to be forgotten. He seemed the simplest man of intellect I had ever met – except Moore, in whom simpleness is indistinguishable from clearness of thought, while Hardy can't think well. He does not strike you even as having the observer's eye – His penetration is emotional, I think, & more like the poet's than the novelist's."

This visit, in April 1902, was the first of several, during which Desmond joined Hardy on walks or cycling trips across the wide grey-green downland near Dorchester to Weymouth, or along the high-hedged lanes through neighbouring villages clustered by clear streams that dried up in summer. Hardy would point out landmarks that had featured in his novels: "Once," Desmond recorded, "when we were passing the scene of some incident in *Tess*, he said to me, 'If I had thought that story was going to be such a success I'd have made it a *really good book*.'"

As an aspiring author, Desmond was very curious to find out what had made Hardy decide to write fiction. Money, Hardy told him: hearing that George Meredith earned £100 for writing a novel, he had sat down himself and produced *Desperate Remedies*, which was published in 1871.[13]

Mrs Hardy on these occasions was disconcertingly jealous. Once she walked Desmond up and down the lawn, uttering "a ripple of quietly violent abuse of H. and his family. 'The peasant class, I dare say you do not know the peasant class. You are fortunate. They are very treacherous. I wrote a large part of Mr Hardy's books. Then his family told him he ought not to let me help him, that it would be bad for his reputation. Now I'm shut out. Literary men are not at all to be trusted . . .'"[14] Letters of advice in the same unbalanced vein followed for years afterwards, Desmond accurately dismissing her pronouncements as "crazy"; but he and Hardy kept up their friendship till the writer's death in 1928.

"The Owl", meanwhile, settled in Dorchester above a little hat shop, "building dungeons in the air" as Desmond put it, or falling in love, at a safe distance, with unknown girls in idyllic rural settings. Eventually Chen's unhealthy obsessions with him abated. Her feelings had come close to dislike: "even when he is fond of me," she told Desmond, "he tortures & vivisects one's whole being . . . one interests him only as an experience . . . he cannot love."[15]

In truth Desmond was the only person for whom "The Owl" deeply cared. Like a cat, he still returned unswervingly to Cheyne Gardens, when he felt lonely in Dorchester. It is to Thomas Hardy's credit that he took a kindly interest in Reymond's eccentric life: "I am often telling Abbott", he wrote to Desmond, "that he does not go out enough or see enough people, but I cannot make much impression. He is always much better when he has been to London. He was full of an idea of going to live at Winchester the other day, but he has found out that they have incandescent gas burners in the cathedral, which he says makes it impossible."[16]

It was to take Desmond a long while to accept that he had grown away from Reymond; guilt, affection and a feeling for the past drove him to keep the friendship going; but Abbott seemed fixed in an undergraduate world of inexperienced young men waiting on the brink of life. Haunted, pathetic, fastidious, he would wait there for ever, while Desmond, however much he might hanker after old times, had to go on his way. Desmond's failure during these early years to write the book he so passionately believed he had in him, must ultimately, be attributed to his particular cast of mind and temperament. It is undeniable, however, that the disturbing saga of Chen and "The Owl" played a significant part in frustrating his endeavour.

6   Love and Work

In 1902, when Desmond had his first serious love affair, he was a striking young man of twenty-four, with very dark hair and broad shoulders; his responsive face with its strongly marked eyebrows had an amused quizzical look. He was not, and never became, a fastidious dresser, but there was something debonair about his untidiness; and his clear skin, bright eyes and melodious voice made a particularly agreeable impression. Above all, he was at ease with women, whose company he always enjoyed, for Chen's social aspirations meant that he and his mother moved in circles where much emphasis was placed on feminine charm. In this he was unlike Cambridge contemporaries such as Moore, Forster and Strachey, for whom, as young men, women of their own age seemed mostly both threatening and dowdy: different enough from the male to be alarming: not different enough to be interesting.

Desmond frequently joined Neville Lytton's entertaining house parties at Rake, near Milford in Sussex, and it was here that he began to see much of Irene Noel (1879–1956), whom he had met earlier with Sir Leslie Stephen and his family. Neville Lytton and his beautiful unconventional wife, Judith, seem to have largely replaced the grand but ageing Brownlows as the principal focus of Chen's passion for the well-born. For Desmond the Lyttons' company was exhilarating: Neville was becoming increasingly recognised as an artist, partly through the enthusiasm of his youthful patron Eddie Marsh. Judith Lytton (1873–1957) was the daughter of the swashbuckling poet, traveller and Irish nationalist, Wilfred Scawen Blunt and had his over-masterful temperament. Father and daughter quarrelled ferociously over the family properties and over Blunt's sexual escapades. Desmond concluded after witnessing many years of this: "aristocrats are very dirty fighters".[1] Judith had inherited her father's picturesque, lean-faced looks. She was a champion Real Tennis player and an expert horsewoman. Later she took over the running of her father's celebrated racing stud at his seat, Crabbet Park, to which she was the heir. She also bred dogs. Here she found an affinity with Desmond; he loved animals and they formed an integral part of his literary and conversational imagery – whether it was bears, dogs, tapirs, hippopotamuses or rabbits, they seem to have come at once to mind whenever he sought a simile.

Judith Lytton adored her handsome husband; their days were spent riding, practising tennis and learning French. While Neville painted or played English folk dances on his ivory flute, Judith would write verse, some of which was published. Like many vital young married women who bask in domestic happiness, she had a good deal of affection to spare for her friends, including Desmond and Irene Noel.

Hitherto, Desmond's amorous life had been uneventful. As with many stagestruck young men of his period, his romantic feelings were fixed chiefly on actresses, including at one time, Edna May.[2] In August 1900 he had gone to see a Japanese company acting Shakespeare at the Shaftesbury Theatre; the actor Kawakami had played a powerful Shylock – "The only performance I have seen in which it seemed credible that a pound of flesh was actually going to be cut from a man's breast before our eyes" – but what had really struck Desmond was the entrancing Sada Yacco, who played Portia. Boldly, he sent her a bunch of flowers and secured an introduction. Before their second meeting he felt confident enough to invite her to lunch, writing in Japanese, with the assistance of an interpreter. "She was pleased to see me – really pleased, & we had some delightful broken trivial talk together – but why didn't I tell her I was in love with her?" Desmond lamented to Reymond Abbott.[3] Their tentative little idyll evaporated when she left London with the company.

Such stage door encounters came to an end when Desmond fell in love with Irene Noel. Two years younger than himself, intelligent and good-looking, she seemed to him the incarnation of a Meredith heroine: she was independent but not "modern", wilful and challenging, vital rather than humorous. She was fashionably dressed with luxuriant brown hair piled on top of her small, neat head. Her background made her doubly romantic to him: Irene's grandfather had been a comrade in arms of Lord Byron and had been given a large estate, Achmetaga, in 1832, on the lovely island of Euboea. This had been the Greek nation's gift in gratitude for his championship of their independence. Far more than the men she attracted, Achmetaga was always the dominant influence of Irene's life. Her mother, a beautiful, neglected woman, had run off with a neighbouring Greek landowner and eventually died in England while Irene was still a child. As she grew up, Irene's father relied on her to manage the estate and it was understood that she rather than her ineffective brother Byron, would eventually inherit Achmetaga.

There, for most of the year, she reigned, "vigorously" – a favourite word of hers – cleaning and beautifying the house, gardening, supervising the planting of the vines, managing the servants and visiting the sick in the village. She had a good mind, and set herself a testing intellectual regime, studying classical texts, foreign authors, and English thinkers – Plato, Plutarch, Thucydides, Dante, Walter Pater. She also sketched assiduously, recording the season's changes in that hilly, sunlit landscape, from the first appearance of the violets and roses in the fragrant Greek spring. She learnt to address the peasants in their Euboean dialect and her position as châtelaine intensified her already dominating nature.[4]

One of her responsibilities to the estate was to find a husband and to have an heir. This was partly the object of her extended visit to London every year. She lodged at Hyde Park Gate, near Vanessa and Virginia Stephen, with a close family friend, "Matia" – Mrs Ellen Cobden Sickert, the divorced first wife of the painter. For fourteen years "Matia" (Greek for "eyes") was effectively Irene's mother. If Irene's behaviour towards Desmond and some other young men, including – it is said – Winston Churchill, appears exasperating and selfish, it must be remembered that she was being pulled uncomfortably in different directions. Desmond might have been more congenial than any other man she knew, but however delightful and interesting she thought him, his future was too uncertain. It was Achmetaga to which he had to measure up rather than just to Irene herself. Achmetaga was the bulwark of her existence; it could not again be associated with inadequacy in any form. Though Irene was under pressure to find a husband, and in any case was amorous by temperament, she was mistrustful of close relationships with men; they had been the ruin of her mother, and "Matia"'s life was overcast by her divorce from Sickert. Irene was realistic in seeing that she herself was hard to please and had a difficult temper. She needed someone who would both be a credit to her and submit to her control. Despite an exuberant exterior, within Irene was insecure. Again and again she led men on, charming them, goading them with her vacillations before, half-unwillingly, dropping them. Desmond was only one victim out of many.

But in 1902 his hopes were high, and so, it must be added, were Chen's: she was greatly taken with Irene, with her cultivation and, most of all, with her prospective wealth. So it was with Chen's blessing that Desmond planned to stay with the Noels at Achmetaga in June of that year. His first destination was Turkey.

Free from care, despite the letters from Chen which followed him inexorably, panicking about his "depts", Desmond relished even the discomfort of the tramp steamer on which he travelled. "The food is very plain & will be I can foresee very unappetising to a queasy stomach. . . . the tea is of the kind wh: sends a strong astringent shudder

left 'Bob Trevy', a cartoon by Max
Beerbohm
above G.E. Moore, philosopher and
Cambridge Apostle, who became
Desmond's greatest friend
below left Desmond in his Cambridge
days
below right Eddie Marsh, *c.* 1904
(portrait by Neville Lytton)

right
Irene Noel

below left
Judith Lytton at Crabbet Park. She
encouraged Desmond's and Irene's
'affair'

below right
Neville Lytton, who, with his wife
Judith, was to become a great family
friend

down the back. Well, well – I wouldn't rather be aboard a passenger steam[er] for all that." He quickly made friends with the captain and the other officers for whom his amusing company enlivened the monotonous voyage.[5]

Armed with introductions from Harry Cust, he plunged himself for two weeks into the life of Constantinople, then one of the most fascinating cities in the world, "with Persians Albanians, Turks Greeks Circassians Armenians Arabs, English Russian etc passing passing all the time . . . up & down the rickety wooden streets". On a little Arab horse he rode round the old fortifications, through the winding streets of the ancient Turkish quarter and under dark dusty cypress groves, past neglected Mussulman graveyards. He witnessed a service of dervishes howling in a state of frenzy who were healing the sick by treading on them, and he gave alms to a colony of lepers he discovered living in a huge burial ground outside the city. Once he had visited Smyrna and Ephesus, he was eager for congenial company and looked forward to joining the Noels in Greece.[6]

He reached them at breakfast time on 1st August after a beautiful moonlit ride through steep woods and narrow valleys from the Euboean coast.[7] He stayed for a month at Achmetaga. It was an idyllic existence: he spent much of his time with Irene, reading Meredith aloud with her, bathing, and riding over the vast estate. He also used to accompany her father on his daily inspection of massive irrigation works, returning to jot down a few lines of his novel. After tea, they would all go for a long drive or a ride, finishing the day with dinner outside in the woods or on the terrace.[8]

Clearly in Desmond's mind some "understanding" now existed between Irene and himself, and he was blissfully happy, despite his feelings not being fully reciprocated by her. Nothing marred his visit until he came down with a fever at the end of August, as he was due to leave. After he said goodbye to the Noels he spent nearly three weeks in Athens, ill with jaundice and recuperating; he was moved to tears as he contemplated the Acropolis and recollected, in the fly-blown solitude of his hotel, his magical visit to Euboea, conjuring up a vision of Irene, firm and serious as she taught English to the local priest, or, transformed to a sea-nymph, swimming by moonlight at Kimassi.[9]

He returned to England at the end of September, much surer of himself: "I have become a MAN," he told his friend Arthur Paley proudly, "and am no longer a flimsy fantastic chimera. I have acquired a will of my own . . . and a formidable eye. Seriously Arthur I have had adventures and feel as if I had been tossed in a blanket." There is an obvious way in which this statement can be interpreted, but whether it throws any light on the nature of his relationship with Irene in particular, it is impossible to say.

Later on during the First World War, when Irene eventually became engaged to be married, Molly referred acidly to her numerous "affairs", but it is doubtful that Irene, who was worldly as well as romantic, would have compromised herself to the extent of having an "affair" in the modern meaning of the word. Neither did that most energetic gossip, Virginia Woolf, who commented unfavourably on Irene on many occasions in her diary, ever intimate that she was sexually promiscuous. Unfortunately it is not possible to trace the vagaries of Desmond and Irene's relationship in much detail because nearly all the letters passing between them have disappeared, as has Irene's diary for 1903; it is evident at least that Desmond made repeated declarations of his love, and that Irene's feelings were too indefinite to satisfy him.

It was a relief for him to confide in G. E. Moore,[10] and, later, to be able to reciprocate by helping Moore to sort out some of his own problems. Bertrand Russell, at Bob Trevy's insensitive suggestion, had proposed himself for one of the annual Apostolic reading parties. Russell, unaware how much Moore continued to dislike him, believed that things between them were on the mend. So it was up to Desmond, who always got on well with Russell, to persuade him to withdraw discreetly.[11] For this Moore was grateful: "the fact that you like Russell so much makes me think I ought to like him. But I can't help thinking that even you would have found him embarrassing before a fortnight was over."[12] As well as Moore and Desmond, the reading party which finally went to The Lizard in Cornwall in the spring of 1903 included Bob Trevy, Lytton Strachey and Leonard Woolf. Desmond found Trevy an ordeal: "Bob has talked and talked – address a remark to him & it's like opening a weir hatch."

He was keyed up for a visit to Northern Italy later that spring where he was to join Irene and "Matia". He had resolved to ask Irene to marry him. His mother, who clearly saw this conquest as her own responsibility too, harangued him about every detail, from the length of his shirt sleeves to the state of his mucous membrane; her greatest concern was that he should appear to Irene as a man with the prospect of a remunerative career. She enlisted also the aid of Judith Lytton who had become very fond of Desmond. Judith dashed off a characteristically forthright letter to Irene: "I have just dined with the best looking young man in London (so called) & Desmond is worth 10 of him in every way! I know I am giving you the most desperately unworldly & injudicious advice in wanting you to love Desmond but I can't help it; I *do* like him so much the best of any young man I know! I feel you would be perfectly safe to be loved to the end of your days if you married him. I don't know why I feel such implicit confidence in him, but I do."[13]

Judith's word was likely to carry weight with Irene who was devoted to her; but Mrs Lytton made the mistake of quoting a long and crazy letter from Chen about Desmond's chastity, which also made promises regarding his financial prospects – a curious combination of moral uplift and horse trading which can have done little to raise Desmond or his mother in Irene's estimation. The trip to San Gimignano in Italy turned out to be charming but inconclusive – as Irene probably intended. "My pen sticks a little when I write abt her," he told Chen, "& I sometimes think she does not care for me as much as it is in her nature to care – I sometimes think she does, often that she will."[14]

In that tranquil atmosphere matters went as well as they ever could; but by the time he was writing to Irene in August, it was clear that her feelings had gone off the boil. He found a letter of hers "cold and patronising" and he reproved her for being spoilt and self-centred. Later he apologised for his remarks – though he did not recant them – and declared himself unequivocally: "I wonder whether you will ever love me with all your heart. I am happier now because I love you and with that feeling is mixed so much assurance – tho' I can find no ground to support it, beyond feeling that you want to be loved and love again as much as I do. You do want it. Your whole nature needs it. It is the only thing that can make you all that you are meant to be. You know it in your heart . . . And I want your love."[15]

By the end of the year it was clear that Irene would never marry him. He felt crushed and humiliated but Irene did not repine; she acquired a new admirer, younger than herself – the dashing polo-playing Lord Wode-house, heir to the Earl of Kimberley, shortly to be an M.P. and later a war hero.

Chen was furious: "I cannot think her worthy of the best love you evidently have given her & are giving her now. . . . Like an insect when it has sucked the honey out of a flower goes to another, she can go from one young man lightly and gaily to another." However she reassured her son: "in *the end* it will be a blessing she did not marry you." In this Chen was right. Marriage to Irene would not have suited Desmond. She was much too managing, and he, in his gentle way, too unmanageable for it to have been happy. However his romantic feelings for Irene had not completely evaporated – as will be seen.

His affair with Irene had, however, one important result for Desmond. It forced him to give his mind, for the first time, to earning a living. In 1903 he started to write reviews.[16] His lifelong career as a journalist had begun. During the course of that year he reviewed books and plays for

The Speaker, *The Times*, and *The Outlook*. Bob Trevy introduced him to a new Liberal paper, *The Independent Review*, launched by Desmond's old Cambridge friend, Charles Roden Buxton, with financial aid from the Trevelyans; Desmond was a contributor for several years, during which the paper was renamed *The Albany Review*. He was never well-paid – only 25/– for 3000 words – but he proved a "natural" as a journalist and was given frequent opportunities to write on topics which were close to his heart, like the work of Henry James.[17]

During these early years of the twentieth century, Desmond acquired a growing reputation as a dramatic critic of originality and perception, a familiar figure in the theatreland of the great city. Reluctant journalist though he was, the prospect of seeing any play excited him at that period, even when his more discriminating side told him it was likely to be "bosh". Whenever he was given a reviewing assignment, he would spend his mornings reading the relevant texts, then go on to a long lunch with a friend. One of many he had with the writer Hilaire Belloc at the Mont Blanc restaurant he described as very amusing, "that volcanic person being in considerable eruption, throwing up stones, mud, dust & some passably precious minerals, but obscuring my heavens with a smoky cloud, lit it is true now & then with fine rich fire glow from beneath, but making eyes that love clear daylight smart & tingle. We had a good talk."[18]

Such occasions were often followed by another engagement for tea, with an old family friend he did not much want to see, but about whom Chen made him feel guilty. Cutting it much too fine, he would return to his mother's house in Cheyne Gardens and hurry into white tie and tails; then he would rush into "the carboniferous damp" of London's night, with Chen clucking and fussing around him as he left, and hail a passing cab to take him to the West End – His Majesty's, The Savoy, or The Haymarket. Once there, eager and exhilarated, he settled himself to his seat, chatting to companions and impatiently awaiting the raising of the curtain.

After the performance came dinner. He would join Maurice Baring, perhaps, or Max Beerbohm. Long before he first met Max at the house of Aubrey Beardsley's sister, Mabel, the elegant wit and cartoonist was a familiar sight to him: "I remember walking one night down Piccadilly behind that high-hat with its deep mourning-band which he has recorded. It was then perched above a very long dark top-coat with an astrakhan collar. . . . In a gloved hand this figure held an ebony stick with an ivory knob. . . . I remember also noting the little black curl in the nape of his neck like a drake's tail. His walk was slow and tranquil, such as one could hardly imagine ever breaking into a run."

Max was then the dramatic critic of the *Saturday Review*. He was always delighted to be drawn into a long evening of conversation with Desmond, and how Desmond enjoyed his mischievous humour, and his brilliant impersonations! "I have sometimes found," he wrote, "I was no longer in *his* company, but in that of a dramatic critic whose accent was unrefined and whose mind was coarse, but who invariably contrived (confound him!) to hit nails on the head. I regret to say 'Max' always enjoyed my exasperation." Like Desmond, Beerbohm believed in talk, not chatter. Those were more leisurely days, as Desmond later wistfully recalled, "when the tempo of conversation permitted people to express themselves, and hosts did not prefer emphatic jawing guests, who shift their topic every moment."[19]

With Maurice Baring, nocturnal discourse was likely to take even more farcical turns. Baring (1874–1945), the wealthy, cultivated novelist of Society, and brilliant linguist, whose adventures took him from the steppes of Russia or the Balkans to Belgravia, was a light-hearted master of practical jokes and verbal nonsense. He could talk and write in imaginary languages; he would often enact fantastical scenes between his friends and famous figures, mimicking all of them; and sometimes he would impulsively perform some wild action, such as setting the curtains of his drawing-room on fire. Yet he, like Max Beerbohm, had nothing unbalanced about him; and despite his eccentricities and celibate nature, he was both level-headed and warm – a true friend and an enhancer of existence.

Making his way back to Cheyne Gardens after evenings in such company, as the lights of the Strand and Piccadilly grew dim, Desmond would begin to assemble his impressions of what he had seen; but he often postponed finishing his criticism until he had further studied the play he had been to – a credit to his enthusiasm, but a cause of continual delay.

The Speaker, for which he reviewed increasingly, was a lively Liberal journal; under the editorship of J. L. Hammond, the distinguished Fabian historian, it attracted some of the best-known writers of the day: G. K. Chesterton, Hilaire Belloc, H. G. Wells, John Galsworthy, Robert Bridges and Maurice Hewlett. Desmond eventually became *The Speaker*'s assistant literary editor and, from August 1905, its regular drama critic, in an effort by the editor to increase the paper's flagging circulation. The offices of the paper, up a narrow winding stair in Henrietta Street, Covent Garden, were poky and primitive, without telephone or typewriters; but Hammond was an inspiring editor. From him, Desmond recalled, "I first learnt to honour and enjoy my profession."[20]

Desmond's reviews were outspoken. Years later some of the rising generation of literary men, like Geoffrey Grigson, accused him of blandness, of elevating the mediocre and the well-tried and ignoring the experimental. No such mistake could have been made about his *Speaker* criticisms which had a hard cutting edge and showed an excitement about new developments. As time went on he applied the knife more painlessly but his faculty for spotting false notes never disappeared.

In these years he developed clear views about his role as a theatrical journalist.[21] What mattered, he concluded, was to make his readers think. A critic, he believed, must, above all, be interested in human nature; and secondly he must understand the limitations and advantages of theatre; the first test a critic should apply to a play was whether the playwright had selected a theme which was suitable for the stage; and, secondly, whether the playwright was clear in his own mind what kind of play he was trying to write – too often there was confusion between comedy and farce: "We enjoy a farce most when we forget commonsense and comedy most when we remember it. We cannot do both at the same time." Thirdly, Desmond stressed, a critic must be adaptable, though without lowering his standards.[22] Normally his own approach was very tolerant, for he believed in judging even a lowbrow play on its merits. His favourite actor in this period was Charles Hawtrey who made his name in light comedy. Occasionally, however, a high-minded fastidiousness fostered at Cambridge came out where Desmond felt the piece was pretentious or the production a travesty. He was no respecter of great names: Oscar Wilde he charged with "an extraordinary want of interest in human nature" and he commented that Herbert Beerbohm Tree "makes but a limp Antony", when he saw him in the celebrated production at His Majesty's Theatre in 1907.

His judgements could be devastating: he condemned a Royal Court production of *Pan and the Young Shepherd*, an absurd arcadian idyll by the popular historical novelist Maurice Hewlett. Since the 1890s, a galaxy of trivial and major literary talent had tried their hand at summoning up "the great god Pan" – from writers of real imagination like E. M. Forster, Kenneth Grahame, Oliver Onions and J. M. Barrie, to poseurs like Arthur Machen and Max Beerbohm's fictional Enoch Soames; and authors as distinguished as G. K. Chesterton had regarded this feeble outburst of paganism as a serious moral threat. For Desmond, this "Pan trouble", as he called it, was like a tiresome malady, caught easily in the late romantic fogs which blew in ragged patches over the early twentieth-century literary scene. Judged even by the standards of the "Pan worshippers" however, Desmond felt Maurice Hewlett had failed: "In Arcadia there should be no riot of the senses or of the passions. Mr. Hewlett can no more create its atmosphere than Mr. Conder could paint it and partly for the same reason; he is too preoccupied with sex. His hot and swollen style ill suits the contentment of the woods. . . . One nymph describing what she has done, sings: 'I stood hid to the flanks in the thick of the fern, as the tired day fell, washing my body in blood shed by the sun'. The word 'flanks' absolutely destroys the atmosphere. . . . It seems to me that the author has done nearly all that is possible to unpoeticise Pan. . . ."

An inept production of a good play aroused his indignation: for example, in May 1906, *Othello*, at the Lyric, despite a star cast with Lewis Waller and the younger Henry Irving; Desmond was horrified by the decision to end the play with the suicide of Othello: the final act was "utterly ruined". To him the widely praised Tree production of *Antony and Cleopatra* was also marred because the actors had been encouraged to gabble their lines: "Anyone who is not stone deaf to the music of language, . . . who is even sleepily susceptible to the rhythm of speech, must have left the theatre contemptuous and cold."

But Desmond's initiation as a dramatic critic came at a happy moment; for he became closely involved from the start in a wonderful new era for English theatre. Hitherto, the productions which commanded the most enthusiastic audiences had largely consisted either of hackneyed situation comedy and melodrama – or of spectacular stagings, by the great actor managers, Tree and the Irvings' of Shakespeare and other major classics. Such performances were vehicles for the stars – and Desmond much admired the Irvings, father and son – but too often the general level of acting was mediocre. Recently, thoughtful and controversial drama, such as that of Ibsen and Shaw, had been put on by non-commercial theatrical societies, The Independent Theatre and The New Stage Club, for example, which had come into being in order to break down prejudice against new art; and to a certain extent the gap between the conventionally popular and the modern "theatre of ideas" had already begun to narrow, with new plays of improved quality by such authors as Oscar Wilde and Pinero.

However, the older theatrical tradition continued well into the period when Desmond was reviewing, and critical theatregoers like himself still felt dissatisfied. The influence of the theatre societies was limited, and it was not until 1904, when the youthful and idealistic actor, Harley Granville Barker, and the experienced business manager, J. E. Vedrenne, took the lease of the Royal Court Theatre, Chelsea, that for the first time the combination of good new drama and a much improved level of acting at last began to make their impact on popular taste. This was achieved through Bernard Shaw's money and encouragement, and Barker's inspired direction.[23]

Granville Barker was a reformer, a Fabian socialist who wanted to see the creation of a National Theatre. Attractive but moody, with wan, intense good looks unfashionable in the period of the statuesque Lewis Waller, he was unusual among actors in being an intellectual; and he was not only interested in the message of the plays that he put on, but he understood how to match their performance to it effectively. As Desmond put it, Granville Barker, by rejecting what was artificial and "theatrical", and returning to actuality in gesture, diction and sentiment, persuaded the public to appreciate a more natural style of acting.[24] Desmond soon recognised that his productions were more satisfactory than those of Tree or Irving because they approached the play as a whole and did not over-concentrate on the star roles. Granville Barker's close association with Shaw was a key element in his popular success, not least when it was known that Edward VII had enjoyed a command performance of Shaw's *John Bull's Other Island*. Moreover, despite Barker's strain of moral seriousness, he did not confine his interests to high-brow drama; they ranged widely from dramatised arguments for socialism to fantastical harlequinades. In Desmond, as in Max Beerbohm, in A. B. Walkley and William Archer, Granville Barker found the valuable allies he needed among the critics; Desmond indeed became a lifelong friend.

Barker's enterprise at the Royal Court lasted nearly three years; it opened on a non-commercial basis. It was not quite repertory theatre but there was a core of actors who gave their services to it regularly for a small fee, or were on low-salaried, seasonal contracts. Many particular favourites of Desmond's made their reputations at this time – Lillah McCarthy (Barker's wife), Edmund Gwenn, Lewis Casson, Louis Calvert, A. E. Matthews, Henry Ainley; others, stars like Mrs Patrick Campbell and Ellen Terry, put in brief appearances. Altogether thirty-two plays were staged in nearly nine hundred and fifty performances. From this date both Ibsen and Shaw "took off" as central elements in English theatre; ancient Greek plays – of Euripides and Aeschylus – translated by Gilbert Murray, were made exciting to a modern audience. Much to Desmond's satisfaction, drama from the continent, by Maeterlinck and Hauptmann, reached a wider public and many new English dramatists began to make their impact: St John Hankin (*The Return of the Prodigal; The Charity that Began at Home*), Granville Barker himself (*The Voysey Inheritance*); Robert Vernon Harcourt (*A Question of Age*), and John Galsworthy (*The Silver Box*).

However, Desmond's greatest enthusiasm at this time was for the plays of Ibsen and Shaw. Of the Ibsen productions at the Court, *Hedda Gabler* (March 1907) impressed Desmond the most – the acting was consistently good and Mrs Patrick Campbell triumphed as the destructive, frustrated Hedda.

Ibsen's theatre, as Desmond said, was the theatre of the soul:[25] its struggle to survive disillusion and repression; the tragedy of false idealism overthrowing natural good; the fatal effect of weakness – these were depicted with an intensity only achievable by someone who had experienced them personally, within himself. Desmond understood these well, too, and for him this was true realism, which could never date, even if changing conventions made some of Ibsen's situations seem, superficially, obsolete. Ibsen's drama was the profoundest he had ever encountered.

It was with Shaw, above all, that the Royal Court was associated, and Shaw gave Desmond another kind of stimulus with his effervescent exploration of new ideas. For Desmond, he was the one playwright who could make his audience laugh and think at the same time: he could express opposing arguments with dazzling skill and throughout nearly all his plays he carried his audience along on a torrent of intellectual high spirits: "that fountain of lovely gaiety which went on playing however gloomy the state of the world."

The absence of stereotype in Shaw's plays particularly attracted Desmond – weak men turned out to be strong; firm characters could be inconsistent; the leading women might be quintessentially "Shaw characters" but they were all different from one another; and even minor characters were vivid. The variety was striking, but it was combined with a sense that the stuff of human nature was much the same in everyone and that differences between human beings arose from their conditioning; there were no separate species, "the miser, the libertine etc." Desmond found this a refreshing departure from the shallow clichés of conventional psychological drama. He was excited, too, by Shaw's close look at the relations between men and women, a more realistic appraisal than that of many "love dramas" which dealt with the conflict between "love and convention" or "duty and love", without pausing to consider what "love" might actually be.

Finally, Desmond felt exhilarated by Shaw's elevation of the virtues of courage, intellectual honesty and spontaneity; by his conviction that to mask self-seeking with an idealistic face was far more despicable than self-seeking itself; by his down-to-earth deflation of romantic notions to forestall disillusion; and by his belief in stimulating an "active and gay resolution in the place of an exasperated seclusion of spirit, or indifference, either gloomy or light".

Yet much as he enjoyed Shaw's rational cheerfulness, he could not accept all he preached. He revolted against his valuation of human activity only according to whether it contributed to certain desired goals. Nor could he share Shaw's low opinion of the theatre-going public. Shaw believed that he had to speak loudly, simply and shockingly to the intellectually deaf (otherwise known as the average person). To Desmond, the contempt inherent in this viewpoint was both distasteful and misplaced.[26]

It is also noticeable Desmond's sceptical, libertarian outlook and his deeper observation of human nature made him a more understanding judge of dictatorial psychology than the playwright he so much admired. This showed in his views on Shaw's *Caesar and Cleopatra*, which Granville Barker produced several years afterwards.[27]

Shaw, he maintained, had made Caesar much too rational a man, appealing to reason in others. Such men, said Desmond, never rose to immense power; all "great men of Destiny" were "plungers" and "colossal egotists," impelled by the will to dominate and they owed their success to their manipulation of blind political emotion.

Desmond liked to have a companion when he went to the theatre as a critic. Now that he no longer saw so much of Irene Noel, he frequently invited the charming young Molly Warre-Cornish. For instance, they went to a new production of *Candida*, in December 1904, which he found disappointing. The heroine, played by Kate Rorke, was "insufferably patronising, vulgar, hard. . . . I enjoyed Molly a good deal more than the play."[28]

7   A Troubled Heart

"My hair is twisted into a Grecian knot; skirts wind about my ankles and hamper me. I am full of vague aspirations and questionings as to what I am to do in life; service & sacrifice were the ideals.

"We were not 'thwarted', but our parents seemed to have no other wish for us but that we should flit for ever about their house," Molly Warre-Cornish wrote of herself in the early 1900s. "In that, however, it should not be supposed that they favoured feeble lack of self-reliance, or vapid indolence at home. Seriousness and work must always be there, without being much spoken of."[1]

From both her parents Molly had acquired a spiritual, idealistic outlook. Her sheltered, happy childhood had given her scant knowledge of life beyond her large, cultivated family circle. Her first excursion outside it was not until the autumn of 1902 which she spent as companion to a German princess, the daughter of the Grand Duke and Duchess of Anhalt.

Molly found life in rural Germany altogether strange: for part of the year the court stayed at a schloss in Holstein, near Kiel, where their "country subjects might have been the Marquis of Carabas, Cinderella, and the Miller in Rumpelstilzkin" she later wrote. She felt herself a spectator at some arcane hierarchical ritual enacted by creatures of the same race as herself but completely alien in their social behaviour. Partly, this was because of their isolation: transport was by horse, and there was no telephone or electricity. For the old-fashioned dinner-parties, which took place at the eighteenth-century hour of three o'clock in the afternoon, lackeys in knee breeches lit a multitude of candles and drew the shutters against the sunshine outside. "Grafs & Gräfins, having driven long distances from all about the country would emerge from landaus; the ladies' silks and the gentlemen's coat tails somewhat crumpled from long hours in the carriage. They were cheery, straightforward, plain people. They all seemed to have shrill voices, & they shouted; but they had rather pleasing provincial intonation."[2]

It was picturesque – but dull. Molly suffered from homesickness. Travelling to Halle to watch Joachim perform was a blessed reminder of life at Eton. She returned to England, with relief, at the end of April 1903. That summer Molly was twenty-one, a comely, slender girl with a pleasant, rather round face, serious in repose, with a direct gaze from dark brown eyes under well-defined brows, but ready to break into spontaneous laughter. She was interested in clothes, like most attractive young women, though she did not have a very large allowance to spend on them; nor were she and her sisters encouraged to pay too much attention to their appearance: neatness came first – clean nails, hair and shoes were important. Next came suitability – over-dressing was a fault their fastidious eyes soon picked up – wearing fussy hats or exquisite suède gloves in the country, for instance. Molly's allowance of £11.10s. a quarter was for dress as well as travel, stationery and expeditions. Molly wore her clothes well, but she bought few new outfits, often having coats and skirts "made over" by the family dressmaker at Eton, and buying new gloves – two pairs for 5s. – or blouses – 15s. for a smart one, 11s. for an everyday one – to wear with them. She splashed out on the occasional extravagance, of course, buying a feather boa, for instance, when Loubet, the President of France, visited England in 1903 and she was invited by an old family friend to tea at St James's Palace to meet him (she was disappointed: "Deadly dull person – I can't bear the Republic," she wrote in her diary).

She spent most of the next two years at home, helping her mother run the household at the Cloisters, and enjoying excursions with relations in London and abroad. A plan that she should teach history came to nothing; for although she was much interested in the subject, her schooling had not equipped her for passing the examinations necessary for a teaching diploma.[3]

Housekeeping did not appeal to her. At home it amounted to little more than discussing meals with the cook and dealing with the ever-recurring problems of servants – when they threatened to leave precipitously or were rude. By the time she married she had still only a hazy idea of how food found its way from the tradesman at the door to the dining-table. In her, largely impecunious, married life this meant that housekeeping was a continuous effort to her. Blanche did not encourage any of her children to be practical or well-organised; that was too commonplace. She herself was often sunk in abstraction, so that "you have to turn some household question which you need answered in about six different ways until it attracts her attention," whether it was the numbers for meals or the arrangement of flowers, said Molly. Blanche often punctuated her absent-minded reveries with snatches of her thoughts spoken aloud, but to herself; her enigmatic utterances and sudden outbursts became more frequent with the years.

Blanche's "nerve riots", as Molly called them, increased too: sudden squalls of fury when she would bang doors and wound her family with unsparing personal remarks. Her disappointments – the death of her eldest son; the inadequacy of her two elder daughters in coping with their lives; the unlikelihood that her husband, whose powers seemed to entitle him to a larger sphere, would ever enter one; her own inability to finish another novel – in general, the failure of the outside world to rise to her high expectations of it led to these sudden rages. Blanche was not able to take too much reality. She had little idea of what people were really like – but a clear idea of what she thought they should be like, and she frequently confused the two.

As for Molly's father, now in his mid-sixties he withdrew increasingly into the library or his study, whence he would be summoned from the foot of the stairs. When he finally joined the company it was as an onlooker, sitting apart with legs crossed limply, twitching his free foot and chuckling at the conversation. On winter evenings, he would stand warming himself abstractedly with his back to the fire, from time to time giving the logs a backward kick without turning to look at them – but so quickly that he never burnt his spats.[4]

Romantic and cultivated as she was, Blanche was extremely susceptible to "atmosphere".[5] It was all-important to her, whether it was the "beloved atmosphere" of her female relations or "the atmosphere of genius" of Henry James or Donald Tovey. Now she succumbed to the "atmosphere" of the Roman Catholic Church, "going over" in the summer of 1903. Years later Desmond was to analyse her conversion. "She was always passionate, always anxious to conclude. She could not make a pillow of doubts. The tragic sense of life was never long absent from her mind; serenity was impossible to her" (as it was to Molly); "she distrusted in others the serenity which was based on compromise . . . Roman Catholicism appealed to her because it explained and even dramatised for her the beauty, courage, and tragedy of life, and because it was uncompromising."

Her daughter and son-in-law Reggie and Charlotte Balfour were now living at Ford Place, near the Sussex coast, and in the Gothic church at Arundel built thirty years previously by the premier Roman Catholic peer, the Duke of Norfolk, they, too, converted. Conversions to Catholicism were still uncommon at this time in England, but they were all influenced in their decision by Belloc's recently published *The Path to Rome*; and when Belloc and his wife came to live nearby, the two families became great friends, Charlotte helping to furnish the chapel in the Bellocs' house, King's Land.

Blanche and the Balfours were by no means alone among their

acquaintances in taking this step (Maurice Baring went over to Rome a few years later). At this distance the Edwardian period may seem solidly confident, but many people had begun to rebel against the established Victorian tenets – the supremacy of the Empire, free trade and capitalism, and the subordination of women. At the same time, they groped for certainties; many, such as Desmond and his Cambridge friends, sought a rational view of life free from the mists of religion; but it was natural for others, like Blanche, to turn to the Christian church in its most ancient, traditional and uncompromising form.

All Molly's family, including herself, had spiritual inclinations; they were brought up to believe in self-sacrifice and service and in ideals greater than self, greater than the world into which we are born. Molly's brother Gerald sought spiritual certainty in a life stripped to its simplest form, "working, as a poor man, amongst the poor";[6] to this end he became a country curate on the Welsh border, and then came "a short sharp phase of Tolstoyism", Blanche reported to Maurice Baring. "He went to work in Hull docks, got employed by a Norwegian ship and unloaded ten hours a day with charming Norwegians."

Eventually Gerald came back to teaching, at Manchester University, though not to the Anglican Church, becoming instead a Christian Scientist. This last upset his family more than anything: "I would far rather he became a monk or a Plymouth brother or a Quaker," wrote his father to Desmond. Gerald also became fascinated by Greek drama which he translated, and by the then fashionable system of rhythmic dancing and dramatic expression, taught in Germany by M. Jacques Dalcroze, which he incorporated into the Greek plays and disseminated among the children of Manchester's slums, as well as his own nephews and nieces, making them do Isadora Duncan steps in their bare feet, chanting as they skipped up and down.

Molly's religion was more orthodox. She was pious, said her prayers regularly, and went to church at least once on Sundays and on Holy Days. She believed, like her father, a liberal Anglican, that the Church of England had as much formality as its followers would stand, and the minimum discipline to keep it in shape. When she married Desmond, an agnostic, her faith was shaken for a few years, but by the end of her life it had returned, with greater intensity.

On her frequent trips to London to stay with her Aunt Anny Ritchie in St George's Square, Pimlico, or her Aunt Gussie, in her artistic house on Campden Hill, Molly met Irene Noel, another close friend, with whom, no doubt, she discussed Irene's good-looking suitor, Desmond Mac-Carthy. Molly appreciated Irene's life-enhancing robustness and enthusiasm to which Desmond also had responded. When Molly had been homesick in Germany she wrote, "I often think of Irene and imagine her in my place – How splendid she would be." On 4th July Molly spent a "perfect day in the country" with both Desmond and Irene at Crabbet Stud. The annual summer sale of Arab horses was always festive and picturesque: at luncheon in the great tents put up for the occasion Molly sat next to Neville Lytton, "who is simply the most charming person in the world. Mrs. Neville like a summer queen in pink and white muslin. Eddie (Marsh) Desmond & Irene also at luncheon which was great fun. Mr. Blunt spoke . . . I longed to buy an Arab." Afterwards they wandered up to Crabbet, "the house which is my ideal of a south England country house".[7]

This idyllic day was rounded off by going to *Cousin Kate* at the theatre with Irene, Desmond, G. E. Moore and others of Desmond's friends.

The next day, Sunday, Molly was invited to luncheon with Mrs MacCarthy and Desmond, where the other guest was "Moore the philosopher who did not give out much, but appeared charming & sang afterwards very badly & yet well," a criticism which others made of his engagingly vivacious musical performances.

Chen was not taken with Molly or her parents: aware that the cultivated Mrs Cornish thought her tedious, she retaliated by referring to Blanche as "the old horse".

Desmond and Molly's friendship deepened slowly: they met on various family occasions – at Eton, when he attempted, in vain, to argue Gerald out of his Christian Science beliefs; in London, dining with Aunt Anny in Pimlico, or Aunt Gussie in Kensington – both of whom had a particular fondness for him. It was not until Molly left England in the summer of 1905 that Desmond moved from being a friend of the family into the foreground of her life.

Molly had accepted a post as governess in the household of the Lord Lieutenant of Ireland, Lord Dudley. This was not a menial job; in a grand household such a position was held by a lady of gentle birth, whose manners and cultivation set an example to her charges. Molly supervised the education of two younger little girls, Honor and Morvyth. Lady Dudley was a mother for whom the nursery had few attractions. "It is a revelation how the smart set educate their children – a sad one."

Lord and Lady Dudley were among the rich, sporting, country-house owning friends of Edward VII; they entertained the King lavishly, in Ireland on State Visits as well as in England, being wealthy enough to sustain the expenditure this entailed – Lord Dudley owned some 30,000 acres in England, including profitable industrial areas of the Midlands, as well as estates in Jamaica. Lady Dudley was very much the *grande dame* running her complicated household in Ireland with its hierarchy of staff and the official entertaining, and at the same time managing to enjoy the delights of the English season and travel to Europe, to Paris and Biarritz.

The Dudleys and their friends brought Molly into contact with the philistinism of the rich and leisured class of Edwardian England, evident even in clever and able members of it like themselves: "Conversation at luncheon, respective merits of various shootings (sic), deerstalkings, liveableness of country houses like Chatsworth, Gordon Castle (tabooed) – impossibility of winter in England if you don't hunt – billiards, losings at turf club etc.! and *yet* they're all so clever. . . ."

From Dublin Molly began writing to Desmond who replied with alacrity. The situation in which she found herself was not an easy one perched, as governesses commonly were, somewhat uncomfortably between the nursery above and the drawing-room below. She was mostly alone in the company of her two badly-behaved charges in the Vice-regal Lodge in Dublin, "a huge white classical pillared building with formal gardens, & policemen dying with boredom behind shrubs. . . . I am a tremendous home ruler. The Irish are enigmas – I know nothing about them – but they are *quite* charming – & quite come up to my expectation."

"Do you know you're a decided Dublin type," she wrote later. "I have seen you walking on the quays of the Liffey constantly." As, on the next page, she remarked that "Dublin is terribly without backbone – people look as if they were all waiting to have something done for them" this was an unintentionally two-edged observation! It also seems to have marked the beginning of the pernicious myth that dogged Desmond for so much of his later life, that his failings and weaknesses were due to his Irish blood. Desmond and Molly corresponded regularly, and both much enjoyed each other's letters. Hers were now signed, "Your affectionate Molly".[8]

When she returned to England in October 1905 she saw Desmond for the first time for six months. Now Desmond visited Eton for dinner and the night with her family. But soon Molly was off again, accompanying the Dudleys to Biarritz, then in its heyday as a fashionable resort. The government had changed, Balfour, the Conservative Prime Minister had resigned, and Lord Dudley was out of office. Life with the family on holiday was less formal, though no less smart than before.

She loved the coast at Biarritz, with its "caverns and jutting rocks, all most exciting, which in the warm sun and the Bay of Biscay tonic air is really very delicious" and she wished Desmond were there to see it; but she wanted an end to her Jane Eyre-like existence: the New Year of 1906 was to change it more decisively than she had anticipated.

They were both invited to a dance given by Molly's Aunt Gussie, Augusta Freshfield, on Monday, 29th January. Desmond asked Molly to keep two dances for him near supper – so that they would be able to spend the long supper interval together. That evening he was dining at the other end of town, in Hampstead, with Roger and Helen Fry; afterwards he travelled down to Kensington, to Airlie Gardens at the top of Campden Hill where Aunt Gussie and Uncle Douglas lived in a handsome and unusual house designed for them by Norman Shaw. Its special atmosphere was due to Augusta Freshfield, Blanche's sister. Like Blanche, she was romantic and aesthetic – only rather more down to earth – and she had the good fortune to be married to a rich man which allowed her to indulge her artistic tastes. She filled her house with "a close conglomeration of Italian shrines, caskets, cabinets, marquetrie, against the tangled background of William Morris' pomegranates." The pictures were by contemporary painters – Rossetti, Sir Frederick Leighton, Burne-Jones, Holman Hunt and Watts; the Freshfields were friends of these artists, as well as of the du Mauriers, and many other prominent writers, such as Henry James. Hospitable and generous as she was, dances at Aunt Gussie's were a frequent feature of Molly's girlhood, though none was as momentous as this one.

In her shimmering satin dress, with long white kid gloves, a spray of flowers pinned to the left side of her bodice, her soft brown hair coiled on top of her head, Molly, with her sister Cecilia, greeted the chaperones who were invariably present; though chaperones were going out by now, at dances in this house there they still were, recalled Molly, "massive and comfortable . . . in their rich waisted velvets and long trains . . . [their] elderly heads nodded together over the young things whirling round the centre of the room."[9]

In this familiar, well-loved house Desmond and Molly met again – decisively. On their dance programmes was printed only one word "Valse" all the way down, interspersed twice with "Lancers". Her train swirling first about her feet, then gracefully caught up, Molly whirled with him across the polished floor to the heady tempi of "that old 'Blue Danube' Valse". They no longer doubted that they were in love.

When Desmond "declared himself" that evening, however, Molly asked him to wait – but not for long. Next morning she wrote to him saying "I care for you quite *quite* as much as you care for me"[10] and asking him to come and see her.

Their engagement was greeted with delight by her family. Her father wrote to her at once:

Darling Child,
  I only send this line to give you my love & blessing & most full consent – As you must know I have always loved Desmond, though I never knew that you and he loved each other.

Now you must get married as quick as you can – There is no time
when one wishes one had more money than when the children want to
marry.

Your loving Father[11]

As well as being a model of what fathers should write to their children
when they become engaged, this note also tells one much about Frank
Warre-Cornish's charm. To his future son-in-law he wrote, "I have
always thought you one of the people with whom it would be a pleasure
to live."

The rest of Molly's family were also delighted; Desmond thanked them
all for being "extraordinarily good to me. Long before I ever thought I
should ever marry Molly, I thought you were the nicest family in the
world."

Chen, of course, presented more of a hurdle. But after a predictable
flurry of anxieties she received Blanche and Molly's sister Margaret
warmly at Cheyne Gardens.

Desmond and Molly wrote to one another daily, their letters full of the
joyful surprise of young lovers who find themselves happily and suddenly
united. From Eton, where Molly had now returned, she said, "I must
seem to you to lean and drift all these first days of happiness – but I feel
such strength and power in you. . . . My faith is deep that there is no
happiness without some strenuousness. I am never happy in luxury for
more than a week. I don't believe you would be either.

"You are really *too* delightful – it is almost too splendid to think you
are my own, Desmond."[12]

It was now that Desmond paid a visit, with George Trevelyan, to his
hero, George Meredith at Flint Cottage, Box Hill. Afterwards he
described it excitedly to Molly: "I had an hour and a half's talk with him –
incessant talk. He was first-rate. It was an emotional occasion to me as
you can imagine – looking on him for the first time and hearing his voice."

That dark February day, he had walked reverently up the damp gravel
path between high box hedges, towards the poet's house "with feelings
very like a lover's". These grew when he entered the narrow hall, and
heard the resonant rumble of Meredith's voice through the thin door on
the right of the passage as he talked to his dog. In a fuller account, later on,
he recalled how surprised he had been by Meredith's manner – though he
should not have been, as it mirrored his written style, "full of flourishes
and his enunciation grandiose, as though he loved the sound of his own
words. This characteristic at first, I remember, somewhat disconcerted
me. It struck me that he talked with a kind of swagger, and I was not
prepared for that. Copy-book biographies always insist upon modesty as

a sign of true greatness. I had certainly found out that humility was not the invariable accompaniment of power and insight, but I still clung to the idea that great men were always as biographers say, 'simple.' Now 'simple' Meredith was not, nor was he 'natural', 'unaffected'; in fact none of the adjectives of obituary respect would apply to him."

As Meredith was very deaf, his conversation was more-or-less a monologue; Desmond found something miraculous and heroic in the determination of the old man to sparkle. His infirmity was all the more poignant because, in his prime, he had been a man of great physical strength and beauty, to which his portraits did inadequate justice. Even in his 70s, his appearance was impressive: "He was sitting to one side of the fire, dressed in a soft quilted jacket with a rug upon his knees. On a little rickety table by his side stood two candles and one of those old-fashioned eye screens which flirt out green wings at a touch; a pile of lemon-coloured volumes lay beside it. His face beneath a tousled thatch of grey hair, soft as the finest wood-ash, and combed down into a fringe upon a high round forehead, had a noble, ravaged handsomeness. The vanity and delicacy, as of a too aesthetic *petit maître* which marks Watts' portrait of him was not discernible; rather a noteworthy boldness. . . . That keen look in profile, as of an upward-pointing arrow, had gone. Old age had blurred his eyelids, and his eyes, once blue, were faded and full of 'the empty untragic sadness of old age'; but that vitality which had inspired many a packed page still vibrated in his powerful voice, and told in the impetuosity of his greeting."

For one moving moment, the old man revealed his unspoiled response to life: he was indulging in a grandiose set piece on the uselessness of his crippled existence – "Nature cares not a pin for the individual; I am content to be shovelled into the ditch," he declared. "I remember how in the midst of such discourse," wrote Desmond, "solemn as the wind in the pines, with a humorous growl in it for an undernote, he looked towards the black uncurtained window, past which a few large snowflakes came wavering down, and that the animation of sudden interest was like a child's. It was a momentary interruption, on he went . . ."

On his return to his room in Cheyne Gardens Desmond wrote Molly an account of his visit late into the night, concluding at last, "I must to bed to be fresh for tomorrow. Come as soon as you can and run straight up stairs dearest to me *first* – that I may see you and hold you. . . . I shall expect the jingle of your hansom every minute after eleven has struck. . . . *Will* you tell me all you have ever thought tomorrow? O my dearest we shan't have nearly time enough."[13]

Desmond was about to depart for Biarritz where he was to stay with George Arthur Paley for whom he was going to work and edit a new journal. Before he left England, he and Molly had a franker talk than they had ever had before about their physical attraction to one another – a talk which left Molly feeling "some shame which I feel is to my shame to feel, and brought about by an education which in its silence teaches one to feel that there are feelings which are unworthy".[14]

Desmond replied next day on the train to Paris, "I loved your letter this morning and I have read it many times. Dearest it is natural you should feel a shy kind of shame in talking as we did on Wednesday night, but trust in each other can take the pain out of that feeling – and see how glad we are that we did talk as we did. . . ."

He counteracted her morbid tendencies with his own *joie de vivre*: "I love you and in spite of all the ugliness, disappointment and confusion, I am in love with life – I was before I had you – and now I feel it more than ever – far more. There is no danger that *we* shall live only in contemplation of the sadness of the world." Even the Channel crossing with racing seas and great waves sweeping by "delights me almost to shouting".[15]

Molly, meanwhile, had spent a difficult afternoon with Irene Noel. On the surface still her good friend, Irene had a devastating effect on Molly's over-stretched nerves. "Oh Desmond darling I ought to be grateful to her since she has left you to me," she wrote afterwards. But Irene, the manipulator, the experienced woman of the world, rankled with her. For she wanted her own way with men and was able to get it, with an assurance that Molly condemned as insensitive, while being signally aware that she lacked it herself. In the small hours of the night she scrawled a miserable little note to Desmond, which she probably did not send, dismayed at her "jealousy which has all sprung up so quickly and seems unworthy" (though, to the outside observer, perfectly natural). "It's in the night but I want you so for comfort and understanding and gentleness and strength and all I love you for."[16]

Partly, Molly felt guilty because after Irene had rejected Desmond she had shared her view and run Desmond down – which of course she now regretted. Even Desmond was incensed at this time by Irene's request for the return of her letters to him, made through Judith Lytton, which prompted a reply, wholly at odds with his habitual urbanity:

Dear Irene,
    I wish to see you – I received a letter from Judith tonight, telling me you ask for your letters back. It is unlike you not to write direct to me – I opened the box tonight and looked at some – Forgetting my own shortcomings I felt only the bitterest anger at the way in which you despised all I could give and I said let them go & her too out of my life forever – But I cannot – will not break with you for good in bitterness –

now – without seeing you again. For in the hour of death – if that is a solemn hour, you with two others will only be near my spirit. Give you back your letters of course I will – but not in bitterness before I have seen you.[17]

As a matter of fact it was exactly like Irene to get a mutual friend to write to Desmond on her behalf: "To make bombs and get someone else to fire them off is one of Irene's favourite occupations", Judith once observed about her. When Desmond sent her the letters – "a most melancholy box", she remarked – she destroyed all but a scant few. It was not in Desmond's nature to stay angry with her for long, however.

Despite Desmond's assurance that, "You have put more confidence joy and peace in my heart than anyone has done before," Molly was anxious: "Why oh why when I ought to be looking out on life in a happier frame of mind than I have ever had before, should I feel a want of life and joy in me?" Her love was mingled with fear. For whilst Desmond was all that she wanted in a husband – he was clever, original, affectionate, part of her own world, and loved by her family; he was poised on the brink of a career in literature, a subject for which she had "a passion"; he was popular and gregarious, without being a mere socialite; he was attractive, sympathetic and fascinating, and yet . . and yet . . . Molly was shaken to the roots of her being by the prospect of marrying him. The implications of leaving her home behind her and consigning her life, her hopes, her ideals to another were tremendous. To her mother "and all her idealistic, romantic, highly-sophisticated, delicate-minded contemporaries", the things of the Spirit were paramount: was she worthy, Molly wondered, of her husband-to-be – the first man to whom she had given her heart? Blanche had taught her the importance of music and poetry, of the beauty of nature and the joys of family love: but of sex, nothing. Later medical opinion suggested that her ignorance, widespread in those days, when physical love was not talked about at all in households such as hers, nor part of a girl's education, caused sex to loom before her with something approaching horror. Desmond and she were mutually attracted. But instead of delighting her, evidence of sexual arousal alarmed her. It seemed to threaten, because of its unfamiliar, yet highly intimate nature, the over-close attachment she felt to her home and parents. Molly found herself now unable to cope with the reality of love and the prospect of marriage.

The delicate balance of her mind gradually collapsed under a tumult of contradictory feelings: hope, love, confidence ebbed away; a morbid melancholy, jealousy and confusion took their place. She felt as though she was in a nightmare, in which she was living outside herself – literally, beside herself. Her nerves exaggerated everything: tortured by morbidity and thoughts of her own unworthiness, the actual world was rendered meaningless – only her inner world was overwhelming, terrifyingly real.

If ever a young man's love was tested, Desmond's was tested now. For most of the short time he had been engaged to Molly her mind had been in such turmoil that she had scarcely been herself; now she was confined to a nursing home in London and he was only allowed to see her briefly. He was undaunted: never for a moment in his letters to Molly, or to anyone else did he let a shadow of doubt creep in as to her full recovery and their eventual happiness together. Whatever his innermost fears he kept them to himself; the previous week he had written to her: "Molly my dearest although your letter was a sad one I was very glad to get it. I do not now and never shall love you the less for being sad and troubled. . . . I like best the people who can feel troubled about their own hearts – they are the only hearts I love."[18]

This was his declared belief and he stuck to it in the three difficult months which followed during which they had to be apart whilst Molly slowly got better. All that he could do to sustain and support her he did: he wrote to her daily, reaffirming, in a myriad ways, his love and compassion for her in her wretchedness. "Send your thoughts after me sometimes as mine are always flying to you, & when your mind is clear think how well we will live together."

At that time there were no drugs to help alleviate such depressions; sufferers had to live through them, trusting to a soothing régime, and understanding family and friends. Molly was blessed in these. A restful routine of a simple diet and massage was organised for her, under medical supervision. "It is everything to give your body up to someone else like your soul to a priest," she wrote. Desmond called once a week, to take her out for a drive in a hansom or just to sit quietly with her.

At the end of March, she was thought well enough to go to Bexhill-on-Sea, into lodgings, accompanied by a nurse. But Molly had for some time distrusted her nurse and finally she scribbled a desperate note to Desmond: "Do come or send someone. . . . I must have someone whom I love with me to keep me in a *natural* way off myself. I am so afraid of losing my will, my brain is so tired. . . ."

Both Desmond and Blanche hastened down: it transpired that the nurse was addicted to morphine; she was dismissed, a new, calmer, woman engaged, and, a little later, Molly was able to write to her mother that her depression was lifting, and she could look back on it as a period when "I was beyond control & was horribly alarmed at the whirl of thoughts which others couldn't know of, like deliriousness." She was profoundly grateful for Desmond's patience with her: "Dear love, how wonderful of

you to understand, I am sure many men would have let all their love
evaporate at the utterly depressing spectacle of a nervous illness (I have
always *hated* the nervous, had so little sympathy & understanding)."[19]

She was thinking of her mother and elder sisters, who though not so
much unstable as overstrung, could become, at times, semi-invalids. She,
too, was to be afflicted by nervous agitation throughout her life, though
never as badly as this breakdown following her engagement – the first
emotional decision she had had to make and one which meant a
separation from her parents, something from which her elder sisters
Margaret and Dorothy had shrunk.

Gradually she got stronger until she was well enough to go to
Switzerland with Charlotte for the month. In the meadows above Lucerne
Molly enjoyed the sunshine, writing to Desmond, "I haven't been
thinking much, just enjoying, and rather dreaming about you and the
future, and reading Keats, and enjoying the sun and the delicious
meadows and the pale blossom trees. . . ." She bought him a present of a
bear ("wooden – don't be alarmed").

Her letters reflected a gradual return of self-confidence and optimism.
Desmond's letters from London told of his round of work and visits to
friends as well as his hopes and plans for their future. The date of their
wedding was kept open until Molly's return to health and to England. On
one thing they were determined, that it should not be just "the spicing of a
garden party", but a separate, quiet occasion for close family and friends.
Although Desmond was an agnostic, there was no question but that they
should be married in church, coming as Molly did from an actively
religious family, where a faith, "is the main guide & principle, is a very
sheltering thing, & you will hardly believe that I have never talked to an
agnostic in my life before you – or gauged an agnostic's life, and can't
quite yet," Molly wrote to Desmond, adding that she wanted to talk to
Desmond about religion when she returned to England.

That longed-for day came at last: Desmond and she had been parted for
four weeks when he met her, no longer pale and anxious, but browned by
the mountain air and sunshine, off the boat train at Waterloo on the
morning of 30th May. A little shy at seeing him again after a painful and,
to her, still slightly shaming illness, she was nevertheless confidently
happy to be reunited with her faithful lover.

Before their wedding, which was to take place in August, she and
Desmond visited Suffolk to stay with George Arthur Paley and his
fashionable, somewhat distant wife, Bina; they looked at the various
houses on his estate on offer for them to live in as part of Desmond's

salary for helping Arthur with their journal, *The New Quarterly*. The summer disguised the bleakness of that flat Eastern landscape; the wheat growing tall in the great rolling fields softened the horizon and the magnificent woods were inviting for picnics and rides. It seemed idyllic.

On 10th July came the wedding garden party at Eton: it was a romantic, sunlit day. The bride-to-be was simply dressed, all in white with a rose in her wide-brimmed hat. The groom, with characteristic panache, also wore a hat, of straw, and, instead of morning dress, a grey suit with a pearl pin in his dark blue tie. Crowds of happy friends and relations – aunts, cousins, Desmond's contemporaries from Cambridge – thronged the Cloisters.

Among the older guests was Henry James, who had written to Desmond with congratulations: "I pat you very tenderly and rejoicingly on the back and can take the same liberty with Miss Cornish"; and now here he was to give them his "friendly blessing" in person.[20]

After greeting the young couple and their parents, the guests wandered out into the garden which Molly's mother had planted to look as romantic as possible for "the bridal". She had made a new flower-bed, a broad ribbon of blue and white with snapdragons, foxgloves, delphiniums, larkspur, lobelia and veronica in dense array. There was a profusion of roses; Madonna lilies bloomed in green-painted tubs; and against the deep pink brick of the garden wall a handsome fig tree spread its distinctive leaves.

Virginia and Vanessa Stephen strolled down to the river accompanied by Donald Tovey. Indoors tea was laid out, and the guests could walk along the eighteenth-century gallery and inspect the wedding presents arranged as was the convention with their donors' names; some had been given by Desmond's Cambridge friends: candlesticks from Lytton Strachey, a pair of Chinese lacquer tables from the philosopher Bertrand Russell, himself newly married. After tea, came music: a programme of favourite pieces by Brahms, Schumann and Beethoven played by Donald Tovey.

Then at the end of the month, "the bride has packed her books, her presents, her trousseau, her childhood's Penates, and she will come back no more as one of the household – sad thought! One knows by former experience how completely they are gone!" wrote Blanche.

The wedding itself took place the following month at Burley in the New Forest, from Castletop, a house which they had been lent by Molly's cousin Eleanor (née Freshfield) and her husband Arthur Clough, the famous poet's son. Desmond and Molly were married on the morning of Wednesday, 29th August in Burley Church. As Desmond hated "the sentiment of veils and orange blossoms" the ceremony was kept to its simplest. G. E. Moore, his best man, wrote afterwards to tell Desmond "I did enjoy your wedding. And I don't think it would have been so nice if you hadn't been married in church. Weren't you impressed by the ceremony, and by being told what your duties to one another were? I was. I thought the words of the Church Service were very good; and it would be a great pity if there were no such services."[21]

Desmond agreed that it would be hard to find better words: "We both had an awkward feeling at the passage which adjured us to bring up our children as good Christians; but that was all – and that was not acute."[22]

G. E. Moore stayed on with the family at Burley, where an impromptu dance was held in the evening at which he revealed a hitherto unsuspected flair for dancing the polka.

In Lynton Desmond and Molly enjoyed a month's honeymoon of unclouded happiness, "out all day in the sun, going for long walks, or basking and reading aloud, or eating blackberries & sauntering & amusing ourselves, or going for whole days out," Molly wrote. She was happy to be back in her birthplace, which Desmond knew too, from Cambridge reading parties. The weather remained flawless, the warm days succeeding one another, with clear, starry nights.

The farmhouse where they rented rooms was clean and comfortable. Reading and talking by the sea, in the woods, or, in the evening cosily by the fire in their sitting-room, at last Desmond and Molly had a chance to get to know one another. They enjoyed each other's company as they did the soft Devon sun. "D. is simply an *angel*, & we are angelically happy," wrote Molly to Chen.[23] Safely married, Molly felt no repercussions of the anxieties that had tormented her during her engagement.

Gradually autumn came to the valley: white mist curled up through the woods, and the wind blew them up the hills at a brisker pace. It was time to return.[24] On the way back they spent two nights at Dorchester in order to visit Thomas Hardy: as he later recalled, Desmond had taken Molly to meet the Hardys when they were first engaged: "We had lunch, the extraordinary and never to be forgotten first Mrs. Hardy was there. . . . When I introduced Molly she said, 'I congratulate *you* (pointing to me) but I don't congratulate her.' You might think this was an unpleasant beginning to an hour's conversation. Oddly enough it wasn't."[25]

Later on in the autumn, Molly and Desmond moved into their first house, near Bury St Edmunds in East Anglia.

8   "An Oddity Without Parallel"

"There in this little warm room lit by candles and a green shaded lamp with pipe tobacco smelling fragrantly, with two spaniels lying by the fire we spent our evenings. Desmond had an entirely individual peculiarity . . . of quite suddenly giving a long rub to his eyes with both hands rather like a fly that seems to be vigorously washing its face. This curious spontaneous and unique gesture always meant that he was rapturously contented; and at the same moment he would exclaim out loud 'my happiness is more than I can bear!' which exaggeration made us both burst out laughing, and contentedly enjoy the moment." Molly's recollections of her early married life in The Green Farm, Timworth, were happy ones.[1] The straggling village was set amidst the flat fields of Suffolk. Their house was part of a working farm, its back windows overlooking the cowsheds, from which, twice a day, accompanied by a great clattering of churns, the milk was sent to the London train. Sometimes Desmond went with it, getting a lift on the farm wagon to the early morning "milk train" from the nearby market town of Bury St Edmunds.

Molly hung chintz curtains at the small sash windows of their new house and arranged their furniture, some of it wedding presents, some lent by Chen, to make it as cosy as possible. The house was comfortably built on two floors with a border of trees round the garden as a break for the vigorous winds which blew across the surrounding fields. There was no hot running water or electricity. Desmond's study was a low-ceilinged room on the first floor where shelves were put up all round the walls and immediately filled with books. The floor of simple scrubbed boards had no carpet, just a fur hearthrug. "Each morning, all the winter, ice lay on our water jugs on rising; ice lay on our water butts, puddles, ponds, on into the middle spring – Shakespeare's description & Keats' I read to Desmond in the study . . . and these just described our own cold Suffolk days, but we were young and vital and I look back happily even on all these cold days that later in life I have come to hate."

The Green Farm was on the estate of Desmond's old friend, now his patron, George Arthur Paley, known as G.A.P., who lived at Ampton

Hall nearby. The MacCarthys were frequent visitors to this great mock-Elizabethan pile made the more gloomy by the conifers which G.A.P. obsessed with forestry, planted densely in the parkland and right up to the house. Their monotonous dark green was relieved by an artificial lake G.A.P. created, on which to row or skate in winter. The Paleys lived in a conventionally opulent Edwardian manner: they had two chauffeurs, and large conservatories which were full of camellias, and in the springtime sweet-smelling violets and hyacinths. G.A.P. was fond of indoor games, from throwing bread at mealtimes to racquets, for which he had a court sloping at 45 degrees – perhaps he thought that gave more exercise – and army games of great complexity which lasted for days were spread out on the wide floors of the Hall. These elaborately complicated pastimes confirmed to Desmond once again the strange nature of G.A.P.: "an oddity without parallel in my experience of human nature". Paley achieved nothing in his lifetime and is forgotten now by all but a very few, so it is fortunate that Desmond drew an unforgettable portrait of him for the Memoir Club just after Paley's death in 1947. This conjures up the essence of this strange character.

G.A.P. was exceptional in every way, in appearance, behaviour, outlook – and wealth. His fortune was due not to any ambition on the part of his family who were, for the main part, Yorkshire yeomen, but to a series of coincidences, the most lucrative of which was their owning the land on which the prosperous spa town of Harrogate was subsequently built. Consequently, at the turn of the century, aged twenty-five, G.A.P. came into considerably more than £200,000 worth of gilt-edged securities, as well as the Ampton estate; the land near Harrogate was sold from time to time to bring in windfalls of several thousands.[2] "On the death of his mother, he would also inherit another £3,000 a year and a London house, and on the death of a very aged great-aunt one of the most beautiful small Elizabethan houses in England, with all its contents, St. Catherine's near Bath. Oh, I've forgotten, he had also inherited another historic house, Bowling Hall in the centre of Bradford.

"Now you would think those were corks which would keep anyone bobbing on the bright surface of social life – especially a man with no expensive personal tastes. G.A.P. had absolutely none. Fewer even than I. All he really needed was a comfortable chair and something on which to put up his feet, a bowl of tobacco and a bunch of feathers to clean his pipes at his elbow, and a second chair (he didn't mind whether *that* was comfortable or not) for an old friend to sit on opposite him."[3]

More often than not, that friend was Desmond, for G.A.P. liked nothing better than to bounce his strange philosophical ideas and eccentric farming schemes off this most literate and sympathetic companion. So, as some rich men keep race horses or collect works of art, G.A.P. maintained – Desmond: he now paid him a salary of £400 a year, for starting his new magazine, the *New Quarterly*, and for helping him with his own literary efforts. The Green Farm was part of the deal.

Their friendship was an old one, dating back to boyhood at his preparatory school when Desmond had been asked to look after him – and tipped half a sovereign to do so – by his cousin, the Rev. Egerton MacCarthy, who was also a connection of G.A.P.'s family. The new boy's "huge body (he was instantly christened 'Lubber-Huge') was as white as lard, he was exceptionally muscular [and] addicted to boasting of his strength. . . .

"The cry would start 'Let's build a tower of Babel'. Then four or five little boys would spring on Lubber Huge, bringing him down and piling themselves across his body, one on top of the other, calling on spectators to add weight to the pile which would presently dissolve with shrieks of laughter. . . . Arthur would howl frantically, not with pain but with terror. . . .

"What diplomacy could do to protect him, I did, but nothing I could say to him would check his habit of boasting . . . or, what was almost as provocative, boasting about the prowess of his family butler at home."

The tip that Desmond had been given to look after the new boy was on his conscience and he earned it: he fully earned, too, the salary that brought him, with his young wife, to live on G.A.P.'s estate twenty-five years later. For Paley's literary pretensions were as great as his absence of talent. Despite having installed a literary critic virtually on his doorstep, he nevertheless would not take his advice. He had a penchant for writing interminable detective stories which would have shocked a boy of ten by their improbabilities, and these he read to Desmond slowly in a grave, even expressionless voice from the enormous cashier's ledger in which he had written them. "Of course I did my best to suggest improvements although it was outside improvement. And sometimes I would hail a phrase with the enthusiasm of a shipwrecked man hailing a sail. I remember one such phrase; the hero, on a journey in the restaurant car, has placed before him, 'a thin disc of tepid train-rocked soup.' 'Arthur, stop!' I cried. 'You've written as well as Flaubert!' But that conveyed nothing to him, on he went ungratified."

Paley's seems to have been a case of arrested development. Like Desmond, he was the only child of a doting and over-protective mother who had been widowed young. Unlike Desmond, he did not escape from her over-fondness to attain independent intellectual or emotional maturity. Desmond reckoned that he made a close new friend every year from his schooldays until well into middle age, but G.A.P. never made any new friends outside the safety of his family circle. His wife, a smart, conventional woman, Frances Mary, known as Bina, liked the luxurious life her husband's fortune could provide, but for neither of them was it a love-match: he could only be fond of anyone in a limited way, and she was not by nature affectionate or demonstrative.

Nor was it to be expected that Molly, the romantic and fastidious, would get on with G.A.P. She found his manners boorish; his selfishness extreme and his conversation disconcertingly limited. "He was blessed with a simple sense of humour; he could see a joke – otherwise he never gave a plain answer to any question put to him and was very difficult to talk to, balking all spontaneity by an unhelpful contrariness. . . ." He liked rudely to tease visitors and to shock them: "I myself saw two of his offended visitors not wait for their host's motor to take them away from the Hall after a visit, but leave hurriedly for the station in a hired conveyance ordered by themselves in dudgeon, never to return!" In fact this was because G.A.P. refused to let them leave in motors from his own garages – which led Desmond to suggest that the Hall needed a cab rank outside it for the use of his outraged guests. Women were particularly offended by his suggestion that he would have to smack their bottoms to keep them under control, and by his exceedingly frank talk about sex. "I wonder why they pronounce it *vajina*?" he would muse during a mealtime conversation, "I should have thought *vaggina* was truer to the Latin pronunciation."

"Lubber Huge" had grown up to be a tall, conventionally handsome young man, who, despite his wife's efforts to make him more orthodox, contrived to look as out of the ordinary as he could. Molly often complained about Desmond's clothes: how much more did G.A.P.'s offend! At one time he had a shirt with holes cut in it to expose his nipples – for some obscure reason of comfort or health. Another idiosyncrasy was his great yellow boots, several sizes too big, so that he could wriggle his toes uninhibitedly (a necessity to him, however formal or informal his attire). This eccentricity had its uses: one way of silencing the flow of his insensitive, bawdy talk was to ask him about his boots – he loved to give a jocose and lengthy answer. Bina's old nanny summed him up shrewdly as a man who would be kind if he only knew how to be.

"Desmond, I shall never be able to get on with Arthur," Molly said despairingly. "Well, don't try. You'll get used to one another," she reported Desmond as replying. "And all through my married life there was generally just one oddity or another whom I had 'to get used to', for I was lacking in Desmond's very special gift for interesting himself in people who seemed to me to be difficult."[4]

She had one particular compensation for spending the long inhospit-
able winter with little congenial company: to her joy she found that she
was pregnant. She told Chen: "We are so happy here and have such happy
calm days – It really seems selfish to be leading such a happy undisturbed
life."[5]

Molly's baby was born in July 1907 after a labour which lasted almost
thirty hours, during which Desmond was the greatest comfort. Eventually, from her chloroform-induced doze, she "woke to ask if it was a boy
or girl – a boy – joy joy joy. Enormous son weighing 8 lbs which was why
he was such an age coming into the world. Such a darling – soft & warm –
all the terrible time forgotten in the triumph of having him."[6] Desmond,
too, was instantly devoted to his son who was called Michael and
nicknamed "the Archangel". Mid-August found Molly settled comfortably in the Green Farm with Michael and a nanny, Mildred, a local girl,
engaged at an annual salary of £22, who was to stay with the family for
many years to come.

Michael's godparents were "The Owl", his aunt, Margaret Warre-
Cornish, and G. E. Moore. In his letter to Moore, Desmond told him
about the suicide of his brother-in-law, Reggie Balfour, Charlotte's
husband: "I have not told Molly yet that he killed himself, & I do not like
to do so yet, for she is still in distress."[7] Charlotte was left a widow, after
seven years of marrage, with four small children; luckily, she was not
poverty-stricken, for the Balfours were a prosperous family.

On the surface, Molly's letters to Desmond are those of a loving wife
leading a quiet rural existence; but they contain the elements of all the
stresses to which their marriage was subject over the following years: the
separations – Molly in the country and Desmond more and more in
London – which were to be the pattern of their life and which were to
prove, in their frequency, so trying to her; the worries over work – would
Desmond get it done? And on time? Over money; and above all over his
neglect: would he return home to his family when he promised, or days
later? After a year the carefree period of their married life, the cloudless
beginning, was over. Though she was still very much in love and
especially happy after Michael's birth, the worries about Desmond's
career began to crowd in on Molly in her isolation in the country: "I do
trust you will get your Quarterly out by October 25th," she wrote on
21st August. "Everyone asks when it is coming out, & Bina said rather
crossly to me that 'G.A.P. was utterly slack about it,' – & if it doesn't
come out, what have you done to deserve your £400?

"Oh Desmond darling, do forgive this nagging. You know I'm really
not a nagging wife, as wives go. I often feel anxious about your work for
Arthur, because he really doesn't do enough, for a man with a secretary."

Once the *Quarterly* was out, they could look forward to "a *tremend-ously* jolly 3 weeks. I won't nag once in it – except about shaving – and 'hair & hands' nagging – of course I couldn't relinquish that. Meanwhile you must sympathise with me for being so anxious about the Quarterly. . . ."[8]

On their first wedding anniversary, Desmond penned a brief, affection-ate note: "My darling, I hadn't a moment yesterday to write. I think of you every hour. All's well. Very happy on this day and longing to get back to my dearest. D."

At the end of September 1907, Desmond and Paley took a trip to France during which they worked on – and on – Paley's contribution to the *New Quarterly*. They hurtled south in the motor, stopping en route. It was gloriously hot and Desmond enjoyed the change, but trying to make sense of Paley's article was torture. "They say that a hen is unable to lift its head if you put its beak down on a chalk line; Arthur's hypnotised condition when an idea got into his noddle was as helpless! The long hand of the clock might go round and round, the small hand mark hour after hour, but his mind would remain in exactly the same position. If the topic came up next day, next week, next month, next year – there was his beak at the same spot on the same chalk line!"[9]

For all the exasperating tedium of working with Paley, the *New Quarterly* finally came out that autumn. During its two and a half years of life from November 1907 until the latter part of 1910, it was a vehicle for some articles of real quality; but it was patchy and incoherent; the combination of Arthur Paley and Desmond MacCarthy was not a recipe for success. The new journal had to embrace the broad interests of the two men: literature, science, public affairs and philosophy. This increased Desmond's tendency to be a passive, liberal editor. The *New Quarterly* was Paley's property and he intended to use it for airing his cranky views. The three essays submitted by him – "Biology and Politics", "Conciliat-ory Socialism", and "National Afforestation" – made dreary reading; but at least Desmond was able to secure a lively reply by H. G. Wells to Paley's not unintelligent tilt at socialism which was published with it.[10] Though a few, like Lytton Strachey, produced sparkling critical work, in general, more editorial guidance and discrimination were needed. It was symptomatic that in the first issue there was no explanation of the journal's purposes. The paper was intended for many and attracted, in the end, but few.

Although he generated ideas and cast his net widely among his Cambridge Apostle and journalistic friends to secure articles, Desmond was disorganised and slow in answering correspondence; it took an admonitory letter from his none too efficient friend Bob Trevelyan for instance to stir him to reply after the elderly and distinguished poet, Robert Bridges, had offered an essay on the verse translation he had written of Virgil's *Aeneid*.[11]

Bridges' fine translation of Aeneas' descent into Hades was one of the biggest fish caught in Desmond's net; the poet urged Desmond to use the journal as much as possible to publish extracts from unobtainable books or unpublished manuscripts – an idea with which Desmond was warmly in sympathy. In most of the numbers he included passages from Samuel Butler's notebooks, supplied by his friend, Festing Jones, Butler's biographer[12]: Bernard Shaw criticised them accurately as interesting but unequal, "some of them being the observations of a grumpy old bachelor, not at that moment looking further than his nose, though they are shrewd enough at that. Others go to the ends of the earth. I think with your help, Butler will come to his own presently."[13] Though Desmond did attract an interest in the notebooks, which were later published as a book, he could have done more in his journal to explain the most paradoxical passages. According to Eddie Marsh he had left his commentary on them to the last minute: "One Sunday night . . . I sat up with him from eve . . . to dreary morn, helping him to get into some kind of order the still disjected members of a disquisition on Samuel Butler which he had had six months to write for the *New Quarterly* and for which Monday was the last possible day of sending in." Even so, his promotion of Butler, as Shaw predicted, was important in establishing that author's posthumous reputation, when an anti-Victorian reaction got under way and Butler's attacks on religious bigotry came to be admired.

During his time as editor, Desmond contributed little work of his own. His essay on John Donne was the core of a biography which for years he intended to write. He also wrote an article protesting against the censorship of drama. The theatrical censor had recently struck a blow against the "theatre of ideas" by refusing licences to several important plays, including Granville Barker's *Waste*.

Of the contributors, on the whole the philosophers – Moore, McTaggart, Russell, Lowes Dickinson – put up the most impressive performance, the latter offering a public lecture that he was giving that year. These were generous gestures by distinguished men to a new journal; so too was Thomas Hardy's offer of "House of Hospitalities", a first time in print for a gloomy and – for Hardy – mediocre poem. Worse was Belloc's curious sonnet: "To a Young Married Lady Possessed of a Freehold in the County of Sussex", though it was atoned for by an essay, "The Stane Street", the following year. Max Beerbohm also contributed essays, "The Fire" and "Dulcedo Judiciorum", which are graceful but not in his wittiest vein. Granville Barker wrote a pithy defence of a

yours always
D MacCarthy

I tried to write a play with Donne as a hero. Complete failure. I am either getting stupider or never was as clever as I hoped

The Green Farm

above
Part of a letter written from The Green Farm, showing Desmond's sketch of the house

left
Desmond and Molly in early marriage

left
George Arthur Paley (G.A.P.), nicknamed 'Lubber Huge'

above
Desmond's lifelong friend, Reymond Abbott, known as 'The Owl', seen here in old age (right) with Michael MacCarthy

below
The pageant at Ampton, G.A.P.'s home; Desmond is 3rd from the left; G.A.P. next to throne

repertory theatre system of the kind that he had recently helped to pioneer at the Duke of York's theatre.

Desmond gave foreign literature much space in the *New Quarterly*. Two stories by Chekhov, newly translated by H. R. Stewart, were interesting items in the July 1909 issue; but Maurice Baring's amateurish rhapsodising on Gogol ("irresistibly droll") did less credit to the journal; and a play by von Keyserling about the love life of the Lithuanian peasantry can hardly have excited its readers.[14]

The fees offered to contributors were small and they became smaller: Strachey was only paid £5 per article. J. M. Keynes received (with apologies) £4[15]. To Max Beerbohm a sum of £10 was mentioned for "The Fire", while Belloc became nervous he might not be paid at all; after sending in "The Stane Street," he wrote urgently for his fee "at the proper price of a pound a page . . . if you do not send it I shall go bankrupt very quickly. I shall lose all I have, my house will be taken away from me."[16]

Bertrand Russell proved a considerable support over the paper, not only with his distinguished articles on ethics and mathematics, but also with editorial advice. He kept in touch, too, over another literary enterprise: Desmond had been asked by the Russell family to edit the letters and memoirs of the late Lady Russell, second wife of Queen Victoria's Prime Minister (and grandmother of Bertrand Russell himself). There was a mass of letters and papers; editing them took Desmond three years – far longer than he had anticipated. This was partly because they were of limited interest to him: as he had said, "History lit by the imagination is the only history I can enjoy myself." Lord John Russell's political career, the central focus of these papers, did not come into this category; and Desmond could only muster a lukewarm concern for the minutiae of the Reform Bill of 1832. Bertie's aunt, Lady Agatha Russell, who was supervising the project – a wan spinster who had little in her life but family piety – took against his attempts at making the central characters come alive; Bertie apologised: "She hates psychology & analysis & complication – broadly, everything that Henry James stands for. If I were you, I would not take very seriously the original writing required, but try to make it very simple. . . . And above all, get it done. You see that owing to your laziness you failed to see Sir Henry Elliot [a leading diplomat and Lady Russell's brother] before he died. Don't let us all be dead before you finish!"[17]

But Desmond confessed to having an "incorrigible interest in other people and their relations to each other", and he considered that "of all the observers of the social scene who are tempted to seize an ell whenever an inch peeps out, Henry James is the master," (which was why he so much admired him). The book *Lady John Russell: A Memoir*, finally

came out in 1910, and in the event, Desmond's accomplished and fluent
commentary formed a major portion of it. George Trevelyan was full of
praise: "I only wish we had more of you in the book. You must write a
biography. You could do it splendidly. You have combined historical,
literary and personal *flaire* which would make you a prime
biographer. . . ."[18] He was right: Desmond could have excelled as a
biographer as his articles on such diverse figures as John Bunyan and Sir
William Harcourt tantalisingly showed.

Desmond finally lost his job on *The Speaker* when the paper became
The Nation in 1907 and Lawrence Hammond ceased to be editor. Molly
often later regretted this change, not only because of the loss of some
regular income, but because it ended Lawrence Hammond's steadying
influence. She wished that Desmond would continue to see him and his
wife Barbara, more frequently, for both were eminent historians, high-
minded and well-organised, though not lacking in humour, and should
have been just the right antidote to Desmond's tendency to procrastinate
over his writing; but Desmond was not suited to the kind of abstemious-
ness which "seeing more of the Hammonds", to the exclusion of other
less earnest companions, would have involved.

When his work on *The Speaker* stopped Granville Barker asked him to
commemorate the Vedrenne–Barker years with a book. This consisted of
a digest of his reviews with a complete set of cast lists.[19] Shaw was
delighted: "Certainly, as regards my own plays, you were not only nearer
the mark than other sharp shooters, you were actually in the same valley,
whilst the others, even when they got on the targets, did so mostly by quite
unintentional ricochets or vagaries of spent bullets."[20]

Though Shaw never became an intimate friend, he greatly valued
Desmond's support and their friendship even survived a contretemps
when Desmond forgot to pay Shaw's Irish tailor for a pair of trousers he
had made for him, and Shaw – much against the grain – had to foot the
bill and try to extract the money from him.[21]

As a postscript to Desmond's time of reviewing the Vedrenne–Barker
productions, it is interesting to read some of his criticisms in the light of
his relationship with Molly. For example, he objected to Shaw's
treatment of love in *Man and Superman* and *You Never Can Tell*, as
nothing more than a blind biological force. He felt Shaw had over-
simplified a complex emotion. It was not just the powerful attraction: "It
is also happiness in the contemplation of her mind and character and
experience of them in her person."

Ibsen's *Wild Duck* at the Court Theatre – to which he took Molly in
October 1905 – had particularly interested him, for it corresponded very
closely with what he felt. The play dealt with the perils of "telling the

whole truth" because of a moral compulsion to do so, regardless of the human consequences. Although absolute honesty in personal relationships had been dinned into Desmond by the Cambridge Apostles and by the teaching of contemporaries such as Granville Barker and Bernard Shaw, he was all too aware of its dangers, and how easily spite or callousness could masquerade as frankness. His own relationship with Molly always involved speaking freely to each other and at times, despite Desmond's sensitivity and generosity, this endangered their marriage. It is a measure of their fundamental closeness that they weathered some very stormy passages.

In 1907 Desmond, while working for Paley and attempting to write a play about Donne, also travelled to London regularly, to keep up his literary contacts and to look out for possible jobs as a critic. With the approach of winter, Molly, who, after all had scarcely ever left the circle of her large family before, often burst into rushes of self-pity at her loneliness.

"I missed you so terribly yesterday evening," she wrote in October, "when I came in to solitude — it is really wretched having to live away from you so much. I got depressed, & felt that you would get so used to living a life apart & wouldn't care a bit, but would get to like it best, so that I shouldn't share your life at all." It was a cri-de-coeur that was to echo throughout her letters for the next thirty years. But these early doubts and misgivings were dispelled when Desmond did at last return on Friday evening, or, if he failed to catch the last train, on Saturday morning, and they passed many contented days, playing with the baby, or visiting neighbours. "Returning home in the later afternoon, with the pony going . . . briskly, along the lanes where dusk was coming on, and where October leaves were falling or had fallen a delicious damp hazel nutty scent in the air and then when the pony turned in at our gate and one saw the lamps had just been lit inside the house and Desmond was coming in himself across the garden from a late run, I was just as glad of everything as I could be," Molly recalled in her memoir later.

Many people came to stay in Desmond and Molly's new house: relations, of course, and Desmond's Cambridge friends who were to contribute to the New Quarterly. Both strands of their lives met one weekend when Lytton Strachey and Blanche Warre-Cornish were staying together. What that often taciturn intellectual made of the voluble and romantic mother-in-law of his old friend is not recorded, but Desmond and he ensconced themselves by the fire in the study and discussed both The Speaker and the New Quarterly. While Blanche, at her bedroom window where the sun streamed in, enjoyed "the glory of Green Farm, the show of snowdrops; they carpet the shrubberies and look so lovely at the

gate with the full dark green leaves,[22] Lytton chose to appreciate the
wonders of Nature from a different standpoint, as he wrote in his letter
to thank Molly, "I read Darwin in the train. Tell Desmond that
literature is twaddle, and that the only things worth thinking about are
Melastomaceae, Earthworms, and Metamorphic Schists."[23]

When Desmond had intellectual and literary friends to stay, though
G.A.P. would much have liked to meet them, as a rule he avoided
bringing them together: "I knew that he would bore my clever friends
and puzzle them. Only the most indulgent among them, Moore or
Goldie Dickinson, were really available for that purpose. What would
be the use of asking Bertie Russell or Maynard Keynes to meet him and
discuss those things in which Arthur might be interested? It would only
mean that I should have to sit by, suffering vicarious embarrassment."
G.A.P. was likely to question Desmond about his friends on such lines
as:

"Is he as clever as Bertrand Russell?"
    "No, I don't think so – no; certainly not."
(Pause)
    "Is he as clever as Lytton Strachey?"
    "He has quite a different sort of mind. He is not nearly as original."
    "Is he as original as you?"
    "O Arthur, how *can* I tell? I've no doubt he feels much more
original. Let's abide by what is certain: He's cleverer and more
original than Chilcot." (Chilcot was G.A.P.'s head-gardener)[24]

As for Molly, though she claimed to have found many of Desmond's
Cambridge friends "alarmingly intellectual" she was no uncritical child-
wife, but surveyed them with fresh and fastidious eyes: "I do not
remember that any one of them was particularly artistic or aesthetically
enraptured with beauty of earth; I should say they one & all had tragic,
pessimistic casts of mind; which is not to say that they were not witty &
humorous & most kind."[25]

Desmond teased her by telling her that Bertrand Russell would be
most interested if she talked to him about birds. She therefore launched
into a description of the nesting habits of the chaffinch and was
mortified to find the eminent philosopher showing definite signs of
boredom. She soon ceased to be overawed by him. On a much later
occasion, when Russell – as was his wont with all women – tried to
make urgent love to her, she could not keep a straight face at the little
man's unspontaneous avowals of passion.[26]

She was quick to note the slovenliness which so often characterised these intellectuals. The higher the brow, the lower the standard of cleanliness seems to have been the rule: in a letter to her mother-in-law she enlisted her help over Desmond's untidiness: "to get Desmond to go to his tailor without fail before he comes down here . . . I really get rather out of patience with Desmond's wildness over his clothes – I really don't see any charm in it. George Trevy even looks positively spruce by the side of Desmond . . . & it isn't beautiful to be unkempt – He hasn't a good enough figure to carry it off, & unless a man is of immense proportions, it only makes [him] look insignificant & *most* undistinguished, & entirely unromantic & unpoetical – simply like the kind of man who works in a bicycle shop all day. . . . He seems to have *absolutely* no vanity on the subject. . . .

". . . Janet [Trevelyan] tells me that George simply writes to his Cambridge tailor & says send me a blue suit, the same measure & exactly like the last. How fearful to have to quote *George* as an example. . . .

"Of course I don't want him to dress like Eddie [Marsh] or spend as much! but there is absolutely *no* danger of his being too smart. . . .

"I hope you will bear me out in all I say; I think it is absolute madness to think that one can ignore the body – *Moore* for instance has absoluely no *external* charm for me, because his suits are greasy, & he looks so hot & fat; *Chesterton* to my mind is *as* disagreeable as a hippopotamus in body – or even worse, because hippopotamuses are not usually *bathed in* perspiration. (I *will* use violent language). *Bob Trevy* has *too* distressing a body & face for a poet!

"I don't see why men should be allowed utterly to leave out & ignore poor plain little women with no taste . . . whereas men allow themselves to be as unprepossessing as they like. Desmond *must* keep thin, & give a little attention to shaving, nails, & hair – & *teeth*. I mind his getting fat more than anything."

She might as well have saved her energy. Desmond's clothes and his appearance never improved: he did not get particularly fat, but he neglected his appearance with the single-minded consistency that others lavish on theirs. Virginia Woolf noted in her diary, twenty years on, that he looked "like a man who has sat up all night in a third class railway carriage. His fingers are stained yellow with cigarettes. One tooth in the lower jaw is missing. His hair is dank. His eye more than ever dubious. He has a hole in his blue sock."[27] Unkempt he may have been, but he also had a stylishness of bearing, rather than of clothes, which was always appealing: and his compact, broad-shouldered build contrasted with the often under-developed bodies of some of his Cambridge friends, as Molly noted in a letter to Chen after E. M. Forster had visited them at Green

Farm: "I enjoyed Mr. Forster. He has got a wretched little physique & a voice just like Reymond's ["The Owl"]. Why must people of imaginative brains be so wretched physically – Desmond is really quite a Samson among all these friends with odd bodies. Think of Lytton Strachey for instance."[28] On him she did not elaborate: enough had been implied about that etiolated form.

9   South Africa and the "Artquake"

When, in the summer of 1908, Molly found that she was pregnant again, her feelings were mixed. Money was tight, Desmond's future was uncertain, and she would rather have waited until Michael was a little older before adding to the family.

She decided to have this baby at the Green Farm rather than moving in to Cheyne Gardens as she had for Michael's birth the previous year; for Chen's fussing had been inordinate. Throughout her married life Chen constantly undermined her daughter-in-law, both by overt criticism and by comparing their poverty with her expectations of how they should live. Molly was exemplary towards Chen, dutiful, tactful and discreet, but even early on in their marriage she allowed herself the occasional outburst to Desmond: "from her glowing accounts of Leeds and your wonderful cook, and her clothes and maid and delightful visits to elegant people, and first class journeys to Switzerland, I can see that it has all become a sort of 'fairy story'": it was a constant source of rancour to Chen that "we are not all richer and smarter and more pampered".[1]

January 1909 found Molly waiting quietly at Green Farm for the birth of the baby; it was bitterly cold, but she enjoyed looking at "an exquisite white frost – all the trees and shrubs like coral reefs under the sea". Soon after midnight on 26th February, Desmond bicycled off to fetch the doctor and on returning into the house "I heard the wailing of the child. I went up, found Moll terribly exhausted still, in pain but oh through it – immense relief. Your granddaughter weighs only 1 oz. short of 9 lbs. She is a plump imperturbable baby," he wrote to his mother.[2]

Alone at the Green Farm, Molly, like many women after the birth of a baby, was feeling well but emotionally raw, having "to conquer nerves & perpetual sense of foreboding (like a Maeterlinck heroine) & indecision & anxiety & sense of insurmountable difficulties. However as this has got steadily better the last fortnight I have no fear of any breakdown," she wrote to Desmond. Nonetheless she felt both neglected and anxious. The *Quarterly* was not prospering; the Paleys were bored; life at Timworth was beginning to pall for poor Molly; she felt it was time for change. Meanwhile, Desmond was still employed by Paley, and part of his job was to accompany him abroad: for one thing G.A.P. hated making his own travel arrangements, and for another he could not bear solitude. Now he planned to go to Germany with Desmond in pursuit of his current mania for afforestation; there were compensations for travelling with so narrow-minded a companion – predominantly his wealth, as Desmond observed from the luxury of Der Kaiserhof Hotel in Berlin: "this palace of white marble and soft, deep, cherry coloured carpets".

For all that he was half-Prussian, Desmond was depressed by the "ponderous ostentatious façades" of modern Berlin, and by the Germans' idolatrous worship of the Hohenzollerns. They seemed to him to love whatever was *big* and *new*: as he shrewdly observed, "They have a contempt for the instincts and traditions which were most characteristic before they were powerful; yet in their attempts at achieving the magnificent they can't keep homeliness entirely out, so the result is a mixture of the grand and imposing with the whimsical and simple, extraordinarily unpleasing and comic to anyone with a sense of style." It was a relief "to get into the atmosphere of France and the amiable discriminatingly sensual 18th century" when they visited Sans Souci and Potsdam, with its shades of Frederick the Great and Voltaire.[3]

Paley's new venture was buying sixty square miles of semi-arid land in the Karoo district of South Africa, which he proposed to run as a sheep farm. He wanted Desmond to accompany him there and Desmond urged Molly to go too.

Leaving the children, and Mildred with Chen, in the New Year of 1910 Desmond and Molly and a considerable amount of luggage embarked with Arthur and Bina Paley and a great deal more luggage, as well as their two small sons, Gerald and Percy, their nanny and the French chauffeur, for the long sea voyage to South Africa. Paid for by G.A.P., they travelled first-class on the Union-Castle *R.M.S. Saxon.*

From Cape Town it was a 500-mile journey to the Paleys' farm on the great Karroo: they travelled through vast tracts of stony desert with distant mountains all round, like a Doré picture, thought Molly, "one can imagine Abraham with his herds". After twenty-four hours on the train they reached the little settlement of Victoria West, and then came "a *burning* hot drive across the Karoo. I think I have never felt anything so hot."[4]

Melton Wold, the farm where they stayed, was primitive: it had large rooms with good plain fireplaces, but it was hideously decorated, with squalid flypapers hanging everywhere. Molly did not mind too much as she was out of doors all day, reading or writing in the shade of the kitchen garden, and towards evening when the heat had abated, riding out with Desmond into "the blotchy, sallow-faced Karoo", meaning "thirst-land" in Hottentot, it surrounded the farm for mile upon unlovely mile. "Bright desolation" was how Desmond described it to G. E. Moore, "But when the sun set, the whole place was transformed. I have never seen such apocalyptic glories in the sky."[5]

In the mornings Desmond worked on the veranda at the lectures he was to give the following month, and on the more fruitless task of helping G.A.P. As for Paley he revelled in the primitive life and dressed the part of a pioneer, in "Boots with the toes cut off, like a tramp – & a black overcoat cut into a short coat with a frayed edge – no shirt, & a panama with half the brim off. He really looks worse than the most ragged Kaffir on the place. Bina is in despair, but he declares he can't be comfortable dressed in any other way. Desmond is getting much thinner & is very nicely dressed."

Their isolation from their familiar world, and their proximity to one another, brought into sharper focus for Molly how bad Desmond and G.A.P. were for each other. More clearly than ever she saw that the way ahead for Desmond lay in independence.

The MacCarthys went on to Johannesburg where they made their second acquaintance with a mining millionaire – Lionel Phillips. "I am writing from a wonderful millionaire's house" as Molly put it in a letter to her mother-in-law, knowing how delighted she would be that at last they were mingling with the right, that is to say the richest, people. But Molly was eager to see her children again, so whilst Desmond stayed on to give his lectures, she travelled back to England alone.

She had decided that it was time for them to "plunge into London". While Desmond embarked on his career she was prepared for poverty: "I shall not dread it – it need only be horrid if we let our souls be dreary & we ought to start from the bottom of the tree."[6] But she did not feel he was writing with sufficient seriousness: "It is no use vaguely sitting down 'to do a little work'. . . . The time has come when you must simply *fling* things into the press, or you will never do anything at all." The trouble with Desmond and writing was, and always would be, getting down to it. He had no particular deadline as a spur, but relied on submitting articles on approval to editors. No articles, no income, as Molly reminded him again in July, describing "the terrible indignity of the situation – I now have to pretend to my friends for your sake all kinds of things about your writing. . . . I do really think you are behaving feebly, & in an unmanly way when you say that you are going to make £50 a month, & only make £15 (by an unpublished article) in 5 months . . . flat feebleness I will not face. . . . When we first married you did such a fine year's work – now that you have a second child I appeal to you to do as well as you did then." She ended this letter poignantly by running herself down: "Your Moll – who loves you more deeply than can be told – but what good can that do, for you think she has wrecked your life."[7]

Desmond took no offence at her letter – he almost never did, being just enough to recognise the validity of her criticism; he explained that: "as you saw when we were together, my pleasure in things is at a low ebb and this makes writing still harder for me. However, the only cure is to get something done which I can feel ever so slightly proud of. It is dissatisfaction with myself which is paralysing me just now, and I am of course anxious about our future.

"I have felt sometimes as though my mind and character were crumbling to pieces, as though there was some kind of dry rot in my brain."[8]

Urgency was added to the search for a permanent home when Molly discovered that she was again pregnant. If she had been overjoyed at becoming pregnant for the first time, and taken aback by the speed with which she conceived for the second time, she was dismayed by this third pregnancy. However, her instinctive love of children overrode her fear for the future. She told Chen "I simply could not *believe* this time . . . that it was that, as I had done to the letter all I was supposed to do to prevent it." The MacCarthys' knowledge of contraception was, in common with many couples as intelligent as themselves, rudimentary.[9]

Meanwhile Desmond, whose likeness to Mr Micawber in his faith that "something would turn up" was commented on more than once by Virginia Woolf and others of his friends, was whisked off by the art critic Roger Fry in pursuit of a group of pictures that were profoundly to affect the course of art in Europe – the Post-Impressionists.

Desmond's adventures began when Roger Fry (1866–1934) asked him to be the secretary of an exhibition of such painters as Cézanne, Matisse, Gauguin, Van Gogh, Seurat and Picasso whose works were to be shown, virtually for the first time, to the British public, at the Grafton Galleries in London. It was the first time, too, that Desmond had ever seen them, as he recalled in a later radio talk (broadcast in 1946) on the exhibition, "Fry himself had seen very few of their pictures; but he was a man of exploring sensibility and those he had seen had impressed him." In fact, as early as 1906 Fry had recognised the genius of Cézanne, and since then had become increasingly drawn to modern French painting.

At the time of the 1910 exhibition, Fry was forty-four, some ten years older than Desmond. Although their paths had not crossed as undergraduates at Cambridge, they met frequently as Apostles; and Fry had contributed *An Essay in Aesthetics* to the *New Quarterly* the previous year, which was reprinted in his influential *Vision and Design* in 1920.

Desmond at once realised that he was not being asked to help with the new exhibition because of any special trust in his judgement as an art critic, but because he and Fry got on well together as friends: "what really influenced him in choosing me was that we were happy together. My failings were not the sort which annoyed him, nor (equally important) were my virtues. Masterful men often prefer a rather incompetent colleague to an over-confident one. Fry was capable of making muddles himself; he wouldn't have been comfortable with anyone implacably efficient. And here I must mention that he was also a most persuasive man.

"Hearing that the Grafton Galleries had no show for the months between their usual London Season exhibition and the new year's, he proceeded to convince them that they might do worse than hold a stop-gap exhibition of modern foreign artists – also that Desmond MacCarthy was an excellent man of business which indeed, in *my* opinion (of this you must judge yourselves) he did turn out to be. It was all settled in a tremendous hurry. I had just time to interview the director of the Galleries. He apologised for the smallness of my fee (a hundred pounds). But if – he added, with a pitying smile – if there were profits, I might have half of them. Neither the committee of the Grafton Galleries nor Roger Fry thought for one moment that the show could be a financial success.

"Then I was stricken down with an influenza. However, Roger wasn't a man to be put out by a little thing like that."[10]

Fry, the energetic, the persuasive, was not deflected from the pursuit of fresh artistic discoveries by Desmond's illness; armed with a bottle of champagne, he hustled him on to the boat for Calais where "we drank the champagne and ate biscuits on the dark deck – sky starless and air as oppressive as it can be blowing over a northern sea – and then we went down to a red velvet inferno where I got no sleep owing to the shuddering of the screw and the atmosphere – I should have done better on deck, but R.F. was so afraid of my taking cold that he was not easy till I was suffering suffocation with him down below. Got a short sleep of poor quality in the train to Paris," Desmond wrote to Molly.

Once arrived in the capital, stumbling blearily out of the station they found a cheap hotel. The day took on the strange dreamlike quality being abroad has when one is light-headed from illness. "In my dim, thin-walled, heavily-draped little room I got 3 hours sleep on a bed like an enormous pin cushion. After a delicious déjeuner at a Restaurant where I *must* take you – oh I wish I had time to describe it – I felt much better, though I still felt as though my head were the size and weight of an apple.

"We then met Dell who took us round to the dealers and I enjoyed choosing the pictures (which will by the bye give you the most tremendous shocks). We got about 50."

This was Robert Dell, who afterwards became French correspondent for *The Manchester Guardian* and *The New Statesman*. "He was then more interested in pictures than politics – a delightful man, a friend of Anatole France" Desmond – himself a lifelong admirer of that author – explained in a broadcast. "He had the worst French accent you ever heard – much worse than our glorious Prime Minister's [Churchill]. I used to make Roger laugh by imitating him saying, of some picture, things like 'C'est un po tro ro-co-co.'

"At these interviews with dealers I used to pose as M. le Publique, and on one point my verdict was final: Was there, or was there not, anything in some nude which might create an outcry in London?"

From Paris Fry was to have gone with his great friend Goldie Lowes Dickinson for a few days' bicycling tour, but when he wired that he could not come "Fry persuaded me to get on D's bicycle and ride towards Munich." This was to be the second stage of gathering pictures for the exhibition. From the little town of Meaux Desmond wrote to Molly: "the day after tomorrow we reach Rheims when I take the train. . . . I am enjoying myself enormously. Don't think I am shirking my duty to the Gallery in spending these 3 days in this way – Fry's Quaker conscience would not allow him to persuade me to give up any chance of pushing on the work, if there were any opportunity of doing so. We have done a great deal – got a quarter of the pictures already." The arrival of the two Englishmen at Rheims must have been a bizarre spectacle: Fry was in any case an arresting figure with his penetrating eyes enlarged by great circular spectacles, his grey, fly-away hair and general insouciance over dress; "the most rapid way of suggesting his appearance is to say that it was easy to imagine him dressed as a fasting friar in a brown habit with a rope round his waist. . . . His voice, and his voice was one of the physical qualities which made him attractive, resembled Voltaire's; he had une voix sombre et majestueuse and a deep and ready laugh," Desmond wrote in a tribute after his death.

As for Desmond, his appearance was more than usually eccentric: "As I had fallen into some Tar I was not looking quite so neat as you wished me to look on my journeys," he wrote to Molly. "I have been bicycling in my smooth grey suit, the one you hate. This is (I imagined you will be actually glad to hear it) quite ruined. One leg is black and stiff with Tar and there are splashes and smudges elsewhere. The people of the inns where we have stopped on the way have been most sympathetic. They have rubbed me with minerals, lamp oil, petrol and other essences in vain. Our luggage turned up this morning."

At Rheims Fry and Desmond parted company: Desmond went on to Munich, experiencing the usual lowering of the spirits as he crossed the

German border: "The moment you get to Strasbourg the people seem to be years behind as far as the art of human intercourse goes." The language itself was an impediment to the discussion of art he reported to Molly: "It seems impossible to say anything about a work of art without seeming to analyse it as though it were a prescription composed of doses of this and infusions of that." Still he got on well enough with the German dealer Riefstahl: "A man about my age with a pale face and a thin pointed golden beard, very vivacious in talk, and always *correctly* dressing in black "frack" [tail-coat] and a flat-brimmed bowler on his head, such as is worn only by the outrageously horsey in our country. He is very friendly and anxious to meet the wishes of the directors of the G[rafton] G[allery]."[11]

After the fun of France, his spirits were further lowered by the "gloomy, gone-to-pieces" Hotel Roth where he was staying, which reminded him of Mr Dombey's house after little Paul's death. He settled the contributions to the exhibition from Germany as speedily as possible and returned to England.

For the next few weeks Desmond was taken up with arranging the exhibition with Fry. Neither they, nor the owners of the Grafton Galleries expected to make any money from it: in this they were wrong. They did expect "a howl of fury and derision" to greet the pictures: in this they were right. This reaction was partly due to the suddenness of their appearance, "No gradual infiltration, but – Bang! an assault along the whole academic front of Art. You can imagine the shindy! Or rather you *can't*. For that flabbergasted even those connected with the exhibition" Desmond recalled in his broadcast.

He had himself been disconcerted by many of the pictures at first, and found they needed to be assimilated properly before they could be appreciated: "If people can be persuaded, however, to give them a chance – that is to say not to condemn them on their first impression – they will see something in them," he had written to Molly from France. "There is a postman [by Van Gogh] which I expect will send people to the turnstile clamouring for their money back. He is so wonderfully hideous, alive, and as disconcerting as a face put suddenly three inches from one's own."

The question of a name for the exhibition exercised the organisers a good deal. After various suggestions, such as "expressionism, which aimed at distinguishing these artists from the impressionists, had been rejected", at last Roger, losing patience, said "Oh! well, let's call them post-impressionists. At any rate, they came after them," recalled Desmond. And so "a word which is now safely imbedded in the English language – 'post-impressionism' – was invented."

Then Fry "handed over to me, with a few notes, the ticklish job of writing the preface to the catalogue – the unsigned preface. This work of mine was far more widely quoted than anything I was ever destined to write and phrases from it like, 'a good rocking-horse is more like a horse than the snapshot of a Derby winner', were quoted and re-quoted with laughter. And yet this introduction, as Virginia Woolf in her life of Fry points out, "reads today mildly enough. It has even an apologetic air."[12] For in it Desmond was trying to forestall the outcry they all expected: the case of Matisse's pictures was typical of the other artists on show: he said, "The general effect . . . is that of a return to primitive, even perhaps of a return to barbaric, art. This is inevitably disconcerting"; but in immediacy lay their artistic strength.

The catalogue of over a hundred canvasses, bronzes and pottery shows the outstandingly rich and diverse harvest Desmond and Fry garnered from this revolutionary artistic movement, ranging in date and style from Manet's *Bar at the Folies-Bergère* to Gauguin's Tahitian pictures.

Up to the last minute all involved with the exhibition regarded it as a risk. The day it opened, 8th November Desmond wrote to his mother: "O the exhibition has meant such work! but I have enjoyed it nearly all – but such worry and anxiety and responsibility. . . . Well – the pictures are hung and I have given satisfaction. I *think* we may succeed but it will be a shave."[13]

The hanging of the pictures added considerably to his anxiety; thirty-six years later, he recalled it in his broadcast: "The hurried agonies of that picture-hanging are still vivid to me. Roger was entirely absorbed in deciding which picture would look best next another, while it lay with me to number them. As he was continually shifting them about when I was elsewhere, I was terrified that the numbers and titles wouldn't always correspond, with the effect of increasing the mockery, which I now felt certain the Exhibition would excite. It was four a.m. before I got to bed the night before Press day, and then I couldn't sleep for worrying. When the newspaper was brought to me with coffee in bed, although it happened to contain a long and laudatory review of a book I had just published,* I couldn't even read that. The prospect of public ridicule owing to having, say, catalogued a nude girl as 'Station-master at Arles', made my walk to the Gallery more like a walk to the Gallows. Soon after ten the Press began to arrive. Now, anything new in Art is apt to provoke the same kind of indignation as immoral conduct, and vice is detected in perfectly innocent pictures. Perhaps any mental shock is apt to remind people of moral shocks they've received and the sensations being similar, they attribute them to the same cause. Anyhow, as I walked about among

---

*This was the edited letters of Lady John Russell.

the tittering newspaper critics busily taking notes, (they saw at once that the whole thing was splendid copy). I kept overhearing such remarks as 'Pure pornography', 'Admirably indecent'. Not a word of truth, of course in this. As M. the Publique I had been careful to exclude too frankly physiological nudes and, indeed, at the last moment, instead of hanging two of the pictures, I told Roger they'd better be kept, for a time, in my sanctum downstairs.

"Well, the Press notices were certainly calculated to rouse curiosity! And from the opening day the public flocked, and the big rooms echoed with explosions of laughter and indignation. Sometimes I hovered about trying to explain what I thought was the point of a picture, drawing attention to colour or arrangement, and here and there, now and then, I did find a receptive listener."

He also found a great deal of hostility. Wilfrid Blunt was among those members of cultivated and cosmopolitan society who regarded the pictures as infantile and morally outrageous. "The exhibition is either an extremely bad joke or a swindle. I am inclined to think the latter for there is no trace of humour in it. Still less is there a trace of sense or skill or taste, good or bad, or art or cleverness. . . . Apart from the frames, the whole collection should not be worth £5, and then only for the pleasure of making a bonfire of them. Yet two or three of our art critics have pronounced in their favour . . . and Desmond MacCarthy acts as a secretary to the show." Blunt was old enough to remember when the pre-Raphaelite pictures were first exhibited at the Royal Academy half a century earlier: "it is pretended now that the present Post-impression case is a parallel to it. But I find no parallel. The pre-Raphaelite pictures were many of them extremely bad in colour, but were all carefully, laboriously drawn, and followed certain rules of art." Here he put his finger unerringly on the reason why the Post-Impressionists overtook them: because, breaking those well-established rules of art, they were "an imaginative declaration of rights; the right to be more independent of literal representation; the right to handle nature with more imaginative freedom; and above all, the comprehensive right to experiment them-selves," as Desmond wrote of the exhibition.

But for Blunt, and others of his caste, "these are not works of art at all; unless throwing a handful of mud against a wall may be called one. They are the work of idleness and impotent stupidity. A pornographic show," his diary entry concluded.[14]

Blunt's daughter, Judith, and her husband Neville Lytton – no revolutionary artist he – teased Desmond's mother by saying that it would serve Desmond right if Molly's forthcoming baby resembled Van Gogh's canvas *La Jeune Fille au Bleuet* (the mad girl in Zola's

Germinal).[15] While that talented amateur artist, the Duchess of Rutland, whose own drawings were always very faithful to their subjects, wrote more in sorrow than in anger from her house in nearby Arlington Street, to Desmond, as the exhibition secretary, lamenting that she had allowed her name to appear on the committee without seeing any of the pictures: "I am so *horrified* at having my name associated with such an *awful* exhibition of horrors I am very very much upset by it," and begging him "to keep my name out of the next issue of catalogues" – which it duly was.[16]

It was this sort of opposition from the educated classes which most riled the exhibition organisers, as Desmond described in an article after it closed in January, 1911: in it he acutely analysed why they would not allow such pictures to be art – because they would not provide an acceptable background to their well-oiled lives: "On the whole the classes who were most opposed to the Grafton Gallery Exhibition were, firstly, the cultured – that is to say the people who without necessarily having much imagination, have trained themselves with the greatest care and patience to look out for certain traits and qualities in works of art as the hall mark of true merit; secondly, by the rich and aristocratic classes who, possessing beautiful houses and refined furniture, tend to regard art merely as a background to their own lives. The cultured, though their taste may be impeccable in many directions, are by no means the likeliest people to see merit, even when it is there, in any new development. The aristocratic conception of art as a background to an elegant, dignified life, if it really ever got the upper hand, would sterilise the productive impulse in art."[17]

Despite the hostility and outrage, "Presently we began to *sell* pictures! The Art Gallery at Helsinki bought a very fine Cézanne for eight hundred pounds, I remember; and when we closed, my share of the profits amounted to – what do you think? – over four-hundred-and-sixty pounds – such a lump sum as I had never earned before, and would never earn again!"[18]

But it took more than one exposure to them for the British public to accept the Post-Impressionists: when, the following year, Roger Fry collected together a second exhibition of their works, Leonard Woolf was asked to be its Secretary, and he received exactly the same reactions as Desmond had: "Large numbers of people came to the exhibition, and nine out of ten of them either roared with laughter at the pictures or were enraged by them," finding them either "immoral or ridiculous or both", recalled Woolf.[19] Molly herself admitted that she did not find much meaning in the exhibits: "they are thought monstrous by the average public. I belong to that, and they don't give me much pleasure, it must be confessed, but I don't feel I know enough about them yet, but when Roger Fry shows one a statuette like this [squiggle] and says it's *wonderful*, I can only see it in the light of the comic spirit."

Desmond finally ceased working at the gallery in February 1911: whilst his excursion into the world of art had been exciting, as far as his career was concerned it did not lead anywhere. He wrote one or two articles on art criticism during the course of 1911 and 1912 but that was not his métier. He tended to look at pictures from a literary point of view as though they were either interpretations of literature, or comments upon the real world, similar to those made by poets and writers. As the writer David Garnett said of himself and his friends, "When we first looked at Cézanne, Van Gogh, Gauguin and Matisse we were baffled because we were unacquainted with any literary equivalents. The more literary the paintings, the readier we were to accept them." Garnett was just about able to appreciate Gauguin's Tahitians, for example, because he had read *Typee* and *Omoo* by Melville.[20]

In his 1946 broadcast, Desmond pointed out that Roger Fry did not make one penny out of the Exhibition, nor out of the Omega workshops, which he started later. Indeed, by introducing the works of the Post-Impressionists and of Picasso to the British Public, "he smashed for a long time his reputation as an Art critic. Kind people called him mad, and reminded others that his wife was in an asylum. The majority declared him to be a subverter of morals and Art, and a blatant self-advertiser. . . . Few people know the position Roger Fry occupied in the world of Art when he took this enthusiastic and disinterested step. In 1905, he had been appointed to the Directorship of the Metropolitan Art Gallery in New York . . . immediately after accepting that American offer he learnt that he might have stood successfully for the Directorship of the National Gallery. . . . His reputation carried weight in the world – but it couldn't carry that Exhibition. . . . He was not only the most analytical of English Art critics, but the most open-minded; and this power of making discoveries was connected with a trait in him which was amusingly at variance with his strong intellect. He had taken a double first at Cambridge in science. Yet he was a credulous man. Yes, there were times when I used to exclaim, 'Roger, you'd be the greatest of critics if only you would sometimes listen to the still, small voice that whispers: "Fiddle-sticks".' He was always ready to believe, for a time at any rate, that someone had done something or was trying after something which might prove enormously important."

To all the MacCarthy family Fry was a good friend, getting to know Molly best when she took the children to stay at his house in the country to escape the air-raids in London during the First World War. Neither

Desmond nor Molly much admired the products of the Omega work-shop which Fry set up in 1913, however, finding them at best faintly ridiculous, and at worst, hideous; and as a painter, they thought Fry's works dull. As for Fry, he criticised Desmond for frittering away so much of his time in fashionable company; this offended both his Puritanism and his prodigiously high standards of hard work. "[Desmond] has become fascinated by *smart society* which inspires him to talk and gives him good food and drink. I suppose he'll get sick of it. I tried it and found it very much wanting and thankful that I have no more to do with it," he wrote to a Cambridge friend.[21]

His own hard work and determination did not bring *him* the success he particularly desired – as a painter. He lamented in a letter to Desmond in 1923 "the British public won't have me at any price. It wants lyricism and I ain't a lyric God knows."[22]

Similarly, success as a creative writer eluded Desmond – though not from an excess of hard work; both men were pre-eminent in their fields as critics, as popularisers of art and of literature, which they strove to make accessible to as many people as possible. But both of them carried to their graves a sense of disappointment at their failure as creative artists.

10   Smouldering Ambitions

In that Indian summer of 1910, Molly was invited by Virginia Stephen to Studland on the Dorset coast; leaving her children with her sister Charlotte, she was free to enjoy both the seaside and the company. Desmond joined them just for a weekend, whilst Molly stayed on. It was now that she made friends, as a person in her own right, not just as Mrs Desmond MacCarthy, with key figures of the Bloomsbury group:* Vanessa Bell and her husband Clive, as well as Virginia, who, two years hence, was to marry Desmond's Cambridge friend, Leonard Woolf.

As for her hostess, the rapport Molly formed now with the beautiful Miss Stephen established their lifelong friendship: "Virginia is delightful and interesting; – always rather alarming, but that is fascinating, and she has *so* much more in her than most girls – she is most refreshing."[1] She and Molly were almost of an age, and cousins, but they had never been particularly close. One characteristic the two young women had in common was a sharp observation of their fellow-creatures: "I am making great friends with Virginia and we have heaps of conversation. I abuse the mutual admiration of souls of the young Cambridge and she rather agrees. They are too absurd. Norton talks *and* walks exactly like Lytton," she wrote to Desmond of Harry Norton (1886–1937), mathematician and Apostle.

"Lytton Strachey is *their* Moore," she commented, adding that she supposed they "now look upon Moore and D. & Crompton [Llewellyn Davies] & all the last set as quite passé!" Away from her young family and basking in the congenial company as much as the brilliant weather, her attractions were not lost on Clive Bell – ever observant in that respect – though it was some time before he made her aware of his interest.

This might have been the moment for the MacCarthys to settle in Bloomsbury alongside their friends whom Molly was later to dub "the Bloomsberries"; but "the only houses to be got cheap there are very large.

---

*The Bloomsbury 'group', as they are called, were not in fact a group. Their origins lay in Cambridge, though their locus moved to London. Their members, if they can be called members, included such as Virginia and Vanessa Stephen who had never, for instance, read 'The Cambridge Bible', as Vanessa described it, *Principia Ethica*. Nor was its author one of the 'group', though many of his disciples were of course.

I don't think it matters allowing the spiders to spin in the upper rooms, nor do I mind a coat of dust on the cornices; but Molly thinks we had better get a house into which we fit with difficulty, than one which will be dirty and roomy," Desmond told his mother.[2] So they searched further south in the then unfashionable purlieus of Chelsea. Eventually, in November, they found a house they could afford, "not squalid and yet humble" as Molly described it in her pitilessly precise fashion: this was 25 Wellington Square, off the King's Road which, with some intervals, was to be their home until the Second World War.

Built about 1840, the square combined Regency elegance with Victorian solidity: the houses were stuccoed, with balconies on the first floor overlooking the square; tall and narrow, they had well-proportioned rooms and plenty of space, but the staircases were steep, and the landings cramped.

Several disreputable lodging houses in the square provided good theatre for the little MacCarthy children, peering from the balcony outside their nursery on the first floor. In the centre, in place of the present manicured garden (no children or dogs allowed) was just "a cat-run"; but close by were the Ranelagh Gardens and the Royal Hospital, that most beautiful of Wren buildings. To reach these the children were shepherded down neighbouring Smith Street where the largest house (and now one of the grandest) bore the legend BEDS FOR MEN; its dubious and enthralling floating population made them dawdle, heedless of Mildred's chivvying. A cul-de-sac, Wellington Square, gives on to the King's Road, then dingy and only partially respectable. Drunks and exhibitionists lurked in its ill-lit corners. Its shops were convenient though – bakers, a wine merchant, a dairy and a fishmonger, and, in Sloane Square at the end, a modest-sized drapers, Peter Jones. There was plenty of "street theatre" provided by "organs, flutes, bands, singers and whistlers" who came frequently round the square, as Molly wrote to Chen, "also continual hawkers – the muffin man made six rounds ringing his bell this afternoon."

Desmond and Molly were delighted with their new house – and with the reasonable terms on which they secured it: "The lease is to be five years," she told Chen, "and we can leave by then if we are more prosperous. . . . The rent for the first year is only to be £30 because of repairs – there has to be a new bath and kitchen range." One of the benefits of their new house was its accessibility, especially welcome after the isolation of their first home in Suffolk; all sorts of friends dropped in – some rather too often – or, over the years, came to live nearby. These ranged from Logan Pearsall Smith (1865–1946) who from the time of the First World War shared a house with his sister Alys, the estranged wife of Bertrand Russell, in St Leonard's Terrace near the Royal Hospital; the writer Vernon Lee, who stayed, while in England, in Royal Avenue, the next street; the painter Ethel Sands (1873–1962) who lived in The Vale, further down the King's Road, with her companion, Nan Hudson; Charlie Sanger (1871–1930) and his family who moved into Oakley Street; and later, the indefatigable hostess Sibyl Colefax who added *ton* to the drab King's Road. Within a few years there flourished in this corner of Chelsea as colourful, though more disparate, a social circle as in Bloomsbury; it demonstrated, as well as anything, that Desmond was not exclusively – or even chiefly – a member of the "Bloomsbury set as often alleged.

The MacCarthys needed social life and when they had settled in their new house they began to think about entertaining: in those days even modest entertaining meant servants and those, in turn, meant problems. It was quickly apparent that a house the size of theirs, with five floors, including the basement, needed two servants, besides nursery staff, for "the cooking, washing up, and keeping [clean] of basement and area, and answering doorbell, and boots, knives etc.," Molly wrote to Chen;[3] ideally, "a nice little cook general at about £16 [a year] and a between maid at £10 [a year], I don't think it will be possible without this, to be comfortable *at all.*" It was Molly's opinion that "Nothing is more tyrannous", as she put it, "than to have one's servants unhappy – they must be happy and feel free if they are to do good work," and she set about searching for the perfect pair. It was to be a while before she found them. In the meantime the faithful Mildred was still devotedly looking after the children.

She presided over the nursery on the first floor, two of the prettiest rooms in the house, divided by folding doors. At the windows Molly hung the chintz curtains from the drawing-room at Timworth and she found that she had just enough furniture to go round the new house and just enough carpeting. Desmond's study, on the top floor next to the servants' bedroom, was very peaceful. Off the narrow hall on the ground floor the interconnecting drawing-room and dining-room were furnished simply; a hatch linked the dining-room with the basement kitchen. Meals clattered up in it and nursery meals were carried upstairs on trays. Chamber pots were a necessity in a house with only one lavatory. Part of the servants' morning routine was emptying the discreetly covered "vase of disgrace" as Desmond called it.

Molly prized a well-ordered household, though she found its management difficult with a young family and never quite enough money. She strove always towards a modest domestic harmony, composed of cheerful fires, bunches of fresh flowers – bright anemones in the autumn, for instance, bought from the flower-seller at the end of the square –

well-polished furniture and moderately tidy rooms; she came to prize it the more, perhaps, because of the times of *dis*-harmony, of financial crises, or turbulence which frequently befell the family. But now, just before Christmas, when the new house was finally arranged, she declared herself "most happy with it – it is just what I hoped for," she told Chen.

Relations with her mother-in-law, too, were particularly easy at the moment since Chen was living hundreds of miles from London, near Penzance in Cornwall, where she had removed herself in order to economise – a self-imposed exile of half a year during which she never stopped complaining. Her German life had ended, apart from a brief pre-war visit, with the death of the "Parent Bird" after a terrific struggle, during which he challenged the devil to carry off his soul.

Molly wrote to Chen, proudly, of the hard work Desmond put in recently to make the Post-Impressionists exhibition a success. Immediately, what the exhibition meant to the MacCarthys was – income; its success, and notoriety, meant many visitors, many pictures sold, and financial returns; "So, I can feel that for this year, 1911, *with care* we are safe," she wrote to Chen, reckoning that £500 income would be enough for them to live on – just – with their small additional income from capital for rent, rates and insurance.[4]

There was an additional burden on their resources when Molly's baby, a son, was born in March 1911 at Wellington Square. The new baby was called Dermod and, devoted as Molly was to him, she remained tired. After the strenuous winter moving into the new house, this pregnancy had dragged her down in health – and this was her third baby in the course of four years. Much as she would have liked to continue to nurse him, she had to give up after a week as her milk ran out.

Leaving him with a nurse, she went off with Chen for a week's rest to the Isle of Wight – an ill-conceived plan, as it turned out, because her nerves were in a post-natal jangle, she found herself missing the baby, and Chen was not a soothing companion. Her holiday coincided, too, with Moore's annual reading party and Desmond, with Lytton Strachey, had gone to join him at Lulworth in Dorset. He had not, however, forgotten Molly and wrote full of sympathy and reassurance.

Happily, this spell of post-natal depression did not deteriorate, and later in the year Molly was able to enjoy a proper holiday on the Belgian coast with her sister, Charlotte, for which Chen paid. Molly came back in good spirits and she was further encouraged by Desmond finding new and interesting work on *The Eye Witness*, edited, with the assistance of Cecil Chesterton, G.K.'s younger brother, by his old friend Hilaire Belloc.

Had it not been his only hope of frequent employment, Belloc's paper, which first appeared on 22nd June 1911, selling at 6d. weekly, might have seemed a curious choice for Desmond. It was very far from his political standpoint, the kind of Liberalism which went with consensus and toleration. Belloc, it is true, was liberal in the sense that he put individual liberty on a pinnacle and had been until recently an eccentric Liberal M.P. However, he was never moderate in his criticism, and he relished combat: the purpose of his journal was to root out the deceptions he saw behind the contemporary political world. He regarded "consensus" as another word for conspiracy between the political bosses. He despised Mr Asquith, whom Desmond considered the voice of sense in public life.

During the latter part of 1911 Belloc made one of the lodging houses in Wellington Square his base, and Desmond now saw more of him than at any other time in his life, though theirs was a constant friendship, cemented by the bond between Desmond's sister-in-law, Charlotte Balfour and Belloc.

Desmond always took the view that too many people were put off by Belloc's aggressive self-assertion and failed to appreciate the depths of his humanity; with his highly developed sympathies, he himself understood him and enjoyed his company, even though, as he once said, the two of them "hadn't an idea in common": Belloc's mainstay was his belief in the Roman Church; and his tendency was always to preach, rather than, as Desmond preferred, to increase his readers' appreciation of literature by increasing their pleasure in it. Unlike Desmond's his output was prodigious – 150 books alone, besides lectures, articles and poems: "I remember once meeting Belloc at the close of a day when I have achieved what I thought an almost Balzacian record! 'I have written today,' I told him proudly, '5,000 words. What is your top figure of production?' He said, '23,000 – and they were quite good words too!'" Desmond told Roy Harrod, many years later.[5]

Desmond relished what Blanche Warre-Cornish would have called Belloc's "atmosphere". He enjoyed, too, carousing at Belloc's house, King's Land in Sussex, exhilarated by "the sensation that his low beamed room filled with his voice always gives me of being in the engine room of a small steamer punching through heavy seas." Desmond enjoyed watching Belloc "much as a child does a rhinoceros," he commented.[6]

He responded eagerly to Belloc's rich sense of history: "He certainly has a stronger historical imagination than any man I know. He does not care about weighing evidence or being as fair as it is possible to be – of course; but he can fill the past [with] the courage & beauty of life, which in the teacher of history is the rarest & most valuable faculty of all."[7]

In addition to his contributions to *The Eye Witness*, Desmond embarked in 1911 on writing a play with him, with a political theme: "All my financial hopes for the coming year are now centred on the play – I should think they might make a very good hit with a political one," Molly wrote to Chen in October. Despite her hopes and the fun they had writing it – "Hilaire painting a fan whilst Desmond wrote," said an onlooker – nothing came of their collaboration.[8] Neither Desmond, the great lover of the theatre, nor Belloc, who was as often bored as he was entertained by it, ever produced any plays, either together or separately – to the chagrin of both.

With his customary energy and persuasion, Belloc had managed to assemble a host of talented contributors to his new periodical, many familiar to Desmond from *Speaker* days, including not only H. G. Wells, G. K. Chesterton and Arthur Benson, but E. Nesbit, the children's writer and Mary MacArthur, the woman trade unionist. Although stimulating, their wide spectrum of attitudes could be bewildering.

The Eye Witness was quirky, sometimes disagreeably so. Notoriously, it ran a series on "The Jewish Problem". Its anti-semitism persisted in its successor, *The New Witness*. None of this reflected Desmond's view point; on the other hand, his association with the two papers was no help to him either.

Of the 40-odd articles Desmond wrote for these two lively and controversial journals , the most outstanding were on Granville Barker's production of the *Winter's Tale* – "Startling Discovery at the Savoy" – and his portraits of Meredith and Samuel Butler. In some he displayed his imaginative power, as in his evocation of the seventeenth-century Catholic apologist, Bossuet, whose home at Meaux he had visited when he was in France with Roger Fry.[9] He wrote on a wide variety of topics, art, philosophy, society, manners, morals and memories – though not all with equal success; he remained self-critical, dismissing his more rambling and whimsical efforts: "I know I sometimes wrote well, though at other times with an involved limpness distressing to me," he later admitted.[10] He gave vent, in a piece on Andrew Lang, to his own sense of frustration at having to spend his time turning out journalistic ephemera instead of having the leisure to concentrate his efforts into major literature.

Molly sympathised; but she could not encourage him to give up his journalism, knowing his nature – and her own – as she did: "It is rather trying to have been born so much into the established order of English life as I have been," she observed to Ottoline Morrell in March 1912. "I am not in the least an artist and find it so difficult to meet the precariousness of life boldly, in the gipsy spirit – so I daren't suggest to Desmond that we should live on air for some years while he writes and writes – because I don't think he would with *only* the books to do. Bernard Shaw thinks it is fatal to writing to retire from affairs."[11]

To support his family, Desmond needed to take on more work, not less, as Molly frantically reminded him in the late summer of 1912. Writing for the *Eye Witness* did not profit him financially; despite its rising circulation, it had little revenue from advertising and the paper's owner, an unbalanced financier called Charles Granville, had to bear most of the costs. The limited advertising space was conspicuously occupied by "puffs" for Granville's own writing and publishing. He frequently failed to pay the contributors for months; when he did, it seemed to happen quite illogically, when he was spending massively on a new publishing business, buying another paper or disappearing mysteriously abroad. Desmond and Belloc speculated that "he must be the illegitimate son of a Russian Countess of immense wealth living on the Riviera whom he could periodically tap or blackmail".[12]

Such fantasies might be amusing, but poor Molly was at the end of her tether, watching Desmond dawdle over his articles and book projects, while passing up further opportunities to earn money:

"Your *own* earnings this year from Jan. 1 to August 30 have been £125! . . . I have kept a perfectly accurate account of the items. I tell everyone that you earn £350 a year! . . . At the beginning of January when with hair turning grey I *begged* you to make for a post, you promised to make at least £300 . . . and carried the day with confidence. We can't go on fooling through life like this. I can't take any pleasure in light intercourse and banderlogging until I see something different. You will turn me into a morose, nagging, peevish, lonely woman – disillusioned & disappointed – and our children will wonder *why* you can't give them a better time, as other Fathers do who have made careers, or have honours, if not wealth, and will think of you as a lazy old man. It is you *yourself* who have led us all to expect so much, & let us in for disappointment. Having set out to astonish the world with the fruits of leisure – and giving yourself 15 years of a literary life & written 2 books! I have only just realised that it is now or never! – Hadn't you better go into a garret alone and write write write – you let yourself be distracted by the smallest thing. You lie indolently diffusing thought. It is cruel, that is all I can say. Roger Fry is here – every minute industrious. Don't be too angry at my outburst – I love you always but am utterly unstrung by care & loss of faith in you. Send me some hope."[13]

What followed was not hope, but disaster: Charles Granville's only benefit from owning *The Eye Witness* appeared to be a review of his poems – which had been ignored by all other papers. The reviewer did what he could to praise the proprietor's doggerel, speaking of "the music of his verse and the easy and happy choice of his language".[14] He would have done better to have noticed the signs of manic irresponsibility: "Then up! Enjoy the present time/The wine of life drink deep;/Make most of the great pantomime/There are years enough for sleep."

All heedless of these warning signals, the editorial team were caught off their guard when *The Eye Witness* collapsed in October 1912, as Molly described to Clive Bell: Desmond, on asking for payment for two months' work, "was told that Mr. Granville, the supposed millionaire, had deceived them all – and left for the Continent with the Editress of the *Outlook*, a bankrupt and unable to pay the arrears owed to contributors."

Perhaps because of her letter, a temporary deliverance came when the generous Clive and others of their friends rallied round, as Desmond, delighted and slightly dazed, wrote to Molly: "Dearest, I found a letter from Woolf containing – you'll open your eyes – a cheque for £30! *collected among friends* to make up for my Eye Witness losses – I am somewhat overwhelmed and this has taken the form of not acknowledging it. . . . Just think of it and hardly a rich one among them! It's simply enormously kind. . . ."[15]

"Desmond was overwhelmed by the kindness of his friends," Molly told Ottoline Morrell. "He doesn't know who they all are, who made up for his misfortune . . . I am so afraid it has all come about by my only subjects of conversation being money, and the pains of childbirth."[16]

Not long after, the *Eye Witness* once more revived, as *The New Witness*, under Cecil Chesterton's management (Belloc had already abandoned the enterprise). The new paper ran on sparse funds and the literary quality declined. Desmond wrote regularly for a few months, until Cecil Chesterton lost a libel case brought by Godfrey Isaacs over his part in the Marconi affair and *The New Witness* also came to an end.

Meanwhile to make some ready money in the autumn of 1912 Desmond was forced to return to East Anglia to be an amanuensis to G.A.P. It was a lowering experience, working on a book of economic philosophy which he knew would never come to anything with a man for whom he had lost respect, at the same time as being all too aware of the books of his own he should have been producing. He wrote dejectedly: "Dearest of Molls, The Ampton atmosphere is asphyxiating. Still I live. I work all day. This afternoon I took a solitary – ah the freedom! – walk 5–6.30. I visited the Green Farm and strolled down every path and peeped in at the black empty windows – with rather dreary reflexions. How could I have wasted [those] years of my life! How could anyone capable of letting himself be blown like a dead leaf into any sheltered corner, hope to achieve anything. Still I'm young enough for such regrets to be shot through with a glow of resolution, and belief in the future."

As an antidote to Arthur Paley he had a brief visit to Cambridge and "a satisfying dip into exhilarating talk". The controversy of the moment was the election of the Austrian philosopher, Ludwig Wittgenstein, to the Society. At the root of this was the old rivalry between G. E. Moore and Bertie Russell: Wittgenstein was Russell's "discovery" and it appeared that he wished to keep him to himself and out of the orbit of the Apostles. He was, however, elected, which pleased Desmond.

Regretfully, Desmond recognised the urgency of finding regular work. He had written to Ottoline Morrell: "To accomplish such a thing will be the extinguisher to smouldering ambitions, but anything is better than smouldering without breaking into flame. I have smouldered now for fourteen years – a long time to smoulder, too long to smoulder."[17] At last in 1913 he landed a job which suited him perfectly, though it did not solve his financial problems. That enterprising Fabian team, Sidney and Beatrice Webb, now in their late fifties, had decided they must start a paper to promote the scientific socialist management of society. They wished the reformist case to be presented on their terms, by reasoned argument, in contrast with the radical *Nation* (which had turned down Desmond as an editor), a paper appealing, they felt, more to the heart than to the head. Financial support came from several rich sympathisers including, notably, Arnold Bennett and Bernard Shaw. As the first editor they appointed Clifford Sharp, a capable, moody, hard-drinking journalist who had previously edited *The Crusade*, the monthly organ of the Webbs' Poor Law campaign. Almost certainly on Shaw's recommendation, Desmond became the drama critic of the *New Statesman*, which was launched in April 1913. Before it first appeared, the Webbs invited the paper's future staff to stay with them at their country house near Liphook.

Desmond's terms of employment were not generous, but as good as he could hope at the time – two guineas a thousand words plus ten shillings extra for attending theatres. Beatrice and Sidney Webb introduced him to his fellow-contributors, including the poet Jack Squire, the literary editor, with whom he had played billiards in old days on the *Eye Witness*. Squire at that time was dark and picturesque-looking – with a thick mass of curly black hair and a slim athletic build. Like Sharp, he drank and smoked heavily. He worked hard for the *New Statesman*, and it was largely due to the efforts of Sharp, Squire, Desmond, Robert Lynd and others in the editorial team that by 1918 the new paper had outstripped the circulation of the *Nation*.

At first Desmond found the Webbs awe-inspiring. At their Tuesday lunches their talk took for granted a knowledge of public affairs he did not possess and which he was happy to leave to others; but they were capable of humour. H. G. Wells had guyed them in *The New Machiavelli*

as "the Baileys" (the severely handsome Beatrice, appropriately had been
called "Altiora") and he had portrayed them again in a new novel.
Desmond described their reaction to this latest production: "I remember
Beatrice saying cheerfully, 'I'm in it; I'm the woman whose voice is
described as "a strangulated contralto," but *you* are not, Sidney.' 'Oh yes
I am,' said Webb, speaking from the sofa on which his legs and feet looked
absurdly small in comparison with his broad brow and head, 'Oh yes I
am, I'm described as one of those supplementary males often found
among the lower crustacea.' This smiling serenity made me feel that I was
indeed in high and good company."[18]

Having been advised that too specialised a paper was bound to fail, the
Webbs assembled a team which was far from being a collection of socialist
ideologues. Desmond was a non-political Liberal, while Squire, though
emotionally on the side of the underdog, was a staunch traditionalist.

A genial bohemian, he, Desmond and the ever-reliable Robert Lynd
used to mitigate the strenuously bleak atmosphere of the paper by giving
each other occasional "little warm shower baths of praise as a relief".
Squire wrote a weekly column under the pseudonym "Solomon Eagle".
Although he had little in common with the prophet of doom who
appeared during the Great Plague of 1665, it was descriptive of his wide-
ranging and sensible, if old-fashioned views, just as Desmond's later pen-
name "Affable Hawk" fitted his more penetrating, though kindly, vision.

For the journal's Editor, Clifford Sharp, "Meticulous Vulture" would
have been a fitting nom-de-plume. The saturnine Sharp had the hooded
eyes of a disagreeable bird of prey; and he was obsessed with exposing
clearly for the benefit of readers the bones of an argument, cleaning from
it the extraneous and incorrect. There was about him, recalled Leonard
Woolf, "an atmosphere of intellectual Jeyes' Fluid, moral carbolic soap,
spiritual detergents . . . collectivism and drainage – material or spiritual –
were, I think, the only things Sharp believed in with any flicker of
enthusiasm."[19]

Ideologically, and personally, Sharp was a mass of contradictions.
Though his paper advocated collectivist policies, Beatrice Webb was
disconcerted to find that he became increasingly drawn into the ambit of
Mr Asquith, the Liberal Prime Minister; during the war, though it
opposed conscription, the *New Statesman* took a staunchly patriotic,
anti-pacifist line and Sharp quarrelled with Shaw over articles which in
his view showed sympathy for the Germans. This did not upset Beatrice
Webb, though she was disappointed that the *New Statesman* ceased to be
socialist in the strict sense of the word.[20]

Her early estimate of Sharp shows how little she understood his
strengths and weaknesses when she appointed him. She judged him at first

"a safe though not distinguished writer". Desmond later paid tribute to "the admirable articles of our Editor, arguments released at the end with a whizz like a steel spring". She spoke of Sharp's good journalistic manners. Sharp was arrogant, domineering and as Desmond recalled "very rude". She reckoned him slow, but as Desmond said, he possessed, in an extraordinary degree, the power of decision. She spoke more accurately of his lack of magnetism; certainly Desmond found the ambience on the paper "a trifle wintry". As contributors, Desmond wrote, "We were never encouraged to think of ourselves as indispensible; a persuasion to which journalists of our type are too prone." On the other hand they admired Sharp's efficient management and felt complete confidence in his loyalty. They stood by him, consequently, at times when drunkenness stopped him from working. Desmond himself accepted his editor's strictures on his own writing. In fact one outstanding characteristic Desmond possessed as a critic was his readiness to listen to objections to what he had said, or to his own second thoughts; he would go back to a play and review it if he felt he had done it less than justice – as he did with Granville Barker's *Midsummer Night's Dream*.

In his productions of *The Winter's Tale*, *Twelfth Night* and *A Midsummer Night's Dream*, Granville Barker achieved at this time an atmosphere enhanced by visual beauty without distracting from the dramatic action which he put before everything. His sets were simple but decorative, consisting mostly of sumptuous hangings patterned with striking geometrical designs, with a good deal of gold. The costumes, too, were clear cut in design and showed an effective amalgam of influences – Ancient Greek and Byzantine, Bakst, Art Nouveau and even Beardsley. The poetry of the individual lines was less emphasised than the dramatic power of whole speeches and dialogues; and there were very short spaces between scene changes and only a single long interval.[21] The wonder and power of these productions is attested by the lasting influence that they had on literary scholars, such as Lord David Cecil, who after being taken as a boy to *Twelfth Night* and the *Dream* was fired for life with a love of Shakespeare.[22]

While a child would have been particularly receptive, both to the wonderful golden costumes of the fairies in *A Midsummer Night's Dream* and to a fast-moving production, Desmond was not so simply satisfied: the first time he went, the "ormulu fairies looking as though they had been detached from some fantastic bristling old clock", diverted his attention as much as a Tree production full of sphinxes and shrubbery. However, never one to fail a friend, back he went, and the second time admitted he had underestimated the whole performance. His final verdict echoed his previous one on *The Winter's Tale*: under Granville Barker's direction, as never before for Desmond, Shakespeare had come alive.[23]

For Desmond, the most important discovery of that enthralling prewar season was Chekhov: here was a playwright whose sensibilities and outlook were closer than any other to his own. When he saw, in May 1914, an indifferent production, by the Stage Society, of a magnificent play, *Uncle Vanya*, Desmond regretted passionately that Granville Barker had not been in charge of it. He was of course already familiar with Chekhov's writing, but this was the first important stage production, and his own response and subsequent championing of the plays helped greatly to ensure their success.

Desmond, like Chekhov, refused to sit in judgement on his fellow men, though both might love or hate certain human characteristics. Desmond compared Chekhov with Tolstoy in order to highlight Chekhov's particular genius: "With terrible insight Tolstoy puts his finger on the very spot and tells us we ail there and there. After that pitiless diagnosis, since he is wise, he, too, forgives. But in Chekhov penetration and sympathy are not successive movements of the mind, but simultaneous; a single faculty, thanks to which no weakness escapes him or remains unpardoned. It is a subtler justice."[24] This was, precisely, Desmond's outlook on life.

To Desmond, Chekhov captured the essence of reality: the plots and personalities with their uncertainties and their unfinished business; the inspired evocation of atmosphere, particularly the composite mood of a number of people talking together, and the delicate orchestration required when a number of characters were brought together, "each sad or happy for different reasons, and each with different thoughts, who are nevertheless all involved in the same situation".

Both Chekhov and Desmond observed mankind with a blend of irony and sympathy. Both saw a kind of beauty in the thwarted idealism of people's lives: "These people", Desmond found himself exclaiming, "are suffering from an unduly protracted youth!" In *Uncle Vanya*, as he pointed out, "Vanya's elderly passion for the self-centred Elena reflects something of the humiliation of young longing that expects everything and does not understand itself . . . It is, of course, young to want to prop your ladder against a horn of the moon, but it is also to be not quite an adult not to know that although we have immortal hunger in us, there are — a paradox thanks to which the world goes on — satisfying properties in a little real bread. Chekhov's characters have not learnt that."[25]

Nor had Desmond, altogether. In fact his frequent lamentations about his unfulfilled life were the very stuff of Chekhovian drama, as were the existences of his more eccentric friends such as Bob Trevy and "The Owl" — perhaps the profoundest reason for his affection for them.

For all the success of his work for the *New Statesman*, his other writing – his great purpose in life – novels, the life of Donne, seemed forever to hang fire. Donne's fertility and swiftness of mind still continued to attract him: and over money difficulties he could identify himself with the mystical poet. However he found close treatment of his life uphill work. Donne's sermons were particularly hard to read, for all their energy and lyrical qualities.

Molly, less ambitious but also less easily distracted, was trying to continue with the novel which she had begun soon after her marriage and returned to on and off during the subsequent years of child-bearing and house-moving. She was not a fluent writer, and, like any mother of young children, with a household to run, found that, "Distraction! is simply the lot of women."

She had written to her mother-in-law: "I really despair of finishing my novel. To get one done it must mean three hours work a day in the morning when fresh, & the children seem for ever about, & household duties, accounts, letters, interruptions of every kind seem for ever happening that *must* be seen to . . . I should feel most tremendously pleased if I could help the family income a little by getting *something* for my novel – the *worst* seem to pay a little, but really at present I don't seem to have vigour enough to detach my mind from the children & become absorbed without neglecting them as a result."

She started a new regime of rising at six and writing till nine, "when we have baths & breakfast. A cheap alarm clock wakes us with a devilish scream, and then we have very hot coffee from a thermos flask, & Desmond goes up to the study, & I work in my room in a dressing gown & eiderdown quilt. Doesn't it all sound too dreary for words, – but then getting up at any hour is trying, & we have discovered that it is no worse at 6 than at 8," she told Ottoline Morrell.[26]

Another idea of Molly's for adding impetus to their writing was the Novel Club. Harry Norton helped her to recruit members: on 6th March 1913 he wrote to Rupert Brooke:

> Mrs MacCarthy wishes me to ask you if you will join a club to write novels and read portions of them to each other – at regular intervals. The following people have joined
>
> | | |
> |---|---|
> | Desmond | Vanessa [Bell] |
> | Norton | Molly MacCarthy |
> | Duncan [Grant] | Marjorie Strachey |
> | [Gerald] Shove | |
>
> The following people have refused to join
>   Lytton Strachey [who was living in the country at this time]

James Strachey
If you feel inclined to, there is to be a first meeting on 17th to discuss
what we really propose to do.

There can have been no answer, as, a week later, Harry Norton wrote
again to Brooke, asking if he gathers "you will not join that club?"[27]

Throughout 1913 too we have tantalising glimpses – but no more – of
Desmond's novel which, he wrote to Ottoline Morrell, "progresses
slowly. Henry has fallen in love on the platform of Paddington Station &
is just passing Suttons Seeds on his way to Eton. There are some good bits
of boy in it, but I know people will say I have made him too mature –
though they will be *wrong*."

In the same month, May, he paid an agreeable visit to Asheham, to stay
with the Woolves; Lytton Strachey, who was also staying, noted with his
usual facetious disparagement: "his eternal dispatch-box, from which he
produced the first chapter of a novel on school life – not very inspiring. He
can't make up his mind, he says 'how far to go!'"[28]

Desmond was wondering how much he could describe of the
homoerotic life he had observed among the Eton schoolboys. This had
ranged in character from cynical pursuit and seduction to his own
innocent, Dantesque adoration of a small and obscure boy, espied at
Paddington when they were both aged eleven, and to whom he never
spoke until the day he left school. He used to entertain his broad-minded
Bloomsbury friends with tales of the headmaster's great oratorical
denunciations of "the abomination", and of his meeting, after many
years, with a once pretty and sought-after boy, nicknamed "Angelica"; "I
identified her," he recalled, "behind the heavy white moustache of an
enormous dragoon". Such amusing reminiscence proved much more in
his line than trying to work the material into a sustained piece of fiction.[29]

His life still needed far greater regularity if he was going to achieve
anything beyond his journalism, as was witnessed by the waspish Lytton
Strachey, when Desmond stayed with him at the beginning of 1913.
Desmond was "incapable of pulling himself together," said Lytton:
though he went out riding all day, he also got up in the middle of the next
morning, refused breakfast "and then ate the whole pot of marmalade
with extreme deliberation".[30]

The truth was, he never was going to go any further, neither in self-
revelation, nor in putting together any coherent book. He had found the
real outlet for his talent, though he did not realise it. Once he began to write
regularly and to become a name in the critical world there was no prospect
either, of switching his mind to the very different type of mental discipline
involved in creative writing. His great novel remained for ever a pipe dream.

11 "Companionship & Fun & Friendship"

During their early years in London before the Great War undermined the certainties of the settled, stratified society in which they lived, the MacCarthys enjoyed a widening circle of friends: old ones, such as Leonard Woolf, now back from working in Ceylon, and new ones, such as the flamboyant Ottoline Morrell.*

Desmond had first encountered Ottoline years before in the modest rooms of his Cambridge friend Charlie Sanger, and his wife Dora: "High up above the hustle-bustle and roar of traffic of the Strand lived this couple, not long married – and one day of the week they were at home," recounted Ottoline in her memoirs. (She did not add that she and the MacCarthys found the other guests, all well-informed, and worthy, pretty heavy-going). She remembered "climbing up the endless stairs and at last finding myself in their plain little room with matting on the floors and a gas stove," and how shy she was with their friends, few of whom she had met before. But Desmond, she said, "was as kind then as he would be today to anyone who needed encouragement. I don't remember the subject of our talk ... except that it was sympathetic, ruminating, suggestive and original."[1]

Desmond, too, later recalled "when we met at the Sangers and the fish was done with cheese, so that you did not know whether it was high fish or a new dish and could not nearly finish your helping."[2] (Dora Sanger's slovenly housekeeping was a source of constant criticism among her friends).

After their first meeting, Ottoline invited Desmond to lunch; he accepted, asking if he might bring Molly as well; she also took tickets for a lecture he was about to give on George Meredith's writings. The MacCarthys were just the sort of young couple she liked: intelligent, creative, and not bound too much by the conventions of Society from which she had struggled all her life to free herself.

Ottoline supported all the arts – literature, music, painting and the

*Lady Ottoline Morrell (1873–1938) née Lady Ottoline Violet Anne Cavendish-Bentinck, half-sister of the Duke of Portland, married, in 1902, Philip Edward Morrell (1870–1943), Liberal M.P. 1906–1918.

ballet – with zeal, and wherever possible befriended the artists themselves: so it is not surprising that she and Desmond met during the course
of the preparations for the Post-Impressionist Exhibition of which she
was an active patron. Original, daring, derided, she herself resembled the
Post-Impressionist art. She had cut herself off from her aristocratic
background, which regarded such art as degenerate, and had resolved to
cultivate the society of intellectuals and artists. She always felt herself to
be an artist manquée; her creative temperament found its expression in
decorating herself and the houses in which she lived. "I have just had a
vision of you coming into Roger Fry's room in Paris in your cloak and the
hat you used to have which was like a crimson tea-cosy trimmed with
hedgehogs,"[3] Desmond told her in a letter written some years later. Her
appearance was always memorable and had little to do with prevailing
fashion: in middle age she might wear a large hat trimmed with ostrich
feathers and drape her tall figure in a sweeping skirt of vividly coloured
silk when short, straight skirts were in vogue. "I often think of you, and
see you in a geranium coloured gown at the top of a hill against the sky
straitening [sic] your garters in a blinding snow storm. Do you remember
a delicious walk we had in the winter and how we laughed?"[4] Molly
wrote to her during the dreary days of the First World War.

Her husband, Philip, who came from a legal family, was "very much
the prince consort", according to a younger friend of theirs, Lord David
Cecil, conventionally and romantically handsome "like a very good-
looking footman"; but he was not altogether the complaisant and long-
suffering spouse he is often made out to have been: his long affair with his
secretary resulted in another clandestine family. "Pipsy" also paid court
to Molly, but nothing came of his flirtatious overtures.

Impulsive, passionate and in all her relationships possessive, Lady
Ottoline was also "a rare muddler . . . in her intense affairs", wrote Molly
to Clive Bell: "Don't let people say unkind things about her," she pleaded
– in vain. In a circle notorious for its exaggerated gossip, Ottoline was a
butt for the malice and fantasy of friends, such as Lytton Strachey and
Virginia Woolf who seemed almost to vie with one another in their highly
coloured descriptions of "Lady Omega Muddle", as Lytton nicknamed
her. Desmond told Molly of a typical conversation he had with Strachey
walking on the downs near Asheham: "We . . . had a long intricate gossip
about Ottoline. Of course I did not divulge; but he knew it all and told me
a lot besides . . . about Henry Lamb.* He thinks Ottoline's life is wrecked

---

*In his book, *Memoirs*, Maurice Bowra recalls of Lady Ottoline that "In moments of crisis she
was capable of bold improvisation. Desmond MacCarthy's wife, Molly, once entered the room
and found her embracing Henry Lamb, by whom she was greatly attracted, and with perfect
self-command she said "I was just giving Henry an aspirin."

by Philip. I think *not*. But we will have a talk about this and remain, shan't we? loyal, to the dear bewildered bewitched self-entangled aspiring one."[5] Desmond and Molly stayed true to their friend: both of them enjoyed her larger-than-life personality, whilst recognising her delusions, particularly over her determination to live on the highest plane "of ideas, and imagination, truth of thought, truth as to life" as she wrote in her memoirs. She was constantly being brought down to earth, often by the demanding egoism of her most intellectual or creative friends, such as D. H. Lawrence and Bertie Russell.

To Desmond and Molly she was always open-handed, and they fully appreciated her "gifts for friendship . . . it does me so much good to see the wisdom of the heart which I think you have," Molly told her.[6] Lady Ottoline's was indeed "the wisdom of the heart" rather than of the head, and Virginia Woolf, too, found her intuitions "more penetrating than many of the profoundly reasonable remarks of our intellectuals;" to Virginia, as to Desmond and Molly, Ottoline "always has the pathos of a creature vaguely afloat in some wide open space, without support or clear knowledge of its direction".[7]

However much she distanced herself from her aristocratic background Ottoline retained her innate grandeur: with aplomb, she would sit round her dinner table at her London house, 44 Bedford Square, as on 18th May 1911, for instance, Desmond and Molly, Winston Churchill – "on his way to a Court ball and . . . in full dress uniform, looking like a mock Napoleon," – H. W. Massingham [editor of *The Nation*], Virginia Stephen, Roger Fry, Josiah Wedgwood and his wife, Noel Buxton[*] and Humphrey Paul.[8]

She liked to ply her friends with gifts: she sent Desmond the plays of Strindberg when they were published in mid-1912 "which I am delighted to have" he wrote to her: "No book can be too depressing for me. I look forward to putting on my diver's harness (keeping of course a pipe of communication with the upper air) and weighting my light spirit with what lead I can find, to descending into those cold livid depths."

In her turn, Ottoline was appreciative of the MacCarthys: she called Molly the supreme letter-writer of the day and, indeed, Molly's many letters to her, particularly at this period, are some of the best she wrote. Molly trusted her enough to confide in her her worries about Desmond's career and to discuss personal relationships during the period when Ottoline was trying to extricate herself from too passionate an entanglement with Bertie Russell. "I do *trust* . . . that you felt that you had left Bertie to cope alone again with life at the right moment. Ottoline will you

[*]Josiah Wedgwood (1872–1943), politician and member of the famous Staffordshire family; Noel Buxton (1869–1948), politician and Fabian.

tell me does he know that Desmond & I know? I should like to know as it disturbs me, wondering."[9]

Molly also discussed a relationship which was coming to the forefront of her own life now: Clive Bell was a year older than herself; he was on affectionate, though not conjugal, terms with his wife, the artist Vanessa Bell. As Desmond's friend, Molly had known him since her marriage. He was a fine figure of a man with a loud voice, a ready laugh and a friendly, open face. He still "seemed to live half with the rich sporting set and half with the intellectuals" as he had done at the university.[10] He was writing his book *Art*, published in 1914, and was ardent in support of the Post-Impressionists. At the same time he enjoyed hunting, shooting and fishing – and could afford to do so. Highly sociable, he liked pretty women and conversation, preferably around a good dinner table – his own. Desmond once described dining with him at his house in Gordon Square: "Clive Bell sat at the head of the table, ebullient, blooming, bald and boastful, but immensely friendly. . . . The talk wasn't up to much, but Clive always diffuses a suggestion that it is unmatched and the company not only choice but actually a gathering of the famous to be, which is soothing and stimulating, though it leaves a sense of one's having been a fool behind – when one goes."[11]

Clive always continued to help himself "in a generous manner to the pleasures of life". He was a gossip and many people found him irritating, amongst them Ottoline Morrell, for whom he was but "the sipper, the taster, the professional connoisseur of life, which is easy to him, for he is without depth or passion"; even his sensuality, she said, was superficial, and his charm but "the momentary charm of the flatterer".[12]

Clive used considerably more than "momentary charm" in his pursuit of Molly. This started in the spring of 1912 when he began to write to her, light-hearted, flirtatious letters. She invited him, with Vanessa, to visit them at Eton where they were staying with the children; he came, without Vanessa, who was then closely involved with Roger Fry. When a month later, the Bells left for Italy, with Fry, on a painting holiday Clive's letters to Molly began in earnest – or rather not in earnest for Molly was at pains to keep their correspondence from becoming either sentimental or intimate.

Frequently, though, the romance of his surroundings overflowed into Clive's letters: "I find myself alone on a summer's night in Arezzo – the most sympathetic town, but one, in Italy. . . . Nothing could be better than Arezzo for the temper. No motors, no horses, no streets to speak of, just pavements going up the hill and down the hill . . . and then just at midnight as I was standing under the wall of the Duomo looking over the Apennines towards Perugia, I wished that I wasn't alone. I wished that I could somehow make some human being feel what it is to be in a town where Vasari's piazza seems a vulgar modernism. I wished you were here."[13]

This might, of course, have been a reaction from the company of two such very energetic painters as Vanessa and Fry who worked all the time and in almost all weathers, leaving Clive and his thoughts free to wander.

Molly's replies to his letters, though prompt, were confined to day-to-day affairs and of course gossip, particularly about the romance between Leonard Woolf and Virginia which Clive had no qualms about discussing with her, as "Virginia had been at infinite pains to throw dust in my eyes – Vanessa has been sworn to secrecy etc. etc. – so, of course, I have been at as many to keep them open. And there was plenty to see. No; I feel no shame in gossiping about Virginia" – she being such a gossip herself.

"The facts, I think, are these," Clive continued. "Some time ago, – when I don't possibly know – Woolf, (Leonard she calls him) proposed; Virginia still vacillated, uncertain of her feelings but enjoying them immensely; within a few weeks she will come down heads, and it will all be very satisfactory," except for Leonard Woolf's Jewishness, which set him markedly apart – "and Woolf's family are chosen beyond anything" (as Virginia was to find when she married into it).[14]

Molly, too, had news of Virginia who had been to dinner with them: "She has all my love. It is quite unrequited, I think. I told her I was not going to stump up her stairs to fall breathless at her shrine at the top – I am such a bad worshipper, I failed over God. I just like companionship and fun and friendship. Some people enjoy worshipping. I am quite idiotic now – this letter was begun in the freshness of the morning & now it is midnight! . . . If this is to catch you at Siena I must send it – I have been interrupted all day. I put to bed three children tonight and arrived whispy and breathless at Ottoline's to sit next Henry James at dinner. Violet Asquith* was the other guest – Desmond had her. He is rather in love with her. Henry James is very heavy now. It is agonising talking to him, but fortunately the conversation became general at once. . . . Henry James came home with us in our taxi." Afterwards Desmond wrote to thank Henry James for going out of his way to take them home to Chelsea, to which James replied in typically wistful fashion that "it was delightful to me – and had a wild romantic beauty – that I *could* whirl you twain, in genial converse, through the rich London night. The only pity was that we whirled *through* it too fast – and so through the converse." He hoped they would have occasions for more, although he was not "at the sociable trudge – as distinguished from the conversational creep or crawl". James

*Violet Asquith (1877–1969), elder daughter of H. H. Asquith was to marry, in 1915, Maurice Bonham-Carter.

did not admire Violet Asquith much – "she was too modern – singularly plain – the characteristics of the goat and the sheep combined in her profile!" Molly repeated to Clive.[15]

How far she had embroidered on James' mischievous observations is unclear, but she had certainly been put out by Desmond's admiration for Violet Asquith. He had met her two months previously at a luncheon party given by the Barings, and afterwards, incautiously, had reported to Molly: "In fact you have here a new cause for jealousy! I thought her so clever and so very agreeable." Molly, who all too easily lost confidence in herself, seems to have taken this literally: Desmond always responded to intelligent women who set out to make themselves pleasant, and they in turn found him charming and fun, and not in the least inclined to talk down to them, like so many Cambridge intellectuals. In any case Violet Asquith was everything that Molly was not: assertive, political, articulate and self-assured in a way that grated on Molly's sensibilities. It was hardly likely that she would usurp her place in her husband's affections. Still, Molly's antipathy smouldered; it was a few years before it erupted.

As predicted by their friends, the engagement of Virginia Stephen and Leonard Woolf came about very soon. Desmond described in a letter to Ottoline Morrell how "They came here [to Wellington Square] together to announce their intentions. I found them sitting on the parlour sofa talking to Molly who introduced me to Mr and Mrs Woolf. Virginia has a bad headache, the consequence of excitement, and has gone to bed and no one sees her." They were married a few weeks later, on 10th August 1912.

Towards the end of July Molly wrote to Clive: "I don't really quite know why you & I are friends Clive – You know I can't look at a picture for more than 2 minutes without yawning – and I could like your hair shorter, being full of deeprooted philistine prejudices (I am not apologising for them as, having them, I naturally think they are right.) However in spite of this you have been so nice about writing to me and in Italy you thought it would be nice if I were there so you must like me, and I like your kindness, & appreciate a particular kind of life that you have in you. Often you are not nearly so clever as many of your friends, but you have *all* the vitality they lack, says Molly paying her compliment as disagreeably as she can. Perhaps after this letter you won't feel inclined to be friends any more."[16]

He was though, and so was Molly. She found him entertaining and, as she said, vital – a quality in which she felt deficient. She did not want any more intimate involvement with him – which was why she only reluctantly paid him compliments. There was no harm in writing to him, and exchanging gossip about mutual friends: "By the by hasn't Lytton's appearance quite become painful?" wrote Molly. "Why look bland & grandiose when neither? Last time I visited Ottoline, I found myself feeling a little sick & faint on the sofa. Etchells, [Frederick Etchells, the architect], dirty & dull, Lytton looking like some country prophet, Marjorie Strachey very very nice but wildly excited & not at all clean, & Ottoline exotic & unable to create a game of the party. . . ."

Molly regarded her friendship with Clive as so innocuous that there was nothing between them that Desmond could not know about, or be invited to join in — visits to the theatre, for instance. It gave her pleasurable respite from domestic cares and financial worries. Despite Clive's undisguised physical interest in her, she did her best to keep their relationship light-hearted. She wrote cheerfully to Ottoline after a visit to Clive that "I was so glad to feel so fond of him, & understand him so well. He has got a very poetical & beautiful side to his character, & as I know that, I mind so much less about all the part that will for ever be unsatisfactory in him. It was all very happy — I feel I have not withered anything up by my putting an end to becoming actually important to him, — we shall always understand each other about it all; & I felt there would be no difficulty about having a perfectly restrained & happy sympathy which Desmond would be glad of too."[17]

When their epistolary friendship began, Molly had no intention of allowing him to make love to her, but as his son, the biographer Quentin Bell has pointed out: "Clive could never carry on more than five minutes' conversation with a personable woman and refrain from some slight display of gallantry. . . . An ardent and sanguine temperament such as his was excited by resistance and fortified by the least hint of success."[18] When, eventually, the effort of keeping him at arm's length became too much for Molly she was a reluctant lover. Although she was fond of Clive, and grew fonder, she was never in love with him and she did not really wish to become his mistress — unlike him, she was happily married; she liked the stimulus of his company, but in the end the impact of their relationship was less on her affections than on her marriage. For it meant that Desmond felt free to take an open interest in a series of striking, intelligent ladies over the next few years: he was not unfaithful in the fullest physical sense — but he was quite prepared to be — and Molly was at the least irritated, at the most furiously jealous. Her "trivial affair" with Clive altered the whole emotional pattern of the MacCarthys' marriage.[19]

In September 1912 Molly took the children to stay by the sea at Littlehampton, in lodgings, at two guineas weekly, paid for by Chen. From there Molly visited Clive for a few days at Asheham House, near Firle, on the Sussex Downs. This was a particularly romantic house discovered by Virginia Stephen before she married. Vanessa was living here, and Duncan Grant (1885–1978) with whom she had embarked on a long-lasting relationship. With a fellow-guest, Sydney Waterlow (1878–1944) Molly enjoyed walking: "the down country is simply a revelation to me. In the dusk suddenly villages lit up their lights and twinkled out, like stars on mist," she wrote to Desmond. She continued artlessly, "Oh dearest I do enjoy thinking of you so much when I am away. Sometimes you make me shake my bed with laughing at the mere conception of you – at other times I dream of your mind with grave reverence at your soundness and poetry. . . . I am so very happy in this raté atmosphere. Clive's great merit of vitality is very pleasant. They are all utterly irresponsible and lazy – at least Vanessa and Duncan seem to work away at mysteriously bad daubs of genius."

They in their turn enjoyed Molly's visit, but found her severity disconcerting: "She is we all thought very nice, but it was rather a strain on our tongues which had wagged rather free before," Duncan Grant wrote to Virginia Woolf. While Vanessa, too, wrote to her sister, commenting on Molly's "unexpected moral sense which crops up suddenly and is rather tiresome".[20] This was partly her innate reticence – she did not enjoy bawdy jokes as did her hosts. She might, too, have been unsettled at entering into the Bohemian existence of Clive and Vanessa who were living under the same roof, but not as husband and wife, along with the bi-sexual Duncan Grant who was the object of both Vanessa's and Maynard Keynes's love. Life in the Cloisters at Eton was eccentric, but never like this. Then, too, she was reluctant to be drawn into a greater intimacy with Clive Bell than she felt was either right or desirable. As she had written to him earlier in the year: "I just like companionship and fun and friendship."

After the difficult autumn of the *Eye Witness* fiasco, and Christmas 1912 at Eton in fine traditional style, Molly wrote to Clive, "Desmond & I have had a despairing conversation about drifting & on not getting as much as we want out of life. He wants fame & excitement & honour – & I want adventures & to write novels & plays, & have several love affairs, & to keep young for five years more, & become an actress, & all sorts of things – & all this has arisen from a sudden realisation on both our parts, of the approach of middle age, padding slowly but surely behind late youth. . . . Do you remember writing to me from an Italian town? I felt you were just writing to the moon & was glad to have the letter & interested & liked you, but felt unresponsive; & now I like to write."

To this Clive replied with alacrity, on New Year's Eve: "What's all this about six more years of youth? I give you fifteen on any method of computation. Certainly you're younger than you were this time last year.

And affairs! Your golden age seems only to be beginning. . . . About that six years question – you know Virginia doesn't mean to be middle-aged till she's fifty. She doesn't think about that, at present, though; she's full of conjugal dismays. It's a question, it seems, whether Woolf has any physical attraction for her. She doesn't yet feel it anyway. Consequently unsatisfactory anxiety. I implore Vanessa to be blunt, and I'm sure she is; but apparently it's beyond words."

His letter ended on a personal note: "Do you honestly think I was writing to the moon? I wasn't. I was writing to a very definite woman, whom – I know I ought not to say it – I'd have given one of my eyes to have had beside me on the warm, black steps of S. Francesco d'Arezzo: if she hadn't been alive and close to my feeling I shouldn't have written a word, to the moon or to anyone else. After I'd written I was terrified, I remember. But on the last night of the year all épanchements are licensed."

On his return Molly and Clive arranged to meet for dinner, at Wellington Square, and he invited her to go to the pantomime. Desmond was included in this invitation but though he could always enjoy himself on such occasions, he must have felt at that time that the world was slipping gently away beneath his feet. He knew that it was in part his inability to cope with his life and in particular his family responsibilities which caused Molly to seek consolation elsewhere; and it was not simply a case of finding work that paid, but of making his name as a writer of real distinction.

For their summer holiday in 1913 the MacCarthys took a cottage in County Wexford, in country they loved; but the house was not prepossessing: "Desmond says it looks like a house on the stage, prepared to look *as* poor as possible. He thinks the greatest nightmare he could imagine would be to arrive here with Eddie Marsh, & Henry James."[21]

On their return at the beginning of August, the MacCarthys plunged back into London life: Desmond had lunch with Lytton's youngest brother, James Strachey, and played tennis with Philip Morrell and Duncan Grant under the plane trees of Bedford Square. From Leonard he received news of Virginia who was then suffering from one of her most acute bouts of madness, unable to sleep and refusing to eat. Towards the end of the month Desmond wrote her just the sort of light-hearted account of his thoughts and activities as would be calculated to divert an invalid:

I have been meaning to write to you lately with quite pathetic intensity; but you know how hard it is for one whose profession it is to write to get as far as pen and paper when correspondence is concerned. It is so much more delightful to sit and think to you . . .

The children came back to-day. . . . They are all three asleep now in
the prettiest attitudes – the long and fastidious Michael, the queer and
twinkling Rachel and the marvellously comfortable and sensible
Dermod. Heaven help them – for I can't – much! I bend over them at
night with the feelings of the guilty mother in the play, whose
paramour is waiting impatiently outside in a brougham . . .

Belloc looked in yesterday with a large kite – To sail this and watch it
hovering in the clouds at the end of a mile of string would, he said, not
only amuse Michael, but do me good. I hope it will and that I shall be
able to set it going. I went with him to order planks 10 foot long by nine
inches, and his mastery of the merits of wood, the loss in cutting etc.
filled me with a zestful interest in life. I catch a glow from him every
now and then. . . .

What have you been reading? Don't read too much, and don't
answer this even if you feel inclined – I have been reading Anatole
France with – oh with – *fine* pleasure. I have also worked – but its not
good. I shouldn't mind that if there was more of it. I long to be a
copious writer. I must stop writing now, however, for it is late.[22]

Virginia's mental state deteriorated until it drove her to attempt suicide;
she was then moved to the country, where she made a slow recovery of
which Clive wrote news to Molly, describing the harrowing effect her
mental collapse had on Leonard, her husband of only a year. Meanwhile,
during August, Molly had gone, on her own, to see Clive and Vanessa
who, with a group of friends, were camping near Thetford in Norfolk.
Vanessa's brother, Adrian Stephen, was of the party, and the four
daughters of Sir Sydney Olivier, the distinguished Fabian Socialist. Molly
was enchanted by the unspoiled setting and the atmosphere of physical
ease.

Clive shared a tent with Vanessa and Maynard Keynes – he would have
preferred it to have been otherwise, as he wrote afterwards: "The truth is,
my dear Molly, that in camp, and for some time before, my case was little
better than Adrian's [Adrian was wooing one of the Olivier girls]; only I
have a more masterful nature – masterful of myself I mean. I don't mean
that I didn't enjoy camp: even at 100F Molly is a joy; but at that
temperature she is also a considerable agitation to my not very placid
disposition."[23]

On his return to Asheham Molly went to stay with him, and Vanessa;
he continued to write to her in the same vein after she had gone back to
London: "I have an uneasy suspicion that I made out my feelings to be
much more Platonic than they are. For instance, I did very much want to
hug you & should have done so I believe if it hadn't been for my invincible

terror of your frown." And again, a week later, on 25th September, ". . . now the day has come round again with brilliant sun-shine and no Molly. It's a bore missing you so much and quite against my principles. What do you advise? Violent exercise and a flirtation with Gumbo (Marjorie Strachey) are both quite out of the question. Time, time, time."[24]

They did sleep together at Asheham; but she left the house precipitously next day. And generally she deflected many of Clive's amorous advances; while he made no secret of his pursuit of other women who compensated him for Molly's lack of physical interest. That winter he invited Molly and Desmond to go with himself, Vanessa and Roger Fry, to look at pictures in Paris. For his part, Desmond declined on the pretext of the "cold that whisks about the streets of Paris in winter . . . [it] is less palpable than London cold and therefore more treacherous, like a knife behind you, touches a kidney and the result is diabetes for life. Therefore, I implore you, make arctic preparations. Take as your constant companion the shade of that old bore Dr Jaeger . . ."[25]

So Desmond deflected, in cheerful banter, the chagrin he felt at Molly's continued relationship with Clive. For him to have expressed jealousy would have been counter to his Cambridge philosophy of freedom in relationships. Molly must be allowed to do as her emotions led her; but not to have felt any jealousy would have been unnatural to him. Molly's excursions were usually more mundane and bound up with the children's health and need for sea and air, as she wrote to Virginia Woolf in March 1914: "Oh my dear, family life; – their tonsils & adenoids, their colds & tempers, their boots & lessons . . . I am now at Margate with them. The air comes cutting across the sea in a bee line without obstruction from the North Pole – It is doing us all a lot of good. . . . I have my niece Hester Balfour here as well, a tall flapper with 2 pale plaits. She is very pretty like Reggie Balfour – She looks divine in her bath in my room in the morning; after it she pins a red flannel scolloped sacred heart on to the breast of her combinations, with '100 days indulgence each time' written on the back!"

After leaving Margate, the family were lent Ford Place, Charlotte Balfour's old home in Sussex, now owned by Alys Russell and her brother, Logan Pearsall Smith, for whom she kept house, in addition to doing myriad 'good works'. The house had an ancient, agreeably haunted atmosphere, with its rambling passages, faintly lit by oil lamps; its panelling and its tapestries and a beautiful drawing room, decorated in yellow silk; a giant walnut tree grew outside, and in summer the light filtering through its leaves on to the staircase and landing was dim and green. Logan Pearsall Smith had installed his extensive library at Ford and

Desmond stayed on to work on his never-to-be-finished book on Donne, when Molly returned to London in May.

That last summer before the Great War she and Desmond were invited to many of the celebrated Thursday evening salons held by Ottoline Morrell at Bedford Square. At one, on 14th May, Molly met E. M. Forster, Gilbert Cannan, Augustus John, Boris Anrep, Nathalie Ridley (formerly Countess Benckendorff) and Walter Sickert. She was also considerably irritated, as she wrote to Desmond, by being borne down upon by Irene Noel who "instantly plunged in loudly about *Clive*, & the Bells! so hard & gossipy, & very insensitive I thought. . . . Really the quicker she is got with child the better. It is so distressing to think of her becoming an advanced Suffragette which she might quite well do in a year or two. It is very tiresome when the Virgin point of view is persisted in too protractedly by one who has had so much experience – a great sign of harshness & conventionality of heart. I shall be very firm about it & try & convert her to a better understanding of men even now. She is always rather impressed with my opinions, though you won't believe it. . . ."

It was to be some months before Irene Noel met the man she was to marry; meanwhile she was on the loose in London and that summer she regained a place in Desmond's affections. As Molly and the children spent much of the summer away at Aunt Anny's little house at Freshwater on the Isle of Wight, Desmond stayed mainly with his mother, with whom he frequently saw Irene Noel. Despite Chen's declaration that she "deserves being tortured . . . when she tortured others so much," Irene had succeeded in winning her round. "You would enjoy the theatre of Chen, Desmond and Irene, only if you were here it would not be the same theatre," Desmond wrote disingenuously to Molly. "Chen and Irene get on very well and I enjoy Irene enormously in a curious way. Am I in love? The only thing which makes me think I may be unbeknownst to myself [is] that I am often on the verge of being angry with her. That is the only suspicious circumstance. But Grobis[*] you know how I love ghosts and she is the strangest little ghost to me. We have not yet had an intimate confab. Perhaps that will come off tonight – as we dine together. Anyhow it will be she who will pour out to me not I to her. . . . I read Clive's letter with tolerance only didn't . . . well . . . my Grobis."[26]

Desmond was not as detached about Irene, as he liked to make out. On the contrary he was extremely susceptible to her and that summer, while on the Continent, the Powers moved inexorably towards war, in London another act of the "Ireniad" took place against a background of Chaliapin's memorable performances as *Boris Godounov*; of the sensa-

---

[*] "Grobis" = Raminagrobis, his nickname at this time for Molly; a neologism of the kind Desmond was fond of making up. Molly did not, however, take kindly to this one.

tional season of Diaghilev's Russian ballet; of the effervescent Thursday evening *salons* of Ottoline Morrell; and of Chen's prattling and nagging as she moved into a comfortable new house in Kensington.

Now in her mid-thirties, Irene, despite having had numerous admirers – at this time Hilton Young the future politician – was still unmarried. She was as lively, attractive and gregarious as ever; she enjoyed "going about" and Desmond enjoyed taking her. She needed Desmond's sympathy, too, because of the grave illness of "Matia", for so long her "mother-substitute". Irene was now desperately anxious about her, and Desmond's was a sympathetic shoulder for her to lean on; he often paid Matia and Irene surprise visits to cheer them up. "If you want me – even for an hour or so – wire. I think flying to you under the present circumstances one of the things really worth doing," he wrote to her during Matia's last illness in August.

The day that war was declared, Tuesday 4th August, Desmond had arranged to meet Irene for dinner, writing to her: "you are miserable and anxious – no wonder. I too have felt that dread the last two days which the Italians call la figlia della morte.

"The worst year of their lives is coming for millions of people. And as for our own particular difficulties and troubles, courage – we'll handle them well, though they are now doubled."

Irene and Desmond's dinner that night was an impromptu picnic, eaten in Hyde Park. They met at seven, and walked in Kensington Gardens, sitting by the Round Pond and strolling along the Serpentine, then down to Knightsbridge where they purchased sandwiches, raisins and a bottle of cider which they consumed watching the sun set in a tranquil sky, the last evening of peace for four long and anguished years.

Afterwards they travelled on the top of a bus to visit Hilton Young at No. 35 Kensington Square. He was out to dinner, and while they awaited his return Irene played the piano for Desmond and "D. told me scandals". When Hilton came back they sat talking until midnight, when Desmond walked Irene home. Desmond himself did not return home, but wandered the streets into the small hours, unwilling to bring that momentous evening to a close.[27]

"I was not in the pushing, yelling, chaffing crowds which thronged the Horse Guards or in the cheering ones outside the House of Commons," he wrote. "I had lost my way, and after walking about half an hour I had come out somewhere below Holland Park. How late the buses were running! And the taxis were buzzing one after the other down the main thoroughfare, as if it had been ten o'clock and not two in the morning. This reminded me of public injunctions, already emphatic, concerning economy in petrol. But economy was impossible tonight; night of good-

byes, of intimacies and friendships huddled into climaxes; night of
sociable, equalizing forebodings; night ominous to the solitary, but gay,
positively gay, to the gregarious. . . ."

Like Bertrand Russell and others who paced the streets that night, he
realised with amazement and alarm that average men and women were
delighted at the prospect of war: "A taxi packed with people waving flags
whizzed by, down the now empty road. A girl in a pink jersey and a man,
sitting on the half-open roof, set up a long hooting screech as they passed:
I felt I had sampled the patriotic enthusiasms of Piccadilly Circus. . . .

". . . Clearly the great majority (unless they fear too much for
themselves or those nearest them) loved war. There was exhilaration
abroad tonight, but beneath lay forebodings of dreadful days, and deeper
still a dumb resentment at the cold-blooded idiocy of diplomacy. Yet,
there it was – and it was a kind of happiness . . . the irony of it was enough
to make one cry: people seldom experience so genuinely that sense that
life is worth living, which a feeling of brotherhood gives, as when they are
banded together to kill their fellow-men. . . ."

As he walked on, he encountered a pathetic and slightly ridiculous
symbol of the fratricidal tragedy which was about to begin: ". . . Coming
towards me now under the lamps was a man in spectacles, with a small
straw hat perched on his big square head. He looked Teutonic. 'Gute
Nacht', I said, as we passed. He stopped for a second & wrung his hands:
'Ach Gott, Ach Gott! Mein lieber Freund!'."[28]

12   Ares and Irene

Desmond was a patriot, though no jingoist. As a writer he wanted "to get a little nearer the scene of these tremendous terrible events" in France, he told Irene. His mixed blood did not lessen his loyalties to Britain nor to the France he loved – on the contrary it made him more balanced in his outlook. Following his Prussian grandfather's views he agreed with the philosopher Nietzsche that by submitting themselves like sheep to "beaked and clawed" leaders, the Germans had sacrificed all that was best in their culture for "political and national insanity"; but he refused to blame them alone for the catastrophic diplomacy which had caused the war, or to join the popular chorus in England which denounced them as a race of brutes and cowards.[1]

Of course the talk among the MacCarthys' family and friends, whether pacifists or volunteers, was all of the war. Towards the end of August 1914 Desmond went to visit Roger Fry at Durbins, the house designed and built by him near Guildford. He has left an unforgettable tragi-comic vignette of Fry and his friend Goldie Lowes Dickinson, the aesthete and the philosopher, the latter plunged into gloom at the prospect of the war: arriving at Guildford Station that Saturday evening, he told Irene, he found the streets "full of noisy loitering people – bands were playing and war news bawling. It's some little way to Durbins. The road between the elms was very dark. One comes out on a chalk hill & above me I saw the light fantastic Frenchified house Roger has built – it is nearly all window – shining like a factory working late. I peeped in & saw Lowes Dickenson [sic] bending over patience cards & Roger lying on the sofa. They were surprised to see me – (my telegram had not reached them) and glad. I had a meal of cold peas, cheese and a bottle of claret. We (R & I) talked about the war. Dickenson sitting mostly silent – very wrinkled yellow dusty and depressed. The war has brought the world crashing about his ears. Like a man with an unhappy love affair he keeps getting up and wandering off by himself to ponder disconsolately. This happens every hour or so & Roger keeps saying – 'I don't know what to do about Goldie. His gloom is awful. . . .'

"That night the claret did me good & I went to bed in a solemn dream. I slept in Roger's bed – which has orange curtains and a great pile of books beside it: he slept in the garden porch where the mizzling rain blew in over him all night. Did he mind? Not a bit."[2]

Amongst Desmond and Molly's friends, there were many who were opposed to Britain taking part in the war – Ottoline and Philip Morrell, Bob Trevy, Arthur Ponsonby, Clive and Vanessa Bell; but others were eager to join the Allied Forces on the Continent – George Trevelyan took charge of a Red Cross unit; Neville Lytton enlisted, as did Gerald Warre-Cornish; while Maurice Baring went out to France with the Royal Flying Corps and stayed there for the whole of the war. At the beginning of hostilities Britain relied heavily on the enthusiasm and ability of such amateurs to run her war effort.

In the exceptionally hot weather, Desmond pondered what he should do: "The beauty of the summer is something I can hardly remember equalled but its glories are meaningless to me. I carry about with me the feelings of an extradited criminal. If this goes on I shall have to enlist . . ." he wrote to Irene on 3rd September from Crabbet Park.

At thirty-seven, Desmond was older than the men first called upon to volunteer, and his idea of joining up evoked a forthright letter from his old friend George Trevelyan: ". . . the time has not yet come (it *may* come) for people like you to go soldiering." Rather than "in a moment of generous and noble enthusiasm make a decision which will be grossly unjust to Molly and her children and not even much use to England," he suggested Desmond should join a relief organisation.[3] Eventually Desmond volunteered to work for the Red Cross in France, as did George Arthur Paley. They were to convey the wounded from the front lines to field hospitals. Paley offered his large four-seater Panhard car and the services of his chauffeur, Hall, as well. After a rudimentary training in caring for the wounded they left England on Monday, 19th October 1914. Desmond, in khaki uniform, peaked cap and puttees was waved off on the train in London by Molly, Chen and his children; and on the boat in Folkestone by Irene, who was there helping to organise Belgian refugees.

Desmond stayed in France until January 1915. His detailed letters to Molly give an incomparable picture of life at the scene of battle, both the waiting around for orders whilst the vast war machine creaked into action, and the tense times of conveying the wounded, usually under cover of darkness along hideously rough tracks, to the makeshift field hospitals.

One good thing which came out of his months in Northern France was a lifelong friendship with Somerset Maugham who, with Desmond and G.A.P., and Bishop, a doctor, formed a quartet who worked together.

Maugham was already a popular and successful playwright, though at that time not one who appealed to Desmond, as he later recounted: "I, who either from curiosity or admiration, had eagerly sought out many writers, was not interested at finding myself thrown together with him. A scene in a little bedroom at Malo near Dunkirk comes back to me: a thick roll of proofs had arrived for him; he had corrected them and the long strips were lying on the bed. They were evidently the proofs of a novel. Now, although I was short of something to read, my interest in them was confined to noticing how very few corrections he had made. When I remarked on it, he replied that he always went over his work carefully before he sent it to the printer.

"'Ah', I thought, 'he's as business-like as a novelist as he is as a playwright. The itch for perfection doesn't trouble him; the adequate will do. I suppose the book will sell.' And these were the proofs of *Of Human Bondage*! A novel which, together with *The Old Wives' Tale*, *Farewell to Arms*, *Kipps*, *Babbitt*, and a few others, will float on the stream of time when the mass of modern realistic fiction is sediment at the bottom."[4] Different though they were, Maugham and Desmond became friends from the moment they were thrown together.

When they, together with the rest of their detachment, reached Boulogne, they were sternly warned, as writers, against sending any reports to the newspapers; at that time, the security-conscious military authorities were trying to exclude war correspondents from the fighting zone altogether. Later on Desmond was allowed to write a series of articles, for publication in America, on his work with the Red Cross. He was pleased to hear that the organisation would pay all his expenses including his estaminet bills, and that he would not be beholden further to Arthur Paley. As for their duties, they were being sent with an American Red Cross group to the French zone of the fighting, where they would transport wounded from the clearing stations to Doullens, Montdidier and other base hospitals a few kilometres back from the line. They were also asked to trace as many as possible of the 4,000 British soldiers who had gone missing during the retreat from Mons to the Marne and about whom there was intense anxiety at home.

Their fleet of ten cars was based in Amiens; the ancient cathedral city had been occupied for a while by German forces but was now clear of the fighting zone. Since the battle of the Marne, the previous month, when the enemy had been deflected from their triumphant march on Paris, the Allied forces had been trying confidently but unavailingly, to dislodge them from the deep entrenchments they had since dug. In the Albert-Roye sector, where Desmond's detachment chiefly operated, the French were losing thousands of lives in piecemeal attacks and it was not until late in

the year that they recognised that only by huge mass assaults on the
Germans' lines had they any hope of overwhelming them. Despite the
carnage, however, the fighting was sporadic in intensity and the demands
on the Red Cross intermittent.

Desmond was touched by the gratitude of the French, who were still
feeling the first shock of invasion, towards the British army. All the way to
Amiens, the villages and towns through which they passed gave them a
tremendous welcome: "you can imagine with my natural liking for them
how glad I am that we are fighting for them."

Every evening the colonel in charge of their detachment had to make
fresh decisions, on the basis of hair-raising reconnaissances, about where
they might be most needed, if at all. Within a week, Desmond had grown
used to the sight of death and had learned to detach himself a little from
the sufferings of the appallingly wounded men he loaded into the cars.
The base hospitals, he found, were makeshift and dirty, breeding grounds
for infectious illness. Near the front, churches and barns served as first-
aid posts where casualties came straight from the line, usually at night, in
confusion and haste. The desperation of the wounded was terrible to
behold, but later, away from the battle, most of them became lethargic
and stoical: "It's wonderful," Desmond wrote to Molly, "how easy it
seems to bear what must be borne after a few days have passed. There is
one boy of twenty in the ward I go to to whom I have taken a pitiful liking.
He is educated and sensitive and suffers from a wound in his ankle which
gives him such atrocious agony (far worse than the big gashed wounds)
that I fear he will die from exhaustion. He was five days hiding after being
wounded in a cave and it is the long neglect after the infliction of a wound
that makes it bad."

Friend and foe were victims together in the tragic butchery that
Desmond witnessed. Only once did he encounter from any German the
hatred that had inspired the war: "I asked a wounded Uhlan who was
lying on the floor of the cottage-kitchen if he would like a drink of water
and a cigarette. He said 'Yes, but not from a swine like you', so I told one
of the prisoners outside to go in and give them to him." He made, in fact,
considerable efforts to comfort some of the German wounded men who
had been brought back to Doullens: "There is one without a leg at the
hospital who is dying more from homesickness than the shock. I try every
day to cheer him up – the sound of his mutter sprache does him a little
good, but he is doomed. All day little hurried processions pass through
the streets to the cemetery, a perfunctory priest chanting in front and a
few casual soldiers joining up behind. . . ."

Death had become commonplace, an inescapable fact. But instead of
the racket of war, what struck Desmond was the silence both of those on

their way up the line and those broken by the fighting. "All go past in silence, sometimes they nod – they seem hardly to talk among themselves – only exchange a word or two. The same with the wounded; they are almost completely silent . . ."

Closer to the line, he encountered a similar impassivity in a gun crew near Feschamps where he had driven with Paley. He handed out cigarettes and chatted with them for a while; then: "one of them suddenly looked at his watch and nodding casually to the others, all four set off strolling across the turnip fields, with the air of partridge shooters going to their places after lunch. They were going to their guns to begin fighting again."

Shortly before Christmas he strayed for the first time into a full-dress battle: "We had not gone far . . . when *whack* went a gun quite near us on our left. The violence of the percussion and its suddenness made me feel as though I had received a blow over the heart. It was instantly followed by another and another and another. The concealed French batteries were opening fire. From the willow clumps and copses on either side of the road (the green had come into the grass) I noticed little darting daggers of golden flame leaping out, which a second later were followed by the whacking crashes which had startled me at first. They shook me still. It was as though one's whole body was an eye which winked instinctively at a threatened blow. The uproar redoubled and redoubled. 'I shall be glad to be out of this,' I thought, but there was exhilaration in one's quakings. 'I'm in a battle! This is *it*!' It was the beginning of the attack."

After a while, the thunderous noise of the guns acted as a narcotic to fear, said Desmond. He handed out cigarettes to infantrymen on their way up to the line, some gazing at him "with a somnolent morituri te salutant expression," others grinning . . .

Shortly after this he helped to load badly mangled men from a mill destroyed by German artillery, while other shells continued to rain all round them. "During a pause the little medical officer in the white mackintosh and legion of honour ran to the corner – and began beckoning to us crying 'vite vite'. We started at a pace which along such a road was merciless to the wounded I am afraid and were soon out of the danger zone."

Excitements such as this were uncommon. Desmond had not been prepared for "the *boredom* of war, the prolonged desolating ennui from which everybody apparently suffered." He did, however, help the Comte d'Hinnistal recover his precious belongings from his château behind the enemy lines, driving to there by moonlight with some of his detachment. "The woods were full of French soldiers eating their evening meal in the dark, no lights. In the magnificent stable yard there were more – the trenches were a couple of hundred yards beyond – a great crowd of them there in their blue cloaks; one was cutting up a sheep by the light of a candle . . . the façade of the château was a sad sight, great gappy holes, roof smashed and the old chapel a ruin. . . . The guns had stopped but there was a desultory rifle fire from the German trenches. . . . We crept into the house through a hole in the kitchen and filled our sacks with plate and precious knick-knacks. . . . It was pitiable to see the beautiful rooms, carved chairs, pictures, china all smashed and mixed with stone and mortar. Here and there the moon light showed a corner quite undisturbed, the fine books lying on the table and a vase of flowers and all round it wreckage. . . ."[5]

An excitement which filled further empty spaces in his life as a Red Cross orderly, he did not mention to Molly: Irene Noel, too, was in Northern France. From her diary she would seem to have been in her element nursing in Dunkirk, tirelessly organising hospital arrangements, all the while surrounded by young men. These included the one she eventually married, Philip Baker, who was also in Dunkirk setting up the first Friends' Ambulance Unit, of which he became the Commandant.

Soon after her arrival, Irene visited Desmond in Boulogne; she had lunch and dinner with him and Somerset Maugham at the Hotel Meurice, where they were staying. A fortnight later, on 5th December, Desmond visited her in Dunkirk where he waited to go off on an expedition. He saw Irene every day for a week, going for romantic walks along the pier in the mist and searchlight after dinner; when she felt unwell, she lay on her bed with a hot water bottle whilst he read Somerset Maugham's novels aloud to her and told her stories of his schooldays.

Unsurprisingly, in the heightened atmosphere of the war, with death lurking so close, Desmond seems to have made some kind of "proposal" to Irene at the end of this week when they were constantly in each other's company. On Sunday 13th December he spent most of the day with her and in the evening they went at her suggestion to Vespers at the cathedral; they walked back "& had an unsatisfactory talk. We walked to the end of the pier without coming to any solution," Irene's diary noted. It is easy enough to guess what Desmond suggested and that Irene refused. It would have been imprudent for her to compromise herself at a time when she was more than ever eager to find a husband.

Next day, Desmond left to go on the expedition behind the lines and shortly afterwards Irene returned to England, where she spent Christmas. So the moment passed; the last entry Irene made in her diary for 1914 was: "I wrote to Hilton [Young] and P[hilip] B[aker] for the New Year. I wonder what will happen. . . ."[6]

What happened was that Desmond returned to England for good in the middle of January 1915; he was relieved to get back, as he missed his family and had felt underused in the Red Cross. Meanwhile, Irene's friendship with Philip Baker progressed. Their engagement was announced on 9th April, a day when Molly visited Irene in London. She described the lovers in a letter to Chen: "You mustn't think I would tell anyone this who might be malicious but I can't resist telling you!" she began artlessly to her mother-in-law, an indefatigable gossip. Irene had summoned her to tell her about her fiancé – for whom she then apologised; while he was there she argued with him, and when he had left, after lunch, she listed his splendid qualities, "Great Purity was one of them!" though she did not seem to be in love and "complained of his Bourgeois Origin". At this, Molly "got into one of my sudden tempers . . . and said she was a very selfish woman". She concluded: "I counted up Irene's affairs that I personally know of yesterday and there are 12; and there must be more I don't know of."[7] By now she knew, or suspected, that Desmond and she had seen much of each other in France (in fact on the back of one of Desmond's letters to Molly, written in ink, was "Dearest Irene," in faint pencil, and an October date).

Philip Baker was eleven years younger than Irene, but, according to Judith Lytton, was more up to coping with Irene than Desmond had been. "He is not goodlooking but very reliable & . . . He has a very pleasant sense of humour. . . . No money or prospects,"[*] she wrote to Chen. "She is not in love any more than she has ever been. . . . He is a quaker & goes in for running races. In appearance he has the pinched half starved look of most race runners. He has nice honest brown eyes, long fair hair, a very weak chin & enormous teeth which I have advised them to have filed down, a suggestion which filled them with joy as they hadn't thought of it before."[†8]

Despite the misgivings of friends, and their numerous tiffs, Irene did marry Philip Baker in the summer of 1915. Her name was added to his, becoming Noel-Baker. Their only child, Francis, was born five years later.

For several years afterwards Desmond spun the saga of "the Ireniad" to Virginia Woolf: "Sometimes I have looked into my box of memories to see if Act III is in reasonably good order and ready to be performed" he wrote to her at the beginning of 1918. "Not that I rehearse it, but I remember an incident & try if it reminds me of anything else."[9] But his romantic interest had ended conclusively by 1915. For him, Irene's

---

[*] But Philip Baker was able and clever: having set up the Friends' Ambulance Unit in France, he then became an officer in the First British Ambulance Unit for Italy until the end of the war; afterwards he was assistant to Lord Robert Cecil at the League of Nations and for over sixty years a leading campaigner for peace. He was also part of the British Olympic Team for Athletics.

[†] They did not take up this suggestion, however, as Virginia Woolf noted in her diary ten years later "Phil Baker is standing as a Labour candidate. Irene will have his teeth filed & get him in – (a scrap of *real* dialogue)." (17 October 1924). [VW Diary Vol. 2, p. 319]

combined fascination had lain in the fact that though she had never fallen in love with him, she never discouraged him from flirting with her; and she had seemed perennially unattached, happy to spend time in his company as well as being good company herself.

When Desmond left for France Molly moved into her sister Charlotte's house in Kensington with the children. "Everything is absolutely flat & silent in London," she wrote to Desmond from there on 30th October. "No-one seems to go & see any-one else . . . it shows how all is simply in suspense until the war is over. . . ."

Although she continued to see Clive, their relationship was drawing to an acrimonious end, as Virginia Woolf noted in her diary for 1915 ("Sunday 24 January"):

"In the middle of dinner last night, Molly rang us up to ask whether she & Desmond might come to lunch today. Oliver [Strachey, elder brother of Lytton] exclaimed that Desmond as he happened to know, had promised to lunch with Henry James. We told Molly this. It was news to her. So she came alone, about 12.30. We plunged of course into Gordon Square gossip," in particular into Molly's deteriorating relationship with Clive: "whether he got bored first or she disgusted, I don't know. Anyhow, as I could have foretold, after violent scenes lasting almost 18 months, they have parted, & he abuses her, & she abuses herself – for ever having listened. But she finds that an intermittent acquaintance won't do for him – 'garden party talk' he calls it; & she feels that intimacy in those circles leads to a kind of dustiness of soul. . . . She was incoherent, inattentive, & fragmentary as usual; like a little grey moth among machines . . .

"As Molly sighed 'It must be wonderful to have a husband who works!' I think it would be much odder to have one who didn't."[10]

Molly saw Clive again, of course, since they moved so much in the same social circles, but as it is conspicuously difficult to put the clock back in amorous relationships, so it was not possible for Molly and Clive to enjoy a platonic friendship. He simply was not interested.

The dramatic event which finally ended their affair was an air raid on Chelsea; Clive and Molly were out together when a bomb fell perilously close to Wellington Square: this bomb ended their relationship – as Molly explained in a letter to Clive: "I must write and thank you for my dreamlike evening. It seems that this was the only quarter of the town that suffered, although everything was so quiet when we got here. A wing of the Royal Hospital was bombed a few minutes after the warning & the adjutant's 3 children were killed in bed, & several others; St. Leonard's

Terrace windows shattered & even our house filled with sulphur smoke, which drove my nurse & the children into the next basement. It was for them *far* the worst of all the raids – they were all white as sheets, as the shock of the explosion was tremendous. I am taking them to Guildford [to stay at Roger Fry's house] today instead of tomorrow. I *so* enjoyed the early part of the evening; I don't know when I have enjoyed your company more. I confess the last part was rather a nightmare; responsibility for the young or foolish seems to me the trying part of being out – unrealisable I think for those who have no young in London to look after. I hear the poor colonel & his wife were dining out, when their children at the Royal Hospital were bombed."[11] The thought went through her head, as she later recounted, that if she was to be killed in an air raid, how shaming to be killed with Clive!

Clive did not accept her decision with any good grace. Although at about this time he began to see a great deal of Mary Hutchinson[*] with whom he was to have an affair for many years, his new-found amorous happiness did not prevent him from making bad blood between Mary and Molly – implying that the old love hated the new – as well as spreading unfriendly gossip about Desmond whom he blamed partly for Molly's change of heart. It was a long while before Clive and Molly's friendship was back on a more even footing.

In common with many people the MacCarthys had reckoned on the war being over within a year. The effect of its protraction on people at home cannot be over-estimated: they were not only shocked immediately by the death of so many men but also ground down by the wearisome length of hostilities. Molly's nerves, never strong, were daily exacerbated by worry and dread: "I have been meaning to write," she told Ottoline, "but I think one gets more and more inarticulate as the war goes on. One thinks and thinks – but unless one's words can be like cries rending the air they fall short of expressing one's feelings and one is silent." There was no tranquillity anywhere as long as the war was being fought. When in Wellington Square the family was at the mercy of air raids, particularly at the time of the full moon. Then they would go down into the basement and the children would play, or sleep in their dressing-gowns on makeshift beds until the "All Clear" sounded when they would stagger wearily upstairs again.

Because of the air raids, and in order to economise, Molly and the children lived mostly out of London for the rest of the war, with Desmond joining them whenever his work allowed. For much of 1915, they settled in Freshwater, on the Isle of Wight, in Aunt Anny Ritchie's cottage. Molly

[*]Mary Hutchinson (b. 1889) married the barrister St John ("Jack") Hutchinson in 1910. She was not conventionally attractive, but stylish and fashionable.

taught the children herself, and in the quiet evenings they went out canoeing. Roger Fry stayed nearby with his daughter, Pamela, and they all made an expedition to Alum Bay; the MacCarthys were amused to see that the curious coloured rocks had patterns resembling those of the Omega workshop. Fry's visit was such a success that he planned another one, bringing both his children as well as Goldie Lowes Dickinson, who was still swathed in gloom on account of the war: "so we shall have a lot of jolly, vague transcendental talk from the PostImpQuakerSwedenborgiomaterialist [i.e. Roger], & the Spiritualtruthfulaurasearching sodom combatting racked & tortured Goldie," said Molly.[12]

Throughout the war Fry was generous and hospitable in having the MacCarthys to stay at Durbins. The children were amused by the housemaid staggering in with trays almost buckling under the weight of Omega workshop plates which, when they came to eat from them, were rough and unwieldy.

One relief was that Desmond did not go out again to the front with the Red Cross but found employment at the War Office. He earned £252 a year, translating and helping to decipher intercepted messages and telegrams. His office in Whitehall was "in a huge room with high windows", he wrote to his son, Michael: "It is as big as a little chapel and the walls are covered with panels, carved and ledged. A long table stands in the middle of the room. At the end of which sits an old general in khaki clicking away at the typewriter. I sit on his left hand with dictionaries and papers trying to make sense of all sorts of bits and news and scraps of telegrams the Germans have been sending about to each other . . . The Zeppelins came over London and dropped bombs but they did not do much damage."

As for Desmond himself "The war weighs upon me at times almost as though I had discovered that I had a slow incurable disease. Everybody seems making up their minds that another winter campaign is inevitable."

The Apostles' annual dinner, which he attended in June 1915, was a gloomy one: "The speeches were damp – much obituary reference to Rupert Brooke," who had died in April; Eddie Marsh, Desmond's neighbour at dinner, was hit particularly hard by his death. Later, Desmond dined with him at his club, but failed to tempt him into indiscretion about his new job as secretary to the Prime Minister.

Despite the gloom of the war, Belloc, with whom Desmond had breakfast one morning early in July, managed to lift his spirits. Passionate in the cause of France and the Allies, Belloc had set himself up as an expert on the war, in his magazine, *Land and Water*, which featured numerous articles by Desmond, now one of the many writers involved in war propaganda. Desmond wrote to Michael: "He has a sitting room in an hotel where he sits writing & talking with his coat off & his shirt front bulging like a breast plate. Sometimes he sings a little & as the window is open, the butcher boys passing the railings stop and stare in."

In November 1915 Desmond moved from the War Office when the work he had been doing became more specialised and needed a wireless expert. He was recruited by the Admiralty along with other clever and versatile amateurs such as the brilliant classicist and Jesuit Father Ronald Knox, and Captain Edward Molyneux, later to become a famous couturier, to work for the team in "Room 40", in the Admiralty Old Buildings.

"Room 40" was the heart of British naval intelligence: here the enemy's cyphered messages were decoded and interpreted. Under the formidable Admiral Reginald "Blinker" Hall, the Director of the Intelligence Division, "Room 40" was responsible for many notable successes; these included preventing a German victory over the British fleet at the Battle of Jutland; stopping a huge consignment of German arms from reaching the Irish "Easter rebels" in 1916, and decisively influencing the decision of the United States to join the Allied side in February 1917. His group of intelligence officers were continually overworked, though the importance and excitement of the secret operations, and their devotion to the small, hawk-like Admiral Hall, kept their morale high. Desmond and his fellow-recruits helped to relieve the intense pressure on the intelligence team. His knowledge of German must have been useful, and two letters in his correspondence show that he was also involved in breaking codes. As the details of his job remain classified even now, and he obviously could not discuss it with anyone outside the office, we do not know precisely what he did; but it is likely that besides deciphering, he was also a "tubist", whose work the historian of Room 40, Patrick Beesly, has described as "receiving, sorting, recording, distributing and filing the rapid flow of intercepts discharged with a rattle and a bang into the wire box at the bottom of the pneumatic tube"; this essential preliminary activity left the specialists free to concentrate on their areas of expertise.[13]

Desmond wore a naval uniform, and his annual salary was the standard one of £208, rising to £260. He stayed here over three years, until after the end of the war.

Desmond's sympathy with those suffering or bereaved on account of the war extended beyond his family and friends: in October 1915 he wrote to E. W. Hornung, the author of the best-selling thriller *Raffles*, who had lost his adored only son in the war. Desmond got in touch with him, he explained to Virginia Woolf, because "I had liked the photograph of the boy I had seen hanging up in the gallery of the dead outside an underground bookstall – he was a jolly smiling boy, very goodnatured and vivacious I could see that. He didn't look just set and spruce like the other poor fellows. So I wrote to Hornung to say I had felt very sorry for him that morning and the result of my letter was this invitation to motor out to some Surrey Inn for lunch last Sunday."

Despite its melancholy it was the sort of unexpected, intensely human, encounter to which Desmond all his life responded: Hornung "could not stop thinking about his boy and hardly stop talking about him. He tried to think of war as the great splendid game and now and then fumbled for his pocket book to show me little poems he had written in that vein. The only way he could bear it was to think that his child had perished in the most glorious grand bouquet of fireworks life provides. What could I do but let him talk?"[14]

Whatever brilliance the fireworks might once have held for anyone had been extinguished by the second winter of the war. Molly's nerves were so overstretched that in February 1916 she took up Ottoline Morrell's invitation to stay with her at Garsington Manor, near Oxford. The Morrells had moved into this beautiful old house the previous year; it was an ideal haven for Molly gradually to regain her equilibrium. Like all Lady Ottoline's houses Garsington was ravishing; and she herself did all she could to soothe and cosset Molly. Throughout the war Ottoline and Philip Morrell provided work for conscientious objectors on the land; and they were constant in their support of the anti-war cause. The MacCarthys continued to see them in London, too, where they had kept on their Bedford Square house, although they only lived in part of it. Ottoline and Bertie Russell were still intimate friends, although without the same passionate intensity, and Bertie found other women with whom to have affairs.

Early in 1916 Russell gave a widely-acclaimed series of lectures on war and society, later published as *The Principles of Social Reconstruction*. Desmond and Molly attended some of these, often with Ottoline. She has left a vivid description of going to dinner with the MacCarthys in Wellington Square in March. They talked about authors such as Henry James and Stendhal, and afterwards, recounted Ottoline, "Desmond who was in one of his friendly, drifting moods, wandered out of his house when I left, and wandered on into my taxi, and wandered still further up to my room at Bedford Square for 'a few moments' as he said. We found in my room the bath all prepared before the fire. 'How comfortable it looks'.

"He took up my volume of Villon that I had been reading, and sat down as is his way, forgetful of time, and read poem after poem, with his special and delightful capacity of enjoyment, and on and on we drifted talking of the delights of Poetry."

Ottoline's bedroom was particularly splendid now, as it was in one of the drawing-rooms where "a large, very high four-poster, with Cardinal-coloured silk curtains, trimmed with silver" dominated the room. Even the altered circumstances of the war could not subdue Ottoline's love of colour and enjoyment of sumptuous materials.

Molly, but not Desmond, whose work detained him in London, spent Easter, 1916, at Garsington. Clive Bell and Mary Hutchinson were also there, as well as Roger Fry, Harry Norton and Maria Nys, later the wife of Aldous Huxley. Easter Day was fine enough to have a picnic tea in the wood, and afterwards Ottoline, Molly and Maria walked to Cuddesdon Church nearby to hear the High Church, left-wing Bishop Gore preach at evensong.

A little while later, towards the end of May, Violet Bonham-Carter had proposed herself to stay at Garsington, and, to help matters along, Ottoline, who disliked Violet, also asked Desmond, Lytton Strachey and Maynard Keynes, with "a young Mr. Winterton," a conscientious objector. In her memoirs Ottoline described how, unwisely, she had left Lytton Strachey and Violet alone for a few minutes and "Violet had started to abuse conscientious objectors, although she knew quite well that we all at Garsington were their supporters, and that Lytton himself was one. She said they disgraced England and ought to be deported to a desert island.

"This naturally annoyed Lytton & he answered, 'If these are the Government's views I don't see much difference between them & the Prussians'.

"This made her very angry, for she became very red and gathered up her bag and gloves with an angry wave of her hand and swept out of the room. . . .

"It was indeed a godsend that Desmond MacCarthy was with us, for he is always like oil on any troubled waters. Lytton told him of the scene; he and Maynard carried us through the weekend. But she never addressed a word to Lytton while she was in the house."[15]

Desmond's social life held strange contrasts: pacifists at one moment and patriots the next. He described being taken by his mother-in-law in February 1916 to a recital by Patrick MacGill, the soldier-poet,[*] to which he had not looked forward as being rose-tinted drawing-room propaganda, rhapsodising on the glorious sufferings of the soldiers at the front. In the event, it was just bearable: proceedings were introduced by two pipers who "filled the hall with droning, squealing music; after them Mrs.

---

[*]Patrick MacGill, b. Donegal, 1890, enlisted in the Irish Rifles at the beginning of the war; he was a popular writer of professionally Irish tales, and poetry in the Kipling mould, as well as accounts of the war itself, such as *The Amateur Army*.

MacGill dressed with the bright simplicity of the rustic entertainer, came on and proceeded to read . . . passages from MacGill's articles and the *Red Horizon*. Very sentimental they were . . . Pat MacGill being a simple soul was not excruciated by the situation, so it was all right. He has the simple self consciousness of the actor. He didn't mind his descriptions of his dead comrades being read out."

Two days later, on 13th February, he dined with Clive and Vanessa Bell and Duncan Grant and afterwards called on Bertie Russell: "We had a long interesting talk till 1.15 a.m. I wish I had the energy to write it down for you. We compared ourselves, à propos of the nature of life, using other people as supplementary illustrations from time to time. He is looking again for a religion. Wandering in a frozen continent of whirlwind & dire hail, at present . . . I can ferry over to that land, but I do not understand – at least I suppose he thinks I don't – what it is to be exiled there. You see my despondencies come from not feeling up to life, his from his not feeling life up to him. We laughed & spoke our minds."[16]

13   Jealousies

"I always have moments of sadness there now," Desmond told Molly of one of his last visits to the Cloisters in the summer of 1915. "In the morning when I go down to the bath-room I think of the days when it seemed to me the happiest household in the world. You tell me that was a delusion – but it was, wasn't it, an incomparable home – and it was more delightful to stay there than at any other house in England."

Frank Warre-Cornish, in his late seventies, was failing; his enfeeblement was complicated by Blanche's eccentricity. She "had such a horror of the gaga," as Desmond put it, that she would not recognise that her husband was now fatally ill. His death would mean not only her widowhood but also the end of her life at Eton – the only life she had known since her marriage fifty years before. Arthur Benson remarked how curiously Blanche spoke about her husband, "that he thought so much about ultimate problems – death, immortality. 'A man ought surely to have found a solution by his age,' said Mrs Cornish, with that acrid ring in the voice one knows." Frank reconciled himself to death; Blanche denied it. His children, meanwhile, read aloud to him, and accompanied him as he was wheeled about the playing-fields of Eton in a bath-chair. One September afternoon Molly was reading *Don Juan* to him when he slipped peacefully into unconsciousness. His death meant the end of the household in the Cloisters, too: "the Cornish chapter had closed. But I think those memories of old days bring only a gentle melancholy and sadness and one is so glad that they have been."

In the same month the blow for which the family had been nerving itself finally fell: Gerald, now a major in the 6th Somersets, was killed in the Battle of the Somme. Molly and her family consoled themselves that he had died heroically, leading his men into battle; that he had prepared himself for death, for he knew it would surely come; that "Everywhere there is the same desolate burden," but Molly could not help feeling sad when "I see very living people – young men full of vitality" and Gerald, the scholarly idealist who had acquitted himself so bravely at the Front, dead.

Frank Warre-Cornish's death deprived Blanche both of her spouse and of her standing. In straitened circumstances, she shared a maisonette in Redcliffe Gardens with her eldest daughter Margaret. Earl's Court was a come-down from Eton and, removed from the setting she had created and which exactly set off her personality, Blanche was a diminished figure for the remaining six years of her life.

As well as these family tragedies Molly suffered another loss at this time – of her hearing. Her deafness crept up slowly but inexorably, over the next few years. She consulted specialists, but they were not hopeful of her ever being cured. The most eminent, Hunter Tod, of Wimpole Street, diagnosed middle-ear deafness (known medically as "conductive hearing loss") the cause of which was not known. Deaf aids were not very advanced in those days: Molly tried one cumbersome instrument after another, none of which she mastered properly, nor were they particularly efficient. She experimented with an ear trumpet, and a neat instrument recommended by "the deafest old gentleman in London", the theologian, Baron von Hügel,[1] but her condition was exacerbated by tinnitus, head noises, for which aids are of no avail. This condition came and went, sometimes creating within her head "as much confusion of sound as about six Donald Toveys playing the piano at once – at Derby-racing speed – very disagreeable". She often had headaches and the extra concentration needed to catch what people were saying continually tired her.[2]

She bore her affliction as best she could – and she was not by nature patient – but it had a profound effect both on her way of life and on her spirits from now onwards: afflicted, in her mid-thirties, with a deteriorating condition, she naturally despaired at times; she was often agitated, but she tried to manage the agitation, to calm herself, when she recognised that it was getting out of hand. Sometimes she succeeded in controlling it, sometimes she did not.

Her deafness cut her off from much that gave her pleasure, from so much social intercourse, the interplay of character, quickfire jokes and wordplay. Often, wearied by trying to hear and to manage her instrument, she was tempted to retreat into the country and silence. Her friend Dolly Ponsonby wrote understandingly: "There are some people who might just as well be deaf, for any use they are to their friends, but as you are particularly quick and intuitive and sympathetic it is hard on society to lose you. You certainly must not run away from your friends. But I shall run after you wherever you are." Tinnitus unfortunately is often perceived by the sufferer to be worse in quiet surroundings, where, instead of being masked by other noises – of the street, for instance – it seems to dominate to the exclusion of everything else.[3]

Molly was fully sensitive to the effect that her deafness had on others:

"talk is constantly stripped of nearly *all* charm . . . most things being *half* heard, or just missed – as if one were always reading a torn page – guessing at most of it."[4] As Virginia Woolf, whose sister-in-law was deaf, noted in her diary at this time, "deafness imposes itself upon the mind as well as the voice; it frightens away the quicker, shyer deeper thoughts so that all the talk that reaches a deaf person must be of the same hearty, plain matter of fact kind. Try as one will, one can't do otherwise."[5] Molly was apprehensive about her relationship with Desmond: the irony of being the deaf wife of someone who thrived on conversation and on theatre-going was not lost on her. As much as any of his friends and acquaintances, she loved the originality and imagination of Desmond's talk. But he was also sympathetic and patient; he had a very distinct voice, melodious and carrying, which was comparatively easy for her to hear, especially as she was familiar with it. He sat near to her, and repeated what was being said when necessary. But of course Molly's deafness meant that she went even less into society and though she never had Desmond's exceptional relish for it, it was cruel to feel debarred by her affliction. She preferred a gentler social life; small dinner parties of close friends, tête-à-têtes rather than large gatherings. She was fully conscious that her increasing deafness was an obstacle in their marriage which was not, at this time, especially harmonious. The old troubles of Desmond's lack of order and organisation, and of their poverty, were not so much the problems now as his independent way of life and his consequent neglect of his family.

Their relationship, though based on a firm foundation of love, had ceased to have any sexual expression: Molly felt neglected, and, like any wife who yearns for physical affection from her husband and does not get it, she built up resentment. It came pouring out in angry and uncontrolled scenes. Molly had never been one for holding back her emotions; she did not seem able to help these scenes of furious despair although they left her feeling ashamed and distressed. One of her outbursts at Wellington Square continued in a letter she wrote to Desmond:

Dearest D.

I do not think it will do to have these scenes. I had better come to some decision about your friends in order to guard myself from jealousy. You see at the bottom of it all is something that I daily want to tell you in a *serious* way but feel sensitive about saying. . . . that I myself have felt almost *daily* for about a year a great wish to go to bed with you but am too proud seriously to ask it.

You seem so cold that it has passed by quite unrealised by you that in the last 3 years I have only twice been to bed with you. This at the most passionate age of my life, (I can tell from my feelings) when I feel force of life dying within me of starvation, deafness coming, morbidness getting a clutch on me. But I do not reproach. I suppose it *can't* be helped that you cannot wish it for yourself, but I think you ought to face this with me with dignity & seriousness. (I have been hurt that you have not realised that under light words, I have been feeling *acutely* really).

I feel that I have lately been relegated to the light chaffy side of you. You do not give me *any* serious life at all. . . . But dearest I love only you in this world, even more than Bumpy [Dermod] – if I lost you I would simply *lose* life; therefore you *must* help me to make your life happy by helping me to be generous . . . But how to do it? Oh God. It is no use the way you pass it off in chaff. . . . You cannot treat me as you have always treated your mother when she is morbid (just cheering her up at the moment), it is not the right treatment for me. I am as subtle and sensitive as you are yourself, . . . you must take trouble to help me . . , & to know that each scene makes you love me less & more inclined to find home a bore which is natural, doesn't help me much, does it? . . .

I *must* be the most important person in your life. I *cannot* be left out or patronised by your friends. But *after that* it is my *wish* and my absolute principle that you should be *free as air*. Surely you have seen that whenever you *tell* me things about people I am enchanted & happy, it is always when you *don't* tell me that I am miserable & feel left out of it. Please read this through again & try to believe that I am feeling strongly. I am crying as I write. You are *so* illusive dearest. . . . Your Moll. *Please don't* go out, & come in too tired to speak.[6]

(What Desmond's reaction to this most moving letter was we do not know; but on the envelope Molly added urgently "*Don't* leave this about. Found in *bathroom*.") Molly accused Desmond of being a "shut up character" and it is true that a lifetime's exposure to Chen and her neurotic desire to know – and, by extension, to control – her son's feelings had led him to be wary of exposing too much of himself; to be "illusive" as Molly put it, and cultivate detachment. Twenty years earlier he had written to Chen defending his reserve: "'Your confidence! Your confidence!' how many men and women are crying for that; husbands to wives, mothers to children; every friend to friend. But there is much included in that word confidence which is better hidden, covered up, is better trampled down. The spirit of dignified selection, which we call reserve, alone makes companionship, yes love, possible. There are spiritual indelicacies just as there are physical indecencies."[7]

Now that same reserve, part natural, and part cultivated as self-protection, was flung back at him during the second important relationship of his life.

top left Desmond in Red Cross uniform, 1914
top right Irene Cooper-Willis, the photograph she gave Desmond
below Part of a letter from Hilaire Belloc (1913)

TELEGRAMS,
OOLHAM, SUSSEX.

KINGS LAND,
SHIPLEY,
HORSHAM.

July 19th.,1913.

My dear Desmond,

Though you hate writing, write and tell me how you are getting on. You are bound to do this in return for the lovely portrait which I paste on to this, which I had taken in Paris in order to have a living memorial of my Face-Hair defying death.

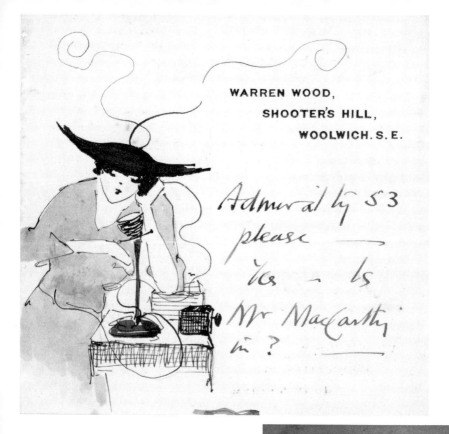

WARREN WOOD,
SHOOTER'S HILL,
WOOLWICH. S.E.

Admiralty 53
please
Yes — Is
Mr MacCarthy
in ?

above
Part of a letter from Enid Bagnold
to Desmond

right
Desmond in naval uniform
during the First World War:
'Room 40'

The absence of sexual relations between them dated back as far as Dermod's conception five years previously. Molly had been terrified of having another baby; their separate bedrooms led also to a deeper separation. To all intents and purposes, their sexual relationship was over within a few years of their marriage. Later, their son Dermod, a doctor, remarked that if they had known more about birth control, they would have spared themselves some anguish. In addition, whilst Desmond was an exceptionally tolerant man, Molly's affair with Clive rankled more than he admitted. He did not like sharing his wife's affections with one who was in many ways an undignified figure, with his preposterous remarks and notorious ladykilling. However trivial Molly may have thought it, repercussions from the affair rumbled on for some time.

Molly's jealousy was to last for the next twenty years, sometimes acute, sometimes in abeyance, but always a source of angry scenes which became an unhappy feature of their life together, scenes in which Molly accused Desmond of neglecting her for other women and his own social life, and he strove to retain some kind of rational equilibrium – but her jealousy was beyond reasoning. On occasion it could become farcical – as when it focused on Violet Asquith, now married to Maurice Bonham-Carter; Desmond still saw her regularly, sometimes with her husband, sometimes without, but never intimately (as the friendly, but not romantic letters between them plainly show). March 1918 found Violet writing urgently to Maynard Keynes, then doing highly important work at the Treasury, about certain "very delicate diplomatic functions which await you" over lunch with herself and Molly. Heading the letter "Confidential – & *very* dreary" she related how she had met Desmond several times at Ottoline's, always without Molly (not strictly true: they had all had dinner in Bedford Square in 1912, as has been seen) – and ultimately got to know him at "the Conscientious Objection party" at Garsington (as we know from Ottoline's desperate account of Violet's tactlessness on that occasion) when Maynard had also been a guest. During the two years since, they had met regularly though not often, wrote Violet, but Desmond had never brought Molly with him when they all went to the theatre, nor mentioned her, even: "About three weeks ago he came to me and told me they had had a terrible row – that she was very angry with him but infinitely more angry with *me* – said I had behaved abominably in never asking her etc. etc.

"Personally I should have thought it was entirely a matter between her and Desmond whether they went out together or alone – and I cannot *conceive* his not having known that she minded after the first three times – still less can I conceive her holding me – a detached stranger – in any way accountable for a lapse in his sensibility or conduct towards her. At any moment during these two years he could have asked me to meet her if he had wanted to – or thought she wanted to."

Feeling it too late to ask them both formally to dinner – "I should have such hopeless fou rire – the only solution we could think of has been suggested by Prince Bibesco – a benevolent Rumanian whom you met at my house who knows them both very well and has suggested that she and I (without Desmond) but with *you* a liaison officer should meet at lunch at the Automobil (sic) Club!! (the spot has been specially selected for its size – noise – bends – & general absence of cramping intimacy) I know I shall have the most awful giggles & I do *implore* you . . . to come. You are my only hope – Yours Violet Bonham-Carter. It is all *too* absurd."[8]

A day or two later the lunch took place, presumably with Prince Bibesco as the fourth; Maynard Keynes must have been amused by his role as "liaison officer", which he was to repeat in international economic affairs at the end of the War. For Molly also wrote to him beforehand making sure that he was coming and to *"please* be kind to me, I shall feel such a fish out of water".[9]

She would not have been, but she was right in saying that this was not her world: she was fond of Keynes but she did not like Violet, and was no more than politely friendly to Antoine Bibesco, whom she regarded chiefly as a friend of Enid Bagnold – another source of her jealousy. Such lunches were not for Molly.

A more understandable cause of her jealousy was Desmond's infatuation with a new Irene in his life, Irene Cooper-Willis. "She was beautiful, a little stern, with a low-quiet debating voice, debating with herself about what was right. The right word, the right action, the right course to pursue. Desmond hadn't a chance," her lifelong friend, the writer Enid Bagnold, observed in her autobiography.[10] It is likely that Desmond met her through Bertie Russell who had been much taken with her when she had worked with him in the newly-formed peace group, the Union of Democratic Control, at the beginning of the war. She was always on the lookout for literary work, and, probably at Russell's suggestion, had recently come to help Desmond with the unending problem of G.A.P.'s book, which he was making a final effort to put into shape. At the beginning of February 1916 Irene had spent the evening at Wellington Square, to the evident disapproval of the MacCarthys' maid Eva: "when we went upstairs to work she knocked so *very* interrogatively at the door. Miss C.W. is coming again. I shall have to break this to Eva."

A week later, on 14th February, he reported that they were making progress on the book: "She does it splendidly. By the by, I like her *very* much. I believe she's 1916. What luck meeting her so early in the year!", he wrote[11] cheerfully to Molly, referring to his claim to make a new friend every year. Irene *was* 1916 for Desmond; but entanglement with her brought him as much bitterness and pain as it did pleasure.[12]

Irene's combination of masculine and feminine attributes was irresistible to Desmond: she was intellectual – earlier she had studied mathematics at Girton College, Cambridge; she was high-principled, an ardent pacifist, as well as a socialist and feminist. She was good-looking; the photograph she gave Desmond that summer shows an intelligent gaze, a clever brow, and a certain stylishness of dress.

When Desmond met her Irene was in her early thirties – she had been born in 1882, within two days of Molly – and wanted to make her way in literature as much as in public affairs. She needed to earn money, and here Desmond did what he could to help her with reviewing books. Irene was living with her family at Blackheath in South London, where they were neighbours of the Bagnolds, and it was through her that Desmond met Enid, who was to become a closer and longer-lasting friend than Irene. The Cooper-Willises were a legal family, and in her forties she was herself to become one of Britain's first women barristers.

One of Desmond's early tokens of friendship was to buy Irene a blue butterfly he saw in a shop near the British Museum, where she was working on Socialism and International Law: she wrote to thank him from her quaintly named cottage, The Old Pest House, near Sevenoaks, in Kent: "I came down late this afternoon still feeling blue and in imagination planting orange marigolds upon my grave. The butterfly has conquered the marigolds – and driven away the dull blue devils. Thank you ever so much for it – it is enchanting and so is your kindness – quite magical. Enid Bagnold cannot come to lunch on Monday as she is having lunch with *titled* people – but she will come on Friday – so will you keep that day?"

Irene was always a little caustic about the literary and social aspirations of her old friend Enid Bagnold of whom she was fond, but who was very different from herself, being affectionate and instinctive, rather than cerebral and deliberate. Enid was eager to see something of Irene's new literary admirer. Eventually, early in March, the three of them did have lunch together; afterwards Irene wrote to Desmond regretting that "The lunch wasn't a success, was it? Enid said it was all my fault – that I was subdued – was I? and that she felt infuriated with me all the time. She also said that I had a dirty face – but I had had a bath that morning so it could not have been very dirty. Arranged lunches never are successful – somehow – and in this one Enid was trying to 'show off' and not at all like she is when she is alone. However I daresay it was my fault – and I ought not to have remarked upon her hat, which *was* horrible, as 'these things are not done' only I always forget."

Throughout the summer and autumn of 1916 Desmond was seeing Irene regularly – but not, he complained, enough. She was tireless in addressing meetings – however ill-attended – of the Union of Democratic Control and of the Women's International League, another anti-war association. Desmond, whose work at the Admiralty made the real progress of the War hideously plain to him, wondered, as did Bertie Russell, the most ardent of pacifists, what actual value the efforts of the peace movement had in bringing the hostilities to an end: he did not say this but he certainly voiced his resentment at being squeezed into Irene's life in between meetings. But she was unstoppable: "I foresee a swarm of meetings – and I know the U.D.C. Executive has only elected me on to it to send me out into the wilderness speaking . . . and we shall have to do with seeing one another in snatched moments – I promise you I will practise snatching," she assured him.

By now Desmond was in love with Irene – so that a letter from her about Bertie Russell sent him into a frenzy of jealousy: whilst she had not been in love with Russell because "there were things in him which I positively hated," still she had felt "violent attraction to him – a longing in a way to get closer and closer even to that which I could not bear but thought perhaps I could only bear if I gave way to him. And sometimes when I was with him I forgot everything and only knew that I was with him and was happy – but that did not often happen. Now what love I had for him is much more a memory of a feeling than a feeling."

Thinking from this letter that Irene harboured "present longings" for Bertie, Desmond wrote to her in great agitation. She reassured him that she had none.

Desmond's resentment and frustration – of which his jealousy about Russell was just a symptom – erupted two weeks later: the cause was Irene's refusal to have a proper affair with him. "I do not want the closer relationship with you that you want," she stated. She would prefer to suffer the consequences – his not coming to see her any more – "than do now something which I have no desire for beyond the desire to please you – and I cannot help feeling that my indifference in this way would make it empty for you. I suppose I am not really in love with you, because just being with you and feeling your companionship is enough for me."

"Good heavens! why I've been making *love* to you. That's what you have enjoyed & what you'll miss," Desmond wrote furiously in the margin of this letter.

Irene said, "I hate the thought of losing you and yet I dislike more the thought of a step that I do not instinctively want to take." "On reflection?" Desmond wrote on the letter.

"All sorts of considerations come in," said Irene, chief among them was her abhorrence "of marching into other peoples' lives and taking what conventionally one has no right to take away from them." Desmond countered this with: "This is painful always but as I explained in M's case far less than usual." By this he meant that Molly's brief affair with Clive Bell, and the cessation of her sexual relations with himself, "justified" his having an affair with Irene. As for Irene's protest about the secrecy of their meetings, Desmond told her, "You keep our being lovers in all but bed dark already."

But Irene concluded that, "I do not believe that my ideas of this kind of shabbiness will ever alter. I think one has to learn to do without things." "O no not *some* things," Desmond added emphatically in the margin.

She ended her letter by telling him that he did not know how much she really cared for him: "I do," wrote Desmond, "But you do write these confounded letters. They are not like the way you talk and feel when you are with me. You give on impulse & take away on reflection."

While Desmond believed in honesty in relationships, he was baffled by Irene who seemed to love him when they were together but refused to take the final step of becoming his mistress. However, she was a woman of firm views; compromise was not in her character. So although she knew that "there would . . . always be pain and perhaps bitterness because I would not be your mistress," she would not go against her nature in this, unlike Molly with Clive Bell or Ottoline Morrell at times with Bertie Russell. She was not cut out for romance; she did not like idling away her time. When she saw someone it was for a purpose or for duty: to stride out for a walk, perhaps, to discuss a book under review, or to go to a play. Not for her the frivolity and leisure which are the essence of a love affair – and she dismissed those who indulged in them: "I would rather hear about the Clive Bell people than know them," she wrote to Desmond, "Clive Bell himself makes me feel physically ill – really physically ill – quite unreasonable no doubt – but I have that feeling when I catch sight of him – something of the feeling one has if one is offered a meringue for breakfast, being accustomed to tea and toast."

Finally, on 5th August 1917, she brought their relationship to an end. She wrote to Desmond six closely-written pages in her neat, flowing hand with never a crossing-out or an illegible word. It was a devastating analysis of her lack of sexual drive, outspoken and harsh in places, but deeply-felt and considered. She weighed the evidence for and against her deliberate denial of her sexual feelings, which Desmond claimed, almost as if she was already the barrister she later became. She had tried spontaneously "to let myself – and what sex feelings there might be hidden away – go – but never succeeded"; but it was no good, she

"couldn't fight against an utter, fundamental indifference in me to sex."
She had never, in all her life, experienced any sexual feelings whatever,
indeed, scarcely been aware that they existed: "Your story of your sex
feelings from childhood upwards hasn't got a single incident in it which I
ever experienced. I knew nothing, wrestled with nothing . . . until . . .
long after college I met Enid [Bagnold] and she told me how preoccupied
girls at school were with it – did I realise it existed." The one man who did
kiss her gave her "no thrill – I was just bored. As for Bertie . . . though he
kissed me I scarcely troubled at all about my indifference there because I
was taken up all the time with trying to understand why in some ways I
liked him so much and in other ways hated him. It was that struggle which
was in the forefront all the time – & which ended things. But it was Bertie
who rubbed it into me that I was deficient in vitality – because he couldn't
understand why I didn't love him – my not loving him had nothing to do
with physical vitality or not – if I had been bursting with it – I should still
have felt there were things in him I could not bear – I might have felt it
more. Which brings me to you, my dear. I needn't go over it all again. I
think the joy of finding someone – unlike Bertie – in whom there was
everything to love and nothing to shrink from, made me at first forget all
the deficiencies in me that Bertie had so rubbed in. Because I loved you so
in my way I have tried to force myself at times into believing I enjoyed
your kisses – but it has been a failure – and there is no-one for whom I
would again make the experiment. All the other considerations which I
have at times advanced – those of your being married . . . I don't want to
go into . . . because I know that if I were really in love with you, whether it
would be shabby or not, or ignominious or not to be secret, or lonely or
not in wanting more of your time than I could have, it wouldn't
matter. . . .

"You have a right to be angry, bitter with me. I have spoilt things for
you – disappointed you. I realise all that. I have not kept back anything in
this letter . . . I have written all I know."

After such a letter as this there was very little for Desmond to say except
to ask Irene for his letters back. She refused, saying: "I want to keep your
letters. They were sent to me, they are mine just as much as what you have
said to me in talking. There is no need for you to fear that I shall show
them to people or talk about you and me. I do not chat about my personal
matters. My memory of you is perfectly safe."

As it happened, it was not: there was a sequel to their relationship, a
novel Irene wrote in 1923, under the pseudonym of Althea Brook (her
mother's maiden name was Brook). Entitled *The Green-Eyed Monster*,
she had been writing it for some time, certainly when she was seeing
Desmond. When it came out, despite the pseudonym and the gap of

several years since their liaison, Desmond was outraged. It seemed to him a final blow delivered by Irene to humiliate him.[13]

The book purported to be a study in jealousy, as its title implied. In fact, it was a portrait of a weak deceitful man, Edward Russell, modelled blatantly on Desmond. The sketch was facile and damning, lacking the subtlety, understanding and humour which tempered Virginia Woolf's critical descriptions of Desmond (and of other friends) in her diaries. Edward Russell, wrote Irene, was "extraordinarily brilliant but completely dependent upon social excitement for the exercise of his brilliancy. He had not made the mark as a writer that he might have made for he was lazy, & insatiably social." "A spurt of self-reproach would now & again prompt him . . . but it never lasted long." He had "rare insight and sympathy and a vivid and witty pen," but "away from the stimulus of good food, wine and talk, his energies flagged. His pockets bulged with invitations, on the backs of which notes for articles were scribbled, so few of which ever got written because of the way he wasted his time."

His wife, Beryl, feared that "he would never do anything but amuse his friends, one of whom had described him to her as "a delightful watering-cart making the road of life very pleasant for us all to walk along".

This last quotation, which Irene used more than once in the novel, particularly incensed Desmond: he accused Irene of making "recognition certain by my friends by quoting a well-remembered saying of Theodore Davies' about me, so that there can be no doubt where you get your conception of your deceitful waster and 'spiritual cad'."

Desmond was further annoyed that Irene gave Edward Russell a German mother and an Irish father – in his unreliability and charm being attributed to the Irish blood – and condemned for his selfishness towards his mother, the result of an over-indulged childhood. But the worst betrayal Desmond felt was the way in which Irene used his old love letters to garnish her text: at least these letters showed that Edward Russell had intellectual breadth, which the heroine, by her own admission, conspicuously lacked. "His appreciation of books, of people, was wider, more adventurous than hers," conceded Irene. "his pursuit and grip of others minds more vigorous and genial"; his "careless, seemingly haphazard yet unerring glance made everything so vivid."

No wonder Desmond asked Irene once more to return his letters. "It will save you from a temptation I never dreamt you would ever feel & me from seeing my affections & passions dangling like old clo', marked 'Very Cheap' in another pawn-shop window." Instead of sending them back, however, she destroyed them.[14]

His future wife Beryl's cottage was, like Irene's, in the Kent country-side. "Beryl had worked manfully at it," as Irene had done, planting the garden even down to the same nasturtiums. And here Edward had visited Beryl. "He had taken her into his arms . . . Ah, should she ever forget his kisses and that afternoon which slipped away, unnoticed into twilight and evening as they kissed." Irene had declared herself only too anxious to forget Desmond's kisses, dismissing them as "unimportant". Desmond had accused her of ignoring "a man's primitive pride"; luckily for his amour-propre she did not attack it further in the novel: that is all that was said about sex in the book. As we have seen it was not a subject which interested Irene.

The story's bleak bitterness – out of all proportion to any misconduct on Desmond's part, who had, after all, not even seduced her – says more about Irene herself than about any of her fictional characters; Desmond's affection and admiration for her had been unstinting and generous, and his only offence had been to Molly, not to Irene. Unintentionally, however, he had made Irene feel badly about herself. In offering his love he had inadvertently held up a mirror for her to see the paucity of her emotions. She had been shocked by what it revealed, and the book had been her revenge. Sheltering behind her pseudonym, she portrayed Desmond as a "spiritual cad", belittling and condemning him. The *Green-Eyed Monster* reads like an effort to prove to herself that she had been right in her denial of him and that he, by extension, had been in the wrong.

Yet for Irene that was how their relationship, after much brooding, had come to appear. Under a cool efficient exterior, designed to fend off unwelcome reality, she was terrified. A germ of the explanation must lie in her home – an over-dominating father, perhaps. At all events though she was courageous and enterprising, she shunned close relationships and feared – even disliked – men. In the novel, Tom Wolfe, based partially on Bertrand Russell, was as contemptible and predatory as the shiftless Edward. Her determination to publish it was more a compulsion than a sober decision, and gave the lie to the rational mask she wore.

When that was finally stripped away, Desmond was surprised – a measure of his innocence and lack of experience in love. The whole affair, indeed, seems more like that of two confused young people in their early twenties, than that of a man and woman who lived in sophisticated and intellectual circles. After the book appeared Desmond rebuked her vehemently, accusing her of setting out to hurt him: "*I* had to bear the humiliation of failure in spite of being towards you the best it was in me to be & to suffer the tortures of Tantalus – for you went very far; *you* had to bear in the end the sudden cessation of an adoration & tenderness which were sweet & comforting & the loss of a companionship delightful to you – a hard thing, I know, to bear." Many years later Enid Bagnold recalled how upset Desmond had been "about Irene's obscure novel, though no-one would have guessed he was 'in' it (and indeed never did guess, I think)".[15] The book was reviewed: the *Times Literary Supplement* commented on its over-intensity – and certainly it is not a light read. Irene never wrote another novel, though she produced books on the Brontës and Florence Nightingale, amongst other heroines of hers, and on legal topics. She was a barrister for nearly forty years.* Her path and Desmond's scarcely crossed again.

---

*She died, aged 88, peacefully, in a nursing home. She is remembered by her nephew, Euan Cooper-Willis, as an aunt to be avoided, as she disliked children and was severe and censorious. Irene lived mostly on her own or shared her house with a female companion, but never, it would seem, with anyone who was more than a companion.

14 "Pincher"

It was still safest for Molly and the children to be out of the capital. Were it not for the unremitting hostilities, she wrote to Desmond, she would have been quite happy in her isolation among infants in the country. For September 1917 the children went as paying guests to Charleston in Sussex, where Vanessa Bell had recently moved, and here they enjoyed uproarious games with Vanessa's two boys.[1] For much of the following year they stayed at the Tudor farmhouse, Big Chilling, on the Solent in Hampshire where Logan Pearsall Smith and Alys Russell had moved. It was only a short distance from the sea: "Wonderful camouflaged liners and troopships looking as if their sides had been painted by Duncan, and some by Wyndham Lewis, glide quietly down Southampton Water, carrying thousands to death or ruin – and I lie on a sofa with a Turgenieff novel, and watch them – feeling not callous, but hopeless."[2]

Wherever she went, Molly took with her the novel which she had been writing over the last few years. She had been at it so long, she told Ottoline Morrell, as to have almost lost faith in "my 2nd-rate, old-fashioned, too near the present date to be good old-fashioned, uninspired, prosaic, rather snobbish feeble novel, like a piece of needlework that, having been begun, might as well now be finished, so one stitches away." Finally, the tapestry was complete. At the suggestion of Arnold Bennett, who told her they were the most intelligent publishers in London, she sent it to Chatto & Windus. Diffident as she had been, Molly was delighted when they at once accepted it. Originally entitled *Love and Land Values*, which Molly changed to the less stark *A Pier and a Band*, the book is about the still topical theme of building over unspoilt land. It was set in her birthplace, Lynton, then in the process of being built over "like some exquisite friend who has married for money and been wrecked by it". This theme was interwoven with the love story of the young squire, Anthony Forrest, who held fast to his father's determination that their ancestral property should never be built on and the heroine, Perdita, who came to realise that she has to break away from her own family estate.

The conclusion of the novel is that one should take risks, said Molly, build your life on your own foundations, and not just accept an inherited outlook. She added that the last chapter, when Perdita decided to join Fitzgerald, the man she loved, was written under the influence of Chekhov. This was picked up by David Garnett who introduced a new edition of the novel in 1931 as "Tchekhov's *Cherry Orchard* in an English setting." Despite minor faults in construction, because it was written intermittently, it is a thoughtful, unpretentious novel, humorous but with a deeply felt central theme about the nature of happiness.

Desmond appeared as the charming Fitzgerald, a philosophy student: Perdita was at once taken with him though aware of his weaknesses, which Molly described with gentle, but devastating precision: "Fitzgerald himself was perhaps too comfortably indolent for a man of 26. . . . He might have been impressive if he had shown the slightest desire to be so; but he never did – a trait which suggested a disconcerting absence of ambition or resolve to use his talents to the greatest advantage. His faults were the kind that only escape notice in noblemen of ancient lineage and vast wealth.

"Perdita sometimes felt as if he were a full jug without a handle – full of precious liquid, but with no means of pouring it out." However she also found him supportive, with a great enjoyment of people and a stimulating intellect. "When with him she seemed to get all the satisfaction and none of the pain of being perfectly truthful. There did not seem to be a single thing he believed because he ought to believe it. His critical faculty was of the order which usually produces cold indifference or savage impatience, but these characteristics were markedly absent in him."

A Pier and a Band was immediately successful when it was published in September 1918. Molly's head, which had shrunk to the size of an apple, according to Desmond, "is now swelling to normal size again," wrote Virginia Woolf, who dined at Wellington Square shortly after its publication. She had written to Molly praising her book as soon as she had read it – praise which would have been balm to any writer, but especially to one with as little confidence as Molly: unlike David Garnett, who thought Molly should have emphasised the building theme more, Virginia had not cared for the building disputes, but "all the rest I thought purely delightful, & how I envied your beautiful, malicious phrases which look so simple to begin with & then give a flick of their tails & sum up an entire character or situation – Perdita's power, of course, which makes her so uncompromising, in spite of the fact that her manners are exquisite – indeed one of the few ladies in modern fiction. Fitzgerald is one of the most delightful characters in real life – But I assure you that you must at once begin another book entirely of letters."

Molly, "astonished & delighted that you had read the book already," replied that she would take her advice about the letters.

Molly called her novel old-fashioned, set as it was in the 1890s, before the women's suffrage campaign, when girls could not yet fly over "the five-barred gate of home oppression," dock their hair and rush into jobs, in "art or medicine or sanitary inspection"; and when "no man could speak his mind at all freely to you without believing he would wound your artificial self-respect". But Virginia Woolf, who wrote so much about individual self-expression, hailed it as a breath of life, away from the suffocating South Kensington atmosphere of their girlhood, their well-intentioned, morally uplifting, spiritually high-flying Ritchie Aunts – Anny and Emily, Gussie and Blanche herself. In her diary she wrote, "The gulf that we crossed between Kensington and Bloomsbury was the gulf between respectable mummified humbug and life crude and impertinent perhaps, but living. . . . Molly, thanks to Bloomsbury, has escaped the Ritchie touch."[3]

As for Desmond, his days at the Admiralty had for some time seemed to him like being back at school, working according to rules of which he had ceased to see the point, as he wrote to Max Beerbohm in April 1916:[4] "I look wistfully out of the window. I fancy the world is a wonderful place and heaps of joys waiting for me, if only I could get at them. I read Don Juan under the desk sometimes; and the other day when a pad-footed bespectacled man came up behind my chair and said in that tone of one conferring a favour, yet respectfully, 'Your work has been shown to the Head of the Department. Perhaps you would like to keep this', while he placed a scrap of paper with 'Very good piece of work' scribbled on it, on my blotting-paper – I BLUSHED. I feel like a school-boy and time drags."

Nothing had mitigated his hostile view of the enemy, but he was disillusioned with his own country's leadership, and this had much to do with his personal friendships. Mr Asquith, whom he liked and admired, had been ignominiously unseated as Prime Minister late in 1916 to make way for the pushful, effective Lloyd George. However, a quick victory – the only thing which might have justified this in Desmond's eyes – did not materialise. On both sides, at giant human cost, the national leaders seemed to him chiefly concerned with saving their own faces. In the spring of 1918 the German army drove the Allied Forces forty miles back – the biggest reversal of positions on the Western Front since early in the War. Eddie Marsh's brother-in-law, General Sir Frederick Maurice, defying military discipline, publicly accused Lloyd George of lying over the government's responsibility for the defeat. Asquith challenged Lloyd George over this in Parliament and called for a debate. It was the most formidable attack that Lloyd George had to face during the war but in the end he saved himself by the skilful use of dubious statistics. Maurice, despite countrywide support, had to retire from the army. Desmond was one of those who agreed with the General and Asquith. An old friend of Lady Maurice, he visited the family in Kensington to encourage and congratulate her husband. He found him, "very cheerful and quite untroubled . . . either by misgivings or by the effect of his action. . . . He is a young-grey-haired soldier, with a quick and pleasant blue eye – very direct and a copious rather nervous-merry talker."[5]

For all the "war depression" which sat so heavily upon him, Desmond was a much sought-after guest for dinner and luncheon; at house-parties and Saturdays to Mondays. He was a life-enhancer; he made a party "go": hostesses could cease to fret that their guests might not get on. Desmond was the magic ingredient whose ease and charm ensured that they did. His limitless curiosity about human nature led him to take an interest in his least prepossessing neighbour at dinner; there was no bore so leaden that he could not divine something of interest in him – their very tedium could in itself be fascinating.

"People are so haunted by the fear of being bored . . . But I like the company of people who go hacking on at the same subject, even if that is only how to get a lawn in good order," he said.[6] But above all he loved to entertain and to be entertained in conversation: many friends and fellow-guests have remembered this with delight. In her autobiography, Enid Bagnold described meeting him: "Ah the first impact of Desmond. Not visually, but when the first words moved, caressing and inexorable, into position: when armed with the weapons of his mind he trod softly like a hunter after the hare of his thought. . . .

"One can't call back that stroking, meandering voice, so sure of its words, or if it hesitated it was for a word as tipped with phosphorus as a match, to set the table alight." He caught a momentary truth, and relished it, dwelt on it, while his mind moved rapidly on.[7] His forte was not so much repartee as the elaboration of a theme or a telling anecdote: this might take as much as two minutes without interruption. He, in turn, was always an attentive listener, but he believed good conversation involved allowing the interlocutors the time to finish what they had to say.

These were the "Pincher" years – the nickname Molly used, sometimes affectionately, sometimes with exasperation, to describe Desmond's social gallivanting. "Pincher" was the dog belonging to his cousin, May Kynaston; incurably adventurous, he went off on escapades night after night, and having had a terrific time, came home to stretch out on his own hearth rug at last.

In Desmond's disenchanted mood the company of pretty women provided something of an antidote. He was always susceptible to them and ready to help in their literary endeavours; at the beginning of 1918 Irene Cooper-Willis's friend, Enid Bagnold, published her first book *A diary Without Dates*, an account of her experiences as a V.A.D. nurse, which Irene asked Desmond to review.

"I haven't read it," Desmond wrote to Virginia Woolf with engaging frankness, "but (A) it is very short and (B) the authoress (whom I have read, so to speak) is charming. . . . Ask for it, do. I am going to ask the N[ew] S[tatesman] for it. If we have nothing to say about it, well, it can't be helped."[8]

He visited the "Woolves" a fortnight later, on his day off. Virginia had decided not to review the book. "After a glance at her mind," she thought her "a disagreeable chit" who had obviously enmeshed Desmond.[9] As a matter of fact Desmond was not at all in love with Enid Bagnold, nor she with him. He responded to the twenty-nine-year-old Enid's vitality and high spirits during this depressing fourth year of the War. She was attractive, with statuesque good looks and a wide, somewhat catlike, face. She herself always preferred the company of older men – when she married in 1920 her husband, Roderick Jones, the head of Reuters news agency, was eleven years older than herself. But many of their friends, and Molly, believed they were romantically involved. Desmond took Enid out to lunch from the Admiralty and she enjoyed being with this distinguished-looking figure in naval uniform. In April 1918, rather on the spur of the moment, he asked her to accompany him on a visit to Garsington (Molly could not come); here "as I was nervous of those total Intellectuals he kept me by his side. I heard Lady Ottoline say (in her extraordinary double voice like the two halves of a wasp) . . . 'that tiresome girl who wouldn't let go of Desmond'. I didn't know that I was holding on to their plum," Enid wrote in her autobiography.

Molly told Ottoline after this visit – which she assumed, wrongly, was at the Morrells' behest rather than Desmond's – that she really could not "entamer" Miss Bagnold. "I have only met her once. I saw she had a 'come hither' eye, and left her to get what she could out of Desmond as that was what she wanted."[10] What Enid wanted from Desmond at the beginning of her career as a writer was indeed what she got: an entrée into literary London (though not into Bloomsbury), help and advice with her writing, and a review not from Virginia Woolf, but from Desmond himself in *The Nation*. Enid was grateful, sending Desmond charmingly illustrated letters, one with a drawing of the "excitement, embarrassment, beatitude, of Obscure Woman on discovering the amount that had been done for her" in the way of advancing her book. Desmond called her "Lionetta" – she was not yet a lion.[11]

Enid was not an intellectual like Irene Cooper-Willis: Desmond found her very crudeness a relief after the fastidious Irene. Enid was a spontaneous, even slapdash, but ambitious writer. She was one kind of "new Woman", a free spirit, amorous and independent in a way that was beginning to become fashionable. Irene Cooper-Willis was another kind – serious, professionally the equal of men, university-educated. Both were determined to live on their own and make their own way in life. That spring of 1918 when Irene told Enid that she missed Desmond and had been re-reading his letters (to what devastating effect was not yet apparent), he visited her in her house at Sevenoaks. But there was little left between them; and, besides, Desmond told Enid that "I don't want to start the useless ache and restlessness again."

A more enduring mutual friendship was with Prince Antoine Bibesco (1879–1951). It was he, not Desmond, who fired Enid with romance – as she was always ready to be fired: (she was long on romance, short on facts, as her writing shows). Prince Bibesco was attached to the Romanian legation in London, but was as much dilettante as diplomat; interested in literature and in women, he was cosmopolitan, having been brought up in Paris (where he eventually lived) and a friend of Proust. He was an exotic – when she first met him Lady Cynthia Asquith likened him to a black tulip; photographs show aristocratic Slavic features, with deep-set eyes. He had a pretty house in Grosvenor Road, on the river near Chelsea, where he entertained hospitably: at his narrow dining-table men and women sat facing one another, and there was plenty of drink and uninhibited talk. Desmond said that Antoine's zest for life, and his capacity for devoted friendship – which he certainly showed towards Desmond – "was the more remarkable for being combined in him with a cynicism which would have turned most people into frigid egoists."[12] Even friends like Desmond, who knew how cynical Antoine was, were surprised at Antoine's choice of a wife just after the war. Elizabeth Asquith (1897–1945), daughter of the former Prime Minister and his second wife, Margot, was a social embarrassment in her circle, notorious for drinking and talking to excess, with an "almost astounding lack of social intelligence which prevented her noticing when her coruscating brilliance was reducing her audience to mechanical nods and smirks," wrote Desmond. He compared her drinking habits with those of others "who live to shine socially – men and women alike – among my seniors, for example, the brilliant Harry Cust and that torrential charmer, George Wyndham; among my contemporaries Clifford Sharp." As embarrassing was Elizabeth's conviction of her attraction to men; so Desmond was worried about the Bibescos' chances of married happiness, especially when Elizabeth, on the eve of her wedding, took a "header into intimacy" with Clifford Sharp.

With characteristic fairness, however, Desmond also discerned in Elizabeth "the pathos of that too variously gifted woman so humbly grateful for immediate applause that she would turn in any direction to secure it from any audience; that 'wunderkind' as the Germans call such people in their youth, who had also in her a magnanimity of feeling, the very opposite of 'vanity'." And he realised that her desperate need to show off had its roots in her upbringing by the Asquiths: "how unfortunate it was for a girl with so swiftly receptive a brain and so gifted, and with so responsive, like-nearly-everybody temperament, to be brought up in a home where the highest achievements were taken for granted, and the most eminent in every walk of life started at scratch again as 'talkers'. It was Margot, of course, not Mr A[squith] who created that atmosphere, in which, apparently, the end of achievement, whether in politics, literature, law or learning, was the opportunity to compete with the best in the discussion of life, public affairs, human-nature, books and to shine in conversation.

"To her father, talk was merely a cheerfully chaotic recreation, and he seldom gave more than the top of his attention to it. (Henry James notes, a trifle ironically, 'the admirable intellectual economy' practised by the Prime Minister on social occasions). And it amused him to hear his little 'Liza' with her magnolia complexion and plum-black eyes, embarrass one of his ministers, or a Lord Chief Justice, by a swift retort; and when some man who had been equally amused, insisted on her staying to have it out when the ladies retired, he would watch her now and then, (stroking his rosy gills as he did so), sipping her glass of port and evidently adding to the liveliness of the other end of the table. Yes: but it wasn't very good for sixteen year old 'Liza'."[13]

Desmond's description admirably conveys the atmosphere of the Asquiths' household at The Wharf, Sutton Courtney, on the Thames, near Oxford, which they acquired in 1912. Here the MacCarthys, Desmond in particular, were regular visitors. Life at The Wharf was unconventional, as was the house itself; converted from two old village houses, one of which had been the inn, "it was less a house than a settlement, an accumulation of dwellings . . . containing enough rooms to house a party of 10 or 12 persons . . ." recalled David Cecil, a close friend of Anthony Asquith.[14] It was a rabbit warren of narrow stairs and passages; upstairs the bedroom walls were too thin to allow privacy – anyway privacy was not highly valued chez Asquith; downstairs the cramped rooms could quickly become claustrophobic "with people sitting about as though exposed on trays. One is at too close quarters to one's fellow creatures and can't see them in the right perspective," said a daughter-in-law of the Asquiths. There was none of the hushed calm to inspire artistic creation or intellectual endeavour as, for instance, at Garsington a few miles away. At The Wharf, as Molly remarked, everybody lived in a passage: Desmond was shocked, when he first went there, that Asquith, then Prime Minister, had no room of his own to work in and had to retire to his bedroom to get away from the perpetual bow-wow-wow of the house. It was, as Desmond said, a most difficult house in which to write even a letter: "conversation, tennis, bathing, moonlight floating on the river – games – but above all conversation. . . . It is a spinning top in which all the colours have blended and blurred. . . ."

Traffic between the rooms and the garden was endless and disrupting: Margot converted a barn into rooms for herself in the garden, from which she would send her maid over to the main house with vigorously pencilled letters.

Margot invited a motley collection of guests to The Wharf, based on an idiosyncratic process of selection. As a result, Desmond said "the atmospherics are terrific": at mealtimes neighbour did not necessarily talk to neighbour, as in conventional dining-rooms, nor was the conversation general around the table in the narrow white room, with its garden windows: rather, it resembled "a sort of wild game of pool in which everybody is playing his or her stroke at the same time. One is trying to send a remark into the top corner pocket farthest from her, where at the same moment another player is attempting a close-up shot at his own end; while anecdotes and comments whizz backwards and forwards, cannoning and clashing as they cross the table. And not only are half a dozen different discussions taking place simultaneously, but the guests are at different stages of the meal . . . for everyone gets up and helps himself as he finishes a course."

Though they were never intimates, Desmond knew Henry Asquith for sixteen years, both in office and out. (Asquith confided in few people, and all of those were women; even with his sons he was remarkably uncommunicative.) Desmond lacked the political insights of Asquith's close colleagues and the evidence available to later historians; but he saw certain sides of him clearly; the vivid portrait which he wrote of him in 1928 illuminates the outstanding qualities of a man who has been underestimated as a political leader – not least because he quarrelled with our two most famous and flamboyant statesmen – Lloyd George and Churchill and has been measured unfavourably against them. Desmond had long admired Asquith's polished, unostentatious public speeches and his distaste for playing to the gallery: "the absence of either magnetism or any desire to impress grew beautiful to me. . . . He sought our solid advantage and not our ridiculous patronage."

Closer acquaintance led him to appreciate the way Mr Asquith could combine a taste for light conversation and flights of fancy "off duty" with a judgement on public affairs which sprang from deep thought and hard evidence. Once, when asked by him after the war to describe the situation in Ireland, which he had just visited, Desmond launched into a character study of the Irish leader Griffith "in a manner which I am quite sure during dinner would have won his attention"; but Asquith wanted informed opinion on political trends, not entertainment: "I looked up and saw on my host's face a look of unmistakable, not to say stern, boredom." Desmond saw this as the response of a man habituated to action, and not of one softened by social frivolities, as was repeatedly maintained; nor was it the response of "a scholar and historian pitchforked into public life" who shrank from practical decisions, another frequent description by critics. Desmond's ideas of what constituted political "action" were based, it must be said, on little real knowledge.

Finally Desmond came to respect, from direct observation, the intellectual integrity which made Asquith draw back from discussing certain subjects such as metaphysical or philosophical matters, even though they interested him, because he did not consider himself sufficiently instructed. He had extremely high standards and "a great aversion from stuffing the blanks in his understanding with provisional thinking".[15]

More surprisingly Desmond, always so keen on pursuing the truth, also delighted in his flamboyantly eccentric wife Margot, who was as extravagant in her fantasies as she was with money. "She strikes me as one who has always made her own code, sometimes superior and sometimes inferior to the current one. . . . The world that her imagination creates has plenty of tinsel about it, but she brings before me the courage and beauty of life – as few people have done."[16] If to Desmond social life was like the theatre, he found the Asquiths good theatre indeed. He liked clever families, perhaps, he said, because he was himself an only child; that is what had attracted him about the Warre-Cornishes at Eton. Now, at The Wharf, he enjoyed the spectacle of the different strands of that talented and eccentric family gathered round the table, presided over, if that is not too strong a word, by the benign, but distant H.H., and the extraordinary Margot, with her bony, witchlike head, and small, restless body, attired in the height of fashion, however appropriate or not that might be.

It was not long before Desmond began to fall in love with one of the clan: Lady Cynthia Asquith (1887–1960) was married to H.H.'s second son, Herbert (1881–1947), known as "Beb". Desmond and "Beb" Asquith had one shared characteristic – they were bad providers for their families. "Beb" was an accomplished minor poet and novelist. His best known books, *Roon* and *Young Orland*, were semi-autobiographical, incorporating his war experiences and some of his feelings for Cynthia.

They were melancholy and poetic in atmosphere, and sold well, but throughout his life the unassertive "Beb" was overshadowed – or allowed himself to be – by his articulate family and, in particular, by his wife.

When Desmond met her, at the beginning of 1918, Lady Cynthia had been married for eight years, and had two young sons. Her wartime family life was not easy: with "Beb" at the Front, in order to economise they, like the MacCarthys, let their London house, and Cynthia was "cuckooing", as she put it, in the large houses of friends and relations of whom she had an abundant supply.

She was the oldest daughter of the Earl of Wemyss and his wife, the beautiful Mary (née Wyndham), a leading "Soul". The Wemyss' house was in Cadogan Square, conveniently close to Wellington Square. While Lady Cynthia "cuckooed" there, it was not her household to run and she did not entertain: she was invited out constantly to friends, or had dinner at the Queen's restaurant in Sloane Square. (So often, and with such a variety of admirers, that she confessed in her Diary "What can the waiters there think of me?") Now thirty, Cynthia was strikingly, but not conventionally, beautiful; her auburn hair, tall, graceful figure, magnolia-white skin and slanting, elfin glance have been described by a close friend, David Cecil, as "the true image of a personality at once intimate and mysterious, romantic and ironical, whose conversation was remarkable alike for its poetic sensibility and its infectious unpredictable humour." She had a talent for friendship, and numbered among her close friends writers as diverse as D. H. Lawrence, and J. M. Barrie, and, of course, Desmond.[17]

Cynthia had a strong, magnetic personality; she was great fun to be with; and it is easy to see why Desmond found himself, during the latter part of 1918, spending more and more time with her, while "Beb" was away at the War, and Molly was out of London. Desmond would have liked to take their *amitié amoureuse* further but Lady Cynthia drew back. She needed, and she gave, deep-seated affection and friendship – but not love. And this kept Desmond in a state of fascination.

Cynthia and Desmond met in January through Elizabeth Asquith, who introduced them at dinner with Antoine Bibesco. Their combined, and not inconsiderable, savoir-faire was much needed during that evening in Grosvenor Road as "Elizabeth's mental, physical and moral archness was beyond all description," and sometimes Cynthia did not know which way to look while she flirted outrageously with Antoine: she twitted him with being cross, "insinuating it was the invariable effect of her *troublante* presence and referred provocatively to her other 'lovers'. McCarthy [sic] and I were puzzled and embarrassed spectators. She engineered a tête-à-tête with him after dinner. McCarthy and I found ourselves alone in the drawing-room."

Altogether Cynthia found the evening enjoyable and she liked meeting
"the delectable Desmond MacCarthy", whose name she now spelt
correctly, on various occasions at Prince Bibesco's house during the
spring, sometimes with Elizabeth, who continued to set her cap at
Antoine, and once with Enid Bagnold as the fourth.

In May, when Cynthia was in the country, Desmond sent her his friend
Logan Pearsall Smith's newly-published collection, *Trivia*, "to be read
with *pauses*, and not too many Trivia at a time they give one a pleasure
which is like sipping a cup of Mandarin's tea."

When Cynthia returned to London, Desmond and she met regularly
again; and on 31st May spent "a memorably delightful evening, first
dining at Queen's and then sitting in the Square until nearly twelve. I must
say I delight in his company." Though very different, Desmond reminded
her of her recently killed admirer, Basil Blackwood, whom she had greatly
loved: "It is, I suppose, something in the responsiveness of a thought,
voice, and laugh which they have in common. Between talking to them
and to others is something of the difference between dancing on a floor
hung on chains and on an ordinary one."

Cynthia had a passion for playing poker, which Desmond did not
share, but he accepted her invitation to play with some of her friends –
and must have regretted it, because he lost £4 that evening which he could
ill-afford. It was now that J. M. Barrie asked Cynthia to be his secretary.
Desmond whose capacity for advising others on how to direct their lives
was equalled only by his difficulty in organising his own, encouraged her
to accept the job; he thought it would suit her, for "I have fancied that you
like being adored – in that being no great exception. Barrie, as I read him,
is part mother, part hero-worshipping maiden, part grandfather, and part
pixie with no man in him at all. His genius is a coquettish thing, with just a
drop of benevolent acid in it sometimes." He concluded this analysis of
Barrie, which Cynthia copied into her diary, with the disclaimer that she
would find out about him for herself, "much better than I do who do it
only by conjecture". Cynthia found Desmond's description quite accurate when she went to work for Barrie the following month – she
remained with him until his death in 1937.

In mid-July Desmond met Cynthia with her husband "Beb", home on
leave; like many people who met him, he could find little to say about him
other than that he was "contemplative" – later he nicknamed him "the
Dog", being the figure who shuffled along behind. In August Molly and
Desmond were invited by Antoine to lunch with "Beb" and Cynthia.
Although she was acutely self-conscious about bringing her husband into
the company of two of her admirers, the occasion was "an unanticipated
success" and they sat over the table until 3.30 talking about the war, of

course, as well as laughing at silly jokes – "whether the lover of animals would or would not give a fly to a spider. Desmond told a story of a Boy Scout who, remembering he had not performed his requisite daily good deed, jumped out of bed and gave the canary to the cat."

The following Sunday, Desmond dined with J. M. Barrie and Cynthia; they had an amusing evening and he escorted her back to Cadogan Square, through heavy rain, and then sat talking to her, "keeping me sitting in wet feet".

He and Cynthia now saw each other regularly; on 11th September they dined as they often did at Queen's restaurant – their dinners, because of prevalent food shortages, let alone penury, were modest and often meatless: whitebait, soup and macaroni being a representative menu. Later on in the evening, they sat out in the summerhouse in Cadogan Square, talking about poetry and Henry James. Cynthia's diary entry ended with, "No further ground covered in our relationship." What further ground she would have liked covered is unclear – not much, judging by her later behaviour.

But as Desmond had correctly remarked à propos of her going to work for Barrie: "I have fancied that you like being adored"; and it is likely that she saw Desmond as an admirer and a support when close friends such as Lord Alexander Thynne were killed. Proximity played a large part too: Cadogan Square was very near Chelsea, and Barrie's flat behind The Strand was near to the Admiralty.

Delightful as he found her, Cynthia did not absorb all "Pincher's" time and attention: he began to be exposed now to the importunate invitations of Sibyl Colefax (1876–1950), later to be one of the most indefatigable hostesses of her day. Like Virginia Woolf, Desmond accepted some and avoided others: sometimes he managed to do both at once, accept *and* avoid, as he did when invited to spend his week's holiday with the Colefaxes at their house in Sussex. "The Colefaxes' house is uninteresting perfection," he wrote to Molly. "Delicious gardens, perfectly restored old rooms, but somehow I can't envy that sort of house": so much for the taste of the woman who was to be a partner in the leading decorating firm, Colefax and Fowler, which has celebrated throughout the world that same, very English, country house style. But such a "worked-on" look inside or out, with no expense spared, seemed forced to Desmond and Molly; it was neither really grand, nor expressive of natural good taste; its very smartness smothered whatever interest it might have had. After a couple of days Desmond made his excuses and left – but not before an embarrassing moment with one of his fellow-guests, Lady Randolph Churchill. This celebrated American beauty (née Jennie Jerome), the mother of Winston Churchill, Desmond found to be "an immensely vital old woman with the temperament of the Wife of Bath. I put my foot in it on the Sunday morning walk. We were walking in twos and threes behind each other and something reminded me of Mrs Patrick Campbell." So Desmond launched into a story about her "adding that she was often so damnably unkind that it was difficult to get people to act with her.

"Lady R. turned round and said, 'She is a violent Italian peasant that's what she is – an impossible woman'." Desmond should have been warned by his hostess urgently tugging his jacket from behind, but on he went, to ask, "Oh have you ever engaged her in battle?"

Lady R., "I should think I had."

"My coat was again dusted from behind, but I did not put two and two together, and went on, 'It must have been a famous battle.'

"Well, I turned her out of my house. But she took my husband away with her."

"*Then* I remembered that Cornwallis West was the old lady's husband and that he had been divorced and married Mrs Campbell. However, I did not mind, for Lady R. is not a sensitive plant, and [I] went on talking about Mrs Patrick Campbell, which turned out the right thing."[18]

Despite this episode the invitations continued – or perhaps because of it, for Sibyl Colefax relished scenes like this at her social gatherings. Sibyl and Arthur Colefax were shortly to move to Argyll House, further down the King's Road from Wellington Square, which was dubbed "Lion's corner house" after Sibyl's ambitious party invitations.

A hearth to which "Pincher" was more content to roam, where he would be safe from the temptation of flirting or the strain of "an impersonally compiled anthology" of guests belonged to Oliver and Antoinette Brett. Chen had met Antoinette (née Hecksher) early in the war and was anxious to include Desmond in her new friendship: a wealthy American, who married her very English husband in 1912, Antoinette was intellectually rather than socially ambitious, though she gave large parties and lived in fine style in Belgravia. But she found the English intellectual scene daunting, and here Desmond was a useful bridge. The Bretts were unexpected friends for him, however: Antoinette was not an easy woman, neither humorous, nor educated, and far from flirtatious, but she was intelligent, rich and hospitable, and eager to improve herself (and her children: "Manners, competitiveness, stoicism, accuracy, these were the four virtues," recalled the eldest of her four children, Lionel).[19] Desmond enjoyed the fine collection of first editions the Bretts were amassing, and wrote to Antoinette about books (there was often an element of teaching in Desmond's friendships with younger women). The Bretts' pleasure in literature was later crucially important to Desmond's career. Oliver Brett (1881–1963) was now attached to the

War Office and Desmond used to call in on them at Chester House, Upper Belgrave Street, on his way back to Wellington Square after his day's work at the Admiralty. It was a friendship which was to sustain him in the gloomy early months of 1918 when victory seemed to him, as to most people, something infinitely distant.

Finally, however, in November the Armistice was signed. In many ways an anti-climax − so much blood had been spilled, so intangible was victory − it nevertheless meant peace, at last; Armistice Day itself became for Desmond a heady moment, because he spent most of it and the evening in the company of Cynthia.

He had now progressed to writing to her as "My dear Cynthia" but his letters were still signed "Your affectionate Desmond MacCarthy", nor were they particularly intimate. On 7th November he wrote that, "Everybody in the Admiralty feels the war is over today. It is the first time that conviction has been abroad in the air like ozone."

They joined the crowd which thronged the centre of London on 11th November.

Nothing much happened but the atmosphere was good-humoured, as they drifted down Pall Mall to Buckingham Palace, and saw on the balcony a little group of figures, one doubtless the King, probably making a speech − what about it was impossible to hear in the din of yells, cat-calls, and whistles.

Back in Trafalgar Square they went into St Martin-in-the-Fields church where a Thanksgiving Service was being held: "The quavering, throbbing and whining of the organ, and the people at the foot of the portico steps dancing 'Nuts in May' harmonised into a single appeal which made me feel I should like to go in, sit still and remember. Pews, a slightly foggy atmosphere, bright lights and soporific warmth − how familiar it all was! . . . I waited for the clergyman to tell us also to pray for our enemies; he was, I thought, the sort of man who might. But he did not. At the close we sang, 'God Save The King'."

Outside in the Square, Desmond described to his son Michael how the people lit bonfires, throwing a roadmender's shelter onto the flames, as well as benches and wooden hoardings. Desmond and Cynthia climbed onto one of the stone lions at the foot of Nelson's column: "round a bonfire is a Cruickshank crowd dancing and bawling. The crowd danced and sang and would not let the firemen come near the flames to put them out: so the firemen turned their hose first on the crowd. This made the people angry. They swarmed over the engines like ants; they pushed and banged the firemen about and slit the hose pipes with their knives. The firemen were helpless; the bonfires went on flaming and sending up high into the air clouds of smoke and sparks. . . ." During the course of the evening, "I separated two fighting drunken men and got a bang on the ear from the fist of one of them, which was meant for the face of the other. It was a disgusting sight – two angry sullen drunken faces dripping blood from noses and lips." At least it stopped them fighting. He did not mention, of course, his companion, except obliquely at the end of this letter, "I have been dining out with pretty fashionable ladies a good deal, which Mummy thinks a waste of time and bad for me. But I enjoy good dinners and being listened to – though I am half inclined to think Mummy is right about it."[20]

Desmond escorted Cynthia home, walking all the way. She wrote that "It was about one I suppose. Desmond came in and raided the nursery for cake. He said 'good night darling – God bless you' and kissed my hand when he went," she noted meticulously in her diary.

In Hampshire, Molly and the children had "a most delicious Peace Day": they gathered wood to make a huge bonfire and put lights in every window of the house; through the leafless trees "the ships at sea saw our bonfire and our lighted house and kept sending up little red and green lights from their decks, like exclamations of joy," she wrote to Desmond. Soon the family was reunited at Wellington Square. Desmond continued to work at the Admiralty until the New Year, coping with arrears which had been put to one side during the pressure of the war. He continued to see Cynthia regularly and they both sought one another out, whether as guests of Sibyl Colefax at luncheon, or of Aubrey and Mary Herbert at Pixton, their house in the West country. It was not long before Desmond made his affection plain to her; he kept his declarations well within bounds, however, writing of her as "the most delightful angel of a friend" (25th November) to which she promptly replied in like manner: "You will never know how much of a *luxury* you are – because you couldn't be made to realize how much more like ponds with green bubbles on them people are in your absence than your presence. I despair of explaining this to you –

"Speaking as a pond you have made me so so much happier during the last months and *please* do in the coming ones too!"

Both used the romantic, artificial, teasing forms of address conventional between the sexes in the cultivated circles of Edwardian and early Georgian Society and which Cynthia, particularly, as a child of that world encouraged in her admirers.

Desmond was cautious – and wise to be; for when he did declare himself and hoped that Cynthia would reciprocate his feelings he was greeted with baffled silence: in matters of the heart she was, and knew herself to be, "as dumb as any fish or Cordelia". On 30th November she even wrote apologising for this, "I want to write *something* though I don't quite know *what*. To begin with I feel ashamed at having been so tongued-tied. . . . Dear Desmond, you have been such a blessed dear to me and I do *loathe* to think that I may only develop into a something which isn't worth while . . . just a disturbance. . . . In so far as you may be a moth and I may be a candle you can tell me to put myself out."

Desmond's reply of one line on 2nd December effectively cut through her somewhat nebulous self-searching – "My dear, don't put my candle out."

Desmond was sophisticated – and realistic – enough not to press his suit; he valued his close friendship with Cynthia too much to jeopardise it with unwanted declarations of love; but he long continued to use the same ritual vein of self-abasing gallantry in his letters to her (which makes them less interesting than his to Molly) to perpetuate the romantic fantasy which he, helped by Cynthia herself, had woven about her. Years later, in January 1944, he wrote to her: "When I think of the happiness you have brought into my life, I am grateful. I am so glad to have been in love with you."

15 Peace

The MacCarthys spent the first Christmas of peace with the Morrells at Garsington Manor. "Garsington certainly is an exciting house to arrive at on a winter's night for the first time," Desmond wrote to Cynthia on Christmas Eve. "A black, bitter cold drive, then a sudden stop in an elmy lane opposite high iron gates, and beyond them, between yew hedges nearly as high as the roof, an old dark house, looking deserted, with just a strip of ruby light showing where one of the double curtains is now drawn. Then the door opened and the children found themselves in a wonderful lacquered box, scarlet and gold, containing life size dolls in amazing dresses.

"Big tea – Pickwick read aloud – Gramophone – kind reception – surprising bedrooms (I fall into the Jingle style: he was in a chapter we came in for)."[1] But, Desmond told Antoinette Brett, "the conversation was not very good – too much back biting".[2] He took himself off on long walks across the wintry countryside. On Boxing Day the Asquith party drove over from The Wharf to look at the "Garsington Menagerie". The post-war General Election was then in progress, the results of which Desmond heard on his way to the west country where he was to spend the New Year with Aubrey and Mary Herbert at Pixton, where Cynthia and her family were also guests. When his train stopped at Taunton he heard that Aubrey Herbert was returned as M.P. and was "just beginning to think that life was after all right and jolly and to enjoy myself when other election results came in by telephone. Asquith out etc. This disgusted me very much and I keep thinking about it still. Though this is a C[onservative] U[nionist] house everyone is depressed about it." After thirty-one years in Parliament Asquith lost his seat, as did nearly all his close associates, and a great many of the Liberal M.P.s who had not thrown in their lot with Lloyd George during the war.

Soon Cynthia and Beb departed to join the crestfallen household at The Wharf (only somewhat crestfallen, however: Cynthia reported that Margot had been "dancing – like Salomé – before some rather astonished American strangers": she did not elucidate). In this same letter of 2nd January 1919, Cynthia told Desmond she was, as she had long hoped to be, pregnant "(that pink daughter I hope) and this gives me a certain placidity and sense of direction". Desmond wrote congratulating her on "the best thing that could have happened to you".

The effects of the war had been insidious; its ravages were not confined to those fighting at the front. Four years of worry and vicarious suffering told on Molly now. The war itself over, in 1919 the ordeal of peace began. She and the rest of the family now succumbed to the influenza epidemic which swept the world. Her health recovered, but her nerves did not. She looked behind and saw disappointment; she looked around and saw dragging responsibilities; she looked ahead – to poverty and disintegration. Desmond constantly reassured her of his devoted love for her and her alone: "Dearest I think of you often as I walk the streets, brush my hair, in the interstices of conversation and *pray* (if there were but a God!) that you may be relieved of these awful fits of angry despair. Please think well of me till we meet. Remember how good, how faithful, how ever near I am to you, how inseparable from you – no matter what happened or how I stray. Dearest – be good to me in your thoughts for your own sake," he wrote.[3]

Desmond had now to take stock of his life and to plan his future. He was forty-one, still with high literary ambitions and all too conscious of how much time he had wasted, how little solid writing he had achieved. It was now that Virginia Woolf wrote an account of his character in her diary: "How many friends have I got? There's Lytton, Desmond, Saxon; they belong to the Cambridge stage of life; . . . I cherish a considerable friendship for each of them"; she identified sympathy as Desmond's leading characteristic, but added that in describing him "one is almost forced to describe an Irishman: how he misses trains, seems born without a rudder to drift wherever the current is strongest; how he keeps hoping and planning, and shuffles along, paying his way by talking so enchantingly that editors forgive, and shopmen give him credit and at least one distinguished peer leaves him a thousand in his will."[*]

A few days later, Virginia continued her profile of Desmond in her diary for 18th February, "Where was I? Desmond, & how I find him sympathetic compared with Stracheys. It is true; I'm not sure he hasn't the nicest nature of any of us – the nature one would soonest have chosen for one's own. . . . I don't think that he possesses any faults as a friend, save that his friendship is so often sunk under a cloud of vagueness, a sort of drifting vapour composed of times & seasons separates us & effectively

---

[*] In fact Baron Lucas, who was killed in action in 1916, left money to three distinguished writers, who were also friends of theirs – to Belloc, Maurice Baring and Chesterton. There is a possibility that one of them, or even all, handed some of it as a present to the indigent MacCarthys although they were not mentioned in his will.

prevents us from meeting. . . . This arises from the consciousness which I find imaginative & attractive that things don't altogether *matter*. Somehow he is fundamentally sceptical. Yet which of us, after all, takes more trouble to do the sort of kindnesses that come his way? who is more tolerant, more appreciative, more understanding of human nature? It goes without saying that he is not an heroic character. He finds pleasure too pleasant, cushions too soft, dallying too seductive. . . ."

Virginia went on to wonder whether Desmond had ceased to be ambitious: "His 'great work' (it may be philosophy or biography now, & is certainly to be begun, after a series of long walks, this very spring) only [takes shape], I believe, in that hour between tea & dinner, when so many things appear not merely possible, but achieved. Comes the day light, & Desmond is contented to begin his article; & plies his pen with a half humorous half melancholy recognition that such is his appointed life."

She also recognised that "he has the floating elements of something brilliant, beautiful – some book of stories, reflections, studies, scattered about in him, for they show themselves indisputably in his talk." Even if "the disconnection of talk is kind to them" and "in a book they would drift hopelessly apart". Still, Virginia went on, "I can see myself however, going through his desk one of these days, shaking out unfinished pages from between sheets of blotting paper, & deposits of old bills, & making up a small book of table talk, which shall appear as a proof to the younger generation that Desmond was the most gifted of us all. But why did he never do anything? they will ask."[4]

This is a question which cannot be ignored in regard to Desmond's life. There are many reasons, but no one explanation. His reluctance to set down in writing what he felt it was within him to express was akin to his detachment from his domestic responsibility – which often seemed tantamount to refusing it. Far from lacking ambition, Desmond had been over-ambitious. He had set out not to write any novel but *the great novel*, to assume the mantle of Meredith, Hardy, Henry James. Similarly, his life of Donne, which he did not abandon until the 1920s, was to be a philosophical biography, spanning the history, literature and theology of the period. No wonder Desmond found his own targets daunting and, ultimately, unattainable. Besides, in the course of his extensive reading, note-taking and thinking he had gradually turned against the seventeenth-century poet and divine: "His religion seems to me a poor one, made out of terror and imaginative ecstasies. He loves Paradise, perhaps, but I can't see much love of God in him," he concluded.

His inhibition about writing was compounded by his having almost no sense of time. His readiness to be distracted led to a familiar pattern of disorganisation which necessitated extra work to cover his tracks and ate

into the empty tracts of time needed to think out and sustain a large
project. Virginia tellingly described a typical visit from Desmond in April
1919, when he spent the morning reading and talking to Leonard until the
Woolves eventually had to invent some excuse, for "without this dear old
Desmond would be smoking his cigarettes & talking about catching a
train in the arm chair opposite at this moment. As it was, he had
reluctantly to take himself off at lunchtime, & fling himself upon a world
of crowded trains, & accurate hours." Later she wrote: "I have just made
this beautiful image – how he is like a wave that never breaks, but lollops
one this way & that way & the sail hangs on ones mast & the sun beats
down – & its all the result of dining and sitting talking till 3 in the
morning with El[izabeth] Bibesco, with whom I had tea yesterday. . . ."[5]

Though Desmond was as talented as Virginia believed, were his gifts
the kind which could ever have made him a great author? Certainly he
had an extraordinary feel for words, was in love with them, quite as much
as G. E. Moore was in love with philosophy; but a love of words does not
in itself make an outstanding writer, any more than a love of art and
aesthetics made Roger Fry the great artist that he longed to be. Few critics
spent more time than Desmond in reading and thinking about books. He
absorbed literature as a cat laps up milk; and he was fascinated by human
nature, from eccentrics such as "The Owl" and G.A.P. to highly
intelligent friends like the Woolves or Belloc and to the chance
acquaintances he continued to make; but did this add up to having
something definite to say? He always felt that he had impressions of life
which were uniquely his own to impart to the world. Yet a clear theme, a
really strong plot, eluded him. His exceptional tolerance, his receptivity
to all experience must have complicated the task of expressing himself –
as did his deep-seated scepticism. On some matters, certainly, he knew his
mind, but he had little fixity of vision.

His fiction, when he did publish it – in the form of a dozen or so short
stories – fell far short of the artistic goals he had set himself. Centred
round some lesson about life and decorated with a few humorous
observations, they could have been, but for their more sophisticated
language, the work of an intelligent boy writing for his school magazine.
He destroyed his other efforts at fiction because they disappointed him. If
he had only shown some of them to friends like Virginia he might have
achieved a short book which would have boosted his confidence; or at
least it would have become clear to him, for once and for all, that his most
ambitious projects were unrealisable.

Some years later, when Virginia began to help him put together a book
from the great mass of his journalism – delving into "the filth packets" as
they called them – she lighted on his chief defect: "he can't thrust through

an article. Now, Lytton or I, though we mayn't think better or write better, have a drive in us, which makes an article whole."[6] She was right – many of Desmond's pieces tailed off at the end, as if he had run out of time – which was often the case. They had no more structure than his conversation. This was only a minor failing in a subtle and original journalist, but was incompatible with sustaining a full-length book. Desmond was essentially a "short-breath" writer, as David Cecil has observed. In his immediacy – his on-the-instant perception, his intimate and humorous charm – lay the genius of his talk and his criticism. It is striking how much less alive his criticism seems when read between hard covers than as a column in a newspaper.

Some essence of this, his real forte, has been preserved in the bound volumes of his journalism that appeared over the years that followed. Several of his selected essays, published in 1918, under the unappetising title, *Remnants*, were deservedly praised by Vernon Lee, who delivered her incisive critique with typical warmth and frankness: "Last night in bed I read your Voltaire, two Merediths, Shakespeare, Krüger and, oh my dear Desmond . . . I go about feeling so pleased that just you should have done anything so good . . . so full, steady, rich; absolutely clear and delicate in expression . . . as literature it is quite as good as Lytton Strachey (& you know that is saying a great deal) [*Eminent Victorians* had just been published] and being much more than literature it is better as literature." She added, however, that Desmond should drop the fanciful political and social *aperçus* which he had made part of his repertoire. Such essays were all very well for accomplished wits like Max Beerbohm, but Desmond's brand of humour was not of that kind – it was bound up with his power of sympathy: "you are serious; this is why you can be a real humorist, but not . . . an *amuseur* . . . where you don't feel, you are apt to be trashy (the price of having a heart is the inconvenience of *not* using it.")[7]

Desmond took her advice and thereafter wrote fewer of the flowery musings so fashionable early in the century, in favour of criticism and direct observation. The improvement was lasting. It is sad, therefore, that his career, distinguished as it ultimately was, disappointed him; that he always regarded it as a compromise, and a falling-off from his ideals as a young man. He deprecated himself so much in the hearing of his contemporaries that as a result they – Leonard Woolf, Roger Fry, Lytton Strachey and the others – took him at his own value. While admiring him as a perceptive critic, they, too, were inclined to belittle his career and to regard it as second-best compared with what he should have been doing, blaming it as a distraction from "real writing"; but in literature there is no "ought" or "should", save only to recognise one's limitations and one's strengths. In his failure to do this, Desmond was rather like his Irish grandfather, who sold off priceless land in Kensington, which would have earned the family a fortune in rent, and spent the proceeds on an unsuccessful lawsuit to recover worthless ancestral acres in County Clare.

Now in 1919, Molly was distraught and the bills were mounting. To placate the one and to pay the other Desmond had to undertake some immediate work. The family decided to retrench by moving to the country and letting Wellington Square. For the next six years, they rented a farmhouse at Oare, in Wiltshire. Home Farm, a traditional thatched dwelling, had neither running water nor electricity but, at £20 a year, it was cheap and suited the family life: the children could run straight out on to the chalk downs at the back, while the front was on a bus route to Pewsey and Marlborough nearby. There were congenial neighbours – the children were allowed to use the swimming pool and tennis court at the big house further down the village, and opposite Home Farm lived the diplomat Sydney Waterlow and his wife Margery. They were friends of the Woolves as of various others of the MacCarthy circle; when Molly moved in, Margery made up in neighbourliness what she lacked in sensitivity though it was hard to get over her habit of feeding hens from a large chamber pot left permanently in the middle of the Waterlows' lawn. Desmond never took to the harsh Wiltshire winters, referring always to the "Oarible weather" which greeted him whenever he came there, and he was reluctant to return from London as often as Molly would have liked.

As for work, Arthur Paley made Desmond a generous offer of £800 for ten weeks part-time work in South Africa as his amanuensis. During the war G.A.P.'s wife had left him, unable to live with his uncouth peculiarities any longer. Soon afterwards he picked up a former circus strong woman, Laure, an attractive-looking peasant girl from Jura who was availing herself of a flourishing wartime demand by prostituting herself on the Charing Cross Road. Her fondness for wrestling and her gifts as a cook suited him and he married her. However when he took her back to Ampton, the local Suffolk gentry and the household staff disapproved. Something had to go: Arthur decided it should be Ampton. So he sold the family estate and planned to settle permanently in the Karroo, to continue his farming scheme; but he had not abandoned his literary ambitions.

Because of the demand for shipping after the war, there was a delay in getting a passage to South Africa and so Desmond had to find what work he could to tide him over the summer of 1919. He therefore approached

C. P. Scott, the eminent editor of *The Manchester Guardian*, with the idea of going to Ireland and reporting on "the troubles" – the Irish war of independence – which were just beginning. As an Anglo-Irishman, he explained, he would have a dispassionate angle on the situation. He accepted Scott's small fee and set off for Dublin in May, working on his articles throughout the summer and going twice again for *The Guardian* in subsequent years.[8]

He was fascinated by the Irish cultural scene; less so by the politics, which he found disagreeable where he understood them. At first he leaned towards the rebels, as against the English authorities at Dublin Castle or those who advocated a compromise. Later, he came to understand how little liberalism and humanity counted in achieving the final breach with England. When a brutal civil war followed independence and the heroic national leader Michael Collins was murdered, Desmond was as repelled as he had been by British atrocities.

On his first post-war visit to Ireland he met many personalities who excited his curiosity. He saw Sir Horace Plunkett, the Irish statesman who sent him on to his fine eighteenth-century house in Merrion Square, Plunkett House, the headquarters of the moderate nationalist movement which he ran. There, on the top floor, Desmond was led into the presence of A. E. Russell, poet, mystic and painter, the soul and organiser of the Cooperative Movement. His office was a spectacle, the walls covered with visionary and sentimental frescoes, and a great litter of papers. Russell himself was big and stout, with "a touselled head and a brown beard clipped but allowed to sprout in all directions in the pointed Irish fashion". At the sight of him Desmond was reminded of both Bob Trevy and G. K. Chesterton and was strongly attracted. "A.E." was open-natured and unselfconscious, with G.K.C.'s powerful memory and gentle yet energetic volubility; he seemed, however, much more aware of Desmond's character than Chesterton would have been: "Though he has the same Troubadour method of discourse – as though he were throwing back a cloak and striking a guitar when he begins a subject, it is not nearly such a performance en l'air."

Desmond fled with relief to Russell's office on several occasions over the weeks that followed: "I said to A.E. the other day when I came up tired and distressed by the babel of voices and opinions heard and reheard all day: 'You are a comforting man.' For after talking to him for a few minutes, that distress which certain cock-sure acrid shrill fanaticism, both on the Sinn Fein side and in (Dublin) Castle opinion, had produced in me, began to melt away. It became easy to make allowances and it seemed unreasonable to despair." Desmond was impressed to find that the temperate orderliness of Plunkett House could co-exist happily with such

top left
Lord and Lady Asquith with
their son Anthony at The
Wharf 1923

top right
Elizabeth Bibesco, seen here in
the 1930's

left
Cynthia Asquith and admirers
at Stanway House: H.G. Wells
(on bended knee); Lord David
Cecil (behind), and L.P. Hartley

left
Philip Ritchie (This photograph
was sent to Molly after his death
by Roger Senhouse)

below
Molly and her children: Rachel,
Dermod, and Michael, 1918

a free spirit, working unhampered upstairs, on his highly effective campaign. During these relaxed hours together, the two men, inevitably, talked of their shared love of literature, and found they both had reservations about James Joyce's "ultra-modern writing". They remained fast friends.

Desmond went to see Maud Gonne, who had inspired the love poetry of W. B. Yeats: "You could guess how beautiful she had once been" he wrote to Antoinette Brett "and you were aware that you were in the presence of a large simple nature – too simple perhaps. I don't wonder that Yeats loved her."[9] It was a pilgrimage, for Desmond was an unqualified admirer of Yeats' poetic art. On the occasions when he had met Yeats in England, however, he had failed to establish any rapport with him: "he is too much of the hierophant, one does not talk with him so much as assist at a solemn incantation before an altar. Yet what an enormous respect I have for him! What a *sloven* that dearer, sweeter, larger nature, A.E., is compared with him!"

Desmond's exploration of the Irish character continued when he paid a visit, on his return to London, to George Moore, the Irish novelist whom he admired most of all. He already knew him well and he often discussed his novels with him. Desmond was keenly appreciative of Moore's superlative skill, developed over many years, as a stylist and story-teller. He was fascinated by his power to evoke a far-off place or time – whether Irish or Biblical or medieval – and by his clever deployment of detail to suggest the richness and complexity of a civilisation. He enjoyed the sensuality and the humour which underlay his carefully woven tales and his endless exploration of human motive. Yet he was quick to spot the writer's flaws and draw his attention to preciosities or unnatural expression, for he found that, egoistic though Moore was, his dedication to his art was greater than his vanity. Later Moore paid him the compliment of "reorchestrating" his novel, *The Brook Kerith* in a new edition, to meet the criticisms Desmond had raised years before, when the book first appeared in 1916. He sent Desmond a copy "in remembrance of a well merited rebuke".

Later, he introduced him as one of the interlocutors in his book *Conversations at Ebury Street* (1924). Desmond was not displeased "at finding myself embalmed, even as a rather fatuous figure" as he put it, fretting about Moore's distaste for Thomas Hardy.[10]

Desmond usually found him much easier to talk to – and more intelligent – than Yeats, though Moore was notoriously daunting and contemptuous. When Desmond called at his little terraced house in Ebury Street, in September 1919, he found the going hard. The old man – while seeming far from old, "A beaming childlike smile of mingled innocence

and slyness removed all trace of age" – proved argumentative on the
subject of Irish politics which, as Desmond told Cynthia, was "a surface
smeared with cobbler's wax – and having sat on it, we stuck. G.M. has his
own solution. He was very anxious I should adopt it and promulgate it.
(Call up to your mind's eye that old white cockatoo, alternately frowning
till his eyes disappear and opening them in a round innocent stare, waving
slowly the while a pale plump hand while his elbow rests on the arm of his
chair – both gesture and stare expressing a suave astonishment that
people should not see how absurdly simple it all is.)" Moore recommended a huge Atlantic port at Galway and a tunnel between Ireland and
Scotland, so that Ireland could for the first time truly taste the benefits of
Union with Britain. The result would be prosperity and no more talk of
separation. The air was finally cleared, however, when they came to
discuss the Catholic/Protestant situation. "I used the phrase 'The Catholic
Mind'. At this the cockatoo became intensely excited, 'The Catholic
Mind! ! ! ! There isn't such a thing! They haven't got any minds! No
Catholic has a *mind*. You can't see God turned into a cup of wine and a
biscuit every morning and keep a mind. It destroys the mind!' We roared
with laughter – I half agree, you know. It is certainly shockingly bad for
the mind."[11]

Desmond's fortunes finally revived at the end of 1919, when Jack Squire
left the *New Statesman* to found his own journal and Desmond was
offered his job as Literary Editor. Before this, however, he had to spend a
typically eccentric autumn with his old friend G.A.P. on the South African
Karoo.

16 "Pincher" Passes Away

Desmond sailed to South Africa in September 1919 on a little tramp steamer – the only berth he had been able to acquire – which was shipping everything from salt to drain pipes. Of the few passengers two were old sea-dogs going out to take command of sailing-ships: "they belong to the age of Smollett," in their drinking habits and conversation, which was of a staggering obscenity. "I have never heard anything like it," Desmond wrote, "not even at Eton. Finally, I had to protest. I said, 'Captain Deaks, when I was your age (he is by the bye over 50) and we were all boys together, we used to think a good deal about those subjects, but not *incessantly*'." This gave rise to tremendous hilarity on the part of the old sea dog who greeted Desmond every morning thereafter with "Hi! Mr. MacCarthy come and tell us what you used to think about when you were my age."[1]

After an uncomfortable journey, Desmond landed at Cape Town to find a characteristic muddle had been made: the telegram announcing "Desmond sails" had been transmitted as "Desmond fails" and the Paleys had not expected his arrival; but he did meet up with them, and they all embarked across the "brown lion-coloured stony land" to the Karoo. Imagine, Desmond wrote to Cynthia, Paley's bungalow isolated on the vast stony plain, surrounded by fort-shaped hills; a herd of horses kicked up the dust; further off was a Kaffir village, "and every evening, over this scene, you must imagine (as best you can) the most overwhelming apocalyptic sunsets – seas of glory, palaces of splendour, aerial perspectives suggesting a yonder beyond all ends, levels of liquid light, of tenderest amethyst and green and rose . . . Then, turn your attention to the verandah where three figures are lying in long cushioned chairs – D.M., The Grand Lunar* [his nickname for G.A.P.] and Laure Paley (the latter a large broad-shouldered woman, petulant and abrupt in manner, who is ripping up a blouse as though she hated it and screaming for the black maid from time to time like a parrot, 'Le-ah, Le-ah'). At their feet lies a confusion of papers – old Sketches, Tatlers, Times, Daily Mirrors,

---

* The name of the leader of the Selenites, in H. G. Wells' *The First Men on the Moon*.

etc. The Grand Lunar, a handkerchief tied round his neck, a pipe in the corner of his mouth, stares with his prominent nervous blue eyes straight in front of him. D.M. I can't describe – I am only aware of two changes in him – that he is burnt brown and has a moustache, like two rampant minnows one each side of his nose." G.A.P. presented an even more eccentric spectacle than usual: in the broiling sun, his skin had peeled and "hangs in tatters like a wallpaper which workmen are stripping before painting."[2]

Even by Paley's standards, the bungalow was chaotic, the poky rooms crammed with bulky furniture and family portraits shipped out from Ampton Hall when it was sold. Nothing worked properly: the beautiful old clocks did not tell the time; all kinds of silver, bottles, trays, were littered about, but no water tumbler was in Desmond's bedroom; there were looking-glasses of all sizes, but sprinkled with bird droppings and out of their frames, so Desmond propped one up in order to shave. It reminded him of one of the half-plundered houses he had seen in France, where troops bivouacked among rich clutter before marching on.

G.A.P.'s huge book on Social Questions was "as out of date as Newton's on Pentateuch Chronology to deal with. I am ripping it up and stitching at it in the same kind of furious impatience that Laure exhibits when she overhauls her own wardrobe. On the top of that he is writing a Detective Story – with psychological sauce!" This was equally impossible, and, though Desmond did his best to suggest ideas, neither book was publishable and this was the last time Desmond was employed to make them so. "I am not happy," he confessed, "but to say I was miserable would be absurd. The Grand Lunar and I have a childish antediluvian immovable affection for each other."[3]

At the beginning of December he was relieved to embark from Cape Town back to his family at Home Farm.

That wet and windy Christmas Eve, Molly and the children listened impatiently for the village taxi to draw up outside the little iron gate: at last it arrived and they flung themselves at Desmond. Then Molly gave a horrified cry, "'Des – how terrible! No! I really can't bear it.' 'Why? What's the matter?' we cried." The "rampant minnows" as Desmond had described his moustache, were not a success. By Christmas Day they were off, remembered Rachel.

As they grew up, Desmond and Molly's children, strongly individual, affectionate and humorous, were the greatest pleasure to them: Desmond encouraged Dermod's interest in anatomy, and Michael's in the countryside and in animals, which foreshadowed their careers in medicine and in farming. In a household crammed with books, the children read widely, but theirs was not a rarefied home education, as Molly's had been.

The MacCarthy children were unimpressed by the endless flow of conversation from their parents' literary friends – conversation in which children had no part: "When the children come, *always go!*" Rachel, to her indignation, heard Lytton Strachey exclaim in his high-pitched voice with its exaggerated "Bloomsbury" intonation – a remark directed not at the MacCarthy family in particular, but at the whole species of infants.[*4]

But such figures as Lytton, with his falsetto tones and drooping beard were the source of much amusement to the children, too. So was Bob Trevy, now a fully fledged eccentric who embarrassed friends by bathing naked and by his primitive eating habits. "Spearnose," or "the Mandrill" (Virginia Woolf's nickname), so called because of his projecting features and uncouth ways, would often arrive unannounced on the MacCarthys' doorstep in London. If he found Desmond, the two would spend hours playing chess and giggling over their memories of Cambridge life; but even if their father were away, Bob would submit the children – and Molly – to his unstoppable monologues, in his loud, harsh voice. "Mandrill trouble" became a family phrase for having to deal with an importunate, though in this case lovable, caller.

For all their parents' affection, the children could not but be aware of their constant anxiety about money. As the eldest, it was Michael, particularly, who bore the brunt of this, as well as of Chen's remorseless agitation over every detail of his upbringing. As a result he became reserved: "Michael appears as hard as an unripe apple but he is really most sensitive," remarked his father; Desmond understood how awkward children could feel, and did his best to talk to his eldest son, to make him "less jerky and farouche ... O my dear what an anxious relation parenthood is! I don't know that it is true that I *love* my children more than I love anybody else, but when anything goes wrong with them the clutch at one's heart is mortal."[5]

Cut off from civilisation as he had been for so long with the Paleys, Desmond was happy to find himself once more within it, but he resolved to "let sleeping friends lie". "Have you heard the sad news?" he wrote to Antoinette Brett. "Poor Pincher passed away in South Africa."[6] In particular, the closeness between Desmond and Cynthia diminished. She had been suffering from depression, partly post-natal – she had a son, Simon, in August – partly a result of the sorrows of the war. Each morning "was like being strapped on to a rack for the day". She had written pitifully, "I really can't afford the luxory [sic] of Neurasthenia & I have always had a contempt for women with 'nerves'." She was oppressively conscious of her responsibility as the mother of three little

---

[*] Michael Holroyd's version of this (*Lytton Strachey* Vol. 2 p. 23) is: "'When Lytton comes', Desmond MacCarthy used to tell his wife, 'the children must go'."

boys, who were people, not creatures stuck away in a nursery: she had had to come to terms with the fact that her eldest son, John, was mentally abnormal.[7] This, too, filled her with anxiety for his future. Desmond, extremely sympathetic, wrote to her at length, to help her to find the necessary detachment to live with this anguish: "Keep your heart for life," he advised, "if you do, if you defend your own life as you have been doing, in what you do for John will be a sweetness and satisfaction there could not otherwise be, and if you think of yourself (it sounds a paradox) you will also think more disinterestedly about him."

Their former intimacy was never recaptured: her depression, from which she took a long time to recover, and the increasingly central role which J. M. Barrie played in her life, and she in his, combined to distance them. Their relationship, Desmond wrote wistfully in the summer of 1920, drifted inexorably "from the good the true and the beautiful towards the ordinary". The swirl of their lives meant they could not spend long periods of time together: "Perhaps," he went on significantly, "you have spoilt me in the past, doing so much of the arranging and planning and ringing up, so that I grew to expect you would do it *all*, and when you could not do that any longer owing to the exigencies of your life, I, against my reason, felt it like a coldness. . . . Then, I have made great efforts in our relation to sink the He and She . . . in doing so, I extinguished that ardour which is best able to melt reserve and make even 10 minutes to bear fruit in intimacy; . . . Then I began to realize that in the part in your life to which I had confined myself I was no longer without a rival. In Barrie you had that kind of loving, considerate intimately appreciative friend, and not only could he be far more useful but he had oceans of time in which to make you aware of what he was to you and you to him. No woman *needs* two Barries or two Desmonds, though she may hate losing one of them."[8]

Desmond accurately remarked that Cynthia was reluctant to lose him as an admirer; but so conscientious had he been at sinking "the He and She" between them, that in the process, his own feelings had gone off the boil. They remained friends, but he regretted the passing of a passion which had illuminated the last despairing months of the war.

Molly had been irritated by his friendship with Cynthia, writing bitterly to him that "Desmond cares only for women in silk and velvet who run about in a hungry rush and flatter him – he despises the humdrum – and so life has become horrible for Molly – and all is vanity." She was convinced that he squandered money on Cynthia; but he was not extravagant – except with his time; he enjoyed spending long hours with her and writing his thoughts and ideas on literature to her; this made their correspondence less intimate, but it was regular enough to incense Molly – more than the letters, fond, but not loverlike, warranted. On one of Cynthia's letters she scribbled "*Dishonourable* correspondence dishonourably read by Molly (sufferer) on April Fool's Day" and added a squiggle in the shape of a furious spider, while to Antoinette Brett she declared that one day she would write a pamphlet about "Pincherism: its cause and cure, and dedicate it to Antoine Bibesco, Cynthia Asquith, Mrs Colefax, Violet Bonham-Carter."[9]

Though "Pincher" had gone adventuring to fashionable hearths, he had not abandoned well-loved old ones. When G. E. Moore called on him unexpectedly in London, even though "we had not met for a year and only written one letter each, yet it might have been we had been talking all night, and he, having risen earlier, had come in to see me dress. With one who is 'dans le vrai' the splinters keep so fine and fresh – a touch and they unite again. And when he was lounging sideways on the settee, comfortable, ungainly, plump, like a small sea-lion that has flopped upon a shelf of rock, we talked as we used to talk at Cambridge. . . .

"I thought of my letters and invitations downstairs, representative, some of them, of such dubious and faked relationships; thought how often from love of excitement or vanity I had put such ones before those with people tried and trusted." If Desmond had hopes of resting in the bosom of the unchanging past, however, he was mistaken; for at the age of forty-three G. E. Moore had married, in 1916, an undergraduate at Newnham twenty years his junior. She had given birth to their son two years later. When he visited George and Dorothy Moore at Cambridge for the first time since the war, Desmond was depressed, both by the domestication of his old friend and teacher and "because it was borne in on me . . . that I now belong to senior Cambridge. My place is on the Dais, well up at the high table," he wrote to Cynthia. Moore's home life struck Desmond, who had retained many of his bachelor traits despite years of marriage, as "a closed little place with a door to it which shuts behind me when I go. As I walked moodily back from supping with him an hour ago, . . . walked do I say? – dragged my feet with cannon balls round the ankles and with a head of feathers and a heart of lead! He has a splendid pink and white Rubens baby and a short robust quiet wife. He adores the cherub with a beautiful tenderness, tending it, feeding it, playing with it, smiling and nodding at it with the most delicious complacency for hours together. But I remember a summer evening when the King's Parade was full of loiterers and we two walking through them in a bubble of thought of our own blowing, quite alone in it, and talking about the things in life which are most excellent, what they were. 'And children?' said I, 'What about the relation of father and child' – 'O there are better things than that.' And so there were – then. *Then* – then and now, then and now – that is the contrast which has been exhausting me to-day." Their friendship was too deep-rooted, however, to be extinguished by Moore's innocent marital happiness and once Desmond had become used to the change, their pleasure in each other's company continued as before.

Whilst on his visit to Cambridge, Desmond had supper in Maynard Keynes' rooms: "we supped 13. Vanessa Bell the solitary woman, but not infectiously conscious of her sex, streams of young men till 3 in the morning" – but Desmond felt himself an outsider at revels of which he could not see the point: he described to Lady Cynthia the "tobacco, talk and laughter and Sheppard the professor of Greek at Kings playing the fool in a wild heartbroken way like a Dostoievsky character. Suddenly he stopped in his clowning and shouted, 'I have been going on to find out who here is shocked by me. I know now – it is Desmond.' Sensation – animated discussion if D was in the habit of only pretending to be shocked or being easily shocked and pretending not to be, on which I could throw very little light. I could not speak the truth which was that I was not shocked, but that I did not think Sheppard funny! I was afraid he might cry if I did."[10]

If visits to Cambridge depressed Desmond, much worse was the one he paid to the Isle of Wight where Reymond Abbot was now living at Ventnor in a half-furnished house with a half-mad housekeeper; "The Owl" hooted reproachfully at Desmond, blaming him for his loneliness; for the uninvigorating air, for the deterioration in his health: "the desolation of the Owl chills my heart and frightens me," Desmond told Molly; but even this twilight friendship survived; and over the years Abbot acquired a deceptive air of eminence – so much so, that just before the Second World War Desmond's brother-in-law, Admiral Sir William Fisher, felt he could with credibility do the old man the kindness of inviting him to inspect his flagship.

A link with the island, and with the past century, was severed with the death at Freshwater of Molly's Aunt Anny, Thackeray's daughter, in February 1919, aged eighty-one. Desmond felt, as did many, that the war had brought the curtain down finally on the Victorian period with its certainties and confidence and a more troubled age was now beginning.

Desmond, sometimes with Molly, sometimes without, was still a frequent guest at The Wharf. They also stayed with the painter Ethel Sands at Newington, nearby. Although she, with "her large perfect pearls, her large perfect teeth, her black eyes, and white dress, her kindness, her smile, her fine sense of honour, her air of being out of the battle and being ready just to be kind, in that large stone-grey house, so perfect in every respect, filled me with a wistful sense of rest – &

dissatisfaction," wrote Desmond who preferred the vivid eccentricity of such unattached females as the author Vernon Lee, trying though she sometimes was.[11]

Newington, though undoubtedly the house of an artist, was too perfect; other visitors besides Desmond and Molly noted its carefully arranged colours: Vanessa Bell's eye had been irked by its "fatal prettiness". There are photographs of Desmond and Molly taken during various "harmless idle dainty week-ends" they spent there, looking unanimated even in such distinguished company as that of W. B. Yeats. They were neighbours of Ethel Sands in Chelsea, where she also lived, and Wellington Square benefited from her generosity when she gave the MacCarthys a pair of handsome curtains, dark green with pink tassels. She was a punctilious hostess in The Vale, where the house which she shared with her companion, Nan Hudson, was decorated with mosaics by Boris Anrep, and hung with Sickert's pictures.

It was now that Molly gathered together a group of close friends, a variant on the Novel Club she had started before the War. The Memoir Club would meet regularly, in London, to read papers which were generally, though not necessarily autobiographical. Their one criterion was that they should be absolutely truthful – that characteristic upon which "Bloomsbury" always prided itself. Molly's creation was a long-standing success: the Memoir Club lasted until the mid 'Fifties, by which time the second generation of members had been elected. It was of wider significance than just as a group of old friends, for it was one of the ways in which the "Bloomsbury group" defined itself. It also served as a means by which they met regularly and maintained their friendships. Even when she was staying at Oare, Molly came to London to organise and attend meetings. The papers which this highly original, intelligent and articulate group produced were diverse: some were unexpectedly dull, such as an interminable discourse by E. M. Forster upon his aunts in Weybridge, others were just unexpected, such as the "paper" Desmond "read" from behind the open lid of his attaché case which was revealed to be empty and the "paper" to be an extempore delivery.[12]

Molly sent out invitations to the first meeting of the Memoir Club to be held in Desmond's study at Wellington Square. "The Members at present are:

Roger Fry	Mary [Mrs. St. John Hutchinson]
Desmond	Sidney Waterlow
Vanessa	Clive Bell
Duncan	Maynard Keynes
Bertrand Russell	

3 more will be elected at the 1st meeting. It is a secret club," she wrote to Mary Hutchinson.[13] Bertrand Russell appears never to have come to any meetings, and the original members also included Leonard and Virginia Woolf, for they dined with the MacCarthys beforehand on Thursday 4th March 1920 and Virginia described the "highly interesting occasion" in her diary.

Seven people, not including Leonard and Virginia, read on that occasion: starting with Sidney Waterlow, going on to Clive, Vanessa, Duncan, who was "fantastic and tongue – not tied – tongue enchanted" and Roger Fry. Molly discoursed on her family: she was "carefully composed at first, & even formal; suddenly saying 'Oh this is absurd – I can't go on' shuffling all her sheets; beginning on the wrong page; firmly, but waveringly, & carrying through to the end." The tone of it was that in place of "these mild weak Cornishes", her antecedents, she wanted "to be the daughter of a French marquise by a misalliance. . . ."[14]

It was the first of many happy, stimulating evenings; having started tentatively, the club gathered momentum over the years, and its members produced a marvellous variety of papers, from Clive Bell's account of dallying with one of his first mistresses, to Maynard Keynes' reminiscence of the Paris peace conference. That summer of 1920 Desmond read another instalment of Molly's autobiography for her as she was in Oare and found it impossible to return to London for the meeting. His letter telling her of its success conveys admirably the atmosphere of the meetings:

"My darling Moll, Your Memoir was a tremendous success. I am to convey to you the congratulations of the whole club. All the funny bits were greeted with laughter & it was agreed that the picture of the home & the atmosphere of the time were admirably done. I felt very proud of you & I enjoyed reading it *enormously*. I began, as you would have done, by breaking down after the first sentence & saying it was impossible to read a word more – as it was too stupid. I tried to do this in your voice & with one of your desperate gestures. Maynard was very interesting. Both he & Clive stopped like serial writers at the thrilling point. Maynard's fragment was an account of a journey with Foche [sic] to meet the German delegates & next time he promises us – revelations! Clive stopped on the threshold of his first amour – the one with Mrs Raven Hill. The beginning of his fragment was a little mannered & *affektiert*, but it became interesting. Duncan's ancestral stories were a queer fascinating muddle. Clive proposed that the practical writers (the novelists) should alone read because they enjoyed writing & reading aloud, while the others (himself modestly included) should listen. This proposal was, however, rightly vetoed. 'It was agreed that everyone should be obliged to read in their turn.' Your memoir was the triumph of the evening, though all were accounted good & the meeting was a great success."[15]

Molly's memoirs were eventually published; Virginia Woolf was encouraging about them, suggesting that she should submit them to *The Nation*, of which Leonard had just been made literary editor: "A little comb and brush is all that's needed. You know how Clive conceals his bald patch? Well, that's how to treat your memoirs."[16] *The Nation* brought them out between September 1923 and June 1924 and then they were published as a book by Heinemann, entitled *A 19th Century Childhood*.

Like her novel, *A Pier and a Band*, Molly's memoirs are entertaining and unpretentious; they are an evocative and exact description of growing up in an eccentric but happy household in the last years of Victoria's long reign. Desmond once again appears as "Fitzgerald", the favourite escort of Molly and her sister in London at the turn of the century: "He seems to have unlimited time, and though he strolls through life as if it were a vast exhibition, at any booth of which he can tarry as long as it pleases his fancy, he never appears in the least demoralized by leisure; though there are grave head-shakings over his 'career'. Everyone may be concerned about him, but he quietly goes his own way." Fitzgerald freed the Warre-Cornish sisters from "the pressure of social primness" and its artificial, conventional restraints.

Molly's book was greatly appreciated at its first publication and a quarter of a century later, in an introduction to a new edition, John Betjeman wrote of "the insinuating charm" of its style. It was set apart from other "charming" memoirs of the period because, said Betjeman, it was written "as a true poet writes true poems, not for self-glory or money but for love of doing it . . ."

Betjeman also appreciated Molly's use of English and noted, as Virginia Woolf had too, her idiosyncratic prose rhythms, which she varied as the moment demanded: "With unerring dexterity she knows when to walk, when to soar, when to stop and talk, when to run, so that the quiet journey is always varied."

By the time the book was published, the central character of Molly's girlhood who gave it so much of its comedy and eccentricity was dead: her mother, Blanche, died in August 1922, at the age of 74. This added piquancy to Molly's descriptions of her – relentlessly romantic, idealistic, vague and spiritual. She recalled Blanche sitting out on "the leads", the roof outside the drawing-room window at the Cloisters, of a summer evening while Maurice Baring read Ronsard aloud, and every moth and insect in the Thames Valley fluttered about their lamp. Such heightened moments of romance were lost beyond recall when Molly described them in the 'Twenties; they belonged to another world – as had Blanche herself.

17   "Affable Hawk"

Money continued to be short for the MacCarthy family, despite Desmond's job on *The New Statesman* and his work for other journals. There was never enough for the school fees of Michael, now boarding at Dauntsey's School in Wiltshire, Dermod, who went to Gresham's School, Holt, and Rachel attending a London day school: a parent, wrote Molly, "practically has to go into lodgings while his child has white flannel trousers and a little Gladstone bag and all the rest of it."[1]

Chen's generosity was patchy and always accompanied by such vindictive lectures that Molly and Desmond hesitated to approach her over money. Now in her late sixties she was as trying as ever. In 1922, she decided to enter the Roman Catholic Church, and Desmond hinted that this might enable her to see things in more proportion: "Think what happy and successful lives we have really had, how satisfactory the children are and what a full life in spite of lack of money." He encouraged her "to try to combine your ever youthful responses *somehow* with the wise detachment of old age!"[2]

He urged in vain. Meeting her at tea with Molly in January 1924 Virginia Woolf found her "the most arrant & pernicious bore in the world; like a child, but not to be put down; insisting on her story being heard; utterly unable to see beyond her own plate of bread & butter; must know what kind of jam it is."[3]

Chen was now settled in an ugly mansion block just off the Edgware Road, well to the north of the park but rejoicing in the name of Hyde Park Mansions, liver-coloured apartment buildings wrapped in ineffable clouds of gloom. Here she lived with whatever servant would put up with her neurotic interference in every aspect of domestic life; and from here she penned her daughter-in-law pages and pages upon such subjects as Rachel's knicker-elastic and Michael's growing up a hobbledehoy if he did not go to school with little gentlemen – that is, boys from rich and smart homes.

Molly endured these as best she could; she had long since learnt to keep on neutral topics and to hide from Chen the truth about the family's financial perils – such as the occasion in September 1921 when the bailiffs came to Wellington Square because of arrears of Income Tax.

In a letter to Vanessa Bell Molly made light of it – non-payment of tax being, of course, more respectable than of a common bill, "I came fluttering downstairs like Mrs Micawber, grandly holding my cheque book with the self assurance of a millionaire inclined to be vague about trifles. But they would not take my cheque." They wanted cash, by the evening, and in the meantime they catalogued all the effects in the house; fortunately there was just enough money in the bank, and Molly went and drew it out: "and at 6 one of the bailiffs with a *short thick stick* and a cynical smile came back to fetch it! I felt very sordid and depressed after he had gone – in spite of having carried it off with high handed nonchalance." It was too near the feckless Bohemianism Molly dreaded.[4] As a result of the bailiffs' visit Molly realised she had to take the drastic step of once more letting the house in Wellington Square and moving the family into bleak lodgings at Ladbroke Grove, Notting Hill.

Molly reckoned she saved £75 by letting the house for the winter; but at what a cost in terms of their marriage! She dreaded driving Desmond away by her nagging and was equally worried that if she did not keep on at him he would fritter away his time while the unpaid bills mounted. She reckoned that they needed £800–1,000 a year clear to live comfortably at Wellington Square with the minimum domestic help to run that tall old house with its few conveniences. Their income was several hundred pounds short of that. It fell to Molly to do the household accounts and, even taking the greatest possible care, if she was out by so much as £15 for an overlooked Rates Bill, then woe betide her!

Although the MacCarthys could not entertain very much, they continued to be invited to stay away, with the Asquiths at The Wharf and the Morrells at Garsington, for instance, and to dinner with friends like Virginia and Leonard Woolf. It was at the Woolfs' house in Richmond in May 1921 that the experiment of recording Desmond's conversation, unbeknownst to him, was tried. Desmond told Cynthia that he was dining with "the Weir [sic] Wolves – carrying my own wine" and Roger Fry also came, "loaded with bottles of Chablis", he said.

We had a most successful party last night," Fry wrote to Vanessa Bell on 20th May. Leonard's secretary "Miss Green (whom Virginia calls the chest of drawers – it's a terribly exact description) managed to take it all down. I'm sure Desmond suspected nothing."[5]

Although Desmond talked well and fluently, according to Miss Green's account it was not interesting, but then was Miss Green (plain, high-minded and not noted for her sparkling conversation) a good judge? The record of the evening does not unfortunately survive, but Virginia Woolf herself, two years later in July 1923, wrote down some of what was said when Desmond came to visit them at teatime: Leonard was then literary editor of *The Nation* and Desmond was in the same position on *The New Statesman*, using the pen-name, "Affable Hawk":

"Desmond asked whether anyone had seen Murry's *Adelphi* magazine?

"Have you read Murry 'I have been a miserable sinner (acting & striking his breast). I have lied, I have swindled. I have laughed at what I love; but *now* I am speaking the truth.' He's like a revivalist preacher. . . .

"V. I don't object to opening the heart, but I do object to finding it empty. Murry has nothing whatever to reveal. Yet he has sold his reticence. . . . I say Desmond, whatever the reason may be, the Hawk gets daily better & better. It's never been so good. People talk about the Hawk: about reading the paper for the Hawk.

"Des. Oh come Virginia, it wasn't as bad as all that before!"[6]

The truth was that from the beginning, in early 1920, Desmond had set a mark on the literary pages of *The New Statesman* which was decidedly his own. His influential editorial column, which he wrote weekly under the pen-name "Affable Hawk", gave him an opportunity to mingle his views on literature with those on life and to draw from his abundant memory. On the death of the poet Wilfred Blunt, he was able to write a commemorative piece describing him: "All the objects which surrounded him roused a romantic curiosity: the obsolete long gun above the mantelpiece; the portrait of the poet himself painted by himself at the age of 14 . . . the beaded camel-charms; ostrich eggs; blazing blue butterflies; bunches of immortelles; the Botticelli tapestry as fresh in colour as when it came off William Morris's looms . . . the freakish and fastidious collection of books; and last, but not least, the magnificent romantic old sheikh himself, asleep, beard on breast, in his chair opposite me. He was a very vain man, but what is rare in the vain, extremely dignified; theatrical, but with far more taste and discretion than Byron."[7]

It was Desmond's imagination and erudition, rather than his openness to the latest developments, which made him outstanding as a critic: the publication of a translation of Proust or Tolstoy: the appearance of a new book on Shakespeare, or Thomas Love Peacock; a novel by George Moore – all these would provoke an illuminating plunge into literary history, reminiscence and philosophical discussion; he was sometimes over-discursive – a rival critic, Frank Swinnerton, spoke slightingly of "his yards, my inches" – but always humorous, unexpected and cosmopolitan.

The 'Twenties were years of revolutionary change and experiment in the arts and literature; this stretched back before 1914 but seemed now to break on the world with tidal force, as the old sea walls of artistic convention collapsed. It was a cultural world being reshaped by Freud and

T. S. Eliot, by modern technology and Bauhaus architecture. Forms of expression and the very meaning of words were questioned in new poetry, fiction and criticism. Traditional morality and family ties were dropped by many in the search for new ideals: Communism, sun-worship, earth-worship, free-love and free expression of all kinds.

Desmond read T. S. Eliot's new critical paper, *Criterion*, with interest when it appeared in 1922 and for all his own mockery he had some respect for Middleton Murry's *Adelphi*,[8] in which Murry expressed his imaginative though often cranky views. However, the avant-garde was not a milieu in which Desmond felt at home. Young authors who belonged stylistically to a classical tradition, like Evelyn Waugh and, later, Christopher Isherwood, he could praise without reserve; but where the writer was experimental in form and outlook, he was rarely receptive. He also felt profoundly that those authors who ignored the meaning· of words while expecting to be treated seriously, like Edith Sitwell, were guilty of a kind of blasphemy. He attacked the slavish reverence for fashion which led critics to sing the praises of Gertrude Stein:

"Miss Stein is not to be blamed for indulging in automatic writing. I remember once composing a piece of prose under the influence of gas, which struck me as singularly beautiful. Alas, only the last cadences could be recaptured on waking: 'I prefer snails. Long may they continue, those black, blithering and blasted animals, to salt the rainy ground of virtue.' However, even as I remembered those words, they seemed to lose their magic significance. I was not to blame for having composed them, but if my friends had persuaded me to mesmerise myself back into the state in which that sort of stuff is produced, and if, when I wrote a thousand pages of it down, they persuaded me that I was doing service to art by publishing it, they would be very much to blame indeed."[9]

A more serious deficiency in his sympathies showed in his ready dismissal of those who set themselves to explore the subconscious. Awareness of its influence was one thing; but it was bad art, he argued, to linger in that murky underworld. An admirer of Joyce's early work, he was repelled by *Ulysses*, which he thought a confused failure.[10] For different reasons, he also disliked Virginia Woolf's "stream of consciousness" technique. Of her novels, he used to say that she could evoke very well the sensation of a train passing, the wind buffeting the watcher standing near the track; but she would not describe the train itself, which interested him more. He preferred a book with strong characterisation, a rational, detailed analysis of motive, and a story line. Desmond's qualified appreciation of her novels was a cause of tension between them, disturbed as she was by *all* critics.

As an editor, Desmond was frequently disorganised; and like "Mr Ossory", A. G. Macdonell's amusing caricature portrait of him, in the novel, *England Their England*, he was very much dependent on his secretary for seeing off unwelcome callers and for pulling together his work on "those awful literary supplements" which the paper put out periodically: "she would stay with me till after eleven at night, doing my work with me, seeing that Edmund Gosse did not figure as Edmund Goose and that other hardly less disastrous errors were avoided."[11]

Accuracy as well as punctuality were often problems to him. Despite his enormous literary knowledge he could misquote even well-known lines: "I know a bank where (whereon) the wild thyme blows," and "oh what a base (rogue) and peasant slave am I." On one occasion he confused George Villiers, Duke of Buckingham, with John Sheffield, Duke of Buckingham, and wrote a review attributing a play to the wrong duke.[12] Arnold Bennett watched fussily over The *New Statesman* which he largely financed, and was quick to point out even minor misprints.[13]

The fundamental cause of Desmond's more slapdash habits was not so much his social life as the amount of work he had to undertake to supplement his meagre income from *The New Statesman*. In the mid-twenties he became, simultaneously, the literary editor of *The Empire Review*, which earned him £300 a year; a reader for Heinemann's, the publishing house; a contributor to the socialist *Daily Herald*, to *The World's Work*, to the American press and, anonymously, to *The New Statesman*'s rival, *The Nation*; and a pioneer broadcaster for the BBC.

His "Affable Hawk" page was prestigious, but a tie; over the period 1920 to 1928, he averaged 51 "Affable Hawks" a year and could only get away for a holiday by writing several at a time. He tried, yet again, to write a full-length book, this time on Byron, a more popular subject than Donne. He failed, but his Byron notes were the basis of the Clark Lectures which he gave at Cambridge in April and May 1929.

In spite of all this work, the debts continued. "I shall have to go on scribbling three articles a week to the end of my days," he grumbled to Lytton Strachey. "It seems sometimes an intolerable life; and to say farewell to the last chance of writing anything which can have value in my own eyes is to part with hope, vague enough in my case, which nevertheless makes journalism bearable."[14]

Falling in with Lytton's own style, he over-dramatised; in fact he enjoyed his work. As reviews editor, his choice of contributors was interesting and frequently original; they included Hilaire Belloc, Leonard Woolf, Lytton Strachey and Clive Bell. He tended not to select specialists unless they were entertaining writers. However, he always favoured those whom he spotted working diligently on their reviews at the London library, as he himself did. That private lending library, a tranquil pool of civilisation in the heart of the West End, was one of his favourite haunts, where he learned endlessly by browsing: "Where else in the world is there a library of that size where one has free access to the shelves? How much knowledge of at any rate *where* to seek for information as for pleasure, I have got by merely wandering about those steel catacombs, pulling out a book here and there and glancing at it, or taking it down to the reading room! How steadying it has been to my sense of proportion as a critic!"[15]

He attracted some notable authors of short stories and poetry, such as Siegfried Sassoon, W. H. Davies, H. E. Bates and Liam O'Flaherty. He was prepared to take risks if a writer intrigued him. Roy Campbell, with his "vigour, fire and vision", was by way of being a "find" of his; he even planned to review the virile South African poet's first book of verse, *The Flaming Terrapin*, before it found a publisher. He was always an admirer, though later he criticised Campbell's glorification of fighting, militant Catholicism and acquiescence in cruelty in his verses.[16] Even where Desmond's judgement was faulty as when he published the ponderous ballads of Herbert Palmer, the liveliness of his literary pages was memorable. On some, neglected authors – like Vernon Lee – he was singularly perceptive in his praise.[17]

Violet Paget – "Vernon Lee" – was a woman of remarkable intellect and imagination. A close friend of Irene Cooper-Willis, she was more than twenty years older than Desmond. She had been brought up in Florence, and while still in her teens had begun to "discover" Italian eighteenth-century culture at a time when it was ignored by the cognos-centi. An aesthete and a polyglot, with a sensitivity as refined as Walter Pater – who praised her work enthusiastically – her penetrating reflec-tions on philosophy and the arts achieved her a *succès d'estime* during the 1880s and 1890s. Her most interesting writings were her reflective vignettes on historical places in Europe – above all the primitive, culturally rich Italian landscape. Her "genius loci" essays transported the reader to the towering rocks and enchanted woods of Tuscany; or Pulcinello-masked, through the haunted courts of Venice, with the strains of Goldoni drifting faintly over the water.

In appearance angular and myopic, with prominent front teeth, Vernon Lee possessed none of the physical beauty to which she was so responsive. What she had was distinction. A portrait by Sargent shows her, when young, dashingly dressed in a wide-brimmed hat and collar and tie. Some who met her were daunted by her intense, questioning manner. Lacking a child's due of affection, she grew up emotionally insecure, over-conscious of her precocity and apt to take over the conversation. Her repressed emotional life came to centre round a succession of young women towards whom she was at once domineering and fickle.

Opinions varied as to whether she was one of the finest or the most tedious talkers of her age.[18] Those who were attracted to her salon in the 1880s and '90s, like Browning and Sargent, were dazzled. Desmond, with his love of "going into things" thoroughly, and always a good listener, found her fascinating when he met her with Bertrand Russell a few years before the war. Her writing appealed to his aesthetic side. He was distressed, too, by her increasing loneliness and by her undeserved neglect. During the latter part of the war, the MacCarthys spent many evenings in her company and Desmond encouraged her to write further pieces on places and atmosphere for *The New Statesman*. She agreed readily, eager to be back in circulation, though her known opposition to Britain's part in the war did her faded reputation little good. It was not easy for Desmond to keep her in good humour – cuts in her prolix pieces annoyed her – but they remained close friends until her death in 1935, at her villa at San Gervasio, near Florence, where, deaf and decrepit, she passed her last days amid the surroundings she loved.

In the late 'Twenties, the Bodley Head, her publishers, began to issue a collected edition of her works; and a tribute by Desmond in *The New Statesman* did much to revive her reputation: "Few writers", he asserted, "are at once so sensitively receptive and so passionately curious as Vernon Lee." Much moved, she wrote to thank him "for the wonderful passage – alas, I fear, of obituary. Obituary not because I intend to die quite yet . . . but because I often think that I have written far far too much and seem to be losing the knack of writing as I used to . . ."[19]

Later she thanked Desmond also for the volumes of his collected writing that he sent her in 1933. "I spent the evening yesterday over your Butler (but my admiration for Butler is equalled by intense personal aversion – sly and hirsute – detestable) and your beautiful Meredith which I remembered from years ago. And I realised what a boon, especially in a solitary silent life like mine are such delightful conversations with such a person as you. I always read your New Statesman articles for this kind of company."

A central part of Desmond's work for *The New Statesman* was still drama criticism. Yet his compulsive theatre going was on the wane. He found the post-war theatre much less stimulating. "The monotony of our modern plays is deadly," he complained. His earlier hopes of a theatrical renaissance led by such producers as Granville Barker were unfulfilled and he realised he had gauged the public mood incorrectly when he believed they were awakening to good drama through the Royal Court productions of the 1900s.[20] This change he attributed to the censorship, because it had treated dramatists, even of Shaw's stature, with contempt; to the pre-war Russian ballet mania, because it violently eclipsed the less showy triumphs of the English stage; and to the war, which favoured propaganda plays or third-rate light entertainment.

There were magnificent post-war productions of Chekhov and Shaw, and he applauded the Capek brothers' satire on humanity, The Insect Play; but the majority of the plays he thought trivial, like the reaction of their modern audiences. These seemed to Desmond no longer capable of responding at the level of moral passion required for playwrights like Ibsen. As he observed, the spirit expressed by "Pack Up Your Troubles In Your Old Kit Bag" might have been an invaluable defence mechanism in the dark days of the war, but it persisted as a superficial response to life generally.

He found himself increasingly bored by the proliferation of theatrical "realism", narrowly defined; the novelty of seeing ordinary people mouthing well-recorded banalities in predictable situations wore off rapidly, and he began to miss the richer, more varied techniques of the now taboo "old stage", with its asides, its soliloquies and its short drop curtain scenes. He tended therefore to concentrate his criticism on the productions and the acting. Eddie Marsh later recollected: "I believe he would have made a first rate 'producer' for I seldom read a notice of his without wishing he had been called in to a rehearsal."[21]

He would write to actors whose performances he admired; Diana Wynyard proudly kept the letter he sent her when she played in Wild December and three years later asked him specially to come and see her in Shaw's Candida: "I nearly wrote to ask your advice about playing one or two scenes," she told him, "because I know you have great understanding of the play!"[22] Theatrical directors, like Michael MaCowan in the 'Thirties realised that they could look to him for advice. Desmond established a partnership between critic and producer on the English stage which was almost unique.[23]

The actress he most admired at the time was Mrs Patrick Campbell, who excelled in refined poetic tragedy, as well as in parts where the "veneer of convention is broken by uncontrolled impulses, and the seriousness of passion interrupted by the broad comedy of nature or a sudden harsh matter-of-factness". He implored playwrights to continue to create roles for her. By the 'Thirties he singled out Charles Laughton and Cedric Hardwick for praise. He was also to recognise the exceptional powers of John Gielgud, for him a rarity: "It is far from being an age of great acting, but the range of his emotional scope, and the intelligence with which he conceives his parts, put him right at the top of his profession."

Desmond repeatedly pointed out a great fault of production at that time
– "that on the English stage seldom more than two people act at once". This
infuriated him at a performance of *Hamlet* in 1925. While Laertes and
Hamlet (John Barrymore) trampled the body of Ophelia underfoot as they
fought in her grave, the cast of onlookers showed no signs of horror at this
appalling scene; whereas in the Jewish Vilna Company's production of
Yankel the Smith at the Kingsway Theatre in 1922, "we often heard three
or four men and women speaking at once, as people do when they are
quarrelling or in moments of excited discussion. How often do you hear
that done on the English stage?"

He also felt that many modern productions failed to capture the correct
spirit of older plays, particularly of Shakespeare. It was very clear, he
believed, how Shakespeare wished his characters to be interpreted, since he
had put the explanations into their own mouths or into those of other
people in his plays, for the benefit of a more naive sixteenth-century
audience. "Shakespeare's art," Desmond asserted, "remains the art of
clear and precise statements"; it was pointless, therefore, to try and find
over-complicated psychological interpretations.

Of course there was still some new drama which interested him. He
welcomed every fresh Shaw play as, miraculously, year after year, they
poured from the old man's pen – *Heartbreak House, The Apple Cart, St
Joan* – intellectually lucid, provocative as ever. Since they had worked
together on *The New Statesman* Desmond had come to know Shaw better,
though they were never intimates. At one time they had a lively exchange of
letters over the personality of Christ in the correspondence pages of *The
New Statesman*. Desmond was impressed by Shaw's patience and good
nature with Clifford Sharp, who had been ruthless – and graceless – in
cutting and criticising his articles during the early part of the war.[24]

He was still interested in plays which made "good theatre" even if they
were of a lesser calibre than Shaw's. In particular, he noticed those of
Somerset Maugham, whom he had begun to treat more seriously since they
had served together in the Red Cross in 1914. Previously, he had not been
drawn to his dramas: all he had ever found to say of them was that they were
"eminently actable", with "the handy compactness, the shop finish and
alluring shininess of a new dressing case" – that now vanished emblem of
man-about-townliness.[25]

He came, however, to enjoy his friend's "clear-sighted, hard-edged
cynicism", a quality more Latin than English. Having identified this
characteristic, he was pleased to see it repeated in play after play – the
remorseless exposé of snobbery and greed, the vulgar panache and
hysterical malevolence of the leading characters. He was not put off by
Maugham's approval of selfishness, because the plays were strictly light

comedy and no more to be treated as a profound comment on life than the plays of Noel Coward: comparing the two authors, he rated Coward higher for wit and lower for realism.

He never over-estimated Maugham – for he had no illusions about his limitations and said so; but he identified what he did well and gave him full credit for it. Maugham and Desmond always enjoyed each other's company; they dined together frequently at the Café Royal and Desmond stayed with him at his home, the Villa Mauresque at Cap Ferrat in the south of France. This prickly writer accepted advice from Desmond that he would never have taken from anyone else; it meant much to him to have the approval of the man who had come to be Britain's leading dramatic critic; for Maugham was forever insecure about his reputation, resenting his rejection by so much of the literary world. Desmond had intellectual cachet but he was no threat; he was not himself a novelist or a playwright; he had no money; and though urbane he was without the kind of patrician self-assertiveness that would have inflamed Maugham's feelings of inferiority. Even so, Desmond was too sensitive not to be wary of his lonely, malevolent friend. Just before his own death he wrote him a letter, which like so many of Desmond's letters was never sent: "I used often to dwell with pleasure on that standing invitation you gave me to the Villa Moresco, where I twice enjoyed the comforts of friendship and perfect hospitality – but I could never summon up the courage to face the chance that my company might *no longer* give you pleasure."[26] This was said with a smile but as was usual with Desmond, he did not shrink from holding up a mirror to his old friend.

In 1928 Desmond began to sever his connection with *The New Statesman*. He resigned from the job of literary editor after an insulting letter from Clifford Sharp complaining about an article being rushed. The board of the paper begged him to stay and he agreed to carry on with the "Affable Hawk" column and the drama, though not with the other work. In June 1928 he also accepted the position of chief literary critic of *The Sunday Times*, which was to increase his influence still further. The terms were twice as good as those for *The New Statesman* and included four weeks' paid holiday. He was able to drop *The Empire Review* but he continued to be an exceedingly harassed "Hawk" until June 1929.

During all this time, Sharp's disastrous alcoholic habits had thrown an increasingly heavy weight of responsibility on his subordinates, including Desmond. In the end it was recognised that he was "very ill and dilapidated by drink" as Desmond told Molly in July 1928. "He will have to turn to Kia-Ora in future; Bacchus has handed in his bill." Shortly

afterwards, Sharp was replaced as editor by Kingsley Martin, who took the
paper along a more clearly socialist path, but this was not the end of
Desmond's association with *The New Statesman*. He continued to write
articles for it and remained a drama critic, though with declining frequency, over the next decade.

Unlike many in that world who regarded Sharp as a debauched cynic,
Desmond never condemned him morally and in 1935 he dedicated his
book of collected essays, *Experience*, to his former editor. It was a generous
gesture, for Sharp had given him a difficult time. Their approach was
absolutely different but Desmond accepted that Sharp had been a genuinely creative editor who imposed a discipline essential for blending the
paper into one homogenous whole.

"Seated opposite each-other at the make-up hour he would glare and I
would despair – but not reform." Desmond's catholic tastes led him to
prefer an uneven paper in which some inspired reviews stood out, even if
they contained bad grammar and flouted the "house style"; but Sharp
regarded such faults as "*blots* on the paper, symptoms too of a confounded
inefficiency. . . ." He insisted on a firm macadamised surface, while
Desmond "quite liked it to be broken by those wild green sprouts of folly
such as are apt to appear in the work of writers when they care about their
subject."[27]

Yet Desmond was subsequently convinced that their disagreements
made for a better paper. If Sharp had not been the editor he was, the literary
side would have been slovenly; if Desmond had not disagreed with him,
readers "might hardly have known whether they were reading a current
issue or one a month old". The two men also saw eye to eye in ways that
really mattered to Desmond: "we had in common a strong dislike of every
type of brilliant, pretentious nonsense, and a well-concealed respect for
each other which made our collaboration interesting as well as tolerable."

As Arnold Bennett acknowledged, "Your part of the paper certainly
shows evidence of increased interest and journalistic imagination."[28]
Among Desmond's contemporaries, such as Squire and Lynd, his criticism
stood out as profounder and livelier, while to the ordinary reader it was
more accessible than T. S. Eliot or Herbert Read.

As he reached his fifties, he was still unreconciled to the changes that age
demanded of him. Buses were something to be caught at a sprint; candles
were for burning at both ends; drink – though he was never a soak – was
something that was seldom refused. Endowed with a naturally good
physique, he had taken too much advantage of its resilience. However,
though the lines of weariness showed now in his amused clown's face, his
intellectual vitality was unabated; it remained so to the end, and the
evidence was in his writing.

18 "The Young Adonises"

By the time she was forty, in 1922, Molly had aged noticeably; her figure had spread, though she never grew fat – Virginia Woolf's comment that she had "grown as plump as a ptarmigan" was an exaggeration. She cut her hair into a fringe, a youthful style which she kept for the rest of her life. She sometimes attempted to alleviate its greyness by dyeing – rather ineptly – "the dye is too much like the yolk of an egg on the top, leaving black beneath", observed Virginia, who thought it gave her rather a common look, like someone at the seaside. On a small clothes allowance she managed to dress always neatly, sometimes elegantly, "much better than I do" allowed Virginia on one occasion. She sported "two minute cows horns above her ears" as deaf aids.[1] She was not yet so deaf that she would not take part with great success in various evenings of amateur dramatics staged in Bloomsbury: the most elaborate was a revue performed at Maynard Keynes' house in Gordon Square in 1926, a squib, aimed at Bloomsbury, on the subject of the Hayley Morriss scandal: a rich young man, Hayley Morriss, seigneur of Pippingfold Park in Sussex, where he kept Irish wolfhounds and a harem of pretty kennelmaids among the Oriental splendours of his mansion, had been accused of debauching a young lady in his employ and sent to prison. This revue, *Don't Be Frightened*, or *Pippington Park* was written by a Cambridge don, Dennis Robertson, with songs mostly by "Tommy" Tomlin* who was to play the part of Hayley Morriss; Molly played Vanessa, as "Clarissa" whom he abducts: she at first turns a deaf ear to him until he offers her a Cézanne and a Giotto, whereupon she succumbs. That Molly could not have looked less like Vanessa added to the audience's amusement, and she was diffident about impersonating her, even writing to her old friend asking whether she minded her doing so. The revue necessitated much rehearsing at Wellington Square, amidst laughter and chatter, which young Dermod MacCarthy overheard from the stairs, but was not allowed to listen to the show, it being too risqué for a fifteen-year-old.

---

* Stephen Tomlin (1901–1937), sculptor.

The songs, adaptations of popular ditties were elaborate, as was the staging. The programme opened with a Beauty Chorus, of three "ladies" in full evening dress with pearl chokers, played by three strapping men, including Dadie Rylands, later a Cambridge don; their partners, three small "gentlemen" in white tie and tails, included Frances Marshall, who was later, with her husband, Ralph Partridge, to become a great friend of the MacCarthys.[2]

Many of the performers in this revue, and among its audience, were part of a new, young generation who now mingled with "old Blooms-bury". The MacCarthys got to know them during the 'Twenties: Ralph Partridge and his current wife, Dora Carrington, were among them; Carrington was devoted to Lytton Strachey, and had many admirers: one of them, the writer Gerald Brenan, confided in Molly, "May I confess that it has been for a long time one of my great ambitions to know you better?" He wrote her entertaining letters describing his adventures abroad. Arthur Waley, the poet and translator of Chinese verse, was a new and affectionate friend now, as well as Cyril Connolly and the fantastic, die-away Eddy Sackville-West, aesthete and accomplished pianist. "I liked Sackville West," Molly wrote to Dolly Ponsonby after meeting him at The Wharf. "I see he is not as limp as you would think as he played beautifully and every now and then went upstairs and had a good write at his novel."[3] Of these young men, limp and otherwise, one became the particular focus of her affections: Philip Ritchie, born in 1899, was in his early twenties when Molly met him, either at The Wharf, or at Garsington where Lady Ottoline invited many undergraduates from Oxford, among them Philip's contemporary there, David Cecil.[4]

On the face of it Philip Ritchie seemed an unlikely choice as a close friend on Molly's part: he was an attractive young man, who charmed a great many people, of both sexes, but his affections were devoted to his own. At Oxford he lived for pleasure in an amusing circle David Cecil called "the fast highbrows"; he liked a drink, particularly the newly-fashionable cocktails; was musical, with a fine baritone voice – he sang compositions by Hubert Wolf, for instance; and he also gambled. "They called it 'reading from Sir Thomas Browne'," recalled David Cecil. "Would you like to come round to read from Sir Thomas Browne?" went their invitations to play poker in one another's rooms. Philip's family were devoted to him: he was the eldest son of the second Lord Ritchie of Dundee – his grandfather, the Chancellor of the Exchequer, had been ennobled. But despite his easy-going, pleasure-loving exterior, Philip was essentially unhappy. A conscript, he had served in the Near East during the last year of the War and something had apparently been crushed in him. Perhaps Molly responded to his sensitivity and his unhappiness. He was also fundamentally weak; he came down from Oxford without taking a degree – for which he had anyway done little work – and began reading desultorily for the Bar in the London chambers of Charlie Sanger, Desmond's old Cambridge friend.

Like many of his Oxford contemporaries Philip had a complicated and overheated love-life. Lytton Strachey was infatuated with him and enjoyed writing him poems – "What need of more, when I have had my fill?",[5] and so on; he attracted all kinds of people – the notoriously tenacious Elizabeth Bibesco pursued him.

This, then, was the young man whom Molly came to know and eventually to love. Attractive, rather than handsome, he had red hair brushed to one side, with the typically freckled, fair skin of redheads. He had an open, responsive face, good manners, consideration and tact; he was not effeminate. When she met him, in the summer of 1924, Molly took to him immediately. She was then living at Oare, and she invited him and his close friend, Roger Senhouse, to visit the farm. "Oh, how delicious are the young and intelligent!" she wrote enthusiastically after the two young Adonises, as she described them, had been.[6] They had told her all about the new house, Ham Spray, near Marlborough, which the homosexual Lytton Strachey had moved into with Ralph Partridge and Carrington a few weeks previously.

After this Molly saw Philip regularly in London. He took her to concerts and to the opera and to the Ivy Restaurant, then in its heyday. Frances Partridge recalls a dinner party there with Raymond Mortimer[*], Frankie Birrell[†], as well as Roger Senhouse[‡], Philip and Molly. Everyone was in high spirits; the food and drink were delicious, the laughter and discussion lighthearted. Philip loved jokes: Frances Partridge remembered how he once started an argument "as to how much money one would require to change one's name by deed poll, and maintaining that he would gladly become 'Sir Philip Filth' for a very small sum."[7] All this Molly found infectious: the company of so many young people did her good. Philip and she had another bond – they both read the Russian writers widely and enthusiastically – Tolstoy, Turgenev and Chekhov in particular.

Molly and he were both guests of Sibyl Colefax at Argyll House in Chelsea. Philip shared the common view of her, writing to Molly in the summer of 1925 that "a certain sense of restfulness is produced by the sight of the blinds and shutters of Argyll House. They enable me to visit the other end of Oakley Street [where the Sangers lived] with a slightly

[*] Raymond Mortimer (1895–1980), literary critic.
[†] Frances Birrell (1889–1935), bookseller.
[‡] Roger Senhouse (1900–1970), publisher.

mitigated sense of guilt. I feel that each end symbolizes my better and my worse self. I hardly know which of the two selves I most dislike.

"Wellington Square, on the other hand, is half way between the two, and exactly what I like.

"Every year at the end of July I count up the new friends I have made. This year is the richest for a long time since it contains both you and Lytton.

"I hope I have not seemed detached or indifferent. I know I do sometimes. It arises from that very unpleasant English quality of not wishing to give oneself away. I am none the less happy and proud that you should say the charming things which your letter contained. I hope I shall never do anything to lose your friendship.

"I have been through terrible storms of jealousy and other miseries since I saw you, but they are all settled now, and my life has resumed its almost uncannily happy course."[8]

Molly also entertained Philip and other young people in London. The house in Wellington Square was rearranged now that the children no longer needed a nursery. The fine room on the first floor overlooking the square gardens became the drawing-room, where the light poured in through the handsome pair of French windows. "Mummy has a tea-party going on downstairs," Desmond wrote to Michael early in 1925, "Lady Ottoline, Mr Sanger and Philip Ritchie – you remember him, the fair and gentle young man who used to come to Francis Birrell's lectures on French history. Her pleasure in 25 Wellington Square has taken the form of mild but incessant entertaining. Having no liking for tea-parties I'm content to be writing to you." The following year, at Raymond Mortimer's instigation, Molly invited two dozen people to a lecture on "L'esprit contre la Raison" by a young French intellectual, René Crevel. There was tea at five o'clock, followed by the lecture: Logan Pearsall Smith gave a characteristically catty account of the occasion to Cyril Connolly, as "an anti-intellectual gospel and attack on reason, chanted and bellowed at us in a kind of figurative and bombastic prose which, though we pretended to follow it, I am sure none of us really understood. The whole thing – the brazen pretentious boy and the anxious pretentious audience, was extremely funny, but I was sorry for Molly, though I hope she didn't realise, being deaf, how absurd the lecture was." The audience, he said, consisted of "all the young lions, or rather the young tom-cats of Bloomsbury" and "a few older celebrities, trembling for their thrones and reputations among those hoping to replace them, and a few ladies of fashion anxious to be in the intellectual swim."[9]

Logan Pearsall Smith, nicknamed "Uncle Baldhead" by the MacCarthy children, was still living at St Leonard's Terrace, nearby, with his sister Alys, Bertrand Russell's estranged wife. He was a frequent travelling companion of Desmond's – whose expenses he paid. Like Desmond he was a man of letters, educated, erudite and a lover of all things literary: but there the resemblance ended. Logan was touchy, worldly, a snob; eventually he was possessed by manic moods which made him an impossible companion. Waspish in his relationships, and not generally popular, he was a generous friend of the MacCarthy family, who stayed for long periods with him in the country, particularly during the First World War.

A crucial difference between Desmond and Logan was money; Logan's came from his rich American family, and enabled him to enjoy the good things of life; he revelled in the success of his books of literary anthology, notably *Trivia*, the harvest of his wide reading. As a literary assistant, he employed "what I call a 'Milver' – a fellow-fanatic whose thoughts chime in a sweet ecstasy of execration with our own!" In the late 1920s this was Cyril Connolly; later Robert Gathorne-Hardy worked for him, and was of great help to Desmond in collecting and editing his articles for publication by Putnam.

Whatever the intellectual content of such lectures in Logan's view, giving these parties shows that Molly now felt able to invite both "Old Bloomsbury" friends like Lytton Strachey, the "Woolves", and Clive Bell, as well as the younger generation; her niece, Clare Balfour, recalled: "When she asked me to a party at which her friend Francis Birrell was to give a lecture on Women in French literature, she said, 'I want the front row filled with a bévy of beáuties.' She pronounced the last words with the Bloomsbury voice. . . .

"A whole row of such was no easy thing to achieve in the Bloomsbury world which was mainly homosexual," certainly at this time. Molly managed "to fill rather a short front row. I remember Julia Strachey (Lytton's niece), Frances Marshall, Janie Bussy (another of his nieces and a talented painter)." Behind these were "some startlingly handsome young men. It was they rather who made up a bevy. . . .

"Lytton Strachey sat on a low chair near the lecturer's table and sideways to it with Carrington crouched on a cushion on the floor to one side of him and Philip Ritchie to the other." Carrington wore a suit of corduroy, then usually for workmen's clothes, and she had no hat on her bobbed hair.[10]

Molly introduced Francis Birrell to the audience, beginning in the usual formal manner and reverting to a humorous intimacy which provoked a lot of laughter. How much Molly's self-confidence as a hostess, on even such a comparatively modest scale, was due to the renewed self-confidence her friendship with Philip Ritchie brought her is impossible to gauge, especially as her letters to him no longer exist. They met regularly though not frequently, and his letters to her, which she carefully preserved, are fond, indicating both that he had emotional problems in his relationships – with men – and that he was happy to be the recipient of her affection if that is what she wanted to give him: "Please, Molly, do not think I was offended or upset or shocked, or indeed felt anything but pleasure in the things which you have said to me from time to time," he wrote to her on one occasion ". . . you occupy a unique place in my heart, and if you have feelings which at all correspond, I am very happy . . . Yours as always, Philip."[11]

It certainly seems as though, through her friendship with young Bloomsbury and Philip in particular, through founding the Memoir Club and being able – just – to afford to live in London once again where she could entertain as she pleased, Molly came into her own and had a social life independent from Desmond's. The friction between them unfortunately continued.

Desmond and Molly seemed to have got into a habit of impatience and irritation with one another. Part of the trouble was their shortage of money, part was Molly's deafness which exasperated her. "The inability to catch the voices of my fellow human being drives me almost to Bedlam" she confessed to Vanessa Bell. Although Desmond took on all kinds of literary jobs now, his output was never prolific and there was still not enough money to go round. He had never been one for practicalities, and Molly accused him of neglect: of herself, of the family, of household affairs and of his appearance – but not of society. Despite his determination to hoard his health and not squander it on social life, he found great difficulty in organising his time to have enough for work *and* society. "I haven't news" he wrote to Lady Cynthia on one occasion "unless you count a lunch with Lady Essex when I was very late and found the Duke of Connaught was a guest, who with royal tact asked me for news from the City, supposing only a deal in millions could have delayed me."

He enjoyed social life as much as ever and gave as much enjoyment in his turn. "Desmond of course does his jolly delightful tricks – eating and drinking meanwhile – acting an actress who cleans her arms like a fly in Nassau" recorded Virginia Woolf of luncheon at Lady Colefax.[12] On this occasion the guests left at the customary hour of three o'clock; on others, Desmond did not rise from table until four or even five in the afternoon. David Cecil, who met him now, showed him part of his first book, on Cowper, and he was most helpful about it, criticising it and taking trouble over his suggestions. But the first time he did so, they met for lunch and lingered over the table until well on into the afternoon. The young man had the impression that this was a regular pattern of Desmond's life.

If an unexpected crisis arose in the MacCarthys' lives there was no reserve of money to pay for it: this happened at the beginning of 1924 when Desmond injured his knee running downstairs, in his usual precipitous fashion, at a supper party given by St John and Mary Hutchinson. An operation was needed to put the knee cap right, followed by a month in a nursing home at 8½ guineas a week. Luckily, he reported to Chen, "a number of my friends have subscribed over £100 to see me through!"

Shortage of funds and Desmond's irregular way of life constantly caused Molly anxiety. Virginia recorded in her diary at the beginning of March 1927 that Molly "could not get her mind off her troubles, first laughing at them – Desmond all right, & so on: then brushing laughter aside, & becoming more & more openly worried. Sibyl Colefax had cross examined her about her debts. To such indignities poverty exposes one. So I told her the truth, or what I hope will be the truth: that friends are subscribing enough to send them abroad, Oh how wonderful! she exclaimed, she never having seen Italy or Spain all these years. . . . 'Of course I was extravagant about doing the house up . . . but then we can let it. . . . Oh Desmond's hopeless – he's like a dog who runs out if the door is open.' So we laid our heads together over the fire; & felt very sisterly & sympathetic."

The organisation of the fund became as comical as any arrangement to do with the MacCarthys seemed bound to be. It was left to Virginia to transact the delicate diplomacy between the two formidable fund-leaders, Christabel Maclaren* and Sibyl Colefax. "I have now seceded, after setting them by the ears, & only hear from Chrissie how unreasonable Sibyl is, & from Sibyl how much she fears that Chrissie etc. etc. I rather expect that the MacCarthys will be set up for life, & keep a motor in the end."

On 24th March, Virginia wrote to Molly with a cheque for £300 "which your and Desmond's friends hope you will both spend on taking a complete holiday abroad for three months.

"Nobody wants to be thanked or named or to have any notice taken of this whatsoever . . . I'm afraid I shan't see you before we go, but I implore you to remember the existence of the inkpot and pen, and let me know what happens to you, whether you fall into a crater, or kiss the Pope's nose, or whatever it may be. . . ."[13]

The MacCarthys were enabled both to pay off their debts, particularly those incurred by the improvements to their house, as well as to go abroad. They planned a European holiday which started with Desmond taking a cure at Vichy: here he drank the waters and did breathing exercises to strengthen his lungs against the asthma attacks which he regularly

* Christabel Maclaren (1890–1974), writer, later Lady Aberconway.

suffered. They were "like running uphill with a portmanteau" he said, and left him feeling old and debilitated.[14]

Molly and he were not on the best of terms when they parted – the usual accusations of neglect from her and of nagging from him – and this made him miserable; he was determined that they would have a delicious time when they met at the end of the month to travel further south: "We haven't been abroad together for years. We will enjoy 'observing' together & we won't quarrel on the journey – we will enjoy it as our children do . . . When you join me we shall have such delightful fun," he wrote.

Because Desmond had another asthma attack they stayed in the Hautes Alpes. Afterwards, they returned to northern France, where Molly stayed with Rachel at Giverny on the Seine. They were paying guests in a farm just above Monet's colourful house and celebrated garden. Molly's room overlooked the haystacks he so often painted. "I am looking down from my room with grey river, poplar trees & alders beyond & windy sky" she wrote to Dolly Ponsonby. The Ponsonbys' house, Shulbrede Priory, had been let to the MacCarthys for the rest of August, for only 3 guineas a week, and it was to this lovely sixteenth-century building that Molly returned, to stay with Dermod and Rachel, Desmond joining them at the weekends.

They had many visitors: some were invited, like Gerald Brenan, who came at the same time as Cyril Connolly. Cyril had "taken a shine to Rachel, and made a sulky scene because I talked to her for a few minutes in the garden," remembered Gerald.[15] Others were inevitable, like Chen, who stayed for a week; and some just turned up, like Arthur Waley's friend Beryl de Zoete. Molly had mixed views about Beryl, who was some 10 years older than Arthur Waley. She found her insensitivity and crudity real, her culture and refinement sham, while her cult of the body was ridiculous especially as it entailed doing violent exercises dressed in the minimum clothes. She was, at least, good theatre.

"I am sitting in the Prior's room – very lofty & 700 years old – as good as new, & good for another 700 years I should think," Molly recounted now to Gerald Brenan. "I feel that Beryl feels it rather infradigue to be sitting under oak beams and would like to see them jazzed over but that can't be helped.

"I must send her up to Hindhead to dance at the hotel if she gets bored tomorrow (Disloyal)."[16]

She discussed with him "the Beryl complex", the all-consuming desire to be younger than you are: Molly seems to have been afraid of having it herself – probably because of her feelings for Philip Ritchie, "that's why I speak of her with the poison of asps under my tongue. I think falsely

construed subjective sex in those who are no longer young the most
depressing & pathetic spectacle! So I keep her as a banner of warning,
waving."[17]

In that summer of 1927, Gerald Brenan, thirty-three years old, had
confided to Molly the anguish of his love for Carrington, which left him
defeated and battered. Now it was Molly's turn to ask him for
consolation. After her delicious summer abroad "some horror must be
awaiting me, to balance" she had written. The horror came when, back in
London, she was telephoned out of the blue with the news that Philip
Ritchie had died. He was twenty-eight.

Two months previously he had had a routine operation for the removal
of his tonsils, but, performed whilst he had tonsillitis, it was a disaster.
There was haemorrhaging, and then he contracted pleurisy. On 13th
September he died of septic pneumonia. With more intelligent medical
care his death need never have happened. Molly was devastated. Because
she had been out of touch with him that summer she had never even
known he was ill. Now he was dead, and the loss of him made her realise
all the more acutely how much Philip meant to her.

On the day she heard the news she wrote brokenly to Gerald, "Of all
the younger generation I loved him the best – he was the one I found the
most loveable [sic] of all – I never knew why. I often thought badly of him
& wished he was not so weak, & yet he always was so far nicer than he
made himself out to be – and it hadn't to do entirely with *charm*, which
people can have without being loveable – It is impossible to write – I am
not used to his being dead – I can hear his voice. Oh how I do *wish* he had
not died."

Molly wrote to Philip's family, and received a poignant note from his
father, "I know how much he cared for you. You knew him really & you
knew his sweetness and large heartedness . . . always I feel him near me all
the time. I want you to know how bravely he met the end – only thinking
of us – & smiling at the last."[18] Though she comforted herself that "to die
young is distinguished," Molly continued to mourn Philip: at the end of
the month she wrote again to Gerald saying that "Philip's death has
disconnected my days with the normal stream of life this last fortnight,
very much – it is impossible not to be preoccupied when such a thing as
that happens."[19]

Roger Senhouse sent her a photograph of him, inscribed "with
thoughts of our dear Phil"; Molly pinned this up in her room, where two
years later Virginia Woolf noted it was still there.[20] To Eddy Sackville-
West Molly wrote, "I loved him more than I can say and miss him more
than I can say." Desmond consoled her: "Dearest I know you loved Philip
very much – I think your relationship was a pure delight to him and now

that is a blessed thing to remember."[21] Desmond was correct — their friendship had been a pure delight by contrast to her more complicated and tempestuous relations with her husband. Her relationship with Philip, which had no suggestion of an "affair", was yet agreeably spiced with flirtatiousness: it was never complicated by the jealousy which distorted his male relationships and her marriage; stimulating and fun, Philip appreciated and admired Molly as she enjoyed being appreciated and admired.

Now he was irrevocably gone, she knew how much she would miss him, and everything she did and everyone she saw seemed flawed with its own mortality. Of a performance of *Façade* she went to that winter she wrote to Eddy Sackville-West: "The Sitwell play seemed to mark the cracking up of a short epoch! The 'Façade' scenery was much the worse for wear & shook & trembled, & then to my mind the saxophone seemed to strike up a march of death for itself & the Sitwells — & in the stalls the Façade faces, ice-packed, of the hostesses, — pneumaticised, — galvainised [sic] — ray-ed (sun-rayed?), & giving out electric sparks from the vibro massage, began to jig & work. The Cunard [Lady Emerald] anyhow I assure you (game & gay as a canary as she has been to the last) limped to her car, turned all ashen, & with palsied lips jibbered a goodnight to the young shingled man she had brought, & went out of life (To return, to return — & why shouldn't she? if she really still enjoys it)."[22]

19 Editor, Critic, Broadcaster

In June 1928, Desmond's friend, Oliver Brett, launched him as editor of a new literary magazine. *Life and Letters* was conceived as a more unconventional rival to J. C. Squire's *London Mercury*, also a monthly journal; it was shorter and less artistically produced, but even so, its patterned cover of red and pale brown, its attractive print and good paper, gave it a well-designed, dignified appearance. Desmond aimed for a high standard of writing at a low selling price and until the end of 1931 *Life and Letters* only cost one shilling as against the *Mercury*'s three. It was to be published by the New Statesman Publishing Company, sharing printing and production with the left-wing journal.

By dint of a personal letter sent in facsimile to thousands of addresses, Desmond was able to drum up 2,600 subscribers to the first year's issue; encouragingly fifty pages of advertising were guaranteed at the outset. His principal object was to set up an editorial job for himself which would be less demanding than "Affable Hawk" and for which he would be better paid. With customary optimism he talked to Molly about an annual salary of £800 for life. Oliver Brett was prepared to underwrite a loss of £4,000 a year for its first three years while it became established.

Desmond intended it to be a review with many short pieces on books of all kinds, as well as longer commentaries. There would be reports on the literary scene abroad – in Paris, Berlin, New York. There would be debates on new poetry and novels. A monthly bibliography of the best books available on different subjects – Dr Johnson, for example – would make the paper indispensable to libraries, universities and book dealers.[2]

He was particularly keen to give writers a chance of publishing work normally regarded as too long for a small magazine; and on reviving neglected authors – something which most journals failed to do. Above all, he aimed at variety.

As with all small papers, Desmond could offer little money. He was only just able to pay André Maurois enough for the first "Paris letter" and that series soon tailed off. Desmond's list of contributors was nonetheless impressive and many of them wrote more than once during the journal's short life. They included Virginia Woolf, Vernon Lee, Robert Byron,

David Cecil, Erich Maria Remarque, Lytton Strachey, Vita Sackville-West, E. M. Forster, Peter Quennell, Bertrand Russell, Robert Graves and Edith Wharton.

In the early issues he relied on work commenced well before 1928; for the first number, George Santayana furnished an interesting piece he had written on Hamlet in 1908[3] and Thomas Hardy, just before his death, an essay on fiction written in 1891. Max Beerbohm penned an article specially for the paper, dipping into his store of memory for an entertaining portrait of the writer Andrew Lang; but he warned Desmond against relying too much on vintage stuff: "Dreary old men with 'names' will not avail you much. The brilliant young are what will matter."[4]

Quite soon *Life and Letters* gained a reputation as an original and entertaining journal stirring public interest at a time when Middleton Murry's much acclaimed periodical *The Adelphi* was losing ground. The "brilliant young" – in the form of Aldous Huxley, Cyril Connolly, Osbert Sitwell and Evelyn Waugh – were certainly in evidence. The avant-garde had its place: Sherwood Anderson offered two satirical pieces on modern industrial society; Constant Lambert discoursed on Jazz; Cyril Connolly's excellent essay on James Joyce and Dilys Powell's stylish pieces on T. S. Eliot and Edith Sitwell represented an important part of Desmond's policy, though the controversy he hoped to stimulate over modern writing seldom got off the ground.

In *Life and Letters* for October 1928 he made a cogent attack on government censorship of books and plays – a subject on which he had always felt strongly.[5] This was sparked off by the Home Secretary's efforts to ban a courageous, humourless novel, *The Well of Loneliness* by "Radclyffe Hall", which depicted the persecution of lesbian women by society. Though no admirer of the book, Desmond was indignant that legal machinery for dealing with low pornography should be used to suppress, arbitrarily, a work of artistic merit.[6] On the strength of his article Desmond was called to give evidence for the book by its publishers,[7] Jonathan Cape, at Bow Street Magistrates' Court. He tried to drum up further witnesses himself, unsuccessfully; Arnold Bennett's excuse was his "almost invincible stutter". The Woolfs and E. M. Forster, however, accompanied Desmond. It was all to no avail, as the Bow Street Magistrate ruled their evidence inadmissible. "I spent a miserable day in court," Desmond told Clifford Sharp, "as you will see from the account of the trial it was perfectly useless and all I have done is to associate myself in the minds of the ignorant with things which are thought detestable."[8] The book was duly burnt as obscene, and Desmond had to content himself with joining Shaw, Wells and other literary leaders in a "round robin" to *The Times*, pointing out the absurd injustice of submitting serious works to such antiquated prejudice.[9]

In May 1930, partly for personal emotional reasons which will shortly be apparent, Desmond was also moved to defend D. H. Lawrence's descriptions of sexual intercourse. He praised him for making the subject a "beautiful and serious" element in his fiction: "a daring, salutary and considerable achievement . . . and what he did has made it easier for those who follow to take into poetry and literature the whole of life."[10] In September 1929, too, he had joined Bertrand Russell and Bernard Shaw in addressing a large audience on censorship at the Congress of the World League for Sexual Reform in London.[11] This pioneering mood did not stay with him; a few years later he looked back more critically at Lawrence, who, he told a correspondent, had written "a good deal of pornography out of the persuasion that he was revealing the secrets of the universe! . . . Lawrence said that one of the glories of his philosophy was that it would extirpate two odious things, the sentimental love-lyric and the smoking-room story. Well, I much prefer, and I would defend my preference, for a conception of life which admits of both these modes of feeling, than *one* which makes copulation the deepest experience possible to man, and sex the sun round which everything revolves."[12]

While he was shocked by purposeless violence or real pornography in literature, Desmond himself saw nothing wrong in bawdy humour, written or spoken. He liked to tell the story of a railway journey he made with a writer (probably either W. H. Davies or Wilfrid Blunt?). The route taken by the train seems strange; precision presumably was sacrificed in the interests of the anecdote:

"I was travelling once with an old poet – one of the few whose verse in my opinion is likely to survive – and our train passed a place called Rucking; our destination was Rougely [sic]. Presently, he leant forward, his face lit-up with a joyful inspiration, and he whispered:

> The people of Rucking don't care about fucking,
> But the people of Rougely enjoy it – HUGELY!

"Well I would not repeat that couplet in the presence of an engaged young couple or of a church dignitary . . . yet in the railway carriage, the poet and I shared a laugh which certainly did not do our morals any harm, and felt as though it was, for the moment, doing us good."[13]

One of the most successful parts of *Life and Letters* was the coverage of continental literature – particularly French and Russian – though nothing very experimental was included. "Without Elder Blossom" by Panteli-mon Romanov, published for the first time outside the Soviet Union, was a clever, squalid satire on the casual sexual habits of Soviet young people and was what Desmond had in mind when he told Molly that he wished to publish "unpopular but meritorious short stories". However, the quality of fiction in the paper was distinctly uneven. Outstanding were an extract from Evelyn Waugh's forthcoming *Black Mischief*, Richard Hughes' *High Wind in Jamaica* – which occupied, abridged, a whole issue – and L. P. Hartley's accomplished spine-chiller "Three or Four for Dinner". Others in contrast were very feeble, not least compositions by writers as well known as David Garnett, Hilaire Belloc and Osbert Sitwell. Desmond's best tale, "The Bear", attracted compliments widely but his insipid story about an Italian shop girl, "The Face", revealed only an old-fashioned, sentimental vein in Desmond, which occasionally surfaced in his short stories and frequently in his relations which the opposite sex where an element of fantasy was present – as with Cynthia Asquith.

On the whole, however, what he wrote for his paper – notably on Samuel Butler and Mr Asquith – was as good as his best *New Statesman* contributions; and usually he was well served by other essayists who wrote for him on historical and biographical themes: A. J. A. Symons on Baron Corvo; Somerset Maugham on Arnold Bennett (a catty piece); and G. M. Young on the Victorian age – all can be read appreciatively to this day.

Characteristic of Desmond's choice as an editor were some bizarre reminiscences, including Arthur Symons' "Confessions – A study in Madness" – recollections of his own lunacy, and "A Murderer's Confession" – a reprint from *The Sun* of a series of sensational interviews with a convicted murderer, which Desmond had collected and preserved in 1903, when they first appeared.

The verse printed in *Life and Letters* ranged from some vivid lines by Roy Campbell about a palm tree, to Desmond's latest efforts to convince people that Bob Trevelyan was a talented poet. In "Two Slaveries – Epistola ad DM", a poem of well over 100 lines (in iambic pentameters), the industrious bard of "The Shiffolds" lamented his own (regrettable) enslavement to the muse of poetry and Desmond's to journalism. "Now is our need . . ./With courage and critical sternness to reject shallow doctrine/ . . . Yours friend be the task then/Both to reveal and to interpret; since yours in abundance/Are knowledge and candour, wise hope and sensitive insight."[14]

Desmond was a self-effacing editor. The first number contained no editorial. After the magazine had been out some time, he did write an article appraising its achievement and trying to meet the criticisms that *Life and Letters* lacked an identifiable "soul". In general, however, it was true to say that the paper was marked more by an enterprising choice than any purposeful direction.

By 1931, it was clear that *Life and Letters* was failing financially. "Subscribers fall off all the time and advertisements are practically non-existent," Oliver Brett told Desmond sadly in April. He had carried the editorial loss of £2,000 a year over the past three years; now he found that even the publishing costs were not being met, while his income had been depleted by the depression in the world's stock markets. He was inclined to wind up the paper at the end of the year, reluctant to spoil it by reducing its quality. Knowing Desmond's financial situation, he generously offered him £1,500 to write three books of his choice, sharing the profits of these with him at the end. "This will give you three and a half years to find the ideal job and it will give me the very great pleasure of feeling that I've had a hand in producing the works we have all so long awaited."[15]

Mistakenly, Desmond decided that it would be better for him to go on with *Life and Letters*. From early 1932 to the end of that year it continued to run under his editorship, as a quarterly, priced two shillings and sixpence. For a further year Desmond shared the editing work with another journalist, Hamish Miles, after which his own connection with the paper ceased.

He deserved little blame for this outcome. Nearly all small journals tend to peter out in a few years – chiefly because they cease after a while to attract the interest of advertisers. As much because of its strengths as because of its weaknesses, the paper made little lasting impact and earned no place of importance in literary history. Spiritually it belonged to an earlier period. Max Beerbohm was full of nostalgia when he received a copy late in 1931: "how it makes me ache to be living in those days of serious refinement and happiness! How it cheapens this thin, sad, hectic little era!"[16] If *Life and Letters* had been more the product of a coterie it might have had a greater missionary force: Though Desmond had the Catholic taste and intelligence of a great editor, wrote Cyril Connolly, years later, he could not tolerate obscurity and insisted on regarding literature as entertainment. There was nothing in *Life and Letters* which he could not talk about at a dinner party.[17]

Looking back, Connolly could refer generously to the publication of *Life and Letters* as "the literary event of the late twenties". In his diary for 1928, however, he expressed his disappointment that Desmond's paper, which, because it was well-subsidised, could afford to experiment, seemed bent on pandering to a die-hard English public. The whole tone of the paper was that of a literary *Punch*, he concluded as "august and readable as any late Victorian arse wiper, and as daring and original as a new kind of barley water". Such remarks highlighted the limitations of the paper, but Connolly was always an unsafe judge of literary depth and underestimated the seriousness of Desmond's purpose.[18]

Desmond had become friendly with the precocious, petulant young writer a few years before; he had responded to his wit and his infectious literary enthusiasms. He had encouraged him to review novels for the *New Statesman*. At twenty-five, in 1928, Cyril Connolly was still locked in a prolonged Etonian adolescence, moving uneasily away from homosexuality towards the exhibitionistic courtship of much younger women whom he felt confident of impressing with his brilliance. He laid ardent siege to Molly's niece, Cecilia's daughter, Horatia (Racy) Fisher, a lovely fair-haired girl of seventeen; divinely English, unawakened, staid, as he described her with his brand of self-mocking affectation. In the summer of 1927 he joined the MacCarthys at Shulbrede Priory; Molly had liked him at first, but now went off him. She warned her sister against him; as a result he was forbidden to communicate with Racy. He became convinced that the two Cornish sisters had ganged up on him because he was poor; but it was his character, not his circumstances, which repelled them. Molly was to tell a friend: "The odd thing is that the only person I have ever met in the large and varied community to which we belong whom I consider crude enough to be described as Bogus is Cyril Connolly."[19] She doubted his passionate protestations to Racy and told Cecilia that he was really still "a bugger", which Connolly, when he heard about it, violently resented.[20]

Above all Molly disliked his shameless sponging off his friends. He would frequently take a girl out to dinner, order expensively and then find that he had come without money or had one enormous bank note which he could not change. Molly's daughter Rachel who, at seventeen, thought him an entertaining and sophisticated dining companion, was painfully embarrassed to be confronted one evening with a bill for the two of them which she could barely afford.[21] He took an intermittent interest in her as well as her cousin Racy, but ruined his chances by such inconsiderate manners, "mean with his own money and perpetually extravagant with everyone else's", as Molly said.

From 1926–9 Cyril Connolly worked as a literary assistant to Logan Pearsall Smith.[22] For this he received an annual allowance of £400, even though his secretarial duties effectively ceased after about a year. For much of the time he lived at Pearsall Smith's country house, Chilling. It was an ideal existence for him – delicious food and the prospect of a legacy from his patron – but it appeared parasitic, and Molly despised the way he clung to it, bored and self-pitying and unable to exert himself to write the major work which his talent seemed to promise. "Therefore when he is grand and beautiful about freedom, he simply seems to me a little ass now," she told Desmond.

Cyril found Molly's attitude something of a challenge. In his diary for

March 1928 he made a resolution to associate with the people he was afraid of most. Resenting her, but respecting her judgement, largely because it was so severe, he continued to "pour out" to her, as she put it, in a way that only increased her dislike. Desmond took a more kindly line; he felt some responsibility for the young man whose career he had encouraged. He rightly appreciated the perceptive criticisms that Connolly had written for *The New Statesman*, though he found him at times involved and obscure and asked him to "keep an eye on your long, draggle-tailed sentences."[23] Connolly seems to have accepted this advice readily enough, judging by his development of an excellent style in the years that followed.

He was less pleased when Desmond, exasperated by his behaviour, told him that his opportunism was vulgar. Having sent this letter, however, Desmond at once felt, typically, that he had been too hard on a vulnerable youth; he wrote again, "I lay awake all night thinking of the pain and worry my letter may have caused you," but he continued to press him to clean up his tarnished reputation. "You have no idea how quickly the attitude of gossips will change if you determine upon independence and guard against those habits into which fascinating, hard up people slip and out of your wounds & your capacity for enjoyment will come something which will lead to triumphant recognition – sooner or later. You have got the intellectual daring necessary as well as the indispensable power of perception. I believe in you, & I don't readily believe in people's gifts."[24]

Cyril took deep offence, admitting opportunism without shame, but indignant at the suggestion that he was a "scheming cadger". He accused the MacCarthys of persecuting him, preening himself peevishly in the role of martyr to conventional opinion, over his love for Racy Fisher. He dwelt on his own need for affection and admiration and his fatal temptation to wound. Yet a sentence or two later, he could not resist his compulsion to score off others, which was all too frequently the source of his malice; his riposte had the saving grace of frivolity: As to his "vulgar streak", it seemed inopportune to indulge this while still poor, but he considered it valuable, as there was so much unexploited beauty in sheer hedonism. The piece "England Not My England" which he sent to *Life and Letters* at that time, narrating his ever-increasing disgust with England, was Connolly's writing at its worst and its best: egoistic, conceited, and uproariously funny.

His marriage, soon afterwards, to a rich American heiress of eighteen, enabled him to be kept comfortably in the style to which he aspired. Despite this, he was preoccupied with his failure to live up to a brilliant promise. His nagging sense of inferiority was a legacy of an unhappy childhood and the socially and academically competitive life he had led as a scholar at Eton. He felt keenly, too, the stigma of his physical ugliness – the flattened nose, the flaking skin and the simian jowl. Like his personality, however, his looks were far from insignificant, and he had little difficulty in charming attractive women. His growing obesity, the result of good living, did nothing to beautify him in the years that followed. During the war, his contemporary John Sparrow, then in the army, noticed how closely Cyril had come to resemble the "Squander Bug", a caricature monster, which featured in advertisements put out by the National Savings Committee to discourage the public from waste. Sparrow's joke, which rapidly spread round the common rooms of Oxford, was that Connolly had volunteered to pose for the "Squander Bug"; such was Cyril's reputation that the story was treated seriously by one distinguished historian, who took the statement at its face value and commented acidly: "How typical! That man would do anything for money."[25]

By that time Cyril had become the editor of an influential literary journal, Horizon, which was regarded by many, including both Desmond[26] and himself, as keeping the flag of literary civilisation flying in England at a dark hour of the world's history. It was a successful and interesting journal for which he deserved the fullest credit. He continued deservedly to enjoy a controversial reputation as critic and author; and he remained a friend of Desmond for whom he had by now a great affection.

The careers of the two men invite comparison, for both were highly talented literati who were often regarded as never having realised their potential, and were their own severest judges in this respect. Both were old Etonians, gregarious, humorous and pleasure-loving. But their personalities were quite different. Connolly was a true hedonist, while Desmond's appetite was for friendship and experience rather than for pleasure as such. He was also without an inferiority complex and hence without the ill-humoured desire to score over his fellows and to show off to the world.

Connolly had a more scholarly brain than Desmond, and he could cope more subtly with the complex, the obscure and the paradoxical; but he had less intellectual honesty and his range of human sympathy and general interests were narrower; nor would Desmond ever have descended to the ridiculous follies which Cyril sometimes displayed – as when during the Second World War, he wrote an editorial in Horizon envying the literary world of occupied France "their moment of glory" in "their fraternal conspiracy against the enemy".[27]

Yet at the moment Desmond occupies an obscurer place in the history of letters than does Cyril, partly because he was so much less concerned with bruiting his own reputation abroad. Popular or not – and he had many close friends – Cyril Connolly had ways of making himself remembered; his rudeness, his flamboyance, his gluttony, his wit, his way with women, his self-advertisement. Moreover Desmond's outlook was that of the world of letters *before* the First World War. He did not understand the modern movement and disliked the American-Paris school. In contrast, Cyril Connolly was, by dint of his youth and an unusually acute intellect, an expert on that turning point in the arts, the significance of which still exercises the mind of commentators today.

Even more important than *Life and Letters* was Desmond's decision, in 1928, to accept the position of chief literary critic for *The Sunday Times*, in succession to Sir Edmund Gosse.[28] How would he compare with that eminent late Victorian? Virginia Woolf, who had no high opinion of Gosse, feared that Desmond might fit only too easily into what was – to her – an uninspiring and conventional mould. However, apart from an enthusiasm for literature – particularly Ibsen – and for society and conversation, the two critics had little in common. Gosse had been a sure-footed climber up the ladder of literary fame. For years even poorer than Desmond, he had subsidised his writing by slaving for museums and government ministries and, later, by becoming Librarian at the House of Lords – a disciplined path of the kind Desmond had shunned. Gosse's too seldom expressed artistic gift had enabled him to write one work of genius about his childhood – *Father and Son* – but his deft, unoriginal critical work had none of Desmond's spontaneity, nor his breadth of cultivation.

In May 1928, after Gosse died, Desmond was asked by *The Sunday Times* to write a commemorative article: he praised the texture of his prose, "smooth as silk and shot with wit and iridescent with fancy", but he also hinted at a lack of creativity and a spiteful streak in his journalism.[29] For Gosse, despite his renowned kindness to young authors, could be vindictive, easily offended by real or imagined insults. At a literary dinner Desmond once heard himself denounced by Gosse for calling him "a vicious ape"; he thought Gosse had gone mad; only later did he discover he was being blamed for allowing a *New Statesman* reviewer to compare Swinburne's early ordeal at the hands of critics (who included Gosse) to a journey through a wilderness full of monkeys.[30] Despite the frequency of such unbalanced behaviour, Gosse, who was desperate for social recognition, achieved the knighthood he made no secret of craving. On *The Sunday Times* he was treated with reverence by Leonard Rees, its elderly editor, for whom he had worked since 1919.

It was not easy for Desmond to step into Gosse's tight little shoes. Rees had chosen Desmond, as, over his long editorial career, he had carefully picked other leading lights of the paper: Gosse himself, Ernest Newman, James Agate and, recently, Dilys Powell. This did not prevent him from being exasperated by Desmond's lateness with copy, his failure to keep appointments and his informality. The punctilious Gosse had communicated by letter when selecting books for review; Desmond preferred to telephone Rees (who came to dislike his habit of ringing off without saying goodbye) or to drop in unannounced, or suggest a meeting at his club. Rees, on his part, Desmond complained, treated him as a man might a second wife: "Rees looks at Gosse's picture on the wall then looks hard at me, and says 'How different from my dear Jemima'."

Though by most accounts a much nicer character than Clifford Sharp, Rees quite as insistent that his journalists should work as a team, and while he seldom quarrelled with the substance of what Desmond wrote, he was pernickity about the way business was conducted. His ignorance of literature – "he didn't know a book from a sponge," Dilys Powell realised after a few weeks with the paper – grated on Desmond, who was increasingly exasperated by the editor's fussiness and reluctance to give him a free hand in the choice of books.

Desmond recognised that his own dilatory ways put him at a disadvantage in arguing with Rees. Jack Lambert, who later worked with Desmond on the literary editorial side, remembered his incurable habits. He would arrive at the printing room at the end of each week: "Books pages had to be away by seven on Friday night. Desmond was there, and some – on good weeks, most – of his article was written; he would hand it out and then potter off and then the proofs would arrive, 150 words short, because he'd stopped. He would have instant asthma: 'Now come along and stop gasping,' I would say. 'You must write another 150 words'."

As often as not it was the other way round: Desmond's article turned out to be too long and then Rees would reduce it arbitrarily. "The wretched man out of spite I think *will* cut my text and alter words," Desmond grumbled to Molly after only a few months at the job. "Of course he would not have done that to Gosse." After several rows, he undertook to present his work at the office earlier, on Thursday, and not at the last minute: "If I do that," he told Molly, "he must respect my text and let me write on subjects on which I can write well." This, however, was a resolution he could not keep; occasionally he lost his copy altogether, or a part of it, like his article on André Maurois' life of Voltaire, and it had to be finished by another journalist.

Despite his eminent position, Desmond was often reproved for his spelling mistakes; but it was only the editor's governessy manner with him to which he objected, for he freely acknowledged his shortcomings in this regard: "Spelling reform", he later wrote in a review, "is [a subject] . . . in which I take a pathetic interest, being probably one of the worst spellers alive among educated writers. . . . I remember writing for an editor who had so much respect for my contributions that he was apt to think there was some subtle intention in my mis-spellings, and once permitted me to head my article 'The Pidgeon'. He could not believe that I did not know how to write the name of that bird."[31]

Although Desmond did not get on with either Rees or his successor, William Hadley, he always found the atmosphere on *The Sunday Times* congenial. There were regular convivial lunches organised by the proprietors. He liked the other journalists – notably the flamboyant James Agate, who wrote the theatre criticism; and the public enjoyed Desmond's weekly column, "The World of Books", which was as lively as "Affable Hawk", even if Rees seemed unimpressed. Desmond's friend, F. L. Lucas, the learned Cambridge literary scholar and fellow Apostle, wrote asking him, in 1929, "How can you be so sensitive, and entertaining, week *after* week? I simply love your articles in that stodgy paper which nothing else would induce me to buy. But your gift for hitting nails on the head astounds me: and there's so much more in your criticism than in the T. S. Eliot type. . . ."

By the late 1920s Desmond had also become nationally known as a radio broadcaster. The British Broadcasting Service was in its infancy when Desmond was first approached by a young producer, Mary Somerville, to take part in the new cultural series she was organising. His work, mostly reviewing, began in an atmosphere of idealism about mass-enlightenment through the radio.[32] He took to the medium naturally. It combined his two loves, literature and conversation. It suited his fondness for instruction and for "good expressions". He was in frequent demand until his death in 1952.

In adapting his journalism to a wireless audience, he kept up his standard, even though he had to compress two or three reviews into each of his brief book talks. Many of the broadcasts were about writers who especially intrigued him. Avoiding the more conventional subjects, he introduced listeners to figures who were less well known to many of them, such as George Moore or Leigh Hunt. In the same spirit he brought them the playwright Molière, who had taught him so much about the art of comedy through the brilliance of his characterisation: and the sixteenth-century sage, Montaigne, who had shown him that the wisest way to approach life was with a kindly scepticism and a liberal dash of gratitude.

He also talked to the Russian authors – Chekhov, Pushkin, and, most of all, Tolstoy.[33] His interest in Tolstoy, whom he had admired since Cambridge days, had grown with the latest translations of his work, and with so many new memoirs constantly appearing. On the subject of Russia and its great creative writers he often consulted a close friend and contemporary, Count Constantine Benckendorff. "Conny" was a figure straight from the pages of Tolstoy, combining *joie de vivre* with deep speculation. "I love that dear old bear very much," Desmond told Molly. A prisoner of the Japanese in 1904, Benckendorff bore a Japanese dragon in three colours tattooed on his forearm. After the Russian Revolution, he served in the Red Navy and was repeatedly imprisoned on mysterious charges before leaving his country finally in the early 'Twenties. When they met at fashionable parties – sometimes with the Asquith circle or Maurice Baring – Desmond would argue about politics and literature with the robustly built "Conny" and would ask him about life in communist Russia: "How many people in Russia do you think are discussing the things we are discussing?" he would enquire. Benckendorff's reply, with its affirmation of his nation's indomitable soul, always thrilled Desmond: "Thousands – at this very moment."[34]

Such picturesque contacts enriched Desmond's broadcasts. For a while, also, during the 'Thirties, he hoped to bring out a book on Tolstoy;* but as with so many earlier projects, this came to nothing, and all that remained were a handful of talks and review articles.

One year he reviewed plays for the radio as well; but he found this embarrassing and soon stopped; the new critical medium was alarmingly potent in its impact; he had constantly to restrain his language on the subject of modern theatre, most of which he disliked, lest he should enrage theatrical managers who had been complaining bitterly to the BBC about the rude comments of his predecessor, James Agate.

As a free-lance, he had no long term contract with the Broadcasting Service. His heaviest spell of work came in the early 'Thirties when he wrote and read over 120 different talks. Thereafter, until war broke out, he was offered few topics that attracted him and was only an occasional performer. The pay was poor: for a theatre review – which involved attending three plays – he received 20 gns, and initially, for book reviews, 10 gns – then 12 gns – for 15 minutes. During the year 1934–5 – when he spoke no less than 23 times – he only earned £320. In time, he learnt to bargain, and to claim a publishing fee when his talk appeared in *The Listener*. This infuriated the accounting department who did all they could to trim a few pounds from his pay; a short rehearsal or a slightly briefer talk than usual were common excuses for cheese-paring and once, when it was discovered that his expenses only amounted to £20, the

---

* It is erroneously alleged that Desmond once visited him: see A. N. Wilson, *Tolstoy* (London, 1988. p. 481). But see also Frances Partridge, *A Pacifist's War* (London, 1978. p. 107) who supplies the name of Tolstoy's visitor – Turgenev on the occasion in question.

estimate for his allowance the following year was reduced. It was not encouraging.

He always gave careful thought to technique. To reach the listeners, he said, it was essential to keep them in mind and not to become egotistically wrapped up in an idea, however interesting. Pace was crucial – a brisk trot through the easier parts, a slower speed where the talk became more difficult or significant. He used to gesticulate as he spoke and BBC producers encouraged this after they found it improved his fluency. He aimed at an informal style and regretted that broadcasting had not begun earlier when, as a younger man, his reactions to literature were at their most spontaneous. He avoided sententiousness by careful choice of words: "a little bad grammar, failing a really excellent style, is rather a good thing".[35]

One of his great assets on the wireless was his voice. He had the agreeable, well-enunciated delivery of a cultivated gentleman from the pre-1914 era, as did another distinguished broadcaster Max Beerbohm: unfortunately, over the air, the distinctive mellifluous tone, which added particular charm to his conversation, was missing. This was partly because the sound equipment was insensitive to his full vocal range; instinctively, too, he adjusted his speech to a public audience, as Dolly Ponsonby noticed when she heard him broadcast; she told Molly: "Arthur and I sat up alone yesterday evening in the servants' hall listening to Desmond! He began, 'Will you give me a glass of water?' It was most amusing, and those words, which we shouldn't have heard, of course, were in Desmond's own voice, while the rest, though excellent, might have been anyone speaking. I could only very occasionally recognize his voice."[36]

By 1932, when Desmond's editorship of *Life and Letters* was coming to an end, his career as a broadcaster was already well launched. Following on from "Affable Hawk", his "Book Talk", his *Sunday Times* appointment and his short-lived, but admirable, journal had together set the seal on his success as a literary journalist. Fame had been long in coming but at last his reputation was secure.

20   Betsy

"I appear as a sort of bald battered Roman Emperor whose face is a trodden foot-ball field of all the passions," wrote Desmond when he had his life-mask made in 1930. It was a fairly accurate description: bald he was, and battered – when some of his teeth were extracted he was dilatory about replacing them; Margot Asquith told him the gap in his front teeth was reminiscent of Death: "I only grinned and showed my gap."[1] He was frequently rendered breathless by asthma attacks. As for the passions, his face reflected the intensity of those, particularly now when he embarked upon the greatest love-affair of his life. It caused him anguish, as well as pleasure, arousing as it did a jealous fury in Molly which was often unbalanced.

Nevertheless, Desmond remained an attractive-looking man, not dandified, but distinctive, even distinguished whenever, which was rarely, he gave thought to his appearance. Visitors to the house in Wellington Square might encounter him changing to dine out: the first time a young friend of Rachel's, Mary Pakenham, called, she was shown into the dining-room, and "there was Desmond, telephoning and shaving before going out to dinner. He wasn't a bit non-plussed at meeting this young girl for the first time with lather all over his face," she recalls.

Before changing he also enjoyed a rejuvenating hot bath; in this, as in all things, gregarious, he liked company in the bathroom. "Come and talk to me in my bath," he would call out to his son, Dermod.

"The bathing arrangements at Wellington Square were inadequate, primitive and squalid by present-day standards," Dermod recalled. "But however much my father revelled in the luxury of bath rooms in the country houses of friends we went to stay with, their roaring hot water taps and huge towels, he never complained about the wretchedness of our own." Desmond liked a really hot bath, hotter than most people could stand. "Having stepped in and sat down rather gingerly, he took a sponge and began douching his back and chest with it . . . making loud gasping sounds, aah! aah! aaah! as when pleasure is on the border of pain. Then he would lean rather violently backwards and slide down the slope of the bath with a swish, creating a surge of water which rebounded from the other end, rushed back and broke over his chest like a miniature tidal wave. This he repeated again and again.

"It is his early middle age I am visualising. His chest was very deep, rather barrel shaped due to emphysema, his general build strong, staunch, not exactly stocky but 'cobby' to use his own adjective; strong legs, small buttocks, narrow hips; abdomen no longer flat but not a paunch, not ventré. And genitalia smallish, well made, rather neat as in Greek statues. He was not a very hairy man, but I used to watch with fascination the to and fro swing of the fine black hairs on his chest and belly with the movement of the water, like seaweed in a rockpool."

If Desmond had time, he took a bath in the morning, and then he might be visited by old friends: some, like the barrister Charlie Sanger, would call in on their way to work; but there were also the arch timewasters, G.A.P. and Bob "Trevy". Their "loud noises of conversation, splashing and roars of laughter came from the matchwood compartment on the first landing. . . . My mother, who thought that people should not come upstairs at that time of day, especially to go on with what was really Cambridge life of 20 years ago, hated it."

Failing any company, Desmond was quite ready to talk to himself in the bath. He liked inventing euphonious nonsense or nicknames, "Ramina-grobis" for Molly, "Bobolinka" for Bob Trevy; "it was words like this or long nonsensical rigmaroles, interesting to the ear only, that came floating up the staircase with a watery accompaniment. . . . But what one most often heard, especially in the morning bath, was just a tired repetition of "My life, my life" – "My life, my life!"[2]

Neither for Desmond nor for Molly was there tranquillity in their middle age. Particularly not when, in his early fifties, Desmond fell in love for the last, most intense time.

Betsy Graves Reyneau was an American from New England, an artist and would-be writer (of somewhat doom-laden prose, little of which was ever published). Desmond first encountered her during the summer of 1929 whilst he and Molly were on holiday in France; she had recently separated from her French husband, by whom she had one daughter, Marie, then still a child. Ten years younger than Desmond, Betsy at forty was no beauty, but she was attractive, and made herself agreeably flattering to him; but above all she gave him something he had never enjoyed so intensely before – sexual pleasure.

The few surviving letters between them – most of their correspondence was destroyed at his death – are unlike any other of his love letters in the strength of their passion. The sexual satisfaction which their affair brought him, for the first time in his life, made him refuse to relinquish this relationship, though it blighted his marriage for a decade: at the end of which, their affair over, he wrote to Betsy, once more in America, acknowledging "the fact that I have had to pay, pay, pay in happiness and peace of mind in other directions to keep you in my life," but it had, he emphasised, been worth it.[3]

A literary friend, the poet Sheila Wingfield whom Betsy got to know in England, wrote of her, "To know Betsy is to be given back enthusiasms lost since youth. If Betsy didn't smoke the whole time, with a trick of holding the cigarette out to glance at it through lowered lids while talking, and if she hadn't a dry sense of humour, and weren't an indulgent parent, and didn't speak in an engagingly deep New England voice, you might, just, imagine her as Joan of Arc." An ardent, if simplistic, left-wing campaigner, "adept of picket-line, soap-box and civil rights meeting, everything she does springs clear and straight from the heart" – though there was not always a corresponding link-up with the head.[4]

Betsy was unlike anyone Desmond had been attracted to before and singularly different from Molly. Not for Betsy the subtleties of Cynthia Asquith, nor the scruples of Irene Cooper-Willis. Although, like Irene, she espoused unpopular causes, such as racial inequalities in her native America, she was not well-educated, nor an organised career woman – she stretched her small talent as far as she could, picking up, at random, commissions to draw people for magazines. Desmond helped her in this as best he could, writing to well-known friends like Virginia Woolf and, later on, Ruth Draper. These two did not sit for her, but others, Oliver Esher for example, agreed, and she also had the dubious pleasure of drawing Chen. Above all, Betsy was an outsider in England, and her friendship with Desmond did not substantially alter that. Molly extracted a promise from him that he would keep their affair quiet. "I have done what I promised with regard to B.R.," he told her, "we never go about together". Although Molly patronised her as "fast and flattering with men – but all the while *had* to be mercenary to get along!"[5] Betsy was not really on the make: she was poor and Desmond could not help in supporting her (though Molly was convinced that he was squandering money on her). Nor did he provide an entrée into literary or aristocratic society (much as she would have liked one). Although their relationship was an ineradicable part of both their lives, it was more-or-less clandestine. This rankled, but it had to be. When Desmond was invited to stay with Sheila Wingfield and her husband, for instance, Betsy did not accompany him. Nor did she visit Leonard and Virginia Woolf with him or others of their old friends, or even go with him to many large parties. She did not go to Wellington Square, except infrequently and when Molly was away. Desmond's children scarcely saw her, though they were very much aware of her existence, if only as a source of bitter argument between their parents.

Desmond and Betsy enjoyed happy, intimate times together, such as the holiday they took in Europe in the late summer of 1930. Earlier that year Betsy had returned to America to clear up her affairs before settling in London to be near Desmond. While she was away they wrote to one another constantly. "How I long to hold you Betsy and share your body and everything with you that lovers can. Today and yesterday the physical longing has let me alone, but I don't get peace for much longer than two days together. Tonight I fear your ghost," he wrote to her on 2nd July 1930. Letters were a comfort to them both. Desmond wrote that he took all of hers with him when he went to stay with the Eshers at Watlington. "O my beloved no lover could be loved more as I understand love," he had told her on 24th June. "It is the kind I want I have from you, I only pray that mine may seem just what you want. . . . My dear, I spent such happy hours. I read them all, and then when I turned out the light I imagined that you were within reach of my arms in the great four poster bed. And when I was called with tea I went on reading, and often words in them made me turn to the empty pillow besides me. And after the disappoint[ment] I said to myself 'Soon, soon she *will* be there.'" He would meet her boat when it docked – "I'll be there, waiting for THE INCREDIBLE TO COME TRUE". For their leisurely holiday in Europe, he reminded her to pack "the famous but superfluous black night gown" (a present from him, which became somewhat of a cause célèbre between him and Molly).[6]

From the start Desmond had been open with Molly about his love-affair, feeling, as they both did, that honesty in relationships was always for the best: "I have been more at peace in my mind while with Betsy and yet you have been more constantly in my mind than ever before. You have won this for me, given me this ease of mind. I owe it to you . . ." he wrote to her on the eve of his departure for Luxembourg where he was to stay with Betsy. "I do hope dearest you will be fairly happy while I am away. I shall think of you much more often because the thought of you will not give me so much pain. Indeed, it is strange how close *I* have felt to you since we parted. If I had not been so frantically busy I should have tried to find you today. . . . Though I know I shall be happy at Vianden with B.R. – especially if I work well on the M.S. – I shall be happy in coming back. . . . Please dearest believe it. . . . Send any letters which you think I ought to answer. Tell me that I may write to you about B.R., if I may without causing you pain. I should like to, as it would mean that our intimacy was not injured by this. Good bye my dearest and generous one."[7] But Molly was not able to be generous about his relationship and the intimacy between them was irretrievably injured by his affair with Betsy: having to accept the unpalatable truth that her husband loved a women with whom he enjoyed a sexual passion such as he had never known with her, having to live with constant reminders of her – telephone calls to Wellington Square, Desmond's elusiveness about his plans and whereabouts – these caused Molly agony; nor could she disguise this. So Desmond soon stopped telling her about Betsy and tried to play the affair down. Subterfuge worked no better than honesty: Molly unleashed her unhappiness and jealousy – which in turn infuriated Desmond, and scenes between them were frequent. Soon they could spend almost no time together without her resentment and bitterness, and Desmond's impatience and, finally, anger bubbling to the surface. Molly's deafness drove her too much in on herself and when she was in company, either with Desmond or with other people, she was liable to explode into wild accusations. It is painful to read a scrap of a letter Desmond wrote to her now, and perhaps did not show her, describing how she needled him in front of other people – old friends such as Roger Fry and his companion, Helen Anrep, or their children, "about my being a woman chaser and not a proper man. . . . If I leave the house you will turn on the gas and commit suicide. Why? Why? Why anything so utterly different from your letters? . . .

"You see I live in a perpetual state of apprehension. I may have been extra-considerate for a day or two, but suddenly something will remind you of my having left you without letters at Oare and the explosion will come. Even if it does not amount to 'a scene', I never know when you won't say something on purpose to hurt me. I happen to catch sight of myself in a glass – 'Don't for God's sake put on that expression – that is not what your face is like.' Implication: silly old coxcomb, he doesn't know what a feeble look he has, and so on."[8]

These incontinent rages were unfortunately reminiscent of Molly's mother, Blanche's "nerve riots", explosive, wounding, unpredictable, the result of over-stretched nerves, as much as of Molly's specific cause for jealousy. Part of the trouble was that Molly was not physically strong – unlike the vital Betsy – and she had an unusually early change of life, with complications, involving a spell in hospital. Now in her late forties, she looked much older; photographs show her face looking as if it had been dropped – her features going downwards, the corners of her mouth severe, her expression impassive, her eyes guarded. Molly's father had dealt with Blanche's "nerve riots" by retreating – into his study or the library, or simply his own thoughts. At times Desmond tried to be understanding in the face of his wife's compulsive behaviour, to reason, to cajole – he had, after all, had a lifetime's experience of dealing with his mother. He wrote a lengthy letter answering her cry of anguish at losing him:

"I was very much touched by your note.

"You have not lost *me*. Even if we lived apart which Heaven forfend you would not lose me. . . .

"It does not matter *now* that years ago we drifted away from physical intimacy. It was neither my fault nor yours in a sense, but that of our ignorance of the importance of that physical tie, which your religious and my philosophic education was responsible for, contempt for the body. But marvel of marvels in a sense we have weathered that blunder which has caused you such pain & left this disposition in you to hate me as well as love.

"I do recall that unwittingly I did you a great wrong and my own happiness a great injury, by never lying with you all these years. But you must remember that neither on your side nor on mine was physical attraction strong between us from the first. Our marriage was based in a perfectly spontaneous delight in each other's natures & minds, and that that has proved so lasting, though it has often been buried under pain & disputes, shows that the marriage of true *minds* is also a lasting marriage. . . .

"While we lived as man & wife our physical relations were delightful but not deep." Desmond now regretted that "in my ignorance of human nature (my own, yours) I did not know that much might still be made out of the physical tie between you & me," even after it had been severed by the all-too-frequent arrival of children, by Molly's affair with Clive, and Desmond's vain courtship of Irene Cooper-Willis, and his "sweet but not very deep" (and unchronicled) affair with Angela Lavelli (one-time mistress of Roger Fry). "Then," he went on, "you fell in love with Philip Ritchie. Dearest, if only you had not been afraid of the difference of age, or if he had been more of a woman-lover, that might have brought you consolation for what our marriage lacked. We should have both been spared much misery. . . . You would not have envied me & been so resentful of my having had a mistress. . . . And then when you reached the most trying time of a woman's life when *nature* makes her revolt against the prospect of being no longer fertile & the passing away of ~~sex~~ love chances, confusing all her emotions, I took another mistress. It was very hard on you & I did not realize *how* hard . . ." but he concluded, this was no reason for her to be a dog-in-the-manger.

"Just as with regard to your deafness I have felt because you cannot oh! it is terrible – get the amusement & fun of general talk & the pleasures of variety in social life – why should I give up so many things which my nature fits me to enjoy? . . .

"My love for you is not perfect or I would have given up everything to relieve to the utmost your solitude – given up all sex-life all social life to make your loneliness as tolerable as I possibly could. My love is far from perfect or unselfish but it is real and strong."[9]

For a while Molly was soothed, but not for long; the compulsion in her which caused anger to spew itself forth in scenes, often in the night, left them both shattered and drained. So Desmond lived, as he told her, in a continual state of apprehension, never knowing when the rage would manifest itself, nor what would trigger it. Particularly now that Betsy had come to London to live, Molly found it expedient to retreat, to stay with old friends at Oare, or for a "brace" by the sea, to get away from "The whole *disaster* life is – over and over again! So Godforsaken and *insane*. It drives one's heart into one's boots; and it's difficult to keep one's faith in it *at all* – don't you sometimes feel? . . ." she wrote, half-humorously, to Dolly Ponsonby.[10]

When she was at Wellington Square her children could also become a focus of her fury. Michael was abroad, farming, but Dermod and Rachel were living at home, Dermod studying hard at St Bartholomew's medical school to become a doctor. Pretty and popular, Rachel naturally enjoyed going out with friends to the theatre; but often, on her return to the house, her mother would waylay her and accuse her – groundlessly – of loose living, perhaps just for having the emancipated girlhood she herself had never enjoyed. Rachel, who was an obedient and sweet-natured daughter, did her best to allay her mother's needless anxiety and to placate her. She now became the confidante of both her parents; late at night her father and she would talk over their evenings, where they had been and who they had seen. They had an easy, close relationship, which Rachel always valued. He talked to her about Betsy, too, insisting always that their relationship must run its course otherwise, as he also told Molly, he would be left with a feeling of bitterness and resentment towards his wife. So as she entered her twenties, Rachel found herself a reluctant go-between in her parents' troubled marriage.

She herself was falling in love with the younger son of the Marquess of Salisbury, Lord David Cecil, now an English Literature don at Oxford. Much to Desmond and Molly's delight, they became engaged in the summer of 1932. The MacCarthys found David "an angel – has a clever heart as well as a clever head, which is rarer than a clever head." His family, "one of the dozen greatest and proudest families in England," was more daunting; "the most honourable and kindly people, but they would consider R a very poor match, which she is – I haven't a thousand pounds even to settle on her," Desmond had written to Betsy Reyneau before the engagement.[11] It was still usual for the aristocracy to marry among their social equals, although Lord Salisbury's own parents had made a love-match which had not been well-received; (his mother, a woman of exceptional personality, having, like Rachel MacCarthy, no money). But the MacCarthys need not have worried: "his parents have been charming about Rachel. I think it is perfect of them," Molly wrote to Dolly Ponsonby. ". . . for the uniting of the great house of 25 Wellington Square with Hatfield is ludicrous if seen from the point of view of the world, or from a malicious point of view – & if they are so kind and unsnobbish well then that washes out all that kind of thing."[12] (Chen as usual had her own idiosyncratic view of the social background of the alliance, which was that the Cecils were upstarts compared with the de la Chevalleries with their plethora of ancient quarterings.)

The wedding, in October 1932, was to be a simple morning ceremony, which required weeks of elaborate preparation and was preceded by "a tremendous number of beanos, and receptions organised in fine Victorian style by Lady Salisbury. . . ."

Chen of course made mischief about the arrangements. There was to be a small luncheon party after the ceremony at the Eshers' house in Hill Street, Mayfair. The MacCarthys omitted to ask Chen's sister, Aunt Zelma, of whom they had anyway never seen a great deal. Now in her seventies, Zelma was as energetic and disagreeable in her own different way as Chen. She and her brilliant and eccentric son, General J. F. C. (formerly "Fritz") Fuller, had joined the fascist "Black Shirts", whose rallies they attended. On learning of the party, for relations and close friends, to which she was not invited, Zelma, like the bad fairy in *Sleeping Beauty*, penned Chen a furious letter; Chen in turn wrote Molly "a 14 page stinger of the most insulting order", saying that it was entirely Molly's fault that Zelma had not been asked; it was a letter of downright hatred, said Molly, which attacked her about everything from the way she brought up her children to how she organised her finances. She begged Desmond to soothe his mother down and to protect her from such venom.[13]

The wedding itself, in the ancient church of St Bartholomew-the-Great in Smithfield, passed off serenely. "They seemed rather like two medieval children being wedded I thought both so very young in looks," wrote Molly. While Virginia Woolf observed how "very small, smooth, pale and sleek appeared Rachel and Desmond arm in arm. I have never seen him as a father. now he was that – gentle, kind – leading his daughter . . . Molly was much as a pouter pigeon in some maroon dress with a yellow bunch."[14] The best man was the novelist L. P. Hartley, one of David Cecil's closest friends at Oxford. Over the following years Leslie Hartley also became a great friend of Molly's. Sympathetic and good-natured, he appreciated her humour, and somehow managed to overcome her deafness: he once remarked that Molly was always the youngest person in any gathering.

Rachel and David Cecil's marriage was not only of itself exceptionally happy, but also brought happiness to Molly and Desmond. The young couple were affectionate and family-minded and their house at Rockbourne near Salisbury became a second home for Molly and Desmond in the years leading up to the Second World War. Molly was comforted to see the state of marriage reaffirmed, her own being under siege from Betsy Reyneau. She was habitually anxious about her children, but for once there was nothing to worry her in David and Rachel's lives. On the other hand, Michael, though a fine, strong young man, took some time to settle on a career. He had worked on G.A.P.'s estate in South Africa, until that was sold off at a loss. It was a relief to everyone, including himself, when, in the mid-thirties, he became bailiff on Bryan Guinness's farm at Biddesden in Wiltshire.

Molly and Desmond continued to see their friends though not as much as they would have liked, Desmond being inundated with work, and Molly hampered by her deafness and depression. Desmond and Betsy remained very close although the sexual intensity of their relationship did not last longer than a couple of years. Betsy was now settled in a flat in a pretty mid-nineteenth century house, number 51 St James's Gardens, to the north of Holland Park. She would have liked more of Desmond's time, but he was habitually bad at organising it and behindhand with his work so that arranging his days was never easy for him.

Molly herself was no more practical, but took sporadic steps at tidying and organising the rackety household in Wellington Square. To this end, she asked her young friend Frances Marshall to help arrange the library: about ten new books were tossed into the house each week, she told her; Desmond rarely replaced anything in the shelves, which were consequently in great disarray. There were books everywhere in the tall house, in specially constructed bookcases on the narrow landings, in Desmond's study-bedroom on the top floor, and of course in the hall, where parcels of review copies arrived weekly for Desmond, who never lost his eagerness at cutting the string and opening up the brown paper. When Frances Marshall was undertaking the "literary charring" as she called it, Desmond would talk to her at length about each book and its author – Vernon Lee, for example, which was fascinating but time-consuming. Desmond's interest in the books themselves was greater than any desire to see them logically arranged; for a devoted literary man, he had a certain insouciance about books as objects. They were to be used and enjoyed, like everything he appreciated in life. This was in contrast to the carefully tended library of his contemporary Lytton Strachey, in whose household at Ham Spray in Wiltshire Frances Marshall now spent most of her weekends with Ralph Partridge whom she was eventually to marry.

Desmond and Molly were frequent guests at Ham Spray, too, and were fond of Carrington as well as Lytton, though his "intellectual arrogance" by which she meant his narrowness, his dismissiveness, grated on Molly: he was an integral part of Desmond's life, and had been since their years at Cambridge. In the winter of 1931 Lytton fell gravely ill; Desmond wrote to him, sending the note, as a sign both of his affection and admiration, with Frances to Ham Spray: "as a substitute for talking with you I have been re-reading you. How well you have written! Ease, subtlety, clarity, consistency, and the wit and the grace – I am enjoying all your qualities again and feeling a despairing admiration."[15]

This was the last communication he had with his old friend; it would have been read out to Lytton as he lay, growing weaker and weaker from the cancer which killed him in January 1932. Soon after his death, Desmond, in *The Sunday Times*, sketched Lytton's qualities as a writer with all the perception of a close friend and fellow essayist; he singled out his brilliant powers of selection, no matter how great the forest of information confronting him; and the beguiling smoothness of his prose; more surprisingly, he stressed his seriousness – despite an appearance of frivolity, Lytton was a moralist defending the values he rated highest, sometimes disregarding historical facts to do so. Desmond saw all this expressed in "the soft and steady gravity of his eyes" and his two voices: "one as tiny as the gnat's in *Alice in Wonderland*" in which he would puncture any remark he regarded as nonsense; the other grave and deep, when speaking of matters that touched him deeply.[16]

The immediate problem after Lytton's death was Carrington's inconsolable grief for the loss of the companion she had idolised and who had given shape and meaning to her life: she could scarcely drag herself through the bleak days and sleepless nights without him. One idea that their friends had was for Desmond to collect and edit the unpublished works, essays and short pieces which would give Carrington something to work on connected with Lytton. With that in mind he visited her at Ham Spray a month after Lytton's death. The only account of this is the touching, scrawled note Carrington wrote afterwards thanking Desmond for coming and telling him some more about Lytton's reading: "I was slightly in a dream, and couldn't pull myself together. I forgot to tell you – but you probably know it already – that Lytton read Jane Austen more than any author I think. A winter never passed without our reading all her novels – Donne, Marvell, Shakespeare's sonnets, and Pope perhaps most often in poetry. On walks he took Keats, and Milton. There used to be note books with all the books read every month but I don't know if I can find them for you. The Russians depressed him, although he admired them tremendously. Their habits, and the cold, I think were too much. It was a comfort seeing you – I wanted you to talk to me about Cambridge days, but I was conscious you came down here to work, and I ought not to distract you perhaps. – I feel you understand because of your remark about Lear. For that is the clue to Lytton's character, which only people who cared very much saw. My love to Molly and to you. Your Carrington."[17]

What the remark about Lear was we shall never know, but this letter brings home the depth of Carrington's love for Lytton, how much of his reading was shared by her, and, by extension, how much of his life. She could not survive without him; a few days after Desmond's visit, she shot herself. Her husband, Ralph Partridge, who had done all he could to protect her from suicide, was devastated by her death, especially following so soon upon Lytton's. Desmond and Molly both wrote to him, Molly hoping that "we shall always be able to talk naturally about Lytton and Carrington; also that I shall always be able to see them quite clearly. I can always see Philip Ritchie – and now I see Lytton exactly clearly – and I see Carrington as she used to look in the garden at Ham Spray, on rather a chill spring day – with her fair hair – with a spade running down the lawn to plant something."[18]

Molly and Desmond became close friends with Ralph Partridge; fair, handsome and robust, he was an invigorating presence: exclusively heterosexual, he had never been physically attracted to Lytton, though devoted to him; but he had been captivated by Carrington, as Molly wrote to Dolly Ponsonby, describing the household at Ham Spray: "Carrington had left Partridge before he took up with Frances. . . . But they were all complete pagans together – rebels and outlaws with strange inner histories. Not ignoble; and they were very sincere. – but arrogant intellectually – with Lytton as their support in that! and all the while too human; and quite misguided. It is impossible to know how Ralph and Frances will make out their life. The whole party – Lytton – Ralph – Carrington and Frances were bound up together in affectionate and comradeship at Ham Spray – though not in love affairs – and the bravest thing they can do, is to pay no attention to the world – and live and make the best of a life together – but at present they are utterly shattered . . ."[19]

Ralph and Frances Partridge married soon afterwards; they continued to be amongst the MacCarthys' close friends; and Ham Spray was always one of their favourite houses to visit. The talk; the delicious, simple meals, so carefully prepared from fresh garden produce with occasional exotic imports; the sunny verandah where they ate when the weather allowed; the walks across the Downs – everything about the house was congenial to them. They had many friends in common, such as Raymond Mortimer, and many tastes, among them a love of France. It was to France that

Molly decided to go, early in 1933, to recuperate from the pain which still bedevilled her, despite her operation, and to review the turmoil of her life by distancing herself from it. Her Aunt Emily Ritchie had died and left her a few hundred pounds and so Molly planned a lengthy stay abroad to take stock of her life. "I shall write often, and hope to be in really good rapport with you," she reported to Desmond from the little hotel at Nice where she began her stay.[20]

One of Lytton's older sisters, Dorothy, had married the painter, Simon Bussy, and Molly arranged to stay as a paying guest at their villa in Roquebrune. Here Simon Bussy painted much and spoke little; Dorothy was hard at work on translating André Gide's works; their only child, Janie, who lived with them, was also a painter. The atmosphere of studious calm was just what Molly needed after enduring what had been, she admitted, virtually a nervous breakdown in the preceding months. Not since 1906, when she was first engaged, had her thoughts and feelings been in such tumult. Both of her breakdowns were triggered off by Desmond and both had sexual connotations: the first arose from the prospect of the sexual and emotional commitment of marriage; this later one from the prospect of that sexual and emotional life coming irrevocably to an end, her ill-health, depression and deafness driving Desmond and herself apart, and Betsy Reyneau usurping her position in Desmond's life.

Her search for tranquillity was not without disturbance: her sister, Charlotte, who was also staying in the South of France, collapsed in church from a heart attack and Molly had to tend her; luckily, she made a good recovery. An unexpected visitor at the hotel one morning was Beryl de Zoete, wearing a forage cap and smiling away, like a dog, Molly told Ralph: together she and Beryl strolled about the shops of Nice where "I dissuaded her from a pale blue nauch-girl frock to her knees".[21]

In the Bussys' pretty pink-washed villa, La Souco, Molly was given a charming bedroom, with green shutters at the windows: it reminded her of her girlhood paradise at Lynton, but instead of the Bristol Channel, this looked out over the vast sweep of the Mediterranean, and orange and lemon trees grew beneath the window in the steeply terraced garden. At night Monte Carlo lay twinkling before her, "like a marvellous conglomeration of brilliants round the headland's neck making the Southern Cross seem like an old dingy piece of real jewellery up in the sky".[22] Immediately behind the villa was the main coast road, which Molly crept along, in the gutter, like a humble goat while ruthless machinery tore by; she went up to the little village of Roquebrune with its clusters of tiled roofs; she visited Menton and the other coastal towns, which were peaceful out of season. And she enjoyed being part of the Bussys' talented, unusual household without feeling obliged to join in everything: "I don't speak much – to save the shouting," she wrote to Ralph Partridge. "I feel inclined to be very silent and I only hope they don't find me very dull and deaf."

She never saw Bussy's paintings. Matisse, with whom he had studied, paid visits, but Bussy was, and felt himself acutely to be, neglected as a painter in his lifetime. This increased his bitterness and disinclination to have much to do with the world. "Bussy works, & laughs with his harsh laugh – he still alarms me a little but the fact is he likes to be alarming! Dorothy translates her Gide at top speed, spectacled, and bent over writing table nearly all day."[23]

Molly's letters to Desmond reflect her struggle to gain mental equanimity; "the day Reyneau steps on board her liner, you can send me a wire, and I shall reclaim my own property; – but till then . . . I really want to stop. . . ." In another she said that her menstrual period, "my crise", as she called it, brought bad headaches and some depression "but much less fury, and all *much* shorter – only 2 days." Whilst her mood varied, "I never go right back again. I have had *one or 2 nights* of nightmare when the thought of returning to Wellington Square fills me with a terror-twinge, and I look at it round the corner, and again round the corner, and then smother the monster; and then out comes remembrance of the scream of the phone by my bed, and myself all dishevelled lying back tortured by Reyneau. Then at dawn I get off to sleep and oh! the relief that there has been no *scene* – no *scene* – when I wake! The *gain*. The sure certainty that I am nearer love than that *awful* hate; that will not grow less but must increase with increasing deafness combined with marriage with a Pincher; and if not faced generously, all is up for her."

She read Browning, and found him as beautiful as ever, especially compared with "the little books of incomprehensibility we discuss for hours *now*". But she begged Desmond, "Don't read Browning to Reyneau will you dearest? I don't want to think of it – one or two poems made me have a twinge thinking of you and she – using poetry for expression. However it's pretty early Victorian. . . . Oh how far you drifted from me Des! and oh what happened to me – with every nerve alive? I am *sure* I am getting stronger now – I can forget more, and have been much less at the mercy of my thoughts, and this is one of my *bad* times just now so you see I *am* better."

She looked forward to Desmond joining her in France for his holiday and resolved that she would not storm at him when he came: "We shall have calm and delightful times, and you will be so good to me too, and will do things for my pleasure. I feel you will make up for the poor arid years (when I was too proud to speak of my sense of perpetual unfulfilment) *in other ways*, – and I forgive you now *everything*. – and *I* shall make up for my terrible storms *in other ways* – and now there will be born a new era": she determined it will be one of self-reliance on her part. In an excoriating passage, however, she showed that that era was not ready to dawn quite yet: "I wonder if *you* have *ever* known the *hate* I hated Reyneau with? Sometimes Irene? [Noel] Did you hate? Tell me.

"Simon Bussy is reading St. Simon's memoirs. He told me yesterday with his own odd fierce laugh how St. Simon sometimes *hated* a character at the Court – so much so that he had to go to bed and lie there and just *hate*. – and I laughed so much when he told me! – in a kind of burst of merriment! and he laughed – and *oh* we did laugh! At the idea of St. Simon's tremendous hate! Sympathetic to both of us. He is a very masculine little man; and I think he *has* a lot of hate in him; don't you?" It is an odd glimpse: the furiously humorous Frenchman and the over-wrought Englishwoman, so different from each other but sharing the same grim little joke.

Molly complained that Desmond did not write to her, and she imagined "you are so wrapt up in Reyneau that you can't write, and that she is doing her best, in her heart of hearts, to undo all she can of what is sacred to me, though *outwardly* and *nominally* eschewing such an idea!

"There is a new type now – 'The Sex prig'. I see it growing. I see it in Lawrence's satelites [sic]; in Dorothy Bussy-votary of Buggers and 'anti-marriage' because of her feminism . . . and the abolition of the home is very sympathetic to types like Ray, Karin, Dorothy and Marjorie Strachey, because they have no sympathy with domesticity, and believe in dropping the child at the earliest possible moment into Bertrand Russellish schools, and 'getting on with the work'. I think D.B. (who is a dear – I like her very much) is all the same eccentric like Marjorie; she has no ordinary *human* common sense – only the intellectual experimental sense. I don't suppose Janie will ever marry – she says she doesn't approve of marriage; and I think she doesn't care for infants."

This abandoning of conventional family ties was deeply antipathetic to Molly, struggling as she now was to maintain hers, despite the attempts of Betsy Reyneau, whom she regarded as the worst type of the "New Woman". She saw Betsy and herself as opposing ends of the female spectrum battling for the same goal: Desmond. The one, both from necessity and, it must be said, inclination, accepting the conventional lot of women, to marry, have children and run a home; the other advocating "Free Love" and avoiding the squalid, or indeed any other, results and responsibilities of her affairs; ultimately she put the Strachey women, who were not noted for their domesticity, into the same camp along with Betsy and other irritating examples of the New Femininity such as Alys

Russell and Enid Bagnold. "I think 'Freedom' as a positive 'slogan' in some women is bad, and leads invariably to trouble" she wrote later of Betsy.[24]

Now at the beginning of March 1933, Molly left La Souco as André Gide was coming to stay and her bedroom was needed for him. She moved along the coast to Hyères, which was topped by "Edith Wharton's frowning restored castle. . . . The place is all guarded with glass-bottled walls, and 'Defense d'Entrer', 'Gard aux Chiens' and 'Gard aux Loups!' – 'Gard aux *Lions*' is *my* cry as I skirt the hill on my walk! jealously grudging the *amazing* results of on the whole rather dreary literary output!" Molly was not in the mood for entering the caves of such literary lions at the moment, but presently the two women met and became friends. Edith Wharton turned out to be kindness itself. "She likes me and we get on very well. I respect her . . ." Molly reported to Desmond.

Whilst Wellington Square was shut during Molly's absence abroad, Desmond stayed in Chelsea with Alys and Logan Pearsall Smith. Molly was always irritated by Alys's relentless do-gooding, her espousal of causes and overlooking of people, and now in particular by her well-intentioned postcards from London to the South of France giving her news of Desmond, who she knew had not written to her himself. Before joining Molly in France Desmond spent some time at I Tatti, near Florence, the villa of Logan's sister Mary and her husband Bernard Berenson.[25]

Desmond enjoyed the company of his host, though B.B.'s extravagant judgements on people made Desmond protest frequently; nevertheless, "He is one of the most learned men I have met and I enjoy turning him on to the history of art and civilisation," he told Molly. Conversation played as large a part in the Berensons' life as it did in Desmond's, though their interests were different – aesthetics and gossip being central to the Berensons. Their guests, drawn from international society, were invariably invited to luncheon – the food at I Tatti was delicious. "About 3 the Babel became rather trying," Desmond said. "Then, if 'B.B.' hadn't a beautiful lady to accompany him, I would go with him for a walk, which always began with a motor drive into some wood or among the hills, or I would go for a little independent sightseeing in Florence or to call on Vernon Lee, who is my delight."

The rest of his day was equally civilised: in the morning he was called with coffee on a prettily laid tray which he would take into Logan's room "and we would talk eagerly about what we talk about at St. Leonard's Terrace, the magic of words, the faults of our friends and the dubious but divine consolations of literature; and he would translate a little news from the right Italian papers which seem to spend their space entirely on repeating that there never, never was such a wonderful race as the Italians, day after day. Then after lying like a crocodile in hot water I would take a stroll in the ilex grove among white mossy statues, up and down the terraced garden with its gurgling basins and cypresses like candle-flames shedding darkness instead of light; and every morning I would say to myself 'one day I shall get something very important from all this, something of inestimable benefit will happen to my mind – I shall understand.'

"But nothing ever happened and I would soon go indoors to the books. At the backs of these I would gaze in an ecstasy of depression, feeling how little I know and how old I was and that I need however never be *bored* again. . . ."

After a fortnight, Desmond joined Molly in Hyères; he found her better, and more cheerful. Edith Wharton invited them both to the heavily-fortified château Molly had derided, and there they stayed in great comfort. "We rambled about her perfect garden, eat [sic] her perfect food, went for drives in her perfect motor and ignored her far from perfect little dogs. She read us part of her Memoirs, and I secured a slice about Henry James for L.[ife] & L.[etters]. I enjoyed some of my talks with her and conceived respect for her intellect and brilliant thorough cultivation. But until I began to read her books in bed at night I was rather puzzled why so robust an old lady should cling so fast to the sheltered corners of life. I felt I wasn't really her sort. I wasn't safe and considerate enough. One day I might say something which would let the wind into the orchid-house – and then! However she was kind; very kind, anxious kind – and we were grateful."

Molly and Desmond parted at Toulon, he to return to London, she to have a water-cure at Aix-les-Bains. Both had enjoyed their holiday: it had brought them the contentment in each other's company that had for too long eluded them. From Aix-les-Bains Molly wrote, "Dearest D. I felt so united to you as we sat in the setting sun, and having our dinner before we left Toulon. We are as natural together as two human beings can be, mutually, and it *is* very happy that. . . . Both of us are people rather specially gifted for life, and extra endowed, coupled with lamentable weakness. We *must* go on trying to manage our weaknesses, if we are to be happy old people, now that period is not far off. . . . Well dearest . . . I am stronger for bearing all the things that *must* make me unhappy, if I am not to be a liar – but able to look forward to using my own resources again."

Her return to England in May demanded fresh effort from her; nothing had changed at Wellington Square, and Molly still had to cope with her own swings of mood from depression to equanimity. Rachel wrote sympathising with her mother: "I have been thinking about you a great deal all day, and the more I think of it, the more do I feel that it is really cruel for you to have to come back to the same old thing with Madame R. again: I mean Daddy's tactlessness, and dining out again so soon. As you say, he had all the time when you were abroad – and I am sure anyone *would* mind acutely – I don't believe time does make much difference, and one doesn't get used to being disappointed continually."[26]

For the rest of the decade Molly had to reconcile herself to the reality that she and Desmond would live more apart than together; that she had perforce to make her own life, to achieve spiritual calm on her own. Not until the outbreak of war did she find the longed-for peace.

21 "Our Tip-Top Paper"

During the 'Thirties, the circulation of *The Sunday Times* began to rise rapidly, outstripping its rival *The Observer*. Desmond, as chief literary critic, had a readership which reached 500,000 by the end of the Second World War. The tone of *The Sunday Times* was that of "a forthright and unalleviated Toryism", which continued when Gomer Berry (later Lord Kemsley) became the sole proprietor in 1936.[1] In the late 'Thirties, Kemsley strongly supported Neville Chamberlain's belief that a reasonable agreement with Hitler could be achieved. Politically, therefore, it did not reflect Desmond's views, and in spite of lively cultural journalism the general tone of *The Sunday Times* remained stodgy: "One of the shortcomings of our tip-top paper," complained Desmond to Cyril Lakin, the literary editor, "is that, with the exception of Agate's article there is hardly ever anything in it from beginning to end which makes anybody smile."[2] This he had always felt to be essential to any publication.

Since 1933, Desmond's job had, in important respects, become more agreeable. He began to work with Leonard Russell, an enthusiastic younger journalist, whom he liked, and under their combined influence the book pages improved greatly; in the same year the paper moved from premises in the Strand to smarter offices at the brand new *Daily Telegraph* building in Fleet Street, which had such modernities as rapid lifts and blue rubber floors.

However, no sooner had Desmond's old persecutor, Rees, retired as editor, in 1932, than Desmond found himself frequently at odds, too, with his yet more punctilious successor, the tiny, whispering William Hadley, who occupied the post until 1950. Desmond despised Hadley's timidity. For instance, in 1939 during the course of a review, Desmond quoted a proverb from China: "Even in a flood it is unsafe to save yourself by catching hold of the tail of a tiger." This, he commented, might well have an application in public as well as in private life. Hadley took exception: "Out it went, proverb and comment, without my knowledge. Of course, I know why," Desmond told Cyril Lakin. "The Sunday Times believes in the policy of 'appeasement'. . . . This excision seemed to me to show an extraordinary lack of confidence on the paper's part in its own policy." This was only one of a succession of cuts made without consultation, and in January 1939 Desmond threatened to resign, unless he was consulted in future.

Luckily their very ignorance of the arts meant that the editor and proprietor tended only rarely to interfere with the actual content of a review. There was no objection when Desmond wrote sympathetically on the poet Housman's feelings of persecution about his homosexuality – a piece which was praised for its courage. Over one particular, however, Hadley and Kemsley were always insistent – the rigorous application of the blue pencil to "unsuitable" language, if the agitated printer, Mr Bloxham, reported its appearance. Once, when Desmond used the word "copulation", the whole sentence was removed. He could not resist the temptation to bait his narrow-minded employers; writing his last-minute lines of copy on a Friday afternoon in the printing office "with Mr Bloxham himself hovering around like a bald-headed bishop of the sweetest disposition, and saying every now and again anxiously, 'only waiting for you, sir'," Desmond, on an impulse, scribbled down a sentence later remembered as: "there is some trace of wildness in his outlook and one is always trembling lest at some moment he would seize the chalice and piss in it. . . ."[3] He did not expect to see it printed; the ensuing panic was satisfying enough vengeance for the annoyances from which he was suffering at the editor's hands.

At first Desmond was paid £750 a year and this sum rose gradually to over £1,500 after the Second World War. Except when there was a paper shortage during the war he was allowed up to 1,800 words a week for his "World of Books" column. He put this allotted space to good use. His colleague in later years, Jack Lambert, was endlessly impressed: "His pieces contained as many aperçus as most full time writers of long works could deliver in half a lifetime. In his articles one felt one participated in an interesting civilised conversation about books. He was a man with a great interest in other people's ideas. He would sit with me in the horrid little *Sunday Times* composing room and discuss Ibsen as if he and I were old cronies. He conveyed a feeling of warmth in his reviews, not the exclusive feeling of Bloomsbury." At one point, when Desmond's health was uncertain, the successful novelist Charles Morgan was given a reviewing position equal in prominence; but despite his prestige his contributions looked dull beside Desmond's.

Desmond similarly eclipsed the ever more pathetic and Falstaffian figure of J. C. Squire (1884–1958), whom Rees had also recruited for *The Sunday Times*. Molly shared the widespread "highbrow" view that Squire was unattractive and crude, but Desmond retained his old

top left Ottoline Morrell in 1935

top right Sibyl Colefax, the society hostess, seen here
with Lord Esher (Oliver Brett) in the 'Thirties

below Desmond with his daughter Rachel at Garsington

left
Desmond and his mother 'Ch
at Rachel's wedding to Lord
David Cecil

above
The 'Parent Bird', Desmond'
Prussian grandfather, Otto d
Chevallerie

below
Charleston 1928: left to righ
Frances Partridge, Quentin a
Julian Bell, Duncan Grant, C
Bell; centre: Roger Fry

affection for his generous, uninhibited friend. He lamented, however, his metamorphosis from the Baudelaire-haunted, self-questioning young man, with a keen sense of beauty, he had known during *Eye Witness* days in 1912, to the "positive, combative, hearty person", who became, in literary terms, the very epitome of Stanley Baldwin's England: "I sometimes felt," he wrote in a frank review of Squire's memoirs in 1937 "I had nearly lost sight of my friend behind cricket-pads, bats, pewter pint pots, pheasants, shot guns, runabout cars, footballs, committee agenda. . . ."[4]

Such conscious English oakheartedness helped to earn Squire his knighthood in 1933, but it, and his title, were at variance with his genuinely bohemian, chaotic nature and the sensitivity he had buried. This inner division, and his natural bonhomie encouraged him to drink; he became increasingly unpresentable, flaunting an unconventional sexual life, shocking Lady Salisbury by turning up drunk at Hatfield with his mistress and all the while clinging to the social perquisites of knighthood. As a poet, he was almost a spent force, though an occasional shoot of genuine poetic emotion could still peep out suddenly amidst the neatly bedded banalities.

Both Desmond and Squire, during the interwar period, became identified by a younger generation of critics, like Geoffrey Grigson, with the backward-looking element in the English critical world epitomised by the title "the Squirearchy". Yet they were not comparable. Squire had become an out-and-out populariser of English culture, whereas Desmond always assumed cultivation in his readers and never lowered his standards, save for the forgivable motive of – occasionally – giving an old friend like Bob Trevy a boost. It was a difference which was grudgingly acknowledged in 1932 by a rising star in the Cambridge academic world, F. R. Leavis, when he wrote an impassioned plea for more original and discriminating literary criticism in his crusading journal *Scrutiny*. Though he dismissed Desmond as "the journalistic middleman of cultivated talk", the austere Leavis did not see him as being in the same commonplace mould as Squire and Lynd who belonged to the world of the Book Society and its choice of "worthwhile" books for the masses.[5]

An interview Desmond gave to *The Book Window* magazine in 1932 shows how unsatisfactory he himself regarded lists of "Best Books". He had no great enthusiasm for many of the upper-middlebrow authors such as John Galsworthy, John Drinkwater or Hugh Walpole at whom Leavis had directed his stream of venom. In general, however, he did not greatly care how he was rated by the new critics of the Cambridge English school like Leavis, whom he thought arbitrary and parochial.

Keeping abreast of new trends in the 'Thirties gave him little pleasure.

He lived, he said, like a camel off its hump, nourished by literary food garnered in an earlier era; and though he praised where he could, writers such as Herbert Read, Auden and Spender were irritated by his lack of understanding. He shared neither the hopes of the younger generation nor the disillusion and *angst* they saw articulated in T. S. Eliot's *Waste Land*.

Even so, he never dismissed Eliot, as other older critics like Squire had done. He met – and liked the poet, during the war, probably at Garsington, near the time when Eliot's *Song of J. Alfred Prufrock* first appeared in the USA, changing world poetic vision for good. He respected his high intellectual standards and reverence for tradition. As an admirer of Donne, he praised Eliot's championship of the then neglected seventeenth-century metaphysical poets; and he applauded his later poems, Christian in vision, which made up the *Four Quartets*, for the delicacy of their imagery and language. Eliot's most renowned early verse, however, always left him cold. Nurtured on the optimistic Meredith (whom Eliot despised) and the cheerfully sceptical Montaigne, he could not respond to Eliot's powerfully articulated despair and disgust; to him the *Waste Land* and *Prufrock* were unimpressive both morally and as poetry.[6]

He was enraged therefore when Dr Leavis provocatively announced that Eliot had now displaced Milton from his pre-eminence in English letters, "with remarkably little fuss". Apart from his indignation at the absurdity of treating two such dissimilar talents as being in competition with one another, Desmond cast doubt on Leavis's knowledge of Milton. To denigrate Milton's influence, even in a modern industrial age, he thought nonsense; for as he pointed out earlier, had not John Bright, one of the greatest orators to emerge from the grime and commerce of Victorian England, learned his classical eloquence from studying Milton? and were there not passages in Eliot's *Waste Land* which were actually themselves "Miltonic" in their cadences? "Poor poet", Desmond wrote of Eliot, "how embarrassing is the praise of coteries!"[7]

Yet his admiration for Evelyn Waugh, Richard Hughes and Christopher Isherwood showed that he was far from underestimating all new writing and he picked out, as so often – some unusual and still neglected talents; these included David Lindsay's *Voyage to Arcturus*,[8] one of the most powerful imaginative writings of the twentieth century, also spotted by Victor Gollancz; in the 'Thirties he promoted Lindsay's flawed, mountainous epic, *Devil's Tor* on behalf of its publisher, Putnam. He was enthusiastic too about the books of his friend and contemporary, L. H. Myers.

Contemptuous of nearly all the literary world of his day, Leo Myers once expressed communist leanings in a novel he wrote in the 1930s, *Strange Glory*. Myers' communist phase was short-lived; he sought an answer to life in a succession of different faiths before finally committing suicide during the Second World War. Like Leavis, Desmond was a particular admirer of Myers' trilogy, set in Akbar India, *The Root and the Flower*, which came out in one volume early in 1935. It was an astonishing work of imagination (Myers had never been to India), of metaphysical discourse and of exciting adventure – also of denunciation: it contained disguised and ferocious portraits of Ethel Sands, L. P. Hartley and members of "Bloomsbury", poor Raymond Mortimer, Desmond's future successor on *The Sunday Times*, was depicted as "Prince Daniyal" an effete sadist.[9] In his criticism, Desmond steered clear of these thorny personal matters, praising Myers' plain and, at times, beautiful prose: "He really is a writer," he told Molly; but he noted, when he dined with him, the conflicting traits in Myers' dark, fastidious face: the wide noble forehead and penetrating gaze – and the sensual mouth with the small irresolute chin.

Friendship commonly played a part in helping Desmond to single out authors for attention. He praised Sheila Wingfield's admirable poems in the "imagist" vein after he had come to know her through Betsy Reyneau. He also helped the young poet, Robert Waller, to whom Eliot had introduced him and who became his secretary for a few months before the Second World War, and he encouraged the deranged war poet, Robert Nichols, who tried, unsuccessfully, to re-establish his reputation in the 'Twenties and 'Thirties. Nichols, a shell-shock victim, would often visit the MacCarthys, while they were at Wellington Square, in floods of tears over a love affair or a publisher's refusal. When he died, aged fifty-one, in 1944, Desmond remembered him generously as "an ardent, disinterested man, an impetuous muddler in life who nevertheless kept a straighter path than most people who are perpetually taking their bearings";[10] but the pathos of Nichols' disappointed life interested him more than his poetry.

The same poignant note was often to be found in the Book Column portraits he presented of writers from an earlier period; these continued – as before – to be his best journalistic pieces. His ability to bring the reader into intimate contact with the personalities and minds of past authors was always his outstanding gift. Indeed he seemed as close to some of these as if they had been personal friends. In January 1937 he reviewed an edition of the letters of Samuel Taylor Coleridge's failed minor poet son Hartley – a clever, original man with a talent for enjoyment and for making friends in every walk of life; drink was his downfall. Desmond quoted Hartley Coleridge's sad lines:

        . . . Nor child, nor man
        Nor youth, nor sage, I find my hair is grey,
        For I have lost the race I never ran,

and he added, characteristically: "That will do very nicely for my epitaph
and I knew it would rather early."

His frequent evocations of the poet-journalist, Leigh Hunt, the
contemporary of Carlyle and Byron, are so vivid it is almost as if they
were drawn from the life. He could sympathise with Hunt over his
disordered existence and financial dependence on his friends and he
admired his outstandingly fine literary palate, although he found him
superficial, often no more than "a purveyor of bottled chatter", and
disliked his vein of chirpy, genteel vulgarity; all the same Hunt's
indomitable cheerfulness disarmed him and his antics appealed to
Desmond's sense of comedy.[11]

Comedy, too, was an ingredient in his delight in the eccentric Walter
Savage Landor, last of the great romantics of the age of Shelley and
Coleridge, with his violent changes of opinion, his follies and his King
Lear-like humiliation when an old man.

Desmond repeatedly urged his readers to dip into Landor's writing, as
he himself loved to do, browsing his way through his verse and through
the sometimes incoherent verbosities of his *chef d'oeuvre*, *Imaginary
Conversations*; however impossible Landor had been as a person he had
an extraordinary power with words. "He was subject," Desmond wrote,
"to the most boisterous throes of fury and indignation, but when he
wrote, he decanted the wine of his anger into the finest of crystal vessels so
that the rich glow of it might delight him. This contrast and fusion of
violent sentiments and literary deliberation is one of the piquant pleasures
of reading Landor. . . ." As he frequently maintained, "I admire Landor
so much that I can afford to say he often bores me."

He used to read Landor pencil in hand, marking memorable sayings;
one which pleased him was "clear writers, like clear fountains, do not
seem as deep as they are; the turbid look most profound." Above all, it
was the haunting qualities of Landor's "beauties" of fine writing, for
which Desmond felt the greatest love: "I have often murmured that
sentence from Boccaccio's vision of Fiametta: 'My dream expanded and
moved forward. I trod again the dust of Posilipo, soft as the feathers in the
wings of sleep."[12]

Desmond's lengthy weekly column amounted, over a period of
twenty-four years, to a prodigious critical output. His achievement as
senior critic for *The Sunday Times*, his most influential years of
reviewing, lay in opening up for readers the treasure house of past English

– and also continental – literature; in making vivid for them the characters of the authors whom he admired or who intrigued him, he made them keenly aware of his subjects' lovability, or pathos, or delight in existence. Saddened by life himself, he never lost faith in human nature. Impressive, too, was the patience his reviews revealed: painstaking study to assure himself that Bishop Andrewes' sermons were indeed as tedious as he remembered; insistence, harking back to Cambridge days, that terms must be defined; and readiness to wade cheerfully through acres of lifeless Landorian eloquence to find, at last, an incandescent passage; a willingness, in short, to endure boredom, which contrasted strikingly with his habitual reaction to the mundane duties of his daily life. "If I could not support the boredom often involved in reading many an old master, I should be a poor critic," he wrote.

Desmond's colleague, James Agate, paid tribute to his power of dispassionate judgement in 1944: "A critic, I understand, is one who having no views of his own, or willing to sink his personal opinions, puts himself in the author's place, accepts his ideas, and confines himself to deciding how well or how ill he has expressed them. (Desmond does this fish-like, cold-blooded thing with genius.)"[13]

"Why, if it's not too painful a question, do you waste your talents?" the writer David Garnett asked Molly, in 1937.

"'You might be another Jane Austen – you could so easily create figures like Mrs. Elton and Mr. Woodhouse – and they are actually stirring all round one unseen.

"'Why don't you do something ambitious and a little venomous?'" [1]

Unfortunately Molly did not take his advice; David Garnett's letter was prompted by her slim book of sketches, *The Festival*, especially one which was, in effect, a pen-portrait of Alys Russell: Molly called her Mrs Scrappit, and described her as "so full of the abstract wrongs of humanity, that the deeper satisfactions of people's lives escaped her notice; and there was something most unfortunate about the sympathy she bestowed, for after she came away from a cottage the people she had been visiting were left with an impression that they were . . . downtrodden 'victims', 'household drudges', and they were quite puzzled; for her conception was quite alien to their own naturally cheerful, self-respecting ideas about themselves. When she noticed the impression she had instilled, she thought it very wholesome; the millennium was a good step nearer."

Molly had a sense of period and of place; she was observant and she had a warm heart; but her style was often tentative, and she lacked the staying power to sustain another novel.

Vita Sackville-West upbraided Molly for the silence of her pen, reminding her that "nothing blots out the horror of life as well as absorption in writing. One lives in another and a serener world; one becomes an autocrat instead of a battered puppet." [2] Desmond and Molly stayed with Vita and her husband, Harold Nicolson, at their house, Long Barn in Kent; Vita often entertained her guests at her ancestral home nearby, the Elizabethan palace of Knole. Here Desmond was once present at a particularly stormy passage between Vita and the poet Roy Campbell. Resenting the urbane chatter of his fellow-guests – Desmond, Clive, Raymond Mortimer, Vita's cousin Eddy Sackville-West (who was the heir to Knole) – and Vita and Harold themselves, Campbell was silent and farouche, drinking even more than usual to make up for his sense of isolation. It was his drinking which, shortly afterwards, precipitated his wife into an affair with Vita, an agile seducer of her own sex.[3] Despite Desmond's past kindness to him Campbell subsequently denounced his fellow-diners in a passage of his ferocious satire in 1931, *The Georgiad*:

> When I have watched each mouthful that they poke
> Between their jaws, and praying they might choke,
> Found the descending lump but cleared the way
> For further anecdotes and more to say.

Much later he was to spring – with equal spleen – to Desmond's defence.

Molly very much wanted to complete another volume of autobiography, starting with her marriage and move to Suffolk; she never finished, and what remains shows little of her characteristic sharpness of observation.

She did, however, publish two books of historical portraits, *Fighting Fitzgerald* (1930) and *Handicaps* (1936). The first was of four eighteenth-century figures, chief among them the buccaneering George Robert Fitzgerald who was hanged in 1786. His life was crammed with incidents, many blood-stained. "How I enjoyed it!," Virginia Woolf wrote to Molly. "It's all so new and fresh and incredible – I galloped through Fitzgerald to the end: the bear, the fight, the trial, the rope breaking – you are an amazing woman to dig out these characters, with all the facts and all the fun – so solid and so amusing at the same time. Please write some more to enchant some more Sunday evenings."[4]

Molly's next attempt in a similar line, *Handicaps*, was about people with grievous disabilities which their bravery overcame: perhaps she felt drawn to such subjects as Beethoven's deafness, for example, in view of her own; it includes a poignant account of Arthur Kavanagh (1831–1889), who was born without feet or hands, yet became a sportsman, traveller and an MP. While *Handicaps* was readable, the stories had an old-fashioned ring of improving tales for children.

Ironically enough, the original means Molly had devised as a spur to her own and Desmond's writing, the Memoir Club, of which she was still the secretary, continued to flourish. Its members, grumble though they sometimes did at her chivvying them into producing papers for it, nevertheless kept on writing amusing and stimulating essays to be read out after dinner either at a restaurant, such as the Etoile in Charlotte Street, or a member's house, perhaps Charleston or the Keynes's house, Tilton, nearby. Its membership now included such spouses as Lydia Lopokova Keynes; other consorts, such as Mary Hutchinson, who had broken with Clive Bell by the late 1920s, had ceased to attend. E. M. Forster asked Molly, "please do be severe about us only being the original bunch, and let it be widely known that if Nell this and Gwynne that are brought, all the readers will discover that at the last moment they have mislaid their papers."[5] It is probable that he envisaged Clive, ever the womaniser, indiscriminately bringing his girlfriends.

In the early 1930s Molly and Desmond held a centenary dinner for the club at 25 Wellington Square; of the early members, Lytton Strachey was dead, and this was to be almost the last meeting Roger Fry attended; in September 1934, at the age of only sixty-eight, he died after a fall at home.

Desmond had been abroad on holiday and this sad news greeted his return; it was a great blow. Also awaiting him was the new novel of the talented writer, Evelyn Waugh, whom Desmond liked and admired. It was several days, Desmond wrote to Waugh, before he had been able to embark on *A Handful of Dust*: finally, "I took up your book and read it through. That I could do *that*, shows I think that there is something there besides the wit and point which are delightful . . . if your story itself had been only 'a handful of dust' – however sparkling, I don't think I should have read it through this week. No: it would have been impossible."[6]

He wrote to Waugh three days after Fry's cremation on a hot, September afternoon at Golders Green; the ceremony was "all very simple and dignified. Music. Not a word spoken," recorded Virginia Woolf. Afterwards she and Desmond and Molly strolled in the garden of the crematorium. "Oh we stand on a little island," he said. But it has been very lovely I said. For the first time I laid my hand on his shoulder, and said don't die yet. Nor you either he said. We have had wonderful friends, he said. We walked a little, but Molly was out of it, with her deafness. So we took them to Wellington Square and had tea. A merry natural talk, about Roger and books and people, all as usual."

It is a poignant vignette: Molly's "queer isolation of deafness – breeding this rather peevish but pathetic egotism," Virginia noticed; and mortality, the transience of life, coming to fill Desmond's mind as he grew older. Afterwards, seeing the Woolves off on their drive back to Sussex, Desmond recalled the Memoir Club centenary dinner: "Never again said Molly. Oh yes, I said; and we drove off."[7]

Virginia was right: there were to be many more years of meetings, and at one of them, at least, Roger Fry was discussed. Virginia wrote about it to Molly, who had not been able to come because of illness: "Clive got a bit restive, some old grudge against Roger raising his hackles, and making Nessa as marmoreal as a stone. The stonier she, the more hackled he."[8]

In the years leading up to the Second World War, as the news from Europe worsened, the Club members valued their meetings and their old-established friendships more than ever: "Desmond was babbling as a nightingale," Virginia Woolf wrote after a meeting in April, 1937, "never have I known him in such jubilant good temper as this year. As if he worked only to enjoy to radiate." Few of Desmond's Memoir Club papers are preserved; perhaps because he rarely wrote them out properly, but relied upon the inspiration of the moment, as on this occasion, when he had talked about shooting with Wilfred Blunt (this was published) and with Bob's father, Sir George Trevelyan, the historian, who "came hopping loping like a great gorilla across the wood in the middle of a shoot to say Alfred Lyall's poems are as near poetry as anything I can stand.* Oh but it was beautifully done – and stopped when it might have gone on without boring us," Virginia Woolf wrote.[9]

Desmond himself said to Clive Bell that "after all *we* – at any rate for ourselves – are the best company in the world." One can see why from such hilarious papers as Virginia Woolf's *Am I A Snob?*, which she read during the winter of 1936–7. It was both acute and exaggerated, starting off by asking whether Desmond is a snob? "He ought to be," says Virginia, given his education at Eton and Cambridge; but whatever those institutions did to encourage snobbery in him, she continued, nature did far more, by endowing him with "a golden tongue; perfect manners; complete self-possession; boundless curiosity, mixed with sympathy; he can also sit a horse and shoot a pheasant at a pinch. As for poverty, since Desmond has never minded how he dresses, no one else has ever given the matter a thought. So here then, undoubtedly, is my pattern; let me compare my case with his."

She recalled an afternoon when Desmond, after lunching in Tavistock Square, had spent the afternoon with them, talking. ". . . suddenly he remembered that he was dining somewhere. But where? 'Now where am I dining?' he said and took out his pocket book. Something distracted his attention for a moment, and I looked over his shoulder. Hastily, furtively, I ran my eye over his engagements. Monday Lady Bessborough 8.30. Tuesday Lady Ancaster 8.30. Wednesday Dora Sanger seven sharp. Thursday Lady Salisbury ten o'clock. Friday lunch Wolves and dine Lord Revelstoke. White waistcoat. White waistcoat was twice underlined. Years later I discovered the reason – he was to meet our king, our late lamented George. Well, he glanced at his engagements; shut the book and made off. Not a word did he say about the peerage. He never brought the conversation round to Revelstoke; white waistcoats were unmentioned. 'No,' I said to myself with a keen pang of disappointment as he shut the door, 'Desmond, alas, is not a snob'."[10]

---

* Sir Alfred Lyall, eminent in the Indian Civil Service, wrote *Verses Written in India* (1899).

Virginia went on to mock her own snobbery, and, indeed, more than one friend has remarked on her strange attitude towards Society: "she was terrifically class-conscious in a way that was absurd for a person as clever as she," remarked David Cecil. "In judging people [of the aristocracy or fashionable society] she was like a mermaid who comes out of the sea and looks at the people on the shore": this individual perspective was as often as not wrong. One instance of this was David Cecil's sister, Lady Beatrice Ormsby-Gore, whom Virginia described as "a frank dashing brainless young goddess" with eyes as bright, hard and insensible as greyblue marbles – an absurd misinterpretation of the intelligent, self-deprecating, humorous and kind-hearted Lady Beatrice.[11]

In Desmond's case, Virginia was right; he was not a snob, but he was as energetically social as ever, though often the despair of the hostesses who plied him with invitations. "Desmond lives up to the very edge of his charm!" said one, waiting for his late appearance. As well as being unpunctual, he was apt to muddle engagements, or even to forget them completely. He described to Molly an especially grand dinner party for twenty-four people "who went in [to dinner] arm in arm in Ark fashion . . . the whole thing in splendour was reminiscent of the Nineties" at the London house of Mrs Rupert Beckett. He felt obliged to go to this, in February 1931, "because a year ago I forgot a luncheon to which she asked me and at which the Prince of Wales was present!!! I had forgotten it so completely that I found it difficult to believe I had ever been asked. However she assured me that she had asked me herself and when she asked me to dinner I could not refuse. I enjoyed the glitter and splendour. It cheered me up for the moment. It was a new 'set' for me, rich, smart racing people and I was amused. The enormously rich Lady Granard* was there in ropes of pearls and her mild, exquisitely clinically clean husband with a pearl the size of an electric button in his shirt."[12]

Desmond was invited away regularly, too; he was a frequent guest at house-parties at Taplow Court, the elaborately hideous pile overlooking the Thames, near Maidenhead, which belonged to the sporting Lord Desborough, and his wife, Ettie, one of the last great hostesses of the Edwardian period.†

Over the twenty years that Desmond went to stay with the Desboroughs, he enjoyed houseparties at which fellow guests were likely to be

---

*Lady Granard – the American wife of the 8th Earl of Granard.
†William Grenfell (1855–1945) first Baron Desborough, outstanding sportsman, who crossed both land and water by the most daring means that could be devised: stroking a rowing eight across the Channel, for example, and swimming (twice) across Niagara, just below the Falls; his sporting trophies were displayed ubiquitously at Taplow Court. They owned several thousand acres, and entertained in lavish formality. He and his wife Ethel, "Ettie", had lost two beloved sons, Julian and Billy Grenfell, early in the First World War.

Winston Churchill or his old friends among the Asquith family. "I am here for a mid-week party which is gay and grand and tapers down from the P.M. [Neville Chamberlain] and the Duke and Duchess of Portland to Desmond. I watch the P.M. with the usual amazement: how can men in that position – in these days – take it so calmly? I suppose the truth is that the first qualification for responsibility is not to feel it intensely," he wrote from the Desborough's other house, Panshanger, in January 1938.[13] Molly never accompanied him to either place, though she was asked, "only our parties often have a horrid knack of getting rather big and I know she does not care for that," said Ettie. Winston Churchill was a frequent guest, and a compelling spectacle at all times, such as on a visit to the zoo at Whipsnade: "dear Winston really did behave exactly as if he was seven, running at top speed from one animal to another. Have you ever seen keenness remain unabated and spontaneous so late in life?" asked Ettie of Desmond – this was in May 1936.[14] That keenness was of course to prove his, and England's greatest asset; in August 1938 Desmond reported that Winston was "the luminary in constant, benign, violent irruption" of an elderly houseparty at Taplow. "As usual I liked him extremely; and as usual I felt no confidence that he liked me . . .

"One reason that I feel warmly towards Winston is that he loves his country; and lately I have been disturbed and astounded . . . that, today, the aristocracy and the rich put their own class before their country. He is an exception." Desmond saw no reason to alter that view of Winston.[15]

Desmond was a frequent guest at dinners where Stanley Baldwin, for many years Conservative Prime Minister, was present; for Baldwin liked to think of himself as a man of letters and Desmond could always be relied on to keep him entertained. Desmond could not live by the printed page alone, but delighted in savouring at first-hand the glamorous and trivial world of the beau monde. There was the occasion in 1931 when the luminous Irish beauty, Lady Lavery, gave a luncheon to celebrate the publication of some of Coventry Patmore's poems selected by her lissom protégé, Derek Patmore. There, in Lady Lavery's sumptuously decorated South Kensington House, with its white marble dining-room, frilled organdie curtains and black and gold furniture, Desmond met Lady Londonderry, the official hostess of the Tory Party, and his old Cambridge friend Eddie Marsh, rosy-cheeked, monocle a-glitter, squeaking enthusiastically about the latest fashions in writing. Such occasions were still as essential to Desmond as the quiet hours in his study; and after all, was not the fascinating, doomed Lady Lavery, with her purple orchids and black velvet, the graceful embodiment of some poetic extravaganza by Landor or Browning, writers whom he loved?[16]

But even Harold Nicolson, an alert and fluent observer as he was, failed to capture the appeal of his company: ". . . he got himself tied up in a lot of nonsense," he told Vita of one dinner with Clive Bell, Peter Quennell and his wife, and Desmond, in 1934. "But how we laughed! And what remains of it all? I mean, even to you who know Desmond I cannot reconstruct the thing. No wonder that people like Sydney Smith seem to enjoy or have enjoyed an exaggerated reputation. Dr Johnson is the only conversationalist who triumphs over time."[17]

Desmond could be serious, too: "I discuss seriousness with Desmond. I say that I fear that if one is very happy in life one becomes superficial. He says, 'Yes, my dear Harold, I agree that acute unhappiness is a great assistance to nobility of soul. But it is a mistake to imagine one can achieve nobility merely by making oneself acutely unhappy.'" This was on the occasion of a farewell lunch given by Enid Jones (Bagnold) for her great friend the diplomat Count Bernstorff, temporarily recalled to Nazi Germany by a government he deeply opposed.[18]

Desmond's old friend, Enid Bagnold, had married Sir Roderick Jones, the rich masterful head of Reuter's newsagency; they lived in Hyde Park Gate and Desmond saw them, too, at their house in Rottingdean, though he did not get on with the punctilious Sir Roderick – the two men could not have been more different. Molly rarely accompanied Desmond to either house, except for one particular luncheon at Hyde Park Gate when Desmond brought her perforce. Enid described the occasion in her autobiography and although this book cannot be taken as completely accurate – she twice describes Desmond as having been at Oxford, for example – in broad outline and in describing atmosphere it is very much to the point. "Once I asked Desmond to lunch alone with me in London, but he rang up and said he was bringing Molly. 'We're in the middle of a row and we can't finish.'

"We sat down to lunch. Molly attacked without embarrassment.

"'I've come back from Devonshire this morning and find Desmond has engaged a *valet*. From a prison.' The word 'valet' fairly scorched. It couldn't be true. It was so obvious just to look at Desmond that he hadn't a valet.

"Desmond sat back, far back, in one of those Regency chairs we had then. 'Not a valet,' he murmured, 'and not from prison.' He knew she couldn't hear.

"Molly's indignation never stopped. It seemed to have no basis and no reason. (But all married troubles have reasons). Luckily lunch had only two courses. It was soon over.

"At the front door she said bitterly, 'Take Desmond in your *car*. I'll take a *bus*'."[19]

This tragi-comic description of Desmond's detachment – *his* way of showing exasperation – and of Molly's compulsive bickering, was typical of their relationship during the 1930s. The cause of the particular dispute which Enid witnessed was a manservant named Hall, a lame duck whom Desmond employed at Wellington Square while Molly was away during the summer of 1937.

Molly did, of course, accept invitations on her own account, too; in April 1937 she described going to Covent Garden to see *Blue Beard*, for which Raymond Mortimer had taken a box; the Woolves and Desmond Shawe-Taylor went too; as so often happens, the expedition itself was more fun than the actual opera (by Paul Dukas). The soprano, said Molly, was like a lady selling gowns marked "for the older woman" in the mantle department at Marshall and Snelgrove's department store, with "an enormously competent and haughty organ". Leonard's dress clothes smelt of camphor, and Molly's of similar preservatives, so that by the end of the evening the curtains of their box, too, were impregnated with naphtha. Virginia was in high spirits and cheered Molly up. Desmond Shawe-Taylor remembers her exclaiming with admiration when Molly produced long-handled opera glasses: "Molly, what a hold you have on life! Spectacles upon a golden stalk!"[20]

In the autumn of 1936 Desmond went to his final dinner party at "Lions Corner House," Argyll House in Chelsea where Sibyl Colefax had entertained assiduously for so many years. Recently widowed, Sibyl shortly afterwards sold this beautiful, elegantly-furnished house, which her guests entered through wrought-iron gates and a stone-flagged court-yard off the King's Road.

That evening, Sibyl had excelled even her own standards of lion-hunting by assembling for dinner Harold Nicolson, Winston and Clementine Churchill, Duff and Diana Cooper, Desmond's old friend Somerset Maugham, as well as the pianist Artur Rubinstein, amongst others. At dinner "the great Simpson question" was discussed, since King Edward's friend had just obtained her divorce from Mr Simpson. True to her compulsion to be at the centre of all things smart, Sibyl was an intimate friend of Wallis Simpson. (King Edward abdicated six weeks later.)

The death of friends like Roger Fry, and of Lady Ottoline Morrell four years later in 1938; of relations like Molly's sisters Charlotte and Margaret, and her brother-in-law, William Fisher, all three of whom died in 1937, made Desmond and Molly cherish long-standing friendships which remained: with "The Owl", still perched on the Isle of Wight; with G.A.P., who seemed more decrepit than ever, when he visited London from the Jura where he and Laure now lived in comparative penury; and with Maurice Baring, who was gradually smitten with nervous paralysis. Desmond was wrung when he received a "heart-shaking scrawl from

Maurice in which I could decipher the words 'still in torment' . . . I can imagine him lying there, his bed quivering as though it were a trunk over the screw of a steamer". He visited him in Rottingdean, where he was then living, and did his best, too, to write about Ethel Smyth's book on him, a curious work, "that of a bull in a china shop, but a bull with an intense love of china," Desmond wrote to a friend.[21] Once, in discussing why Maurice Baring was so much more popular as a writer in France than in England (as indeed he still is); Desmond likened Maurice to a junket which the English swallow at a gulp, not realising it could possess subtler qualities.

One relationship which required even more of Desmond than usual was with his mother. Now well into her eighties, Chen repeatedly expressed her desire to die, to "meet those many I have loved . . . my beloved husband and all those who knew me so well when I was younger . . . and had no money cares!"; she was sustained only by her feeling for Desmond whom she loved "better than myself and shall do so till my last moments here on Earth": the last moments were long in coming, though she anticipated them several times, urgently commanding Desmond to fetch a priest.

Towards Molly she showed the reverse side of her love for Desmond; she was petty, malicious and selfish to the last. Molly told Dolly resignedly, "I feel worry for her because she does undoubtedly suffer from some kind of German-Ibsen-Dante-Inferno-frantic brand of distorted agony of nervous suffering encouraged by an indulgent materialistic nature and living alone . . . the loud stop of her mad organ has been out now – and screaming and squealing away, for months."

When Chen stayed with David and Rachel Cecil in the country, she strained even their patience with her "twaddle", twinkling around on high heels – she still minded about her appearance – and boasting about Desmond, unheeding of a word anyone else said until David read aloud in the evenings, just as Desmond had always done, when she did listen, "and enters into the story like a child".

In the anxious summer of 1938, with Hitler's seemingly inexorable advance casting its vile shadow across Europe, Desmond grew more apprehensive for Chen; cancer had now been diagnosed, and, as he wrote to Enid Bagnold, "What will one old woman writhing with cancer pains count in the vast catastrophe? I have told him (the doctor) to leave with her nurse enough morphia to drug her, *if necessary*, till she dies. But he belongs to the Baldwin-type – incapable of facing issues before they arise, when it may be too late."

He went off to Sweden for a rest cure with G. E. Moore, drawing closer to his friend once more as the past came so forcibly back to him. His mother still found the strength to write to him there. But even Chen could not last for ever; by the autumn, she was bedridden and Desmond felt it imperative to sit by her day after day, reading to her or just holding her hand so that she should not face death alone; he brought his work to her cheerless flat, where the silence was unrelieved except by her moans and the subdued administrations of the nurse and housekeeper; down below, in the Edgware Road, the traffic rumbled by, the outside world went on, while Desmond brought his mind to bear on Chen's imminent death: ". . . it has taught me the experience of the majority of mankind, especially the poor: that life does not allow them often to feel anything undistracted: neither grief nor joy nor pure experiences. Yet to respond (and thus to understand) without distraction and with unmixed feelings (this is what the poet does) is a large part of the art of life and perhaps the most difficult.

"Here am I switching my mind off my dying mother – and Death itself – on to heaven knows what . . . practical small considerations, while my response to her departure and my sense that no one after all was so *instinctively* fond of me is contaminated by relief that at last I am going to have the use of her money. The only way I know of disentangling one's feelings and struggling towards that purity and concentration of response which is the essence of religion, is to face the confusing and contaminating elements in oneself."

His own religious scepticism as well as his closeness to Chen inclined him to doubt whether her adopted faith was any use to her in facing death. "Her religion is not real to her," he stated with conviction. The supernatural had only been a means to her of relieving the triviality of her life which she had always lived on the surface. Perhaps, he reflected, she might have got more out of her life if she had faced this triviality for what it was: "The Church persuades you that you are living profoundly when you are not, and so you miss real chances of doing so – and in the end, perhaps, true religion." Desmond could never be anything but hostile to a faith which he saw as denying tragedy; and for him in these later years of his life, there seemed only to be tragedy which denied religion.[22]

One great consolation was that while she was with Desmond Chen ceased fretting: he told Rachel that she was no longer "querulous and small-minded, so I have had happiness as well for those hours and hope often to have true communion with her heart before she dies" – words which were as much a testimony to his close relation with his daughter as with his mother.[23]

Eventually, in mid-October 1938, Chen died; she who had lived, regardless of *their* needs, for her husband and her only son; "the comfort and bore of your life, your tyrant and dependant" was no more. The capital she left, the subject of so many scenes and dramas whenever she was called upon to dip into it, came to less than £10,000.

23   The War 1939–1945

In May 1939 the threat of war in Europe meant that Betsy Reyneau returned to her native America; this was a relief to Molly, for while Desmond and Betsy had not seen each other frequently during the last few years, they remained close and her continued presence in London rankled. From her apartment in New York Betsy wrote anxiously to Desmond after the outbreak of war: "I read and re-read your letters. I am more bitterly unhappy than I have ever been in my life, but not about myself, just about *you* and the young people I care for in England. I still am full of fight, my dear! I was paralised [sic] for a week, but I've come out of that.

"You must read in every letter the things I have said to you and written to you for ten years. *Those things are constantly and absolutely true . . .*

"Please, please write often. Word from you *will mean everything* to me. And can you arrange that I shall know if anything happens to you? . . . I know it is really a better thing that I am here, that it is a tremendous load off your mind, but where I long to be is where I could do something for those I care for. . . ."[1]

Even after eighteen months in Bermuda with a friend, Betsy was writing that she was growing *less* used to being apart from him; she kept in touch with him by reading his articles in *The Sunday Times*, listening to his broadcasts when she could receive them, and re-reading his letters. She thought about him every night. She worried constantly about his safety in the bombing of London; nevertheless her letters ended with the conviction that they would be together again one day.

After her spell in Bermuda, Betsy returned to New York where she had a small apartment in Brooklyn. She made her way by writing and drawing. Her daughter, Marie, married a New Yorker and they lived nearby: but she was lonely, and she never lost the hope of Desmond joining her: "What can I say about us? Here on the wall is your drawing. Here in this room I live with you and talk to you, maybe more than I should. It is three in the morning now and I can look out on the harbor and think that some bright morning, that will seem just like every other to most people, you may come sailing in! *You* – you'll just be here! and the empty, icy feeling in me will be gone. How many people in this world are feeling that way, I wonder? And yet not *quite* that way – they *can't*! . . .

"O my dear – I love you, Betsy."[2]

Desmond, too, wrote of the day when they would be together again in New York, they would "eat great American oysters to our stomachs' content, gazing at each other with rapture across our little table (Yes, yes – that Betsy aura which makes things shine with a gleam). I like to think how puzzled people next us (if they notice us at all) will be to see an elderly man and woman – the man bald and worn, the woman grey as a badger and past her prime – evidently seeing a world of delight in each other, as though they were two beautiful young creatures. Absurd? Yes, no doubt – from outside, but from *inside*? Ah, my pretty one, my charming dear, my play-fellow, my deep, tragic companion!

"It is eleven years now since we sat in Arundel Park and that is a long time for this eagerness to be close to each other to persist – satisfied so often and yet never growing less. It could not be sweeter to satisfy it than it was from the very first." All that they have been through together, the complications of their relationship, the strain, the tangles, the wrenches, have enriched what they feel for each other. Memories of times they shared kept her vivid for him: "I bless my memory; I have more confidence in it than in my character. I never forget WHAT BETSY IS LIKE – never; neither my vision of her nor my understanding of her grows dim."[3]

But Desmond was now in his sixties; the long years of the war divided them, their correspondence petered out and it is unlikely that they ever met again. After Desmond's death Molly had occasion to write to Betsy about some dollars of hers found in a separate bank account at the Bank of England which had been overlooked; from her apartment in Brooklyn Betsy wrote back a very handsome letter – as Molly herself had to admit – urging Molly to keep them, and, if she wanted, to spend them on Dermod and his family, as that would have pleased Desmond. She added, and this was true though Molly had so often been unable to believe it, "I always knew that no-one could change Desmond's feeling for you. Nor did Desmond ever by word or action indicate that his deep feeling for you would or could be changed. If there had ever been any question of a choice, which there never was, I would have been the one to go. And I know after horrible years of the war, that you must have had happy years. I hope you will have many more of them."[4]

Betsy was generous to the last; often wrong-headed – her simplistic left-wing views would have annoyed Desmond considerably if he had not ignored them – she was ever big-hearted. Desmond seems to have been the one real romance of her life, as, in a sense, she was for him: for she was the one woman he loved who gave him everything of herself, without stinting, at a time when he had no thought of ever finding a full-blooded love affair.

During the months leading up to the Second World War, Desmond and Molly were frequently desperately worried about the international situation. But there were compensations within their family circle: most important was the birth in February 1939 of their first, long hoped-for, grandchild, Rachel's son, Jonathan; Desmond had sailed to America that month, for a lucrative series of lectures, returning in March. Soon afterwards Molly had an operation on her kidney, thought to be the source of her frequent bouts of internal pain. In the opinion of their doctor son Dermod, the diagnosis was inaccurate and certainly Molly was never again in good health and had always to live the quiet life of an invalid. She tired easily, and every day she rested after lunch. For Molly's convalescence Vita Sackville-West lent the MacCarthys her romantic house, Long Barn in Kent. The Nicolsons were then living at Sissinghurst nearby. Desmond and Molly spent several happy summer weeks there living "on ham, amid a thousand roses". According to Molly, "the barn itself and garden are rather over pretty and faked up by Lady Sackville (the *wicked* one, now expired) – one expects to see an old Victorian actress smelling a rose at the casement!"[5]

Desmond was anxious that when war was declared, as now seemed inevitable, Molly at least should be out of London; they stayed at Rockbourne with David and Rachel and Desmond travelled to London from there to *The Sunday Times* offices and the BBC. On the morning war was announced, Sunday 3rd September, "to those of us who still held the poignant memories of the Great War, it was as though we had caught again a sickness we had had before," Molly recorded.[6]

The baby Jonathan was the only happy one in the household at Rockbourne, unaware of the tension in the world above his pram. But everyone talked and laughed and tried to live as normally as possible; then, Molly wrote to Vanessa Bell, "I feel they will all go away and leave me, and I shall pick up sticks all the winter, like a witch. I hope to do a little more anyhow than Lady Sackville who said, 'We must do housework you know now. We shall have to turn on our own lights' (to Vita in the last war)."[7] Molly could not sleep at night for thinking of the German bombers preparing for "excitement only fit for devils", not to mention worrying about her two sons.

In London, Desmond wrote to Robert Waller on 30th September, "There is death in the air and it stirs smouldering desires which might otherwise be transmuted into vaguer longings. I felt that myself while in London last week: the motionless hugging lovers under the dark still trees in Hyde Park – no lamps, only muffled moonlight overhead, the inviting voices of loitering women in the almost total darkness of the streets, sometimes showing their faces suddenly, in the little circle of an electric torch, stirred even in my tamed body a longing to hold *any* woman in my arms. The loneliness of the body possessed me as it had in my youth. But I knew at the back of my mind what a flat and dreary thing it is – the joyless unshared spasm and the bought embrace."[8] He had no doubts, however, that this was a war to defend freedom and he was bitter when he heard of Eire's refusal to join the struggle against Hitler, after its own long fight in the name of liberty.[9]

During the comparative calm of the "phony war", the artist, Henry Lamb, who lived at Coombe Bissett, near Rockbourne, proposed painting Desmond's portrait. Desmond enjoyed staying with the Lambs, whose life "is uncorrupted by respectability. . . . There were holes in the sofa cover, and books and mess everywhere," as another visitor, Frances Partridge, described.[10] Apart from anything else, Henry's wife, Pansy (née Pakenham) who was much younger than him, and their two children, were charming to look at; Desmond found the nursery meals agreeably reminiscent of the old days at Wellington Square when his own children were young. His sittings were enlivened by the painter's small daughter, Henrietta, who came into the studio "to entertain me with little mouse-like darts of conversation".[11] As Desmond got to know Lamb better – he had been an acquaintance for years, being an intimate both of Lytton Strachey and Lady Ottoline – "I discovered what you had told me, that Henry is a prey to unnecessary suspicions. . . . If he can explain anyone's speech or conduct in a manner calculated to arouse uneasiness, he does so. It is a great pity for his own sake, but having had a life-long training (thanks to the Owl) in ignoring or allaying suspicion, I do not find it a serious drawback to communication." The MacCarthys were at Coombe Bissett for the first Christmas of the war, when food was still plentiful – as it was not to be for many Christmases to come.

It seemed that as he grew older and balder and his features beakier, Desmond became an appealing subject to artists: "the structure of his head is becoming more marked and interesting and fine and I think if possible it should be recorded" said Vanessa Bell, who painted his portrait,[12] as did Duncan Grant; Joan Cochemé, too, painted a fine oil study of him. Desmond said Lamb's portrait made him look like "a sly old Yid", reported Frances Partridge, who, with her husband Ralph, went to stay with the MacCarthys in Rockbourne in the bitterly cold February of 1940.

In her wartime diary, published as *A Pacifist's War*, Frances Partridge gives an inimitable description of her two old friends, Desmond wrapped up against the weather in many waistcoats, the top one bright red. They walked down the village to look at a fine pen of sows of enormous size, rootling about in the rich Wiltshire earth. "Desmond delighted in scratching their backs with his walking-stick, making them squawk and grunt. Molly stood aloof, saying she didn't like pigs, she couldn't see any point in them whatever. At dinner, she suddenly dropped a bottle of claret on the floor with a bang; it fell over but didn't break. It is, I suppose, the sort of thing that happens daily and Desmond didn't turn a hair. Afterwards Desmond and Molly sat one on each side of the fire and Desmond read aloud to us while Molly lay back and snored gently. Then she woke up and read us Joad's views on picnic food (which had somehow fascinated and repelled her) with great expression and explosions of laughter. Conversation with these two masters of the art charmed till bedtime."

Desmond related how he was once sitting outside in a garden with Logan Pearsall Smith (probably at I Tatti) "in front of a stone path with a bust at the end of it. I said 'Logan, what would you feel if that bust came hoppity hop along the path towards you?' 'Disgust'."

He also recounted how one dark night when he and Molly were walking through the woods back from Ampton to the Green Farm, "I suddenly said, 'Molly, are you sure it's *me*, Desmond, you're walking with and not a spirit from another world?' and Molly *screamed* and *boxed* my ears."

Next day the morning hours similarly flew by in talk, Frances saying that "If conversation were always so absorbing and effortless one would never want to do anything else"; Desmond, for whom it was both, rarely did.

Old friendships, old memories, these were precious to the MacCarthys and their generation now, to "spin a kind of gauze over the war: wh. is broken by papers: & at listening in time," wrote Virginia Woolf of a visit Desmond was long to remember:[13] "two days of indestructible happiness" with Leonard and Virginia and G. E. Moore to the Woolves house at Rodmell, near the Sussex coast. They sat out under the apple trees in the garden, "Desmond & Moor[e] . . . reading – i.e. talking" said Virginia, while across the Channel the Germans pushed forward through France, Belgium and Holland towards the Channel. "Desmond and Moore together, the one talking, talking, the other silent in the armchair, were inextricably a part of my youth, of the entrancing excitement of feeling life open out in one and before one" wrote Leonard.[14] If he shut his eyes, he could feel himself back in 1903 in Moore's rooms at

Cambridge, or on his reading parties in the West Country. Moore was now sixty-seven, but "the extraordinary purity and beauty of character and of mind were still there, the strange mixture of innocence and wisdom" which Leonard had never encountered in any other human being. And so were the silences: from Rodmell, they visited Charleston, and over tea they took Moore up on his famous taciturnity: "'I didn't want to be silent. I couldn't think of anything to say' he said, rebutting, I think with some feeling that he'd carried this influence too far – our charge that he had silenced his generation. Hence his dependence on Desmond; who started talking, to the towel horse, to the cat, when he was a baby," wrote Virginia.[15] Despite his age "every now and again memory, which could make an artist of Desmond, and his amused devotion and affection for Moore, inspired him so that the years fell away and one again felt to the full the charm of his character and his conversation." (After Desmond's geniality, Virginia found T. S. Eliot, whom she encountered a few days later, ossifying into egotism: "A very self centred, self torturing and self examining man, seen against Desmond's broad beam, & Moore's candid childs eyes.")

So there, in May 1940, they sat, Desmond and Moore, Leonard and Virginia, in a cocoon of friendship and nostalgic memories, while the whole weekend was dominated by the threat of impending destruction; the tension was unrelieved; nor were their memories, of course, all good ones: when they recalled the first stages of the 1914 war, then even hope became a kind of self-indulgence and self-deception.[16]

Molly spent that weekend, when the weather, "Hitler's weather", was as brilliant as the news in Europe was bad, with Ralph and Frances Partridge at Ham Spray. She arrived off the London train looking pale and tired from the heat and the effort of lugging her "deaf-box" with her; talking to her via the box added to the strain in the household, although she was animated and funny; Julia Strachey and Frances' old mother were staying too. On the surface everything seemed normal – sitting on the lawn, playing Snakes and Ladders with Frances' young son; entertaining Gerald and Gamel Brenan who arrived on their bicycles for tea. But in the evening, the nine o'clock news and Churchill's speech warning that the fighting would soon reach England, dissolved the conventional social surface and "We all sank into our private worlds of despair. Julia sat with her head thrown back gazing at the ceiling. I stared woodenly in front of me. Molly buried her head in her hands," wrote Frances.

Molly and Desmond at least had their minds taken off the bad news in Europe by their move from Wellington Square to Garrick's Villa, at Hampton Court, just outside London. For years Molly had hankered after a house in the country. Her choice was restricted by Desmond's asthma which was exacerbated by grass and flowers, and by his reluctance to live in the country all the time. "Anything flowery and bowery won't do at all. It will have to be on a bare wide treeless plain," Molly had written to Florence Beerbohm.[17] Now at last the MacCarthys had found the next best thing to a treeless plain: Garrick's Villa was an early eighteenth-century house, embellished in 1775 by Robert Adam for the celebrated actor, David Garrick; Adam added a graceful pillared portico in the front and the large garden, really amounting to a park, was planted with trees which were particularly fine by the time the Mac-Carthys moved there nearly 200 years later. Across the road which had been rudely thrust through the grounds in the nineteenth century, remained Garrick's riverside temple, a graceful tribute to Shakespeare. It was reached from the villa by a subterranean tunnel, and was sheltered and sunny even on winter days.

The MacCarthys' spacious rooms on the first floor had a wonderful view south over the Thames; their rent was a reasonable £175 a year, inclusive of hot water, and rates. They kept Wellington Square, which still had several years' lease to run, and let it to a variety of tenants, including Julia Strachey, who lived at the top with Lawrence Gowing, whom she was to marry, and eventually on the ground floor the elderly Alys Russell.

At Garrick's Villa "each room had a large bow-window, in which stood a writing-table awaiting literary inspiration, from which could be seen green lawns with an orangery or elegant villa in the distance. Opening what I thought was the door of the lavatory, I found myself face to face with Desmond in a vast study as big and high as a theatre, lined with books and busts" wrote Frances Partridge, on her first visit there in July.[18] Garrick's Villa suited them from the first: they were able to enjoy space, and peace, and yet easily reach London by train.

Soon after the unimaginable catastrophe of the fall of France, the country they had loved all their lives, and regarded as the bastion of civilisation and culture, Desmond asked G. E. Moore, "Can you still enjoy pleasant things? Work? I can enjoy them. I forget tragic possibilities for the greater part of each day (measuring time in hours), but *no* separate hour is uninterrupted by moments of anxiety . . . the danger threatens all those one is fond of as well, and also to destroy those things which have most meaning to one's past."

He had just attended a continuing part of their past, the annual dinner of the Apostles; as he described it to Moore, it seemed a Society with one foot in the past, the other in the present. There were about sixteen present, old members like Desmond himself, Bob "Trevy", E. M. Forster, and Eddie Marsh, and younger ones, like Guy Burgess, Anthony Blunt, later to be revealed as spies for the Russians, "Dadie" Rylands and Sydney

Waterlow's son, John. The dinner was more informal than usual, and more intimate, "Owing to the sense of a common disaster threatening everything that the Society stands for." When Desmond was called on to speak after dinner, he recalled the last war during which he had been President and the painful cleavage it had brought about between the Pacifists and the rest, so that when Desmond had wanted to nominate Bertrand Russell as his successor Russell had refused, because, uncharacteristically, he thought it would be too provocative. Desmond finished his speech by saying that they must preserve their integrity of mind and believe in each other's existence even though it might be imposssible to communicate with each other.

They talked, of course, about the war and that it might destroy the Society, but at any rate they agreed to dine again the following year. Guy Burgess, whom Desmond found a crude man, and who would certainly not have heeded his injunction about preserving integrity, belligerently told his companions that they and their like were done for.

At the end of the evening Bob "Trevy" saw Desmond off in a taxi to Waterloo where he caught the train back to Hampton Court and "my roomy and quiet and stately new home".[19]

Another old friendship was revived for Desmond that summer when Virginia Woolf's biography of Roger Fry was published; given the constraints placed upon her by the fact that Fry's erstwhile love, Vanessa Bell, and his last love, Helen Anrep, were both still alive, and that most details about his private life had to be omitted, Virginia's book is a model of understanding, selectivity, illumination and restraint. As usual she was apprehensive of Desmond's opinion, preparing herself for his criticism by pretending that she was not, and that anyway he would just "gently hum and haw . . . and then proceed to give his own version of R. which will probably be more amusing than mine."

So Desmond's review in The Sunday Times of 4th August was "oh a great relief," she wrote in her diary. "And it gave me a very calm rewarding feeling – not the old triumph, as over a novel; but the feeling I've done what was asked of me, given my friends what they wanted . . . Now I can be content . . . for Desmond is a good bell ringer; and will start the others."[20]

Despite the success of this book, and starting on another novel, Virginia's old mental trouble never left her. Cut off from the Woolves by the difficulties of travel in wartime, the MacCarthys were not fully aware of her deterioration the following year. Leonard suffered weeks of anguish before the terrible outcome, for so long a nightmare possibility – Virginia's suicide. In March 1941 she threw herself into the river in a fit of black despair. It was weeks before her body was recovered. Shocked and saddened though Desmond and Molly were, Molly emphasised: "I think she had a *happy* life," and she wished Leonard peace in his memories of her; that when he was out in his beloved garden "in the midst of all the beauty there, at such moments, the thought of her voice, her perfect charm, and tremendously amusing comments, will give you *happiness.*"[21]

Leonard agreed the only comfort was that "despite the horror of the disease which she always had hanging over her life, that life was fundamentally happy. It was so because in day to day ordinary living she herself, her character and outlook, were fundamentally happy, gay. . . .

"There are no two people for whom Virginia had greater affection than you and Desmond and it is the same with me."[22]

Molly wrote sending all the love she could give to Vanessa wishing she could have "One last sight of the perfect handwriting on the envelope, always pounced on to open quickly. . . . I had just read two of her old letters to me, which had set me off writing to her . . . and suddenly she must become a *memory!*"[23] Molly greatly prized her correspondence with Virginia whose letters she regarded as "the most delightful of this century" – a view which many share. Virginia valued Molly's letters, too, once suggesting that she should be under contract to write to her every month. They had shared a good deal – from similarities of background, to flirtation with Clive. Virginia had never had to submerge herself in domestic life and Leonard was an efficient breadwinner; but in independence of outlook, and amused, wry observation of fellow mortals they had had much in common and her death would leave a gap in Molly's life.

Vanessa replied gratefully to Molly's letter, saying that "one can at least be glad that this did not happen as it so nearly did years ago – when nearly all her gifts would have been wasted. It is thanks to Leonard that it didn't. He is amazingly sensible and sane."[24]

Molly and Desmond were relieved to have moved out of Chelsea, where the German bombs soon began to fall; nevertheless their new home was still in the line of fire, as Molly described in a paper for the Memoir Club. One cold February afternoon in 1941 Molly sat writing it, warmed only by the small glow they had in the fireplace instead of the large blaze she loved, and which was needed to heat the big eighteenth-century rooms to any degree of comfort; when darkness fell it was time to do the blackout, according to wartime regulations. Every evening their apartment echoed with prison-like sounds of bolts shooting and bars pushed into clasps as the tall old shutters were banged to. If the air-raid warden glimpsed a chink of light from outside, he would come bursting in, shiny as a wet seal in his black oilskin suit, to point with fateful finger at "the crack"; then Molly would hastily stick back the black paper which had come adrift from the shutters. "Passing along from cold window to cold window, evening after evening, throughout the miserable years of war, creating pitch darkness and then groping for the doors, I feel my unspoken dirges . . . are shared by many others everywhere, silently drawing, pulling, shutting shrouding." At six o'clock Desmond came into the drawing-room, well wrapped in thick jacket and scarf against the cold in his library, for the invariable ritual of "listening in" to the news. Afterwards he would twiddle all the knobs on the wireless to pick up whatever foreign stations he could get while Molly went to help their housekeeper, Blanche, prepare their evening meal, not yet drastically curtailed by food shortages and rationing, but still reduced from peacetime. Desmond set himself chess problems as a distraction; for long periods "The Owl" would come and stay, forced to leave the Isle of Wight owing to the heavy bombing of Portsmouth across the water.

At bedtime, they put out warm boots and outdoor clothes ready to clamber into in case the Banshee should come wailing out their way – the air-raid siren, whose wailing was so expressive of lamentation. In bed, Molly settled down to read Gray's letters which transported her back to the eighteenth-century: "Hardly had I got into Paris with Mr Gray (travelling with Horace Walpole) . . . than the Banshee's wail was heard." Some of the elderly inhabitants of Garrick's Villa took refuge in Desmond and Molly's flat. For three hours they waited, hearing bombs fall, but unable to tell where; a warden, returning from duty, looked in with the news that bombs had hit Hampton village itself, and nearby houses, and that there was a fire at Hampton Court Palace. Molly, whose widowed sister, Cecilia, lived in a Grace and Favour apartment at the Palace, was alarmed; next morning, as soon as they had had breakfast, Molly and Desmond walked across the Park to visit her.

Cecilia had spent the night outside, watching the firebombs burning like prettily-coloured fireworks against the ancient brick of King Henry VIII's palace. Her rooms were charred from the bombs which had fallen on the roof and sodden from the water of the firemen's hoses; her carpets were ruined, her grand piano shattered, but she was making a nest for herself in two small rooms.

Molly and Desmond left to walk back across the Park, peaceful in the morning sun. The deer had all gone for venison, but the venerable trees still stood; they took a detour to avoid the disposal men who were defusing an unexploded time bomb. Back in Garrick's Villa Molly looked out over the serenely flowing Thames: two tankers slowly moved downstream, *Highly Inflammable* painted on their rust-red sides.

The house itself never received a direct hit, though shells fell yards away in the garden, shattering windows and destroying trees. Although travelling in wartime was not easy, occasionally the MacCarthys left London to stay at Rockbourne or Ham Spray. From Rockbourne, Desmond and Molly visited Lady Juliet Duff,* one of Desmond's fashionable female friends with whom Molly remained on distant, though cordial, terms. They went with her to Wilton House, now so full of the military as to resemble a garrison of the Middle Ages, a helmeted soldier at every window. In the grounds they met its owner, Lord Pembroke, disoriented by the takeover, who nevertheless seemed to like saying, "You see, I feel the house is *doing its bit*."[25] The Pembrokes lived in the magnificent drawing-room, while every other room had become a guard room or mess.

Lady Juliet gave them news of Maurice Baring, of whom she was a great friend. When Desmond had visited Maurice at Rottingdean at the beginning of the war, he had found him bed-ridden but in good enough spirits with the budgerigar, Dempsey, given him by Enid Bagnold, running up and down his poor trembling arms or perching on his bald pate. "It was a blessed inspiration," said Desmond. "He loves 'Dempsey' . . . and the poet and the child in him are comforted."[26] But Rottingdean, on the coast, was vulnerable, and Maurice had moved to Scotland, to Eilean Aigas, the house of a devoted friend, Laura Lovat. When Desmond went north for a live radio broadcast for the troops, he visited Maurice there; to Enid he described the romantic wooded island on which the old stone house stood in the rushing river Beauly; the hills around it were peaceful, "the drone of a plane is never heard, only the steady sound of distant rushing water. We have plenty; and plenty includes fresh butter, yellow wine and cream."[27]

As for the invalid himself, Desmond found him less tormented than he had been by his nervous agitation; sitting up against his snowy bank of pillows "as alert as ever and so beautifully patient that sympathy seems almost out of place". Desmond saw him at regular intervals through the day when he talked or read to him. Until Maurice's death in 1945, Desmond wrote to him with news of their friends, such as Hilaire Belloc for whom a birthday luncheon was organised in the summer of 1944. After lunch they drank a toast to Maurice and then Belloc, a still powerful-looking figure dressed all in widower's garb of rusty black, sang a nonsense song:

> My Bonnie has tuberculosis,
> My Bonnie believes in Couee;
> She's awfully bucked by the process;
> So send back my Bonnie to me.

* Lady Juliet Duff (d. 1965) daughter of the Earl of Lonsdale.

"Sang it in a voice perhaps a little less resonant than we can hear in imagination still, but with perfect rhythm and wagging of the head and finger we remember so well. Wouldn't you like, Maurice, to have over again one of those luncheons at the Mont Blanc or elsewhere?

"Part of the music of heaven – not the most celestial part of course – consists of 'records' – humble happy tunes played over again when we want one; illuminated of course by being at last in their proper relation to life."[28]

Desmond broadcast a moving tribute to Belloc, saying that he was not only one of the most original humorists of his time, but also one of England's best poets. Although seven years older than Desmond, Belloc was to survive him by a year, dying peacefully at his beloved King's Land in Sussex.

Desmond also paid tribute to his old literary friend and mentor, Max Beerbohm, on the latter's seventieth birthday, in August 1942, when the Maximilian Society, a small band of admirers of his work, was inaugurated at a dinner in London. Soon after the war the Beerbohms returned to their quiet life in Italy, and Desmond and Molly did not see them again; Max, too, survived Desmond, and broadcast a tribute to him after his death, for which, although not well-off, he refused any payment, saying it was done in the name of friendship.

Their friendship went back to the end of the last century, the 1890s, a period to which Max still belonged in spirit. Desmond and he were very different, and Desmond cherished their differences. "I often think of you with envy; partly because, as I see your life, it seems regulated by so fine a discretion. I have never been able to say 'It is enough,' but gone on eating till I felt a little sick," he had written to Max as long ago as 1928.[29]

Molly, too, saw old friends, sad ones, like Eddy Sackville-West – "the most depressed man one could ever have" she said after his visit to Garrick's Villa – and mad ones, like her old schoolmistress, Sophie Weisse, now ninety-two and on her own having outlived her beloved protégé, Donald Tovey; Molly found her existing in a fantasy world, "though she only once (this time) told me that Donald had been murdered".[30] She resembled King Lear in appearance, her hair all wild; Molly longed to put out her hand and pin it up for her, but did not quite dare – besides, it would have escaped again at once.

Although in the air raids Molly's deafness for once was something of an asset, dulling the sound of the aircraft and the impact of their deadly cargoes, yet it also added to her depression in the war; in January 1943 she wrote to Ralph Partridge that she found it impossible to be entirely sanguine that they would win; that she had no zest for life: "I am not *heard physically* moaning and groaning aloud as did Sir *Leslie Stephen*" (the father of Virginia and Vanessa who, as a widower, was a byword for loudly-expressed gloom); but her deafness meant that everyone had to write things down for her "as though I were a deaf and *dumb* loony". She was worn down by her condition: "After all, what describes deafness? *Failure* of hearing . . . every day a sense of *strain* and *failure* . . . There is a perpetual natural bourdonnement dans la tête, and then the *canned* sound of the instrument *enervant.*"[31] This had been her condition for a quarter of a century now and, understandably, she felt it as acutely as ever; her "deaf-box" was primitive and, being impractical, she never really mastered it, but felt herself at its mercy.

She was frequently "baffled" to use a favourite expression, by life itself. When she and Desmond went to stay for a weekend with the Partridges in the early summer of 1942, for instance, they "gave a fine display of MacCarthyism – the utmost charm and the utmost lack of consideration," wrote Frances in her diary. Beforehand, no clue as to when they would arrive, except, at the last minute, a telephone call of which Molly could not hear what was said to her; en route, Molly lost her bag, and that had to be telephoned about; they brought no rations of butter or sugar, as visitors were accustomed to doing in wartime, though they took sugar in every cup of tea and coffee. Next, Molly lost her spectacles, and after the garden had been scoured for them "was discovered in bed, having found them, but worn out by the struggle". They left by an impossibly early train and insisted on Ralph waking up and calling them much earlier than was necessary – just in case they overslept. But they gave much pleasure, too, "we had lots of what Desmond calls 'good talk'. I remember there was a discussion about India and that Molly said, 'Queen Victoria was the only person who could manage the Indians. She was a great paper-weight on a heap of fluttering papers'."[32]

Desmond, too, began to have fits of depression especially after Dermod was called up as a doctor to serve with the Fleet Air Arm on an aircraft carrier. His position was acutely dangerous; often his parents heard nothing from him for months. His whereabouts unknown, they fed on rumours, and on the lemons he sent home, the only indication that he was somewhere far away. Desmond could not sleep; "my life is over", he wrote "I plant no more memories". But these were moods; and, in more sanguine ones he could write, as he did to Lady Juliet Duff in June 1944, that he found the new bombardment of London by robot bombs in pilotless planes more endurable than the old Blitz, when "the damned Bosch used to hover for *hours* over us here, trying to get through the barrage to their objectives and sometimes at last giving it up and jettisoning their bombs in this neighbourhood. The drumming in the sky and the raging of our guns made it impossible to sleep or read. One just lay in bed quaking." At least the robot bombs were sudden and quick.

At all costs, he went on, he strove to maintain that modest degree of equanimity necessary to get a certain amount of work done, and to stop the war from being overwhelming. Even small measures helped, such as "thinking of others, a nip of whisky, and a certain satisfaction in reminding oneself that one is sharing – in some degree – the life-in-death existence of our fighting men." The times resembled the middle ages; "death is constantly at our elbow – not a matter for rejoicing!" But at least, he comforted himself – or tried to – living through the war might cure them for ever from being "spiritual muffs", from "the refusal to look at anything that reminds us of the tragic side of life, a refusal which makes a society or civilisation so boringly shallow, and in the end robs also our sweet little pleasures of their proper sweetness and turns even laughter into folly".[33]

He continued to write his *Sunday Times* column undeterred by the Blitz and the "doodlebugs". Against such distractions he would carry a bottle of port with him in his scruffy attaché case. There was one frightening moment when it was feared that he might not be able to continue: working frantically one Friday afternoon in Leonard Russell's poky little office off the printing room, he had a sudden seizure, assumed to be a heart attack. Russell recalled afterwards the pathos of Desmond, worn and frail, almost unconscious, his shirt torn open, with an elderly printer massaging his panting chest – the chest of an old man. But it turned out only to be a particularly bad spasm of indigestion and Desmond was escorted home, where he soon recovered; for ten years more he continued his regular appearance at the *Sunday Times* office.[34]

Throughout the war he had also taken part in "morale boosting" radio programmes on English culture and in numerous broadcasts, and was frequently employed by the Empire Service. Despite his popularity, and his many suggestions – which were accepted – for new programmes, he was involved in frequent struggles with production staff, including even Mary Somerville who had originally chosen him. They were non-plussed by his irregular approach to work. Once in November in 1940 he kept two frantic lady producers waiting for two hours while he tried to finish his schools script at the studio; they had been accustomed to leave at five in the evening to avoid the air raids and finally their nerves could stand it no longer and they fled, asking him to return the next day, which he did – an hour late. Occasionally, too, he overran his time and was cut off before he finished. However, the schools team were conspicuously difficult to please. He found the atmosphere of the South African Broadcasting Service, later in the war, much more relaxed. Desmond explained to a sympathetic producer why it was that he seemed so exasperatingly dilatory about producing scripts: "I put work of any kind off till the last moment, otherwise I spend a preposterous amount of time titivating. This is often vexatious for those for whom I work. I CAN ONLY WORK FOR PATIENT GOOD-NATURED PEOPLE who are willing to accept constant apologies followed by no amendment. I have certainly found them in the South African Service."[35]

Not until October 1944 did Desmond have a glimpse of light at the end of the long tunnel of hostilities; this came with the luncheon which the French Ambassador gave at the Savoy Hotel to celebrate the relief of Paris. The wines brought over from the Embassy cellar were delicious; the food, cooked in English kitchens after long years of war, was disgusting. "Desmond very nearly apologised for the British cooking to the Ambassador – like that mad old Lord Dudley who used to do that at his *hosts'* tables when dining out," Molly told Vanessa. But the whole affair was moving, a sigh of relief at the relief of Paris, "the Ambassador obliged to take his guests out, yet celebrating opening his Embassy – like Noah opening the ark window – by long force of war habit, a little gingerly perhaps?"[36]

24   Last Days

"I really do dare say that we have 'got straight' after 4½ years of war trouble and bombing anxiety," wrote Molly to Florence Beerbohm in June 1945. ". . . I *hope* the war atmosphere of the household *is really over*, except of course restricted – quails, canard à la presse, capons, *tiny* new potatoes, all buttery; sirloins, & saddles, Devonshire cream, crème brûlé & all the old monks' liqueurs in a row – to enumerate some things certainly *not* restored (& it must be said some, at all times not abundant to Desmond & me!) anyhow cookery is very fair, considering all things." Though never particularly keen on their food, shortages had made the MacCarthys, like everyone else, long for things they had taken for granted before the war – peppercorns, fresh fruit, sugar, butter, coffee.

On VE day, in May 1945, Desmond wrote to Cynthia Asquith reminding her of how they had sat together on the paw of the Trafalgar Square lion, on Armistice night 1918. "I don't think I shall try to do so tonight," he said. For a while the war continued to cast its ugly shadow. Peace-time life was slow to resume. Food was still scarce, troops did not at once return; Dermod's aircraft carrier was caught up in the war in the Far East, and he was obliged to spend torpid months contemplating the glassy Indian Ocean before being allowed home.

Desmond was sixty-eight in 1945 and though his health was now almost permanently bad, he still pursued an enterprising social life: "Oh what an amazing small parakeet birdie he does look these days, his crest flying out behind him, red eyes – one bunged up tight shut – and the other peeping out at one slyly – and seeming to hop along and shift up and down his perch as he chatters," wrote Julia Strachey after having him to dinner in January. "He was in very good spirits and recounted how as a boy he had invented his own way of getting to sleep at night by repeating the phrase – 'Fogger was puzzled where to go for his health,' after which he started to think of all the delightful places he knew of in fiction."[1]

He was still busy on his column for *The Sunday Times* – he never retired; and if he fell asleep more often after lunch and could seldom manage more than three hours work a day, he generally rose to the occasion when a memorial article or advice on a radio programme was needed. The general character of his existence – writing, talking, broadcasting, counselling, reading and travelling – altered very little; it was the intensity rather than the variety of his activities that diminished.

Inwardly, he was no longer buoyed up by the optimistic expectation that somehow, sooner or later, he would become the author of a masterpiece. To this he was resigned. As an old man stripped of ambition, he was grateful for having had the opportunity to put forward his opinions as a journalist: "We are admirably successful failures," he had told Jack Squire before the war. He believed however that he still had a constructive role: "The old are aware that wisdom was not discovered yesterday. They are therefore repositories of tradition. Culture with them is disinterested; having no longer personal or impersonal goals themselves they understand its importance better. They are its natural champions."[2]

Serenity, however, eluded him. Ill health lowered his spirits. Asthma attacks meant days spent in bed at Garrick's, the house filled with the painful sound of his laboured breathing. Lord Moran, Winston Churchill's doctor, kept a watchful eye on him[3] but Molly never could persuade him to give up smoking, the cause of his emphysema. He felt bewildered also, like most old people, by the rapidity with which the world was changing. The days when he looked kindly on the Webbs' socialist ideals were long since over. As he and Molly – an "old breathless bag of bones and brains" and "a rather pale and particular looking old lady" – floundered helplessly after an ill-mannered, newly-nationalised railway porter on Good Friday 1948 on Victoria station platform, he reflected ruefully on the imperfectibility of mankind: "It is a delusion that goodwill towards our fellow men is the strongest inducement to doing our jobs properly; without fear of the sack . . . it is a feeble, intermittent incentive, and therefore socialism[,] which aims at getting rid of the harshness of competition, is going to prove the greatest disappointment since Christianity," he told Vanessa Bell.[4]

As the years had passed, Desmond had lost his own private faith without gaining another. This was the profoundest reason for his sadness. When a young man he had followed Meredith in thinking that all that mattered was to seize life with both hands, to be true to himself and to trust in the fundamental goodness of "Nature" or "the Earth". Far from being discouraged by fears of spiritual desolation when he had given up Christianity, he had felt exhilarated by his freedom from creeds and churches. What he had failed to realise was that Meredith's radiant vision had been acceptable to him at the time only because it was really a kind of religious faith – although he took it for agnosticism.[5] True rational stoicism would have been too much for Desmond; and now as an old man

top left Roy Campbell
top right Maurice Baring
below left Vernon Lee (portrait by John Sargeant)
below right Cyril Connolly

left
Desmond and Molly, August 1939

below
Garrick's Villa

he perceived the abyss, the incomprehensible, limitless, indifferent cosmos, and he quailed before it, echoing Meredith's words to him forty years before, but without the same cheerful stoicism: "The more you come to understand nature the clearer it becomes that nature is not . . . [on your side], nor cares a pin for the individual."

The frightful cruelties of the twentieth century, the cynicism, the mass delusion and the belittlement of human values by Hitler and Marx were beyond anything that Meredith could have imagined, and they had effectively killed that poet's appeal for the young, as Desmond now recognised, and though he himself could never return to Christianity, he had come to think that only a handful of moral heroes could face the fearful truth about the universe and still maintain that there were principles of right conduct by which a man should live. The rest of mankind needed a sustaining illusion of its own significance, such as Christianity, with its loving God, could offer. "The longer I live," he confided to J. L. Hammond, "the more convinced I am that men must have a religion that, if it were true, would prevent them feeling insignificant. . . . I'm not sure that you and I and Barbara [Hammond], if we want to do our fellow men a good turn before we die, ought not to go to the nearest priest or parson (carefully concealing our lack of faith of course) and ask to be admitted to the Christian Church as repentant agnostics."[6]

Though he had always been interested in psychological literature since he had read a book called *Insanity and Genius* at Eton, he had become almost obsessively convinced that Freud and psychoanalysis had under-mined the sense of human dignity and had made life and literature seem duller; this was a repeated theme during his last years of reviewing. He did not rate Freud highly as an intellect; his theory of the "death wish" seemed to him contrived: "It was prompted no doubt by his waking up to the dreariness and horror of his own interpretation of life . . . that view of human nature which at best prompts only a little misanthropic charity, and in other moods inspires the verdict, 'better dead'."[7]

The same hardening of Desmond's attitudes shows also in his reactions to avant-garde arts and literature; during the 'Thirties he had tried to distinguish between the talented and the worthless. After 1945, whatever virtues he might detect in some modernists, he had concluded finally that the whole movement was "artistically very foolish" and inferior to what had come before it. Cyril Connolly remembered his uncompromising reaction to what he thought bogus and how his look of warm pleasure or philosophic detachment would change to a strangely bleak and forbid-ding expression when he came across a piece of writing which he considered pretentious."[8]

Coming from a critic with a reputation for tolerance, such responses were particularly provocative. Geoffrey Grigson, the controversial editor of *New Verse*, had spent much of the 'Thirties attacking "the Desmond MacCarthy streak in English letters", and was prompted in 1949 to launch a direct assault on Desmond's criticism in a BBC broadcast. The outcome was a touching, if undignified display of loyalty by the brawny poet, Roy Campbell, who owed so much to Desmond in his career. Spying Grigson one day in London, Campbell, doubtless drunk, limped fiercely towards him, stick in hand, crying, according to one account, "You've insulted my daddy!", and making as if to belabour him. Whether Grigson, as he claimed, stood firm, or whether, as Campbell alleged, he fled into a cake shop, it cannot have been an agreeable experience for the younger – and punier – man.[9]

Public recognition which had been slow in reaching Desmond came finally in his last decade. He had turned down the OBE in the late 1930s because of his bitter opposition to the government's appeasement of Hitler; but after the war he was elected to the Athenaeum along with Field Marshal Montgomery and the Astronomer Royal, under Rule II, by which men of exceptional eminence were invited to join. When the Third Programme, the "highbrow channel", was started in November 1946, he was also asked to become a regular part of its organisation, to help the BBC establish broadcasting standards and to offer new ideas for topics or drama. His services were still most in demand as a speaker; George Barnes, the director of "The Spoken Word" wrote to tell him, in 1950, "more than anything we want you to broadcast, and in your case whether alive or recorded does not matter to me".

In 1945 he became the English President of the International PEN club – "an honour which," he said, "made me at first raise George Robey eyebrows, 'I'm more than surprised, I'm amazed'." The PEN [Poets' Essayists' and Novelists'] Club, dedicated to defending the freedom of the written word and to the exchange of ideas between authors in different countries, was born of inter-war idealism and attracted both "the army of the good" and cranks. It was a sort of League of Nations for writers. Its leading light in Britain was Hermon Ould, a remarkable autodidact who had started life as a nigger minstrel and had been imprisoned as a conscientious objector during the First World War – a variety of experience which had equipped him, as Desmond said, with a mind far more open than that of most double Firsts with expensive educations.[10]

Although the atmosphere of post-war Europe, dominated in the East by Stalinist Russia, was unfavourable to the success of the PEN's aims, the enthusiasm of its organisers was a boost for western writers after the long years of Nazi oppression. For Desmond, all the more welcome after the dreary years of the war, the greatest attraction of the PEN was the chance it gave him to travel. For the annual Congress in Stockholm of June 1946 he stayed at a luxurious hotel, and was a guest at lavish royal banquets. The price was an exhausting week of speeches and international goodwill. Then he went for a few days' rest to the sanatorium amid the pines at Tyringe, where he and Moore had stayed in 1938 and where Chen had sent her last letter to him. He found it almost unchanged; the same kind old doctor, the same stalwart bath women rolling him over in the brown water, slapping the soles of his feet and rubbing him down. Though he enjoyed strolling through the woodland with the reawakened enjoyment of nature that comes to many elderly people, he felt inwardly forlorn; as he confessed to Moore: "I ought to have gone to some place where there were no memories lying about." In a week, however, he had flown back to Britain and austerity, his luggage bulging with cheese, chocolate, delicatessen and schnapps.[11]

More eventful was the trip to the Continent he made the next year: he began, soberly enough at the PEN Congress at Zurich from which he went on to Paris. There he stayed with the British Ambassador, Sir Alfred Duff Cooper and his wife Lady Diana, the reigning queen among English society beauties since the years before the First World War. Witty and dashing, she was the ill-starred Harry Cust's most significant achievement; for there was little doubt that she was his daughter. He had been the paramour of her mother, the Duchess of Rutland, and passed on to Diana his immaculate golden-haired good looks. Like him, she was much cleverer and more interesting than her impassive symmetrical perfection suggested. Her beauty had become a legend that had reached the music halls. The comedienne, Ella Shields, had delighted pre-1914 audiences, including Desmond, with the climactic lines of her song: "I've just had a banana, / With Lady Diana; / I'm Burlington Bertie from Bow. . . ."

In the aftermath of the Second World War, there was nowhere in the world it was smarter to visit than "Duff and Diana" in Paris, though the pace was exacting for an elderly man, even one as gregarious as Desmond – dinner parties and al fresco luncheons in the grounds of the Coopers' exquisite château at Chantilly, in the company of politicians, journalists, and animated society ladies. Desmond was sustained by the delicious food and a judicious withdrawal to bed for a couple of hours every evening before the meal, as well as by the effervescent company of his solicitous hostess. He was amused when the Duke and Duchess of Windsor came to dinner one evening: "I had met both of them separately years before," he wrote to G. E. Moore. "Twice I remember sitting next 'Mrs Simpson' at luncheon in the days when she was recognized as his maîtresse en titre but the question of her marriage to him had not come

up. On both occasions I remember tactfully turning the conversation to
Mr Simpson, and I could repeat to you, if I thought it would interest you,
what Mr Simpson's tastes in music and general reading are. My
impression of her then was that she was a kindly, nice looking, bright eyed
woman; natural, not grasping or thrusting, and a very nice comforting,
simplifying companion for the very nervous self-conscious little prince
who was constantly putting his finger between his collar and his neck, and
jabbed remarks at you as if he was thinking of something else, and
something rather agitating. When I saw them in Paris she had acquired a
distinctly reginal benevolence of manner, and he seemed calm but his
conversation was not at all bright. She was dressed in a dark blue
shimmering silk costume, very tight in the bust, very scanty in the
shoulder and belling out into the kind of skirt women wore just after
crinolines; sparkling dimly with sapphires – no other jewels, to harmo-
nize with the dress. She remembered having met me and recalled our
meeting across the table. I did not like on that occasion to ask after Mr
Simpson."[12]

In May 1948 Desmond's last trip abroad as PEN President was
Copenhagen, a city he liked; but the occasion was spoiled by the
disputatious conference sessions. Desmond escaped when he could to a
café amid the lilacs and laburnums of the Tivoli Gardens, and to lunch
with the novelist Karen Blixen at her old house and her garden full of
cherry blossom. His dislike of the political wrangling of the delegates
made him eventually hand over, as president of PEN, to Veronica
Wedgwood, the historian and daughter of his old Cambridge friend
Ralph Wedgwood.

He was still reluctant to receive an official honour, as he told Oliver
Esher, who was trying to secure a knighthood for him: "I thought Squire
made himself ridiculous by becoming Sir John. It did his good repute
harm. It didn't suit him; and although I think myself a better writer, I, too,
am neither a man of learning nor a well-known novelist. I am an acute and
balanced critic who sometimes writes uncommonly well, but one who has
been compelled by the exigencies of earning a living with his pen to
express what he has to say about literature and drama as a reviewer and
weekly critic of plays."[13]

Finally, at the end of 1950, he accepted the knighthood he was offered
and went to "bend the knee" at Buckingham Palace in February. His
friends were delighted. Raymond Mortimer, his apprentice on the New
Statesman, paid him a handsome tribute: "During almost thirty years he
has been the model in whose steps I have been tottering. He taught me
incomparably more than anyone else about both the proper attitude for a
critic and the careful use of language . . . What he has done for two

generations of writers – and readers – is beyond estimation, always fighting against silliness, prudery, lowness of brow, pretentiousness and every other form of vulgarity."[14]

Desmond had continued to keep in touch with his most flamboyant "pupil", Cyril Connolly. By now the success of *Horizon* had done much to put Cyril in a better humour. At Desmond's prompting, Molly had invited him to Garrick's. She still could not like him, though this particular visit went well; he enjoyed their exquisite and appropriate surroundings and particularly the fresh tomatoes and the stew.[15] He valued the discriminating interest Desmond took in his career. Ever emotionally demanding, he was always nonplussed by Desmond's detachment – his unwillingness to draw closer to him than "the kind of generalized Johnsonian intimacy which he encouraged", but he was constantly cheered by being told how well he had done and how he could go on to write a master work – a theatrical comedy, perhaps? When Connolly's remarkable essay of "inner exploration", *The Unquiet Grave*, came out in 1945, Desmond praised its literary quality without reserve. Privately, as he told Cyril, he did not care for certain passages where he felt that Freud had been too strong an influence; he must expunge such thinking from his mind, or he would continue to be a prey to lacerating self doubt. He had always tried to badger Cyril out of his self-indulgent miseries and made fun of his pompous reverence for Baudelaire.[16]

After Desmond's death, Cyril remained devoted to his memory: indeed he was to contribute a subtle appreciation of him as a foreword to *Memories*, a collection of Desmond's writing; but Molly was never pleased to see him when he called on her: "That horrible Connolly is like Mr Hyde," she told Rachel, "how extraordinary it is that we have to submit to this beastly little fellow."[17] She could never get out of her head the spoiled egoist she had so long thought him to be, unable to feel – as Desmond had – that Cyril's enjoyment of life and power of affection outweighed the posturing and the discontent.

Desmond's relations with Cyril's contemporary, Evelyn Waugh, were on a more purely literary basis, reinforced by Waugh's marriage to Laura, one of the daughters of Desmond's great friends Aubrey and Mary Herbert of Pixton Park. There was some similarity in their communications to those between Desmond and George Moore. In both cases, Desmond admired the precision and stylishness of their writing; and both novelists, because they cared passionately about perfecting their art, paid attention to his frank criticisms, though neither was normally renowned for his equability. Waugh, always susceptible to self-doubt, was delighted at the glowing reviews he received from Desmond: "even at the height of my satisfaction", he wrote about *Brideshead Revisited*, "I never hoped for appreciations as generous from yourself – practically the only person whose good opinion I crave."[18] He was much interested in Desmond's reservations about the book, and like George Moore, promised to consider some of them if he were able to rewrite passages in a later edition.

When Desmond resumed his regular visits after the war to David and Rachel Cecil near Salisbury, he was able to see his friend Siegfried Sassoon at Heytesbury in Wiltshire. They grumbled together about contemporary literary trends – Sassoon being particularly indignant at Auden's remark that "poets wrote only for one another". When Sassoon's life of George Meredith appeared in September 1948, Desmond devoted two full length reviews to it, declaring that the author and his subject were ideally matched: those who wished to understand "the spirit of 1914", needed to enter into Meredith's exalted faith in "the Earth": "Siegfried Sassoon, who springs from that generation which went to the war of 1914 in so Meredithian a spirit, half joy of life, half readiness to die, was the very man to write this biography."[19]

Despite his disenchantment with the post-war world, Desmond still found time to encourage young people taking their first tentative steps in writing and especially authors with something original to say who deserved recognition. One discovery was Jocelyn Brooke, a novelist of rare talent who wrote observantly about his childhood aesthetic experiences in *The Military Orchid* (1948). Desmond was impressed. Flaubert, he said, would have been content with those cadences; but he became critical of Brooke's obsession with his pubescent sensations, especially in his verses; "don't persist too much in following little damp dark paths among the laurels," he warned Brooke, "they too often lead only to the garden privy."[20]

He and Molly enjoyed Brooke's lively, frivolous company, in much the same way as she had relished that of Philip Ritchie. After Desmond's death Brooke told her that though he had only known him for four years, Desmond had been his finest and dearest friend and "his generous praise of my work has been the biggest thing in my life". Brooke himself did not long survive his mentor. His later years were shadowed by disappointment about his undeserved neglect and shortened by drink.

But it was Desmond's longest lasting friendships which meant most to him – with Somerset Maugham, for instance, whose reputation he continued to defend as a master of narrative; he delighted in the good living that he enjoyed on his visits to the Villa Mauresque: "the food!" he told Molly. "I am silent with pleasure at almost *every* dish that is put before me."[21] In a letter (of March 1950) to Marie-France MacCarthy, the young French girl Dermod MacCarthy had recently married,

Desmond evoked vividly the little paradise Maugham had created in the South of France:

"I am sitting in bright warm sunshine on a paved terrace with orange and lemon trees, laden with fruit, growing out of it; with my back to a blue, blue sea, and looking up at a milk-white house, with very long windows, which makes the sky above it look even bluer than the sea." There, while Maugham worked, Desmond idled contentedly by the bathing pool in the garden, shadowed by stone pines and surrounded by flowering arbutuses. "My bedroom is high and small, with a sumptuous bathroom attached. It contains every object one wants, down to a row of perfectly pointed pencils. When I am in my bed, with its muslin curtains and white silk coverlet, I feel like a bride – a wreath of orange-blossoms round my forehead would make the resemblance complete. When next I come to stay at 25 Wellington Square [where Dermod and Marie-France were living] . . . I shall feel like Louis Quatorze on the top of a bus."

Maugham, at the time, was involved in buying pictures in his daughter's name, so that he could enjoy them in his lifetime, while she herself would pay no tax on them. The art historian Kenneth Clark and the director of the New York Museum of Modern Art were there to advise him. Desmond never lived, fortunately, to witness the bitter legal wrangles which were the sorry outcome of this ingenious plan. He felt detached from much of the conversation about art collection and Riviera gossip, and the throng of ancien régime exiles:

"I always find myself sitting next a princess or some forgotten duchess with an historic name. One meets a little bent old woman with a brightly painted face and huge jewels, more like 'knuckle dusters' than rings . . . and one presently discovers that she is the ex-Empress of Brazil or something of that kind . . . Everybody," he told Marie-France, "is very royalty-minded, and has just been with the Queen of Spain or some deposed monarch, or the last of Queen Victoria's daughters, Marie-Louise: 'You know the dear absurd old thing?' Truth compels me to say I do not, but, I hastily add, 'She comes often to tea with my son Dermod and his wife in Chelsea'."

The male element on the Riviera seemed to Desmond to consist mainly of "quietly but beautifully dressed men . . . who you would guess had spent their lives in merely preserving their vigour and appearance. Then you find out that, from youth onwards, they have been dashing recklessly from capital to capital in Europe, or even in scouring the Near East, collecting teaspoons, of which they have an unrivalled collection."[22]

He was able, however, to eschew both royalty and millionaires from time to time and to enjoy an exquisite meal by himself at the villa while the rest of the party went out visiting; and there were moments when he and

Maugham could talk quietly together, as Maugham told Molly affectionately: "as I write now I look at the chair in which he liked to sit and I recall
his gestures as he talked & the sound of his voice. Never again shall we
know such a varied and brilliant conversationalist."[23]

Among his other old friends, the Asquiths were still a part of
Desmond's life. Cynthia was no longer the saddened beauty with whom
Desmond fell romantically in love late in the First World War. She had
long since recovered her spirits despite the anxieties around her, her
schizophrenic son, and her inadequate income on which she managed to
live extravagantly – "recklessly protruding her long horns", as Desmond
put it. "It *is* depressing," she gaily declared after the war, "not to be
treated with the respect that is no longer one's due". Cynthia was a
survivor and to support her family she had not only been J. M. Barrie's
secretary but she had also edited countless children's annuals, poetry
collections, quiz games and ghost stories. Now, as an old woman, she
remained bold and alert, her manner teasing, even a little alarming, her
eyes bright and amused. Her once glorious auburn hair retained its tint
with the aid of a bottle; and her symmetrical cat-like face was still
attractive. Under-educated like most women of her class, she never learnt
to write skilfully. Desmond did his best when he had to review her pot-
boiler reminiscences, but he could not pretend they did justice to the
picturesque aristocratic world in which she had lived or to her own
astringent, stylish nature. Her conversational wit came over more vividly
in her brief letters: their immediacy and wild teasing mischief brought
her, as it were, straight on to the breakfast table at Garrick's villa.

Margot Asquith and her daughter, the ill-fated Elizabeth, both died
before the war's end. Desmond wrote memorial articles on them both.
His piece on the sad, squalidly drunken Elizabeth, was a model of the
kindly art of obituary concealment. He spoke of hopes of great success as
a writer disappointed; he recalled her femininity but not the grossness of
her sensuality.[24] This sensitive treatment of her blighted life delighted her
widower. Prince Bibesco, despite his cynicism, which had led him to make
the prestigious match originally, was far from heartless. His life with
Elizabeth may have been unhappy, but he was, in his own way, proud of
her and, besides, his own career had been inconspicuous. He and
Desmond would meet when Antoine was over from Paris and it was a
shock to Desmond, to whom Antoine seemed younger and more vigorous
than himself, when he learnt from Enid Jones (Bagnold) in September
1951, that he had died. The ebullient Enid, more statuesque than ever,
was always a supportive friend and Desmond was happy as ever to send
her comments and advice on her still surprisingly successful books.

Of the others in the old Asquith set whom he had known since before the first war, he often saw Violet Bonham-Carter and her husband and Katharine, Raymond Asquith's widow. He still kept up, too, with Ettie Desborough; but the world of "the Souls" – the world of Maurice Baring and Harry Cust and of his pre-First World War aristocratic acquaintances was fading away fast. It had been years since he had spent time with Judith Lytton, his champion when he had been courting Irene Noel, though Neville (now Lord) Lytton, long since divorced from his stormy, masterful wife, wrote touching letters to Molly from Paris where he had settled and re-married, reviving their old friendship. As for Irene Noel, she was still the vigorous queen of Achmetaga; but there was no final chapter to the "Ireniad", and he only heard about her from her old friends Hilton Young (Lord Kennet) and his family, with whom Desmond often stayed when he was in London.

As for his most intimate friends of Cambridge days, Desmond saw the Trevelyan clan frequently after the war. Old customs continued: at home at The Shiffolds, Bob used to shave with a cut-throat (like Desmond) every morning in the drawing-room at about eleven-thirty a.m., while Bessy Trevelyan would read aloud "a shaving book" such as Boswell or Fanny Burney's Diaries. Desmond always joined in this shaving ritual when he stayed there. His lifelong friendship with the family could still bring the occasional surprise: George Trevelyan, now Britain's leading historian, confessed to Desmond over dinner in 1946 that he had never read all of Gibbon's *Decline and Fall of the Roman Empire*;[25] though toothless, George was still exceedingly vigorous; he enjoyed the Apostles dinner given in his honour in 1951 which Desmond attended. "The Trevelyans are tough thank heaven," Desmond told Bob Trevy. "Like not a few of the old families in England, they have something of the toughness of peasants: look at your hands, how strong they are and how unlike the delicate tapering fingers of a Van Dyck portrait!" But even Bob's wiry strength was failing him; and after a period of illness he died in 1951. Desmond mourned him. His own faith in the merits of his old friend's poems never faltered: "it won't sell; but it may float, and carry some of its cargo to distant ports. . . . I think myself Bob has earned . . . a place in XXth century poetry equivalent to say that of Collins or Clare."[26]

As for Reymond Abbott, "The Owl", that helpless figure proved tougher than all of them. To rescue him from near-starvation, Desmond took financial advice to rearrange his income so that he could afford to live modestly but securely for the rest of his life at Ventnor on the Isle of Wight. The two friends travelled to see each other regularly and corresponded about the subjects that had always delighted them: Wordsworth, Dryden, Horace, "our beloved Pater", and "Mallock's fine prose and wise penetration". On Desmond's last birthday in 1952, it was

"The Owl" to whom he wrote: "Chen – Chen and you! – are both with me together today. How long was it you lived at Cheyne Gardens – on and off – before my marriage?" In his cramped quarters with his few remaining Indian treasures and fine library, Abbott dwelt contentedly enough, in the care of a kind landlady with whom he would discuss Italian church architecture and read Henry James by the light of many dim candles – on which he insisted for aesthetic reasons.[27] He outlived Desmond by many years, fading away finally when he was over ninety, an obscure yet curiously distinguished figure from another age, whose outlook stretched back even beyond his time at Cambridge to the heroic early Victorian days when his father had defended the Indian Empire. It was as a lone guardian of a past rich in culture and endeavour that Desmond respected as well as loved Reymond Abbott, for he too felt passionately that during their youth they had witnessed the close of one of the supreme periods of civilisation.

Desmond and G. E. Moore corresponded as though they were still undergraduates, entertaining each other with their observations and shared impressions. They discussed foreign countries, philosophical works and Morgan Forster's novels, which both found unsatisfactory though interesting – their endings so incredible and the relationships so unlikely. Desmond came up to Cambridge frequently and when he stayed with G. E. and Dorothy Moore in Chesterton Road would dawdle over leisurely breakfasts, reminiscing and joking. It was a special delight for him that Moore received an O.M. in the same year that he himself was knighted. Moore's ill health was a constant anxiety to Desmond, yet he lived on after him, into his eighties. Desmond's affection for this dearest of all his friends showed poignantly in the dream he recounted to Veronica Wedgwood a few months before his own death: "I was walking along a street in Cambridge with a man and I asked after Moore: he said casually, 'O, he died this morning', I turned and clutched him in a pang of disbelieving fear – and behold! to my joy it was Moore himself! We hugged each other, laughing; Moore's face was quite pink from laughter; I can see him still."[28]

It had been too difficult during the war to bring together the scattered members of the Memoir Club; but soon afterwards Molly, who was still Secretary, set about gathering them all for a meeting, aided by Vanessa Bell who eventually, with her son, Quentin, took over the organisation of the Club, with Molly as President. Despite blackballing – the rule of the Club was that even one blackball meant that someone could never be elected – there were several new faces: David Garnett and his wife, Angelica, the daughter of Duncan Grant and Vanessa; Frances Partridge; Dermod MacCarthy; and when Janey Bussy came to live in London,

Molly invited her to join, without consulting anyone else – but "I don't believe the Memoir Club is capable of democratic procedure," wrote Maynard Keynes to her tolerantly.[29]

As before, the members gathered for a meal in an unpretentious Soho restaurant, after which they adjourned to rooms nearby, usually Duncan Grant's in Bloomsbury, where the papers were read out. Molly suggested that at dinner Maynard should sit "where our Lord sits in pictures of the last Supper" as a nucleus for the conversation.[30] She herself liked to be at one end of the table so that she could remain silent if the effort of keeping up with the conversation become too much for her.

When Maynard Keynes died, in the summer of 1946, Molly wrote to Vanessa that, melancholy as it was to see the original members of the club dropping one by one like the last leaves off a tree, nevertheless she thought it should go on: Morgan Forster had proposed bringing it to an end, but Desmond told Vanessa not to pay any attention to him: "He is possessed with a mania for bringing everything to an end. Last year, at the Apostles' Dinner, he made a speech proposing that the Apostles should come to an end. Imagine their proud faces! Now, I quite sympathise with the desire to wind things up. But let's have *some* sense of proportion. Let's start with the solar system itself, not with the poor little sprouts and flowers of worth-whileness growing here and there below – that's what I say, and I'm sure that everyone at Charleston agrees.

"Draw Morgan's attention to the sun. They say it's covered with spots, and it is certainly getting old. It will never see its prime again. It's wasting away. By all means extinguish it – it would be humane."[31] Vanessa agreed they should continue as they always had, for Molly had started an institution that had "produced some of the most fascinating evenings one has ever had".[32]

The memoirs written by Desmond and Molly now included hers on life at Garrick's Villa during the war. Desmond read his memoir of "my dear old, queer old friend", G.A.P.: Arthur Paley had died in 1941; during his sixty-seven years he had run through the majority of his vast fortune. Luckily his canny old aunt, who was married to his banker, Edward Hoare, had realised what was happening and that her husband had failed to grasp the extent of Paley's fecklessness. She therefore took over the financial reins herself. She managed to garner enough, in a separate account, for G.A.P. to be able to live out his days simply but comfortably and to provide for his two sons, one of whom was in a mental home, and the other who was leading a peaceful eventless half-life.[33]

Eventually Molly found it too "baffling" to hear what the speakers were saying at Memoir Club meetings. "I have reached another step down on the deafness staircase," she said.[34] Her deaf aids were no easier for her to manage. She now had one in a box which she carried about with her – and frequently left behind. Its batteries seemed to fail just when she needed it most and the whole apparatus irritated and tired her. Another member, such as Leonard Woolf or Quentin Bell, would sit next to her at the Memoir Club to pass on what was being said, but she finally gave up coming to the meetings.

Sometimes Desmond's asthma overcame him: at a meeting on 16th May 1949 Vanessa was reading a memoir of Virginia as a child; it was nearly midnight and she had not finished when Desmond, who had been seized by asthma as he ascended the stairs to Duncan's rooms, had to be taken home by Dermod. In the car "Desmond sat frozen with breathlessness, with the muscles of his neck standing out like cords. Dermod was all kindness to him," recorded Frances Partridge.[35] The last time Leonard Woolf saw his old friend was on a cold autumn evening as they walked together away from Gordon Square after a Memoir Club meeting. Desmond was again racked with asthma and Leonard went to find him a taxi ("ran off" to find it were Woolf's own words – he was then nearly seventy). "When I put him into the taxi, he looked, not like an affable hawk or even a dishevelled fledgling, but like a battered, shattered, dying rook." As he helped him into the taxi, Leonard suddenly saw him as he had been in youth, walking in the Devon hills on a reading party with G. E. Moore. "There are few things more terrible than such visions of one's friends in youth and vigour through the miseries of age and illness. I left Desmond sitting in the taxi, affectionate, dejected, unheroic because so obviously broken and beaten by asthma and by life; but brave in not complaining and not pretending and in still, when he could, making his jokes and his phrase."[36]

This was, of course, how someone like Desmond would strike the hard-working, sparse-living Leonard, who remained vigorous until his death when he was nearly ninety.

Desmond and Molly's last years did not only consist of ailments and deafness and other such "bafflements"; as with most elderly people these were part, and sometimes a substantial part, of their lives, but there were pleasures, too, and a new serenity and affection in their marriage. They were both anxious by nature; but at least in their old age they stopped causing each other anxiety. "Dearest of all, remember as we go down the hill together – in spite of nerves – in spite of the scatter-brained moments we both suffer from – we are closer to each other than to anyone else," Desmond wrote to her at the end of May 1947. "We won't always be patient with each other, but we can't help being all-important to each other." The very next day he wrote again to her, reminding her that now they were within sight of the end at last, "my philosophic and your religious mind are in harmony about the things which are most important".[37]

Desmond and Molly's old age was enriched by their children's contentment – for Michael, too had been happily married, since 1948, to Chloe Buxton – and by the arrival of grandchildren; by their renewed affection for one another and by the pleasure they had in living at Garrick's Villa, its lawns replanted, where firebombs had burnt, its craters filled with flower-beds.

Cambridge University awarded Desmond an honorary degree in 1952 and he went there to receive it in June. Molly attended the degree ceremony and afterwards returned to London while Desmond stayed on. An attack of asthma developed into bronchial pneumonia; he was moved into a Cambridge nursing home, where Dermod hurried with Molly. For a day Desmond lay almost comatose; just after midnight, on 7th June, "Dermod and I held his hands as he passed into unconsciousness and was gone from us."[38]

His death was not unexpected, but "I don't see how anyone *can* be *prepared* for the death of anyone loved and so completely part of one's life, even though one *knows* it's as simple to die as to be born – but it's so dismaying to have only the silence – and the silence – and then *for ever* the silence – all come about in a minute," Molly wrote to Leonard Woolf.[39]

Molly continued living at Garrick's Villa, where she moved into a smaller flat. She was determined not to be a widowy widow, moaning in black, but she continued to miss Desmond acutely. She "could not get over the expectation that the door would open and he would walk in again," she told Ralph and Frances Partridge when they visited her.[40] Frances was impressed how Molly built up what remained of her life in the way that suited her best. "I am only an ordinary Molly, much as usual, but now nearly 'over' as one says of all the garden produce," she wrote. She visited her children in the country, Michael and Chloe in Norfolk, Dermod and Marie-France, who had settled in Buckinghamshire, and David and Rachel at Rockbourne. Kind friends took her out: she revisited Ford Place in Sussex, where she had spent so many happy, and unhappy, weeks when she was first engaged and during the First World War: "that dear old house is quite absorbed into a huge aerodrome," she told Dolly Ponsonby.[41] She stayed with Leslie Hartley near Bath and he wrote her charming and affectionate letters, consulting her about the title of his new novel, telling her that Korda wanted him to help with the adaptation of his book, *The Go-Between* for the cinema and how unsuited he would be for this, since "such creative impulse as I have comes from ignoring everything round me, and getting into a tobacco-induced Demi-trance."[42]

On the anniversary of Desmond's death she went to "the only church I know of that is not Roman Catholic that has *candles* and a side altar – which to me represented an Altar in memory of the dead and my candle shone out throughout the service"; this was St Alban's in Holborn. Afterwards, she told Rachel, she strolled down to St Paul's "where I found a seething mass of inconvenient sight see-ers gazing vacantly about, and left rather quickly!" She was glad to have made the expedition to remember Desmond.[43]

Lord Kemsley had offered her a life pension of £260 a year, "although times are not very good in the newspaper world, it gives me great pleasure to do that because of my long friendship with Desmond," he wrote.[44] It was only paid once. Molly's health, always fragile, deteriorated rapidly with bereavement. In the autumn of 1953, her heart began to fail. She spent long days alone in Garrick's Villa. Even at that sombre time of the year the morning light fell brightly in her room and she could look out to see the trolley-buses humming along the main road past her window; the temple to Shakespeare on the river bank, and the Thames, empty of tripper boats, flowing dark and swift downstream from her girlhood home at Eton.

Her rooms, despite the bustling and grumbling of her old servant Blanche, and the regular visits of her sister, Cecilia, who walked over from Hampton Court Palace, seemed desolate without Desmond; but in them all were the reminders of his life and personality: his favourite books in unfamiliarly tidy surroundings; the cat, Wavell, whom he had named after the poetry-loving General; his set of Chinese chessmen, red and white, arrayed on the board; and in the shadowed hall that served as a dining-room, Chen's antique inlaid cabinet with its talismanic contents – the carved ivory hand that had once clutched a snake, a MacCarthy heraldic emblem; a mysterious crystal ball; and, stuffed away in the drawers, fading photographs of Desmond as a child, of his father and his grandfather, the "Parent Bird" and his extraordinary family.

Molly lay in bed, growing weaker, sustained by her memories and the visits of her children. Two days before Christmas, 1953, she died.

Her ashes were brought in a casket and placed in Desmond's grave in the churchyard of St Giles' in Cambridge. Next to them now lie G. E. Moore and his wife, Dorothy. Moore had especially asked to be "buried beside Desmond". This had caused Molly momentary panic: could it be that he really wished to be interred *with* Desmond's remains? If so, how could she refuse?[45] The misunderstanding was soon resolved: but the little episode, with its mixture of muddle, deep affection and idealism, as well as concern as to the *exact* meaning of words, seemed to characterise the whole texture of Desmond and Molly's life.

Sources

The bulk of the material cited is from the Desmond MacCarthy papers (incorporating those of Molly MacCarthy and her family, the Warre-Cornishes) held by the MacCarthys' literary heirs. These include the copies of letters from Desmond MacCarthy to correspondents made by Frances Partridge in the early 1960s, or by Desmond's secretaries during his lifetime. Papers cited from other sources are indicated.

Abbreviations
Sunday Times – S.T.; *Eye Witness* – E.W.; *New Quarterly* – N.Q.; *New Statesman* – N.S.; *Life and Letters* – L. & L.;

Desmond MacCarthy – D.M.; Molly MacCarthy – M.M.; Louise MacCarthy – Chen; Warre-Cornish – W.-C.; Ottoline Morrell – Ott.; Virginia Woolf – V.W. (V.W.'s *Diaries* refer to paperback edition); Leonard Woolf – L.W.; Cynthia Asquith – Cynthia; G. E. Moore – G.E.M.; Clive Bell – Clive; Vanessa Bell – V.B.

BBC written Archives Centre BBA; Harry Ransom Humanities Research Center, The University of Texas at Austin – HRHRC; King's College Library – KCL; Sussex Univesity Library – Sussex; Frances Partridge papers – Partridge; Ponsonby papers at Shulbrede Priory – Shulbrede.

Desmond and Molly
1. B. Russell – D.M., 13 Oct. 1904.
2. L. Woolf, *An Autobiography*, Vol. 2 (1980 pb), pp. 95–102.
3. Sean O'Casey – D.M., 28 Mar. 1942.
4. D.M. – M.M., 22 May 1906.

1. A Nineteenth-Century Childhood
1. Blanche W.-C. – Margaret W.-C., Aug. 1882.
2. Mary MacCarthy, *A Nineteenth-Century Childhood*, 4th ed. 1985. Except where otherwise cited the quotes in this chapter are from this book.

3. A. C. Benson, *Memories and Friends*, 1924, pp. 167–191.
4. Virginia Woolf, *Moments of Being*, 1976, p. 65.
5. A. C. Benson, *op. cit.*.
6. *Ibid.*
7. Clare Sheppard (Blanche's niece), unpub. memoir.
8. *Cornishiana*, priv. printed 1935.
9. A. C. Benson, *op. cit.*
10. M.M. – Ott., (no date), HRHRC.
11. Lord Ponsonby of Shulbrede, ms. typescript memoir, *Brief Glimpses* (1943) (Shulbrede).
12. Blanche W.-C. – Maurice Baring, no date (collection Mrs Nathalie Brooke).

13. See Mary Grierson, *Donald Francis Tovey* (1952).
14. Note by Eddie Marsh, M.M. papers.
15. D.M. – Cynthia, 1 May 1920.

2. *"A Remarkable Child"*
1. D.M., "Eton", *Experience*, 1935 pp. 153–4.
2. D.M., "A Memoir of Youth", *Memories*, 1953, p. 207.
3. See Mrs Stone, of Stonehouse School – Chen 30 Apr. 1885.
4. Evans's Debating Society books, 1892–1894 (held at Evans's House, Eton Coll.)
5. D.M., paper from Memoir Club (no date; typed).
6. See D. M. to C. D. MacCarthy, 12 May 1893 & D.M. "Henry James", *Portraits*, 1931, pp. 163–4.
7. D.M., *Experience*, pp. 150–154.
8. D.M. *Memories*, pp. 212–217.
9. Lionel Ford – C. D. MacCarthy, 13 Dec. 1891.
10. C. D. MacCarthy – D.M., 18 April 1895.
11. D.M. – C. D. MacCarthy, 15 July 1893.
12. D.M., *Memories*, p. 209.
13. See letters from Chen to D.M. partic. 1930s; D.M., "Ancestor Worship", unpub. memoir; *Chevallerie'sches Familienblatt*, 1937, 1938, Berlin; *Fontane, Briefe*, Berlin 1980, Vols. I, pp. 164, 256, & II, pp. 277, 488; D.M. to Betsy Reyneau, 2 July 1930.
14. See also Chen to Harry Cust, 24 Sept. 1884. (Paul Chipchase).
15. Chen to C. D. MacCarthy, letters, 1887–8.
16. Chen to D.M., 4 Oct. 1894 and spring 1897; D.M. – Chen, Jan. 1891.
17. D.M., "Ancestor Worship" (note 13).
18. D.M. to Chen, 19 Apr. 1889.
19. D.M., "The G.O.M." and "Sir William Harcourt", *Portraits*, pp. 111 & 122.
20. D.M., "Samuel Butler", *Criticism*, 1932, pp. 3–4.
21. D.M. in *Eye Witness*, 25 July 1912.
22. D.M. to William Gerhardie, 14 Nov. 1936.
23. Chen to D.M., 30 July, 11 Oct. *c.* 1896.
24. Chen to Harry Cust, May 1879 (Chipchase).

3. *"A Really Strong Swimmer"*
1. For this chapter, generally, see: Maurice Baring *The Puppet-Show of Memory*, 1922, P. N. Furbank, *E. M. Forster: A Life*, pb. 1979, Vol. 1 Ch. 4; Paul Levy, *Moore: G. E. Moore & the Cambridge Apostles*, pb. 1981; Sir Edward Marsh, *A Number of People*, 1939, Chs. 2–4; L. Woolf, *Sowing* Ch. 2 in *An Autobiography*, Vol. I, 1980. Also Quentin Bell, information & letter, Alan Kucia (Trinity Coll. Library) to the authors 26 Nov. 1987.
2. Gerald W.-C. to Frank W.-C., 1895.
3. C. D. MacCarthy – D.M., 18 Apr. 1895.
4. A. R. Verrall – C. D. MacCarthy, 1895; and also see D.M. – C. D. MacCarthy, 7 June 1895.
5. D.M., "Oscar Browning", *Portraits*, pp. 34–38.
6. D.M. in *S.T.*, 1934.
7. J. M. Keynes, "My Early Beliefs", *Two Memoirs*, 1949.
8. Bertrand Russell – D.M., 17 Jan. 1917.
9. L. Woolf, *Sowing*, pb. 1980, p. 90.
10. D. M. 2 ms papers for Apostles.
11. G. M. Trevelyan, *An Autobiography*.
12. G. M. Trevelyan – D.M., *c.* 1898.
13. Marsh, *op. cit.*, p. 48.
14. R. C. Trevelyan – D.M., *c.* 1920.
15. See, for example, D.M. – Chen, 20 March, 3 Apr. 1900.
16. D.M. "Henry James", *Portraits*, p. 165 and D.M. notes.
17. D.M. – Chen, 31 Jan. 1897.
18. D.M., "George Meredith", *Portraits*, p. 184.
19. D.M., BBC talk, 23 Oct. 1928.
20. D.M. in *S.T.*, 19 & 26 Sept. 1948 and D.M., "Thomas Hardy", *Memories*.
21. D.M., "Bloomsbury", *Memories*, p. 174.
22. P. Levy, *op. cit.*, pp. 222–225.
23. P. N. Furbank, *op. cit.*, Vol. I, p. 150.

4. *Aspirations*
1. C. D. MacCarthy – D.M., 18 Apr. 1895.
2. Chen – D.M., 7 Feb. 1896.
3. D.M. – Chen, 20 Oct. 1895.
4. D.M. – Chen, 10 Feb. 1896.
5. Chen – D.M., 13 Nov. 1896; see 20 Oct. 1896.
6. D.M. – Moore, 31 Dec. 1896; 9 Jan. 1897.
7. Chen – D.M., May 1897.
8. In Gerald W.-C., *Beneath the Surface*, 1917.
9. A. R. Verrall – Chen letters, 1–7 June, 1897.
10. D.M. – Chen, 12 Oct. 1897.
11. Chen – D.M., 28 June 1898.
12. Christopher Hassall, *Edward Marsh*, 1959, pp. 76–77.
13. Rachel Cecil, information.
14. Chen – D.M., May 1898.
15. D.M. – Chen, 3 June 1898.

16. D.M., "Ancestor Worship", unpub. ms.
17. D.M., "In Germany", *Experience*.
18. D.M. – Chen, 18 Oct. 1898.
19. Chen – D.M., 25 Aug. 1898.
20. Chen – D.M., Aug. 1898.
21. D.M. – Chen, Sept. 1898.
22. D.M., "Henry James", *Portraits*.
23. D.M. – Henry James, undated, not sent.
24. D.M., notes.
25. D.M. "Henry James", *op. cit.*

5. *Mother and Son*
1. D.M. – Chen, Aug. 1901.
2. D.M. – Lavinia Talbot, 6 Jan. 1901.
3. D.M. – Chen, Aug. 1901.
4. G. M. Trevelyan – D.M., 5 July 1901.
5. D.M. – Chen, 1901.
6. D.M., "Shooting with Wilfred Blunt", *Memories*, p. 218.
7. Maurice Baring, *The Puppet Show of Memory*, 1922, p. 146.
8. W. H. Mallock, *The New Republic*, 1900 edn.
9. D.M. "Memoir of Youth", *Memories*, p. 213.
10. Dr Dermod MacCarthy, information.
11. Chen – Abbott, 14 June 1900.
12. Chen – D.M., 1907.
13. See D.M. – Margaret W.-C., 22 Apr. 1902, and D.M., "Hardy", *Memories*, pp. 108–112.
14. D.M. – Cynthia, 17 May 1921.
15. Chen. – D.M., Jan. 1907.
16. Hardy – D.M., Aug. 1916, and D.M. – Hardy, 5 Nov. 1908.

6. *Love and Work*
1. D.M. – Jim Whittall, 10 Apr. 1929.
2. D.M., "Memoir of Youth", *Memories*, p. 216.
3. Letters of D.M. – Sada Yacco, and D.M. – Abbott.
4. Francis Noel-Baker, Sheila Pitt, information; Irene Noel diaries, 1901, 1902.
5. See D.M. – Chen, 6 June 1902; Chen – D.M., 4 July 1902.
6. D.M. – Chen, 9, 24 July 1902.
7. D.M. – Chen, 5 Aug. 1902.
8. Irene Noel, diary, 1902.
9. D.M. – Chen, 20 Sept. 1902, and D.M. – G.E.M., 24 Oct. 1902.
10. D.M. – G.E.M., 14 Jan. 1903.
11. D.M. – G.E.M., 28 Mar. 1903.
12. G.E.M. – D.M., 25 Mar. 1903.
13. Judith Lytton – Irene Noel, 16 Apr. 1903.

14. D.M. – Chen, 16 May 1903.
15. D.M. – Irene Noel, Aug. 1903.
16. D.M. – Chen, spring 1903.
17. See R. C. Trevelyan – D.M., 14 Dec. 1903; and D.M. – R. C. Trevelyan, 26 May 1905.
18. D.M. – M.M., 27 Feb. 1906.
19. D.M., "Max Beerbohm", *Memories*, pp. 192–8.
20. D.M., "Apprenticeship", *Humanities*, pp. 15–16.
21. D.M., *The Court Theatre, 1904–1907*, Introduction. *Speaker*, 16 Sept, 1905.
22. D.M., "The Ideal Spectator", *Theatre*, 1954, pp. 9–10.
23. See C. B. Purdom, *Harley Granville-Barker*, 1956.
24. D.M., *Court Theatre*, Ch. 1.
25. See D.M. "Ibsen", *Humanities*, pp. 60–70.
26. D.M., *Speaker*, 17 Mar. 1906.
27. D.M. *Shaw, The Plays, 1951*, pp. 93–101.
28. D.M. – Abbott, 11 Dec. 1904.

7. *A Troubled Heart*
1. M.M., *A Nineteenth Century Childhood*, p. 92.
2. M.M., "A German Court Before the War", *The Festival*, p. 63.
3. M.M., diary, 1903 *passim*.
4. Clare Sheppard, unpub. memoir.
5. See A. C. Benson, *op. cit.*
6. Blanche W.C. – Ma. Baring (Nathalie Brooke).
7. M.M. Diary, 1903.
8. M.M. – D.M., May–Sept. 1905.
9. M.M., *A Nineteenth Century Childhood*.
10. M.M. – D.M., 30 Jan. 1906.
11. Frank W.C. – M.M., 1 Feb. 1906.
12. M.M. – D.M., 2 Feb. 1906.
13. D.M. – M.M., 14 Feb. 1906, and D.M. "George Meredith", *Portraits*, pp. 170–174.
14. M.M. – D.M., 15 Feb. 1906.
15. D.M. – M.M., 16 Feb. 1906.
16. M.M. – D.M., 19 Feb. 1906.
17. D.M. – Irene Noel, 2 Mar. 1906.
18. D.M. – M.M., 1 Mar. 1906.
19. M.M. – D.M., May 1906.
20. H. James – D.M., June 1906.
21. G.E.M. – D.M., 2 Sept. 1906.
22. D.M. – G.E.M., 4 Sept. 1906.
23. M.M. – Chen. Sept. 1906.
24. D.M. – Blanche W.-C., 20 Sept. 1906.
25. D.M. – Cynthia, 17 May 1921.

8. *"An Oddity Without Parallel"*

1. M.M. *The Bird is on the Wing*, unpub. memoir.
2. The Hon. Guy Strutt, information.
3. D.M., unpub. Paley memoir for Memoir Club, 1946.
4. M.M., unpub. memoir, *op. cit.*
5. M.M. – Chen, 1907.
6. M.M., Diary, July 1907.
7. D.M. – G. E. Moore, Aug. 1907.
8. M.M. – D.M., 21 Aug. 1907.
9. D.M., unpub. Paley memoir.
10. N.Q., Nov. 1907, Oct. 1908, Oct. 1909.
11. R. C. Trevelyan – D.M., 8 Dec. 1908.
12. N.Q., Nov. 1907.
13. Shaw – D.M., 3 Dec. 1908.
14. N.Q., July 1909, April 1909, and Jan. 1909.
15. Lytton Strachey – D.M., 7 June 1910; D.M. – J. M. Keynes, 21 Aug. 1910 (Keynes papers, KCL).
16. H. Belloc – D.M., 10 Aug. 1909.
17. B. Russell – D.M., 1 March 1909, and 7 April 1907.
18. G. M. Trevelyan – D.M., 9 Aug. 1910.
19. D.M., *The Court Theatre 1904–1907*, 1907.
20. G. B. Shaw – D.M., 3 Dec. 1907.
21. G. B. Shaw – D.M., 26 June 1922.
22. Blanche W.-C. – Chen Mar. 1907.
23. Lytton Strachey – M.M., 20 March 1907.
24. D.M., unpub. memoir.
25. M.M., unpub. memoir.
26. Rachel Cecil, information.
27. V.W., *Diary*, Vol. 3, 7 Nov. 1928.
28. M.M. – Chen, no date, *c.* 1909.

9. *South Africa and the "Artquake"*

1. M.M. – D.M., Jan. 1909.
2. D.M. – Chen, 26 Feb. 1909.
3. D.M. – M.M., 30 Sept. 1909.
4. M.M. – Chen, Feb. 1910.
5. D.M. – G. E. Moore, 16 Feb. 1910.
6. M.M. – Chen, Mar. 1910, and April 1910
7. M.M. – D.M., July 1910.
8. D.M. – M.M., July 1910.
9. M.M. – Chen, 1910; Dr Dermod Mac-Carthy, in conversation, was of the opinion that Molly's precautions amounted to no more than reliance on the notoriously unreliable monthly cycle of female fertility.
10. D.M. *The Post-Impressionist Exhibition*, 1910 Third Programme broadcast, BBC, 16 Dec. 1946.
11. D.M. – M.M., 8 Sept. 1910, 10 Sept. 1910, and 15 Sept. 1910.
12. V.W., *Roger Fry, A Biography*, 1940, p. 153.
13. D.M. – Chen, 8 Nov. 1910.
14. Wilfred Blunt *Diaries*, 1920; quoted V.W., *op. cit.*, pp. 156–7.
15. Judith Lytton – Chen, 17 Feb. 1911, re exhibit No. 67.
16. The Duchess of Rutland – D.M., 17 Nov. 1910.
17. D.M., *The Eye-Witness*, 1911.
18. BBC broadcast.
19. L.W., *An Autobiography*, Vol. 2, pp. 65–66.
20. David Garnett, *The Golden Echo*, p. 200.
21. R. Fry – N. Wedd, in *The Letters of Roger Fry*, ed. Denys Sutton, 1972, p. 429, 2 June 1918.
22. R. Fry – D.M., 29 April 1923 (KCL).

10. *Smouldering Ambitions*

1. M.M. – Chen, 10 Oct. 1910.
2. D.M. – Chen, 10 Aug. 1910.
3. M.M. – Chen, Jan. 1911.
4. M.M. – Chen, Jan. 1911.
5. D.M. – Roy Harrod, 14 Oct. 1947.
6. D.M. – M.M., summer 1924.
7. D.M. – Chen, undated.
8. Nan Lucas, Diary, unpub., 5 Nov. 1911 (information Louis Jebb).
9. E.W., 4 Apr. 1912.
10. D.M., "Apprenticeship", *Humanities*, p. 17.
11. M.M. – Ott., 21 Mar. 1912 (HRHRC).
12. D.M. *op. cit.*, p. 17.
13. M.M. – D.M., 18 Sept. 1912.
14. Lewis Melville in E.W., 16 Nov. 1911.
15. D.M. – M.M., 23 Oct. 1912.
16. M.M. – Ott., 5 Nov. 1912.
17. D.M. – Ott., 7 June 1912 (HRHRC).
18. D.M., *op. cit.*, p. 19.
19. L.W., *An Autobiography*, Vol. 2, p. 92.
20. Beatrice Webb, *Diaries*, Vol. 2, 1981; and Edward Hyams, *The New Statesman, A History of the First 50 Years 1913–1963*, 1963, Chs. 1–6.
21. Dennis Kennedy, *Granville-Barker & the Dream of Theatre*, Cambridge, 1983, Ch. 7.
22. Jonathan Cecil, information.
23. D.M., *E.W.*, 3 Oct. 1912.
24. D.M. "Chekhov", *Humanities*, p. 81.
25. D.M., *N.S.*, 16 May 1914. *Theatre*, p. 23
26. M.M.-Ott., 6 Aug. 1913 (HRHRC).

27. Harry Norton to Rupert Brooke, 6 and 15 Mar. 1913 (KCL).
28. Michael Holroyd, *Lytton Strachey*, 1968, Vol. 2, p. 91.
29. D.M., "A Memoir of Youth", *Memories*, p. 211.
30. Holroyd, *op. cit..*, p. 114–5.

11. *"Companionship & Fun & Friendship"*

1. *Ottoline: The Early Years of Lady Ottoline Morrell*, ed. R. Gathorne-Hardy, 1963, Vol. 1, pp. 136–7.
2. D.M. – Ott., July 1909 (HRHRC).
3. D.M. – Ott., Christmas Day 1915 (HRHRC).
4. M.M. – Ott., 13 July 1916 (HRHRC).
5. D.M. – M.M., 19 May 1913.
6. M.M. – Ott., 26 Mar. 1913 (HRHRC).
7. V.W., *Diary*, Vol. 1, May 1919, p. 272.
8. Ott., *op. cit.*, p. 212.
9. M.M. – Ott., no date (*c.* 1913) (HRHRC).
10. D.M., "Bloomsbury", *Memories*, p. 174.
11. D.M. – Cynthia, undated, 1920s.
12. Ott., *Memoirs*, Vol. 2, 1974, p. 51.
13. Clive – M.M., 17 May 1912 (KCL).
14. Clive – M.M., 22 May 1912.
15. M.M. – Clive, 19 May 1912; and Henry James – D.M., 20 May 1912.
16. M.M. – Clive, 27 July 1912 (KCL).
17. M.M. – Ott., undated, *c.* 1913 (HRHRC).
18. Quentin Bell, *Virginia Woolf, A Biography*, 1972, Vol. 1, p. 133.
19. D.M. – M.M., undated, 1930s.
20. Duncan Grant – V.W., 23 Sept. 1912 (Sussex) and V.B. – V.W., 18 Sept. 1912.
21. M.M. – Chen, July 1913.
22. D.M. – V.W., 27 Aug. 1913.
23. Clive – M.M., 14 Aug. (KCL).
24. Clive – M.M., 17 and 25 Sept. 1913 (KCL).
25. D.M. – V.B., Jan. 1914.
26. D.M. – M.M., July/August 1914.
27. Irene Noel, Diary, 1914.
28. D.M., "August 4 1914," *Experience*.

12. *Ares and Irene*

1. D.M., "Nietzsche & the War", *Experience*, pp. 194–198.
2. D.M. – Irene Noel, 3 Sept. 1914.
3. G. M. Trevelyan – D.M., 9 Sept. 1914.
4. D.M., "W. S. Maugham", Memories, p. 63.
5. D.M. – M.M., Nov. – Dec. 1914; and D.M., *S.T.*, 24 Dec. 1939.

6. Irene Noel, Diary, 1914.
7. M.M. – Chen, 22 April 1915.
8. Judith Lytton – Chen, 18 Apr. 1915.
9. D.M. – V.W., 14 Jan. 1918, and *c.* May 1918 ". . . I will complete the story of my hapless affair. Do get me a bottle of wine that my lips may be loosened."
10. V.W., *Diary*, Vol. 1, 24. Jan. 1915, pp. 27–29.
11. M.M. – Clive Bell, 1915.
12. M.M. – D.M., summer, 1915.
13. See Patrick Beesly *Room 40, British Naval Intelligence 1914–18*, 1982; and Ebba Nielsen – D.M., 27 Aug. 1916, requesting decoding.
14. D.M. – V.W., 14 Oct. 1915.
15. Ott., *op. cit.*, Vol. 2, pp. 97 and 107.
16. D.M. – M.M., 14 Feb. 1916.

13. *Jealousies*

1. M.M. – Ott., 13 July 1916.
2. M.M. – D.M., 28 June 1915.
3. R. Hallam, *Living with Tinnitus*, 1989.
4. M.M. – Ralph Partridge, 22 Jan. 1943 (Partridge).
5. V.W., *Diary*, Vol. 1, p. 183, 19 Aug. 1918.
6. M.M. – D.M., undated.
7. D.M. – Chen, 1896.
8. Violet Bonham-Carter – J. M. Keynes, March 1918 (KCL).
9. M.M. – J. M. Keynes, 20 Mar. 1918 (KCL).
10. E. Bagnold; *Autobiography*, 1969, p. 199.
11. D.M. – M.M., 8 Feb. 1916, and 14 Feb. 1916.
12. Irene Cooper-Willis – D.M., letters Feb. 1916–Aug. 5 1917, annotated by D.M.
13. Althea Brook, *The Green-Eyed Monster*, 1923.
14. D.M. – Irene Cooper-Willis, undated.
15. E. Bagnold – Frances Partridge, 1962.

14. *"Pincher"*

1. M.M. – V.B., Aug. and Sept. 1917 (KCL).
2. M.M. – D.M. spring 1918.
3. V.W., *Diary*, Vol. 1 p. 206, and V.W. – M.M., undated, 1918, and M.M. – V.W., Aug. 1918.
4. D.M. – Max Beerbohm, April 1916.
5. D.M. – Cynthia, 20 May 1918.
6. Lionel Esher, *Ourselves Unknown*, 1985, p. 37.
7. Enid Bagnold, *Autobiography*, 1969, pp. 111 & 199.

8. D.M. – V.W., 14 Jan. 1918.
9. V.W. *Diary*, Vol.I , p. 114.
10. M.M. – Ott., spring 1918.
11. E. Bagnold – D.M., 17 Jan. 1918.
12. D.M. – E. Bagnold, 14 Sept. 1951.
13. D.M. – E. Bagnold, May 1950.
14. David Cecil, "Staying with Margot", *The Observer*, 20 Dec. 1981.
15. D.M., "Asquith", *Portraits*, pp. 1–18.
16. D.M. – Cynthia, 30 Aug. 1920.
17. See generally *Lady Cynthia Asquith, Diaries 1915–1918*, 1968; and Lord David Cecil, information.
18. D.M. – M.M., 28 May 1918.
19. L. Esher, *op. cit.*
20. D.M. – Michael, 17 Nov. 1918, and D.M. "November 11 1918", *Experience*, pp. 244–250.

15. *Peace*

1. D.M. – Cynthia, 24 Dec. 1918.
2. D.M. – Antoinette Brett, 31 Dec. 1918.
3. D.M. – M.M., see 31 Jan. 1919.
4. V.W., *Diary*, Vol. 1, pp. 237–8.
5. V.W. *Diary*, Vol. 1, p. 267 and Vol. 3, p. 27.
6. V.W., *Diary*, Vol. 3, p. 21.
7. V. Lee – D.M., 10 Dec. 1918.
8. See D.M. – M.M., 17 May 1919 and D.M. – C. P. Scott, 25 May 1920.
9. D.M. – Antoinette Brett, 12 Sept. 1919.
10. See D.M. "George Moore", *Portraits*, pp. 192–203, and D.M. in *E.W.*, 23 Nov. 1911.
11. D.M. – Cynthia, July 1919.

16. *"Pincher" Passes Away*

1. D.M. – M.M., 1 Oct. 1919.
2. D.M. – Cynthia, 11 Oct. 1919.
3. D.M. – M.M., Oct. 1919.
4. Rachel Cecil, unpublished memoir & conversation with authors.
5. D.M. – Cynthia, 25 July 1919.
6. D.M. – Antoinette Brett, 3 Jan. 1920.
7. Cynthia – D.M. letters, Sept.–Nov. 1919.
8. D.M. – Cynthia, 1 Aug. 1920.
9. M.M. – D.M., undated, mid-Feb. 1919, and M.M. – Antoinette Brett, 16 Feb. 1919.
10. D.M. – Cynthia, undated, beginning 1920.
11. D.M. – Cynthia, mid-Aug. 1919.
12. E. M. Forster, *The Listener*, 26 June 1952.
13. M.M. – Mary Hutchinson, undated 1920 (HRHRC).
14. V.W., *Diary*, Vol. 2, p. 23.
15. D.M. – M.M., July 1920, undated.

16. V.W. – M.M., 24 May 1920.

17. *"Affable Hawk"*

1. M.M. – Dolly Ponsonby, 24 Feb. 1921.
2. D.M. – Chen, 1922.
3. V.W. *Diary*, Vol. 2, p. 286.
4. M.M. – V.B., Sept. 1921 (KCL).
5. R. Fry – V.B., 20 May 1921, in *Fry, Letters* (ed. Sutton), and see V.W. *Diary*, Vol. 2. pp. 119–120.
6. V.W., *op. cit.*, p. 252.
7. See D.M., *N.S.*, 23 Sept. 1923.
8. D.M. – Herbert Palmer, 27 July 1936 (Palmer papers HRHRC).
9. D.M., "Gertrude Stein", *Criticism*, pp. 262–263.
10. D.M., *N.S.*, 7 Apr. 1923, 5 Sept. 1925.
11. A. G. MacDonnell, *England, Their England*, 1933, and D.M., "Apprenticeship", *Humanities*, pp. 21–22.
12. D.M., *N.S.*, 4 and 11 Feb. 1922.
13. A Bennett – M.M., 22 Mar. 1920, and A. Bennett – D.M., 4 Aug. 1925.
14. D.M. – Lytton Strachey, 28 Mar. 1929.
15. D.M., *S.T.*, 15 April 1934.
16. Peter Alexander, *Roy Campbell, A Critical Biography*, Oxford, 1982, p. 34; and D.M. *S.T.*, 17 Jan. 1937.
17. See, for example, V. Lee, *The Enchanted Woods & Other Essays on the Genius of Places*, 1910. edn.
18. See Leon Edel, *Henry James, The Middle Years 1884–1894*, pp. 52 and 149; and Ethel Smyth, *What Happened Next?*, 1940 pp. 26–28 and 50–51.
19. D.M., *N.S.*, 14 April 1928, and V. Lee – D.M., 17 Apr. 1928.
20. See D.M., *N.S.*, 4 May 1935, and 26 May 1923.
21. Edward Marsh, *A Number of People*, p. 58.
22. Diana Wynyard – D.M., 1937.
23. Jonathan Cecil account of conversation with Michael Macowan.
24. Stanley Weintraub, *Bernard Shaw – 1914–1918, Journey to Heartbreak*, 1973 edn, pp. 131–132.
25. D.M., *N.S.*, 6 Oct. 1923.
26. D.M. – S. Maugham, 3 May 1952.
27. D.M., "Apprenticeship", *Humanities*, pp. 20–21.
28. A. Bennett – D.M., 4 Aug. 1925.

18. *"The Young Adonises"*

1. See V.W., *Diary*, Vol. 2, pp. 22 and 162.
2. Frances Partridge, *Memories*, p. 92, and David Garnett, *The Familiar Faces*, p. 64, & Dr Dermod MacCarthy, information.

3. M.M. – Dolly Ponsonby, undated 1922 or 1923 (Shulbrede).
4. For Philip Ritchie, information from Lord David Cecil and The Hon. Margaret Chippindale.
5. Sotheby's *Charleston* catalogue, 21 July 1980: Lytton Strachey ms., untitled sonnet, lot 284.
6. M.M. – D.M., 1924.
7. Frances Partridge, *Memories*, p. 67, and Maurice Bowra, *Memories 1966*, p. 122.
8. Philip Ritchie – M.M., Aug. 1925.
9. Logan Pearsall Smith – Cyril Connolly, 17 Nov. 1926, in David Pryce-Jones ed., *Cyril Connolly, Journal*.
10. Clare Sheppard, unpub. memoir.
11. Philip Ritchie – M.M., undated.
12. V.W., *Diary*, Vol. 2, p. 275.
13. V.W., *Diary*, Vol. 3, p. 130, and M.M. – V.B. 16 Mar. 1927 (KCL) & V.W. – V.B. *Letters*, March 1927, and V.W. – M.M., 24 March 1927.
14. D.M. – Max Beerbohm, spring 1928, and D.M. – Cynthia, 24 May 1927.
15. Gerald Brenan, *Personal Record, 1920–1972*, 1974.
16. M.M. – Gerald Brenan, 12 Aug. 1927 (HRHRC).
17. M.M. – Gerald Brenan 14 Sept. 1927 (HRHRC).
18. Lord Ritchie – M.M., *c*. Sept. 1927, undated and The Hon. Mrs Chippindale – the authors, 14 Oct. 1985.
19. M.M. – Gerald Brenan, end Sept. 1927 (HRHRC).
20. V.W. – V. B., 10 May 1929.
21. D.M. – M.M., Sept. 1927.
22. M.M. – E. Sackville–West, undated late 1927.

19. *Editor, Critic and Broadcaster*

1. D.M. papers 1927–8, *Life & Letters* file.
2. D.M. – R. Fry, 7 Feb. 1928.
3. George Santayana – D.M., 28 May 1928.
4. Max Beerbohm – D.M., 18 May 1928.
5. See V. Lee – D.M., 16 Feb. 1912.
6. D.M. – Sir Michael Sadleir, 7 Nov. 1928.
7. See Rubinstein, Nash & Co., solicitors – D.M., 7 Dec. 1928.
8. D.M. – C. Sharp, 9 Nov. 1928.
9. D.M. papers "Well of Loneliness" file.
10. *L. & L.*, May 1930 and 1931.
11. Dora Russell, *The Tamarisk Tree*, Vol. 1, My Quest for Liberty & Love, pb edn 1977, p. 219.
12. D.M. – Butterfield, letter unsent, *c*. 1935.

13. *Ibid*.
14. *L. & L.*, May 1930, pp. 378–80.
15. Oliver Esher – D.M., 1 Apr. 1931.
16. Max Beerbohm – D.M., Sept. 1928.
17. Cyril Connolly in "50 Years of Little Magazines" in *Art & Literature*, Vol. 1, March 1964, pp. 96 and 106.
18. David Pryce-Jones ed. *Cyril Connolly, Journal & Memoir*, 1983, p. 147.
19. M.M. – Dolly Ponsonby, 1937 (Ponsonby papers).
20. Frances Partridge, information.
21. Rachel Cecil, information.
22. See Pryce-Jones, ed. *op. cit.*, generally.
23. D.M. – Cyril Connolly, 1927.
24. Pryce-Jones ed., *op. cit.*, and D.M. – E. Bagnold, 1929.
25. Lord D. Cecil, information.
26. D.M. *S.T.*, 24 Dec. 1939.
27. *Horizon*, Dec. 1944.
28. Leonard Rees – D.M., 14 Sept. 1928.
29. See V.W., "Edmund Gosse", *The Moment & Other Essays*, 1947, and D.M., *S.T.*, 20 May 1928.
30. See generally Harold Hobson, Phillip Knightley & Leonard Russell, *The Pearl of Days, An Intimate Memoir of the Sunday Times, 1822–1972*, 1972.
31. D.M., *S.T.*, 23 July 1944.
32. See, generally, Asa Briggs, *The Golden Age of Wireless*, Vols. 1 & 2.
33. D.M., Schools broadcast on Tolstoy, 23 Oct. 1928.
34. D.M., Talk unpub. on Dostoivesky, and see Count Benckendorff, *Half a Life*, 1954.
35. See generally, BBC Written Archives, Desmond MacCarthy, 1930s and wartime; and D.M. – Robert Waller, 11 Feb. 1947.
36. Dolly Ponsonby – M.M., 1927 (Ponsonby papers).

20. *Betsy*

1. D.M. – Betsy Reyneau, July 1930.
2. Dr Dermod MacCarthy, memoir "My Father in his Bath", unpub.
3. D.M. – Betsy, undated, post-war.
4. Sheila Wingfield, *Real People*, 1952, pp. 137–9, and 140–1.
5. M.M. – Bina Paley, 12 July 1953.
6. D.M. – Betsy, 2 July 1930, and 24 June 1930.
7. D.M. – M.M., 30 Aug. 1930.
8. D.M. – M.M., part-letter, undated, *c*. 1931.
9. D.M. – M.M., 9 Feb. 1931.

10. M.M. – Dolly Ponsonby, 1931 (Shulbrede).
11. D.M. – Betsy, 2 July 1930.
12. M.M. – Dolly Ponsonby, 21 Aug. 1932.
13. M.M. – D.M., 21 Oct. 1932.
14. V.W., *Diary*, Vol. 4, pp. 127–8.
15. D.M. – Lytton Strachey, 18 Dec. 1931.
16. D.M., *S.T.*, 1932. *Memories*, pp. 31–49.
17. Carrington – D.M., undated, Feb. 1932.
18. M.M. – Ralph Partridge, 16 Apr. 1932.
19. M.M. – Dolly Ponsonby, 29 Mar. 1932 (Shulbrede).
20. M.M. – D.M., 23 Jan. 1933.
21. M.M. – Ralph Partridge, Feb. 1933.
22. M.M. – D.M., 2 Feb. 1933.
23. M.M. – Ralph Partridge, 11 Feb. 1933.
24. M.M. – Bina Paley, 12 July 1953.
25. D.M. – Antoinette Brett, Mar. 1933.
26. Rachel Cecil · M.M., May 1933.

21. *"Our Tip-Top Paper"*

1. See generally Hobson, Knightley & Russell, *The Pearl of Days*, pp. 157–236.
2. D.M. – Cyril Lakin, 9 Jan. 1939.
3. Hobson et al., *op. cit.*, p. 176.
4. D.M., *S.T.*, 4 April 1937.
5. F. R. Leavis, "What's Wrong with Criticism?" in *Scrutiny*, Sept. 1932.
6. D.M., *S.T.*, 3 Feb. 1929, 7 Feb. 1943 and 2 Nov. 1932.
7. Ibid., 28 Mar. 1937.
8. Colin Wilson, E. .H. Visiak & J. B. Pick, *The Strange Genius of David Lindsay*, 1970, pp. 23–4.
9. L. P. Hartley in conversation with the author, 1969.
10. D.M., *S.T.*, 24 Dec. 1944.
11. See D.M., BBC talk, 16 June 1930 and *N.S.*, 4 Aug. 1924.
12. See D.M. *S.T.*, 10 Feb. 1929, 20 May 1934, 12 Jan. 1947, and 26 Jan. 1947.
13. J. Agate, *Ego Seven*, 29 Dec. 1944, Diary.

22. *"Babbling as a Nightingale"*

1. David Garnett – M.M., 3 Nov. 1937.
2. Vita Sackville-West – M.M., 19 Oct. 1929.
3. Peter Alexander, *Roy Campbell*, p. 80.
4. V.W. – M.M., 1930.
5. E. M. Forster – M.M., 4 June 1928.
6. D.M. – E. Waugh, 16 Sept. 1934.
7. V.W., *Diary*, Vol. 4, p. 243.
8. V.W. – M.M., 11 June 1939.
9. V.W., *Diary*, Vol. 5, p. 82.
10. V.W., *Moments of Being*, 1975, p. 181.
11. Lord D. Cecil, information.
12. D.M. – M.M., Feb. 1931.

13. D.M. – Lady J. Duff, 12 Jan. 1938.
14. Ettie Desborough – D.M., May 1936.
15. D.M. – Lady Horner, 7 Sept. 1938.
16. Derek Patmore, *Private History*, 1960, p. 142.
17. Harold Nicolson, *Diary & Letters*, 1967, Vol. 1, p. 163.
18. *Ibid.*
19. E. Bagnold, *Autobiography*, pp. 196–7.
20. V. W., *Diary*, Vol. 5, p. 81.
21. D.M. – Lady J. Duff, 12 Jan. 1938.
22. D.M. – M.M., Oct. 1938.
23. D.M. – Rachel Cecil, Sept. 1938.

23. *The War 1939–1945*

1. B. Reyneau – D.M., 15 Sept. 1939.
2. B. Reyneau – D.M., 3 Dec. 1939.
3. D.M. – B. Reyneau, unfinished letter.
4. B. Reyneau – M.M., 15 June 1953.
5. M.M. – Dolly Ponsonby, July 1939 (Shulbrede).
6. M.M., Memoir Club on the War, *Retrospect* (1941).
7. M.M. – V. B., 8 Sept. 1939.
8. D.M. – R. Waller, 30 Sept. 1939.
9. Sean O'Casey – D.M., 18 and 28 Mar. 1942.
10. F. Partridge, *A Pacifist's War*, p. 29.
11. D.M. – Rachel Cecil, Christmas 1939.
12. V.B. – M.M., 24 Jan. 1943 (KCL).
13. V.W., *Diary*, Vol. 5, 20 May 1940.
14. L.W., *An Autobiography*, Vol. 2, p. 405.
15. V.W., *op. cit.*, p. 287.
16. Frances Partridge, *op. cit.*, pp. 40–41.
17. M.M. – Florence Beerbohm, June 1939.
18. Frances Partridge, *op. cit.*, p. 52.
19. D.M. – G.E.M., 30 June 1940.
20. V.W., *op. cit.*, pp. 307, 309.
21. M.M. – L.W., 7 April 1941 (Sussex).
22. L.W. – M.M., 4 May 1941.
23. M.M. – V.B., 4 Apr. 1941 (KCL).
24. V.B. – M.M., 20 Apr. 1941 (KCL).
25. M.M. – Dolly Ponsonby, 24 Mar. 1941 (Shulbrede).
26. D.M. – Cynthia, 30 Jan. 1940.
27. D.M. – E. Bagnold, 10 Oct. 1941.
28. R. Speaight, *The Life of Hilaire Belloc*, 1957, p. 524.
29. D. Cecil, *Max*, pb. 1983, pp. 458, 474.; broadcast printed in *The Listener* 26 June 1952.
30. M.M. – Dolly Ponsonby, undated, 1941 or 1942.
31. M.M. – R. Partridge, 12 Jan. 1943 (Partridge).
32. F. Partridge, *op. cit.*, p. 134.
33. D.M. – Lady Juliet Duff, 21 June 1944.
34. Dilys Powell, information.

35. BBA. D.M. file.
36. M.M. – V.B., Oct 1944 (KCL).

24. *Last Days*

1. Julia Strachey – Frances Partridge, 15 Jan. 1945, quoted in Frances Partridge *Julia*, 1983, p. 195.
2. D.M., *S.T.*, 30 Jan. 1944. To J. C. Squire 1937.
3. D.M. – E. Bagnold, May 1950.
4. D.M. – V.B., 26 Mar. 1948.
5. See D.M., *S.T.*, 19 and 26 Sept. 1948.
6. D.M. – J. L. Hammond, 6 Dec. 1947.
7. D.M. – Margaret Knight, 5 Oct. 1948.
8. C. Connolly, "A Portrait" in D.M., *Memories*, p. 12; and see *S.T.*, 18 April 1948, 26 May 1952, and 2 July 1950.
9. Peter Alexander, *Roy Campbell*, p. 215; and Dr Dermod MacCarthy.
10. D.M., *S.T.*, 1 Feb. 1948; PEN Club mss (HRHRC).
11. D.M. – M.M., 7 June 1946, and D.M. – G.E.M., 12 June 1946.
12. D.M. – G.E.M., 19 July 1947.
13. D.M. – Oliver Esher, 13 July 1948.
14. Raymond Mortimer – M.M., 12 Jan. 1951.
15. Cyril Connolly – M.M., *c.* 1940.
16. D.M. – Cyril Connolly, 9 Sept. 1947.
17. M.M. – Rachel Cecil, 1953.
18. Evelyn Waugh – D.M., 3 June 1945.
19. See Siegfried Sassoon – D.M., 30 July 1945, and 12 Feb. 1948; and D.M., *S.T.*, 19 and 26 Sept. 1948.
20. D.M. – Jocelyn Brooke, 10 Apr. 1948; D.M., *S.T.*, 18 Apr. 1948.
21. D.M. – M.M., 20 Mar. 1950.
22. D.M. – Marie-France MacCarthy, 24 Mar. 1950.
23. S. Maugham – M.M., 9 June 1952.
24. D.M., *S.T.*, 20 May 1951.
25. D.M. – R. C. Trevelyan, 25 Sept. 1946.
26. D.M. – Arthur Waley, 2 Aug. 1951.
27. Francis W.-C. (nephew) – Michael MacCarthy, 20 Apr. 1958.
28. D.M. – V. Wedgwood, 20 Nov. 1951.
29. J. M. Keynes – M.M., 2 Jan. 1947 (KCL).
30. M.M. – V.B., winter 1945 (KCL).
31. D.M. – V. B., 4 Aug. 1946.
32. V.B. – M.M., 2 June 1946.
33. The Hon. Guy Strutt, information.
34. M.M. – V.B., New Year's Eve 1947 (KCL).
35. Frances Partridge, *Everything to Lose, Diaries 1945–1960*, 1985, p. 89.
36. L.W., *Autobiography*, Vol. 2, p. 102.
37. D.M. – M.M., 30 and 31 May 1947.
38. M.M. – E. Bagnold, Aug. 1952.
39. M.M. – L.W., 11 Aug. 1952 (Sussex).
40. M.M. – Ralph Partridge, 26 July 1952 (Partridge).
41. M.M. – Dolly Ponsonby, 27 Sept. 1953.
42. L. P. Hartley – M.M., 17 Nov. 1953.
43. M.M. – Rachel Cecil, 7 June 1953.
44. Lord Kemsley – M.M., 27 Aug. 1952.
45. Chloe MacCarthy, information.

Select Bibliography
(See references for other works consulted)

Friends and Acquaintances of the MacCarthys
Ian Anstruther, *Oscar Browning: a Biography*, 1983
Clive Bell, *Old Friends: Personal Recollections*, 1956
Quentin Bell, *Bloomsbury*, 1968
Elizabeth French Boyd, *The Bloomsbury Heritage: Their Mothers and Their Aunts*, 1976
Carrington, Letters and Extracts from her Diary, ed. David Garnett, 1979
The Chesterton Review, XIX, I, Maurice Baring Special Issue, Feb. 1988
Cyril Connolly, *Enemies of Promise*, rev. 3ed. 1949
David Cecil, *Max, A Biography*, 1964
Margaret Fitzherbert, *The Man Who Was Greenmantle: A Biography of Aubrey Herbert*, 1983
E. M. Forster, *The Longest Journey*, 1907; *Goldsworthy Lowes Dickinson*, 1934
David Garnett, autobiography: *The Golden Echo*, 1953; *Flowers of the Forest*, 1955; *The Familiar Faces*, 1962; *Great Friends*, 1979
Miron Grindea, ed., *Adam International Review* 1974–5 (Cyril Connolly edn)
Roy Harrod, *The Life of John Maynard Keynes*, 1951
Roy Jenkins, *Asquith*, 1964
Francis Noel-Baker, *Book Eight: A Taste of Hardship*, 1987
Frances Partridge, *Everything to Lose: Diaries 1945–1960*, 1985; *Friends in Focus*, 1983
S. P. Rosenbaum, ed., *The Bloomsbury Group*, Toronto 1975
The Autobiography of Bertrand Russell, 3 vols, pb edn, 1971
Robert Skidelsky, *John Maynard Keynes*, Vol I, 1983
Logan Pearsall Smith, *All Trivia* (coll. edn) 1933
Frances Spalding, *Roger Fry: Art and Life*, 1980; *Vanessa Bell*, 1983
Barbara Strachey, *Memorable Relations; the Story of the Pearsall Smith Family*, 1980
Arnold Toynbee, "The Hammonds", *Acquaintances*, 1967
A. N. Wilson, *Hilaire Belloc*, 1984
Virginia Woolf, *Moments of Being*, 1976

MacCarthy/Cornish Relations
F. Warre-Cornish, *Darwell Stories*, 1910
Winifred Gérin, *Anne Thackeray Ritchie, a Biography*, 1983
Anthony John Trythall, *"Boney" Fuller, the Intellectual General, 1878–1966*, 1977

Literary and Theatrical Criticism
James Agate, *Ego*, 9 vols, 1935–48
Peter Ackroyd, *T. S. Eliot*, 1984

Walter Allen, *As I walked Down New Grub Street: Memoirs of a Writing Life*, 1981
John Gross, *The Rise and Fall of the Man of Letters: Aspects of English Literary Life since 1800*, 1969
Alfred Havighurst, *Radical Journalist: H. W. Massingham and the Nation*, 1974
Robert Hewison, *Under Siege: Literary Life in London 1939–1945*, 1977
Michael Holroyd, *Bernard Shaw: The Search for Love*, 1988; *The Pursuit of Power*, 1989
George Jefferson, *Edward Garnett: a Life in Literature*, 1982
Henry Festing Jones, *Samuel Butler, the Author of Erewhon, a Memoir*, 2 vols, 1919
J. B. Priestley, *George Meredith*, 1926
Peter Quennell, *Customs and Characters: Contemporary Portraits*, 1982
Frank Swinnerton, *The Georgian Scene*, 1934
Anne Thwaite, *Edmund Gosse: A Literary Landscape*, 1984
Maisie Ward, *Gilbert Keith Chesterton*, 1944
Norman and Jean MacKenzie (eds.), *Beatrice Webb's Diary*, vol. 3, 1989

Journals, etc.

The Adelphi, *The Albany Review*, *The Criterion*, *The Empire Review*, *The Eye Witness*, *Horizon*, *The Independent Review*, *Land and Water*, *Life and Letters*, *The Listener*, (in partic. "Tributes to Sir Desmond MacCarthy", 47, 26th June 1952), *The New Adelphi*, *The New Quarterly*, *The New Statesman*, *New Verse*, *The New Witness*, *The Speaker*, *Scrutiny* (in partic. see VII, 1939), *The Sunday Times*, *New Statesman Archive*, City University Library, London.

Works by Desmond MacCarthy

The Court Theatre, 1904–7, 1907
Remnants, 1918
Portraits I, 1931 (no second volume)
Criticism, 1932
Experience, 1935
Leslie Stephen, 1937
Drama, 1940
Shaw, the Plays, 1951
Humanities, 1953
Memories, 1953
Theatre, 1954
Desmond MacCarthy, the Man and his Writings, ed. David Cecil, 1984

Desmond MacCarthy also edited or introduced a number of books, of which the most important are:
Lady John Russell, a Memoir, with a Selection from her Diary and Correspondence, (With Lady Agatha Russell), 1910
Letters to a Friend (Mrs Hilda Harrison), H.H.A. [Lord Oxford and Asquith] 2 vols, 1933, 1934

Works by Molly MacCarthy

A Pier and a Band, 1918 (reprinted with intro. by David Garnett, 1931)
A Nineteenth Century Childhood, 1924, 1929, 1948 (intro. by John Betjeman) and 1985 (intro. by David Cecil)
Fighting Fitzgerald and Other Papers, 1930
Handicaps: Six Studies, 1936
The Festival etc., 1937

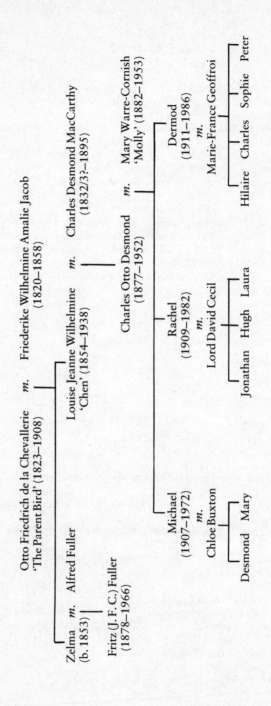

Desmond MacCarthy's family

Molly MacCarthy's brothers and sisters
showing the family connection with the Thackerays and the Stephens

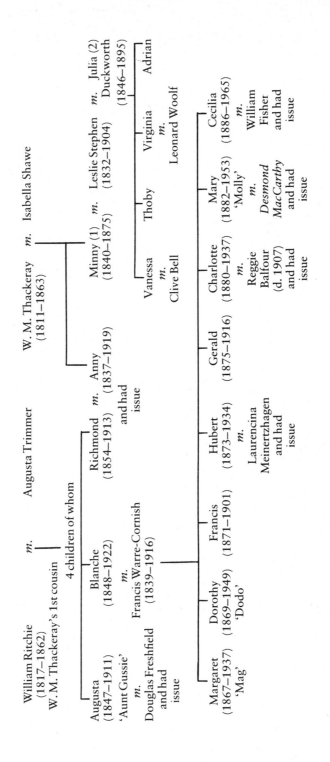

Index